Recent Developments in Southeastern Archaeology

From Colonization to Complexity

David G. Anderson and Kenneth E. Sassaman

Society for American Archaeology
The SAA Press

The Society for American Archaeology, Washington, D.C. 20005

Printed on acid-free paper

Library of Congress Cataloging-in-Publication Data

Anderson, David G.
Recent developments in southeastern archaeology : from colonization to complexity / David G. Anderson and Kenneth E. Sassaman.
p. cm.
Includes bibliographical references and index.
ISBN 978-0-932839-43-5
1. Paleo-Indians--Southern States. 2. Mound-builders--Southern States. 3. Indians of North America--Southern States--Antiquities. 4. Excavations (Archaeology)--Southern States. 5. Southern States--Antiquities. I. Sassaman, Kenneth E. II. Title.
E78.S65A655 2012
975'.01--dc23

Contents

Acknowledgments

In this volume we recount knowledge gained and lessons learned from modern archaeology in the Southeast. The authors wish to thank Ken Ames, Editor of The SAA Press, and the members of his editorial committee for their support in seeing that this was produced in a professional and timely manner. Ken provided many helpful comments on how we might improve the manuscript, for which we owe him a special debt of gratitude. Ken's predecessor as Editor of The SAA Press, Paul Minnis, deserves our thanks for thinking up the idea for volumes like this, and asking us if we would like to prepare one. Since this volume is an overview of a region where a vast amount of recent work has occurred, to ensure we were covering it appropriately, we sent the draft manuscript to a number of colleagues, whom we wish to thank for their willingness to look at some or all of the text: Susan M. Alt, Thaddeus G. Bissett, Ian W. Brown, John E. Clark, Charles R. Cobb, I. Randy Daniel, David H. Dye, David Echeverry, Richard W. Jefferies, T. R. Kidder, Adam King, V. James Knight, Patrick C. Livingood, D. Shane Miller, Michael C. Moore, Timothy R. Pauketat, Thomas J. Pluckhahn, Mark A. Rees, Christopher B. Rodning, Gerald F. Schroedl, Bruce D. Smith, Vincas P. Steponaitis, Lynne P. Sullivan, Victor D. Thompson, Neill J. Wallis, Gregory D. Wilson, and Stephen J. Yerka. Four of them, Daniel, Dye, King, and Rodning, also served as reviewers for The SAA Press, and gave us particularly detailed commentary, and David Dye also graciously provided some of the photographs that are used in the book, as did Thomas Pluckhahn and Patty Jo Watson. Ken Sassaman prepared most of the artwork, and John Neikirk, the SAA Publications manager, produced the final manuscript. Tobi Brimsek and Karen Smith provided membership numbers for the Society for American Archaeology (SAA) and the Southeastern Archaeological Conference (SEAC) in Table 1-2, while the site file managers in each southern state provided the data on the numbers of recorded archaeological sites. This volume represents an even division of labor between the two authors, although the primary authorship of chapters 3 and 4 belongs with Sassaman and the bracketing chapters with Anderson, albeit with appreciable editing of each other's contributions. The conclusions belong to both of us, and we assume full responsibility for any errors or omissions herein. This volume is dedicated to the memberships of SAA and SEAC, two organizations that have done so much to shape southeastern archaeology, and make it a great subject to explore.

1

Foundations of Modern Southeastern Archaeology

The Southeast is a vibrant archaeological research area, home to a large and expanding community of scholars and teachers, land managers, and members of the general public, all of whom have an interest in understanding the region's past. In the pages that follow we highlight new and exciting trends that have been occurring in southeastern archaeology, touching on major discoveries, interpretations, and ongoing debates. Our emphasis is on work published in the last two decades, and particularly the latter half of that range, encompassing research in the new millennium, after A.D. 2000. No single volume, of course, could hope to cover all the important work that is occurring in detail, but we have tried to touch on the major areas of interesting and exciting research. Our focus is on the record of the Native American inhabitants of the region, from initial colonization in the late Pleistocene to the complex societies of the late prehistoric and early European Contact period. The rich and theoretically robust field of southeastern historical archaeology deserves its own volume, although we have drawn on that research where relevant to the narrative presented here. Our focus lies, however, primarily in the precolumbian era, although we recognize that the stories we are telling, and the peoples of interest whose past we explore, continue to this day.

Our goal is to show that southeastern archaeology is a dynamic and exciting field to study and practice, with important contributions to make to archaeological theory and to our broader knowledge of world prehistory. The region has a rich and well-documented archaeological record, useful for the exploration of big questions of interest to archaeologists, anthropologists, historians, and indeed anyone who has wondered about the past, such as how the initial colonization and settlement of the region occurred during the last glacial period; how people, once established, interacted with one another and with the biotic and physical landscape; how people in this diverse temperate forest environment developed and adopted agriculture, in one of the few centers of independent domestication anywhere on the planet; and how complex societies rose and fell over time. Our objectives are to educate and to inspire, to attract new people to work in the region and in the process reinvigorate ourselves and our research community, so that more can be done. We have learned a great deal about the past human occupation of the Southeast, much of it in recent years, but there is far more we can still learn.

In the chapters that follow, we summarize recent developments in southeastern archaeology using a time-honored cultural historical framework, encompassing the Paleoindian, Archaic, Woodland, and Mississippian/Contact periods, terminology adopted decades ago by some of the preeminent founders of modern archaeology in the region (e.g., Ford and Willey 1941; Griffin 1952a, 1967; Willey and Phillips 1958). This sequence is presented in Table 1-1, and includes calendrical (calendar years before present, or cal yr B.P.) and radiocarbon (^{14}C yr B.P.) timescales, as well as major geochronological periods and climatic episodes, which in some cases closely correspond to cultural periods. Thus, the Paleoindian period refers to those events older than 10,000 ^{14}C yr B.P., or > ca. 11,500 cal yr B.P., during the Pleistocene epoch, whose end date was arbitrarily defined by geological convention, since 10,000 is a nice round number and is at least close in time to the end of the last major cold reversal of the Pleistocene, the Younger Dryas period. The Archaic period encompasses much of the early and middle part of the Holocene epoch, from 10,000 to 3000 ^{14}C yr B.P., or from ca. 11,500 to 3200 cal yr B.P., while the Woodland period extends from 3000 to 1000 ^{14}C yr B.P. or 3200 to 950 cal yr B.P., and the Mississippian/Contact era the five or six centuries after that. The divergence between the radiocarbon and calendrical timescales increases further into the past, indicating the importance of specifying which scale is being employed when reporting ages. Radiocarbon calibration and climate change has been examined by archaeologists and paleoclimatologists at a number of geographic and temporal scales in recent years, including in the Southeast as discussed in the chapters that follow, and in recent overviews emphasizing the subject (e.g., Anderson 2001; Anderson, Maasch, Sandweiss, and Mayewski 2007; Fiedel 1999; Kidder 2006; Sassaman 2010a; Thomas, ed. 2008; Thomas and Sanger 2010; Watson 1990:47–48).

Environments Past and Present

What is the Southeast? To some, it is a culture area, to others a geographic region, and to still others, a group of states linked together by historical circumstances. While we, following long tradition (see Bense 1994; Smith 1986; Steponaitis 1986), use standardized maps throughout the text depicting site locations and physiographic zones, it will become clear that the boundaries of the region have never been fixed by either past peoples or modern researchers, but instead have varied depending on the nature of the cultures present on the landscape or the archaeological questions being asked. Indeed, during every period variability characterizes the regional archaeological record, making the establishment of common themes difficult. A major synthesis of the southeastern archaeological record a quarter century ago, in fact, began by showing how the boundary of the region varied from investigator to investigator and topic to topic (Smith 1986:1), making a rigid definition impossible to justify. A flexible approach is followed here. We define the Southeast generally to include those portions of the continental landmass south of ca. 38 degrees north latitude and east of ca. 95 degrees west longitude (Figure 1-1). Essentially, the core of the region lies south of the Ohio and Potomac rivers, and it encompasses the 11 modern states of Virginia, North Carolina, South Carolina, Georgia, Florida, Alabama, Tennessee, Kentucky, Mississippi, Arkansas, and Louisiana, with portions of adjoining states and regions included as relevant.

What is the Southeast like? The human occupation of the region has been profoundly shaped by climate, physiography, and biota, all of which have changed dramatically over the past twenty thousand years, the current presumed upper limit for initial colonization. These changes are briefly noted here, with additional detail provided as warranted in ensuing chapters. The climate of the Southeast in recent millennia has been warm and wet, ranging from tropical to subtropical to temperate, along a transect, for example, from southern Florida to Alabama to the Ohio River. Summers are hot and humid, while winters are mild, with snow and freezing rain occurring commonly only in the northern portion of the region and in the southern Appalachians. Rainfall is distributed fairly evenly over the course of the year, in sufficient quantity to support dense vegetation over much of the region, save in settings of excessive drainage, such as in the sandy soils in portions of the Coastal Plains. Greater or lesser amounts of precipitation occur from year to year and over shorter intervals, a fact that has proven to be of importance to local populations at various times in the past, such as during the later Archaic and Mississippian periods (Anderson et al. 1995; Benson et al. 2009; Kidder 2006; Thomas and Sanger 2010). Holocene climate, while remarkably stable compared to the preceding late glacial era, has been both slightly warmer than modern conditions, as in the case of the Mid-Holocene Atlantic period, and slightly cooler, during the Boreal period that preceded it (Table 1-1). Shorter, somewhat colder episodes on decadal to century scales sometimes occurred, such as the 8200 cal yr B.P. event, in some cases tied to unusual events like volcanic eruptions or glacial meltwater outflows (Anderson 2001). These changes in Holocene climate, while at times significant in their impact on human cultures in the Southeast, were relatively mild when compared with the fluctuations that characterized the late Pleistocene, when warming and cooling episodes were more pronounced and more variable in extent, and in some cases with more rapid onsets and terminations (see Chapter 2).

The physiography of the Southeast is varied but is basically dominated by two macrotopographic settings, the flat and weakly dissected Atlantic and Gulf Coastal Plains and the more heavily eroded Piedmont, mountains, and plateaus of the interior, the latter bisected in the vicinity of the Lower Mississippi Alluvial Valley by an arm of the Coastal Plain extending far into the interior, as far north as southern Illinois and Missouri (Gremillion 2004a:53–55; Smith 1986:3–6; Steponaitis 1986:364) (Figure 1-1). At the Last Glacial Maximum 20,000 years ago, with sea level some 120 m below its present level, the Coastal Plain was twice its current extent in places. As the ice sheets melted and sea levels rose after ca. 15,000 cal yr B.P., shorelines moved inland, rapidly in the late Pleistocene and early Holocene, and then more gradually during the Mid-Holocene. Essentially modern sea levels were reached about 5000 cal yr B.P., at the end of the Mid–Holocene Hypsithermal or Atlantic climate episode, although minor fluctuations on the order of one to two meters have occurred since, influencing Archaic and Woodland settlement patterns in some areas (e.g., Marquardt 2010a, 2010b; Sanger 2010; Thomas 2008; Thomas and Sanger 2010; Thompson and Turck 2009:269–271).

The Southeast is bounded and traversed by numerous river systems that formed natural communications arteries and favored settlement areas throughout prehistory, of which the Ohio/Mississippi system, with its northward flowing tributaries like the Kanawha, Kentucky, Green, and the Ten-

Table 1-1. A Cultural Sequence and Timescale for Southeastern Archeology

Calendrical (dates approximate)	Conventional (cal yr BP)*	Uncalibrated Radiocarbon	Period	Culture Complex	Climatic Event
					Pronounced Warming
AD 1950	50	0	Modern		
				Industrial Revolution	Little Ice Age Ends
AD 1700	300	250	Colonial		
AD 1500	500	450	Contact	European Colonization	
AD1350	600	600			Little Ice Age Begins
AD 1050	950	1000	Mississippian	Mississippian	
AD 930	1020	1100			Medieval Warm Period
AD 550	1400	1500	Late Woodland	Coles Creek	
AD 225	1725	1800			
			Middle Woodland	Hopewell	Subatlantic
300 BC	2225	2200			
			Early Woodland	Adena	
1200 BC	3200	3000			
1800 BC	3800	3500		Poverty Point	
2500 BC	4500	4000	Late Archaic	Stallings Island	Sub-Boreal
3800 BC	5800	5000			
				Watson Brake	Hypsithermal Ends
4350 BC	6300	5500			
4900 BC	6850	6000	Middle Archaic	Benton	Atlantic
5900 BC	7850	7000			
					Hypsithermal Begins
6900 BC	8900	8000			
				Bifurcate	
8200 BC	10100	9000	Early Archaic		
				Corner Notched	Boreal
9550 BC	11500	10,000		Early Side Notched	HOLOCENE
					PLEISTOCENE
9950 BC	11,900	10,200			Younger Dryas ends/Preboreal
10,500 BC	12450	10,500	Late Paleoindian	Dalton/Sloan	
10,950 BC	12,850	10,900			Younger Dryas begins
11,000 BC	12,900	11,000	Middle Paleoindian	Clovis Fluted Points	
11,050 BC	13,000	11,100			Allerod
					Inter-Allerod Cold Period
12,000 BC	14,000	12,000			Allerod
			Early Paleoindian	Pre-Clovis	Older Dryas
12,850 BC	14,800	12,500			Bolling
19,700 BC	21,700	18,000			Last Glacial Maximum

*Calibrations obtained using CalPal online with a 50 year standard deviation, dates rounded to nearest decade or half century

nessee/Cumberland drain much of the elevated interior of the region east of the Mississippi. To the west of the Mississippi, in the trans-Mississippi South, the south and eastward flowing drainages like the White, Arkansas, Ouachita, and the Red drain the interior and the inner Coastal Plain. Numerous rivers drain the Atlantic and Gulf Coastal Plains, many of the larger ones originating in the Piedmont or Blue Ridge, with lesser drainages originating in the

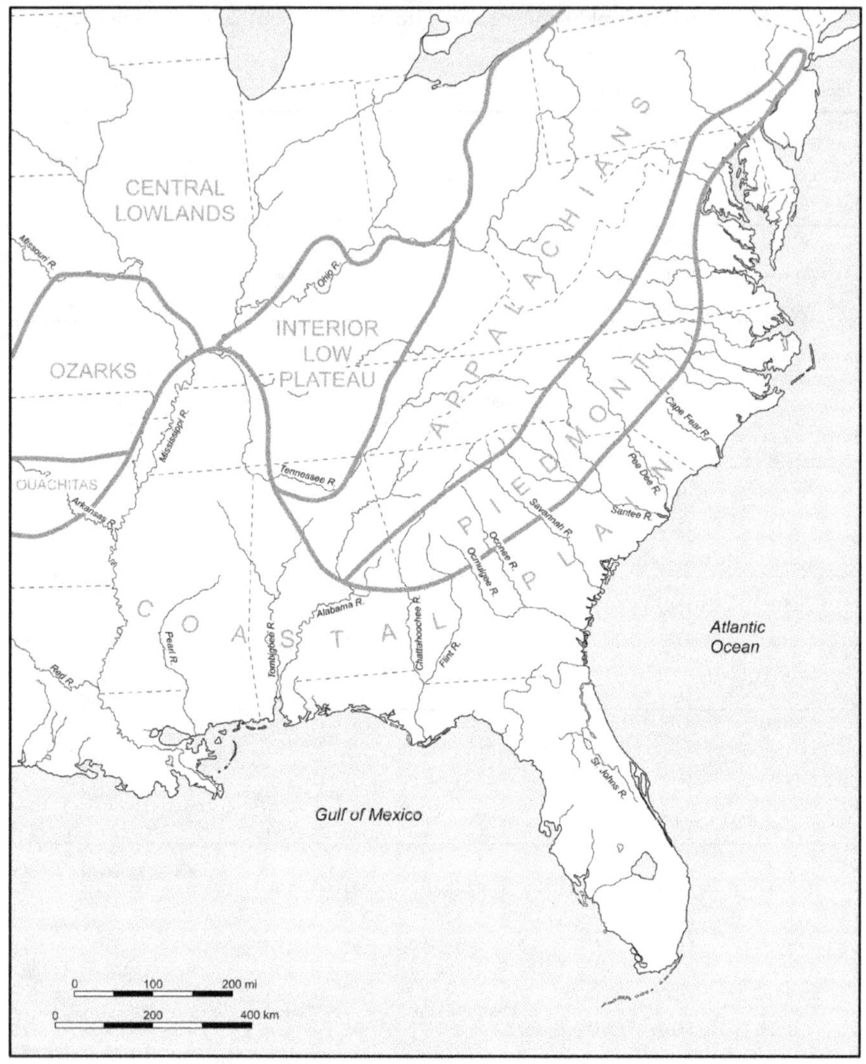

Figure 1-1. Major physiographic regions of the Southeast.

Coastal Plain. The Potomac, Roanoke, Pamlico, Neuse, Cape Fear, Pee Dee, Santee, Savannah, the Ocmulgee/Altamaha, and the St. Johns comprise the major drainages of the south Atlantic slope. Georgia and western Florida lie at the divide between the Atlantic and Gulf watersheds, with the Suwannee, Chattahoochee/Apalachee, Alabama/Coosa/Tallapoosa, Tombigbee, and

Pearl and, across the Mississippi, the Sabine, Neches, Brazos, and the Colorado in Texas the major drainages flowing into the Gulf of Mexico.

Southeastern biotic communities in recent millennia have been dominated by deciduous oak-hickory forests in the interior and mixed deciduous and evergreen oak-hickory-pine forests in the Coastal Plain, with distinctive floodplain and estuarine communities in riverine and coastal areas, respectively (Gremillion 2004a:55–59). A wide array of plant and animal species of use to human populations occur within the region, of which oak, hickory, and walnut mast and white-tailed deer were arguably the most important throughout the period of human settlement (Gremillion 1996, 2002, 2004a:62–63, 2006, 2011; Lapham 2006, 2011; Yarnell and Black 1985). Fruits, greens, and roots were also important sources of food, and a number of annuals like chenopodium, maygrass, amaranth, and sunflower were domesticated in the Southeast and lower Midwest late in the Archaic period, although domesticates do not seem to have played a major role in subsistence until maize began to be intensively cultivated in the Late Woodland and Mississippian periods (Gremillion 2002, 2004b; Simon 2009; B. Smith 1992, 2006). Other animal species important to subsistence practices include fish, of which catfish, drum, and gar were widely taken; birds, both for their meat and plumage; turtles and other reptiles and amphibians; and a variety of shellfish, including mussels in the interior and oysters, clams, and periwinkle in estuarine settings (Claassen 1996, 2010; Jackson and Scott 1995, 2002; Krech 2009; Lapham 2006, 2011; Peacock 2002; Russo 1996a, 1996b; Smith 1986; K. Walker 2000). Biotic community composition changed over time, of course, and floral and faunal communities were appreciably different during the late Pleistocene or even during the early Holocene. As we shall see in the chapters that follow, a fair amount of research has been conducted in the Southeast directed to documenting environmental change and its impact on settlement, including the roles humans played in shaping biotic communities (e.g., Anderson 2001; Delcourt and Delcourt 1985; Delcourt and Delcourt 2004; Delcourt et al. 1998; Gremillion et al. 2008.; Smith 2011; Watson 1990:47–48).

Southeastern Archaeologists Past and Present

In recent decades southeastern archaeology has undergone a profound transformation. Throughout much of the twentieth century prior to about 1970, archaeology in the region was conducted by a small group of scholars, mostly male, and until the 1930s, mostly affiliated with institutions in other parts of the country. Three major periods of intensive research, corresponding roughly to the 1880s, the 1930s, and the years since 1970 have occurred, and each profoundly shaped our understanding of southeastern prehistory. Excellent accounts of this history of research have appeared, both for the Southeast and for the country as a whole (e.g., Stoltman 1973, 2004; Willey and Sabloff 1993), as well as for individual states (e.g., Tushingham et al. 2002). An increasing number of more specialized studies have also been written examining the lives and accomplishments of individual archaeologists working in the Southeast, such as James A. Ford, Clarence Bloomfield Moore, or Jeffries Wyman (e.g., Brown 1978; Knight 1996; Murowchick 1990), or of major female archaeologists of the mid-to-late twentieth century (e.g., Sullivan 1994; White et al. 1999). Histories of research have also appeared directed to specific time periods, such as the New Deal era of the 1930s (Lyon 1996; Means 2012), or of work at specific sites or areas like Irene, Ocmulgee National Monument, or Swift Creek in Georgia (e.g., Claassen 1999; Hally, ed. 1994; Marsh 1998). Most histories of southeastern archaeology written to date have tended to concentrate on events prior to ca. 1970, probably because the amount of work undertaken since that time would have made producing such a history challenging and the resulting size of the document unwieldy. Instead, summaries of recent research trends have been written, for the field of southeastern archaeology or at least the archeology of Native peoples as a whole (e.g., Anderson and Smith 2003; Brose 1993; Brown 1994; Dunnell 1990; Peebles 1990; Steponaitis 1986; Watson 1990), or for specific periods in prehistory like the Paleoindian, Archaic, or Mississippian (e.g., Anderson 1990; Blitz 2009; Cobb 2003; Kidder and Sassaman 2009; Lepper and Funk 2006; Livingood 2008; Meltzer 1988; Pauketat 2007; Sassaman 2010a).

Archaeological investigations in the Southeast prior to the late nineteenth century, or at least those that resulted in publication, were for the most part conducted by wealthy or dedicated individuals. They were typically the accounts of travelers or naturalists, including William Bartram, Henry Brackenridge, or Constantine Rafinesque, who described a number of major archaeological sites and their natural surroundings and in some cases associated Indian groups. Although the presence of artifacts was sometimes noted, careful excavations were only rarely conducted. Thomas Jefferson's

(1787:157–162) examination of a burial mound near Monticello in the late eighteenth century—carefully reporting on his results, including observations about the mounds internal stratigraphy—while oft-recounted in textbooks, was unfortunately a unique exception to the unsystematic plundering of sites that was typical for the period. Jefferson's explicitly problem-oriented research, directed to determining the circumstances under which burials were placed in mounds, and his careful observations and logical method of interpretation, marshaling multiple lines of evidence in support of his conclusions, was an approach not seen again for nearly a century in the region, or indeed anywhere in North America, until the work of Charles C. Jones, Joseph Jones, and Jeffries Wyman in the 1860s and 1870s (Stoltman 2004:17–18). Most excavations into southeastern sites until the late nineteenth century, in contrast, consisted of "probings... by nameless pothunters" with "little controlled excavation... and much fanciful speculation" (Stoltman 1973:120). Site looting remains a major problem to this day in the region, although with the emergence of legislation protecting archaeological sites and human remains in the twentieth century like the Antiquities Act of 1906, the Archaeological Resources Protection Act of 1979, and the Native American Graves Protection and Repatriation Act of 1990, the situation is not as grim as it once was, particularly on federal lands (Harmon et al. 2006). Archaeologists working in the Southeast must bear in mind, however, that many sites have been collected if not actively mined for curiosities and items of value for over 200 years. In the 1850s, for example, a local antiquarian described artifacts uncovered by plowing near Columbia, South Carolina, noting "I have many hundred arrow and spear heads, and many more are in the possession of others" (Howe 1856:159). Even areas now heavily forested may have formerly been cleared, plowed, and collected.

High standards for mapping archeological sites had been established by the middle of the nineteenth century, in Squier and Davis's (1848) magnificent overview *Ancient Monuments of the Mississippi Valley,* based on information collected over the preceding decade and more. The title was something of a misnomer, since most of the sites described were located in the lower Midwest, with particular attention directed to what are now known to be Middle Woodland Hopewell mound and earthwork complexes in Ohio, many of which were carefully mapped using surveying instruments. This was fortunate, because many of these sites have since been damaged or lost to erosion and development. Some southeastern sites were discussed, from the states of Alabama, Louisiana, Kentucky, Mississippi, and South Carolina, although few were mapped in detail. The accounts of sites and artifacts from the Southeast provided by local citizens represented the way archaeological materials were commonly reported at the time, a tradition that continues to this day in some avocational outlets, providing useful descriptive information but less commonly adequate detail on context. Released as the Smithsonian Institution's first "Contribution to Knowledge," Squier and Davis's study remains one of the most significant volumes produced in American archaeology, and helped make the monograph the perceived standard of excellence for professional publication. Site mapping still holds a critical place in fieldwork within the Southeast, and indeed archaeology everywhere, although the mechanical transits of the last century have been replaced with data collected using GPS and total stations, entered in GIS databases, and in some cases superimposed over aerial photographs, or satellite and LiDAR (Light Detection and Ranging) imagery. The origins of the mounds and earthworks mapped by Squier and Davis were the source of much speculation until the end of the nineteenth century, and were frequently attributed to lost non-Indian races (Silverberg 1968), much as tales of ancient astronauts fascinate modern speculators unfamiliar with the rich archaeological record of the Southeast and beyond, and the scholarly literature about it.

Scientific archaeology began to develop gradually in the Southeast following the Civil War, and many of the areas examined then have become foci of much current research. Charles C. Jones, for example, spent most of his life in Georgia and produced maps and wrote excellent descriptive accounts of such famous sites as Etowah, Kolomoki, Nacoochee, Ocmulgee, and Stallings Island (Jones 1873; Stoltman 2004:17; Waring 1968:289), all of which, as we shall see, have received extensive work in recent years. Jones's work has been described as the earliest "information-oriented archaeological excavations" in Georgia (Stoltman 1973:122–123) and he was the first to devote considerable attention to potsherds, an artifact category that has fascinated subsequent generations of archaeologists in the region (Stoltman 2004:17; Watson 1990:43). A compilation produced in the mid-1960s, in fact, listed over 2,000 pottery types from eastern North America, including almost 1,000 from the Southeast as a whole (Broyles 1967), while by the end of the twentieth century 405 types were reported from Georgia alone (Williams and Thompson 1999). C. C. Jones's (1873) *Antiquities of the Southern Indians, Particularly of the Georgia Tribes* contained maps and descriptions of sites as well as artifacts, and included the multi-mound Mason's Plantation site near Augusta, which had been totally lost to erosion when C. B. Moore visited the area in 1898, prompting him to lament, famously, that "The archaeological examination of the Savannah River has been too long deferred" (Moore 1898:168).

The Savannah River has, fortunately, witnessed extensive survey and excavation in recent years, exemplifying a trend in recent southeastern archaeology to exhaustively examine occupations during specific periods in major river valleys, or at least in portions of these drainages, as has been done recently for the Mississippian occupations in the Black Warrior, Chattahoochee, Catawba, Pearl, Savannah, and Tombigbee drainages (e.g., Anderson 1994; Blitz 1993a; Blitz and Lorenz 2006; King 2012; Livingood 2010; Moore 2002; Knight and Steponaitis 1998), and the Late Archaic occupations in the Savannah (Sassaman 2006a). Mason's Plantation, besides illustrating the ongoing loss of archaeological resources in the region to erosion, was long thought to be the location of the principal town of the late Mississippian province of Cofitachequi, which Hernando de Soto visited in 1540 (Hudson 1997; Hudson et al. 2008; Jones 1873; Swanton 1939). Archaeological and ethnohistoric research directed to, among many other things, reconstructing the routes of early Spanish expeditions and the people they met—another hallmark of recent southeastern research (e.g., Galloway 1993; Galloway 2005; Hudson 1990, 1997)—has since shown that the site had been likely abandoned a century or more before De Soto passed through the area (Anderson 1994; King 2012; Wood 2009). The principal town of Cofitachequi appears to have been located at the Mulberry mound site some one hundred miles to the northeast along the Wateree River, in the vicinity of Camden, South Carolina, and near other sites associated with Cofitachequi, including the Belmont Neck and Adamson mounds, the latter the possible site of the Temple of Talimeco, which was described in great detail in the accounts of the expedition (e.g., Cable et al. 1999; Clayton et al. 1993; DePratter 1994; Hudson 1990, 1997; Hudson et al. 1985; Hudson et al. 2008).

Another area where well-conceived archaeological research was conducted at an early date was central Tennessee, where late prehistoric populations had buried their dead in stone box graves (Stoltman 1973:120, 2004:17–18). Unfortunately, these graves were an early target of looters because they were easy to find with a probe or by observing where their outlines were being plowed out, and because they often contained pottery and other grave goods, looting is something that remains a serious problem in the area to this day (Stoltman 1973:124). Joseph L. Jones (1876), C. C. Jones's younger brother, conducted early physical anthropological research with the skeletal remains from stone box graves excavated from ca. 15 sites near Nashville, showing that the smaller individuals were juveniles, not pygmies, as an earlier investigator had suggested (Stoltman 1973:123–124). Importantly, Jones reported the contents of individual graves, a practice that did not become widespread for another 50 years in the region, although less than 30 years later Sir Flinders Petrie demonstrated that such reporting was critically important to the development of ceramic sequences, through the seriation of grave lots from predynastic sites in Egypt (O'Brien and Lyman 1999a:84–91). Since the stone box cemeteries were easier to excavate than mounds, and yielded well-preserved remains, they attracted other investigators, such as Frederic Ward Putnam (1878) and Gates P. Thruston (1890), causing Stoltman (1973:124) to remark that "these Tennessee sites were [among] the most widely known Southeastern sites in the late nineteenth century." Putman's (1878:347–350) work, importantly, included the recognition and excavation of house floors, another practice that eventually became widespread in the region, although unfortunately also not for another fifty years (Stoltman 2004:18). The examples illustrate how early applications of research methods, then as now, sometimes take time to be recognized and adopted, something that typically requires clear and repeated well-publicized demonstrations of their utility.

Thruston (1890) and C. C. Jones (1873), importantly, wrote single-volume summaries of the archaeology of their respective states, offering another model for reporting that, while adopted only intermittently through much of the twentieth century (e.g., Brown 1926; Morse and Morse 1983; Walthall 1980; White 1988), has recently again become popular, with syntheses produced in several states, such as in Florida (Milanich 1994), Kentucky (Lewis 1996; Pollack 2008), Louisiana (Rees 2010), Missouri (O'Brien and Wood 1998), North Carolina (Ward and Davis 1999), and South Carolina (Goodyear and Hanson 1989). These are commonly edited or multi-authored volumes, and in some states encompass multiple volumes, a logical solution given the breadth of material to be covered. Examples of the latter include the Georgia Archaeological Research Design series, comprising some 15 separate overviews covering the state by time period and physiographic region (e.g., Elliott and Sassaman 1995; Thomas 1993; all of these reports are available online at the University of Georgia's Laboratory of

Archaeology website), or the Council of Virginia Archaeologist's syntheses of the archaeology of major time periods (e.g., Reinhart and Hodges 1990, 1991, 1992; Wittkofski and Reinhart 1989). Given the amount of text required to synthesize a single state, the present volume, accordingly, emphasizes recent developments and their historical context, taking a broad rather than a comprehensive approach to the regional literature.

Following a pattern now seen in many other parts of the Southeast, large-scale excavation programs focused on Mississippian-period occupations have occurred in the Nashville Basin in recent years, under the direction of personnel from state agencies like the Tennessee Division of Archaeology and local universities like Middle Tennessee State University and the University of Tennessee (e.g., Deter-Wolf 2004; Klippel and Bass 1984; Moore 2005; Moore and Breitburg 1998; Moore and Smith 2001; Moore et al. 2006; Norton and Broster 2004; K. Smith 1992; Smith and Miller 2009). Some of this work, importantly, has involved the re-examination of the extensive collections made in the nineteenth century (Moore 2004; Moore and Smith 2009; K. Smith 1992). This is another major characteristic of southeastern archaeology in recent years, with appreciable effort directed to writing up materials excavated during earlier periods, some of which had never been reported or were only cursorily reported at the time (e.g., Jeter 1990; Lyon 1996; Moore 2004; Pritchard and Ahlman 2009; Schroeder 2009; Sullivan et al. 1995; Welch 2006).

Shell midden archaeology, while a major focus of modern research, received comparatively little attention in the Southeast until the latter half of the nineteenth century, probably because earthen mounds and late prehistoric cemeteries offered better opportunities for finding elaborate and intact stone or ceramic artifacts useful for exhibition or sale. Scientific work on shell sites began with the excavations of Jeffries Wyman along the St. Johns River from 1867 to 1874 (Wyman 1875; see also Murowchick 1990, Stoltman 2004:18). Wyman was the first curator of the Peabody Museum of Archaeology and Ethnology at Harvard University, and was succeeded by Frederic Ward Putnam, an equally remarkable archaeologist whose work also took him on occasion to the Southeast (Browman 2002; Browman and Williams 2002). Their work, in fact, marked the beginning of a long involvement by scholars and students from northern universities that continues to this day, even though archaeological training began to be offered in many southern states in the latter part of the twentieth century. Whether the shell middens were natural deposits or were created by humans was uncertain at the time (Brinton 1859:180), although work on similar "kitchen middens" by mid-nineteenth century Danish archaeologists prompted gradual acceptance of their true nature in the Southeast, and stimulated explorations by scholars like Wyman (Daniel 1950:87–88; Stoltman 1973: 126–127). Similar concerns, such as whether mounds at the Cahokia site were geological or cultural features, were not fully resolved until the 1920s, with the evidence deciding the matter including information collected during one of the first uses of aerial photography in the field of archaeology (Hall 1968; Moorehead 1923, 1929 [2000]). Debates about the nature of shell midden assemblages continue today, albeit with attention now directed to evaluating whether they reflect mundane subsistence debris or intentionally planned monuments (e.g., Beasley 2008; Marquardt 2010a, 2010b; Milner and Jefferies 1998; Randall 2010; Russo 2004, 2010; Sassaman 2010a; Thompson and Andrus 2011). Recognition and interpretation of sites and particularly artifacts still remains a problem in Paleoindian archaeology in the region, where appreciable debate centers around the existence of Pre-Clovis assemblages at a number of southeastern sites (cf. Fiedel 2012; Goodyear 2005; Hoak 2012).

Wyman's (1875) *Fresh Water Shell Mounds of the St. John's River, Florida*, published posthumously, is another classic work of nineteenth-century Americanist archaeology, and arguably the first scientific monograph produced solely on southeastern materials. In it, Wyman demonstrated that the shell middens he examined were cultural features and that they were formed by gradual accretion and, in an early use of quantification, identified and provided count data for the faunal remains from 12 sites and for ceramics by temper and decorative treatment from seven sites. The former was the first systematic zooarchaeological analysis in American archaeology, while the latter was a ceramic analysis that had "no equal in the literature of American archaeology until well into the twentieth century" (Stoltman 2004:18; see also Gibson 1993; Reitz 1993:118–119), although both forms of analysis are now routinely conducted in the region and, in the case of ceramics, have been since the 1930s (Gibson 1993:23). Wyman proposed a sequence of non-ceramic followed by ceramic sites, and argued that within the latter category, ceramics that were plain and incised were older than those that were stamped. His observations represent the creation of "the first ceramic sequence in eastern North American archaeology... [that] stands to this day" (Stoltman 1973:128).

Developing sequences of diagnostic artifacts to aid in the identification and dating of sites occupied much research attention during the middle third of the twentieth century, during the heyday of the research paradigm known as culture history (O'Brien et al. 1997; Webster 2008; Willey and Sabloff 1993), and remains a research interest to this day in areas or for periods where such sequences are poorly developed. Ceramic sequences were developed in many parts of the Southeast in the middle third of the twentieth century based on both seriation and excavation activity, beginning with Ford's (1936) pioneering work in the Lower Mississippi Valley (Gibson 1993:23; Watson 1990:43). Resolution of Archaic projectile point sequences was accomplished somewhat later based primarily on work at deeply stratified sites (e.g., Broyles 1966, 1971; Chapman 1985; Coe 1964), while the Paleoindian sequence in the Southeast remains poorly documented (Anderson et al. 1996; Anderson, Miller, Yerka et al. 2010; Gardner and Verrey 1979). Work on coastal and interior shell middens in the Southeast, and an interest in multidisciplinary methods, can be traced in part back to the work of Wyman.

While important archaeological work had been conducted in the region in the first three quarters of the nineteenth century, the decades of the 1880s and early 1890s marked one of the three great periods of research in the Southeast brought about through a major infusion of federal support or, in the case of work conducted since 1970, federal and private funding mandated by environmental legislation (Anderson 1997a; Keel 1988; Lyon 1996; Steponaitis 1986; Watson 1990:45). In 1881 Congress appropriated $5,000 expressly for "archaeological investigations relating to mound builders and prehistoric mounds" (J. Powell 1894:xli). This action marked a major turning point in American and particularly southeastern archeology, where a great deal of the work occurred. The funds were made available to the Bureau of Ethnology, which had been established in 1879 within the Smithsonian Institution, with John Wesley Powell of Colorado River fame appointed its first director. Powell appointed Wills de Haas, who had dug at Grave Creek Mound in West Virginia to run the Mound Division and, after de Haas resigned a year later, Cyrus Thomas, a lawyer, entomologist, and professor of natural history at what was then called Southern Illinois Normal University (Keel 1970:9). Thomas in turn hired a number of field assistants to visit, to excavate, and to report on mounds throughout the eastern United States. Over the ten-year period from 1882 to 1891, the Mound Division explored over 2,000 mounds and other earthworks in 140 counties in the eastern and United States (J. Powell 1894:xlv; Smith 1985), seeking to answer the question "Were the mounds built by the Indians?" (Thomas 1894:21). These investigations were reported in the annual reports of the Bureau of Ethnology of the Smithsonian Institution through the 1880s and early 1890s. A massive synthesis was published in the 12th annual report released in 1894, entitled *Report on the Mound Explorations of the Bureau of Ethnology* (Thomas 1894), a volume that is today regarded as a classic of the profession (Smith 1985:5). Hundreds of pages of supporting evidence, and the superb logic employed in its organization and interpretation, led to the conclusion that the mounds were built by "the ancestors of the Indians," helping dispel the overtly racist theories of the time that the mound builders were other than American Indians (Thomas 1894:730). The report provided the "the death blow to the concept of a lost Mound Builder race" (Stoltman 1973:126).

An important lesson to take from the efforts of the Mound Division, still of critical importance in southeastern archaeology to this day, is the need to report the results of fieldwork. The Mound Division examined many sites, and while most received at least some level of reporting, much of that was cursory. Fortunately, extensive collections and records from this work were made and curated, and many have been subject to modern reexamination and reinterpretation, such as at many of the mounds examined in Arkansas (Jeter 1990), and at the Hollywood mound group along the Savannah River (e.g., Anderson 1994; Blitz 1999; King 2012; Wood 2009). Important lessons for southeastern archaeologists are that observations or assertions about the archaeological record are best supported by published evidence, and that the careful and thorough curation of records and collections is a critical part of the archaeological research process (e.g., Sullivan and Childs 2003). This was demonstrated by Holmes (1903) analysis of ceramic artifacts recovered from the excavations of the Mound Division recounted in the 20th Annual Report of the Bureau of American Ethnology, *Aboriginal Pottery of the Eastern United States*, another classic of American and southeastern archaeology. In addition to the descriptive reporting of ceramics from differing regions, Holmes discussed at length the distribution, functional significance, and manufacturing technology of the ceramics recovered, including methods for producing surface treatments that occur widely in the Southeast, such as linear check, cordmarked, fabric impressed, and dentate stamping. Holmes's research, with its emphasis on pottery function and manufacture, as well as its recognition of distinctive regional manufacturing and decorative traditions, was decades ahead of its time, although such work with ceramic artifacts is now commonplace in the Southeast (e.g., Cordell 1984, 1992, 2004; Griffin 1967; Hally 1983, 1986; Pauketat and Emerson 1991; Rice 1987, 1996a, 1996b; Sassaman 1993; Sassaman and Rudolphi 2001; Saunders and Hays 2004; Steponaitis 1983; Wallis 2009, 2011).

Following the cessation of fieldwork by the Mound Division in the early 1890s, archaeological fieldwork occurred only sporadically in the Southeast over the next several decades, until a massive new infusion of federal funding for archaeology occurred during the Great Depression. Investigations during the late nineteenth and early twentieth centuries were conducted primarily by people from museums or universities located outside the region, and was almost invariably directed to sites yielding elaborately crafted artifacts, such as Adena and Hopewell culture mounds in the northern Southeast and lower Midwest, or late prehistoric/early Contact era mounds and cemeteries. Comparatively little sustained archaeological fieldwork was conducted in the Southeast during this interval, although important excavations at specific sites did occur, at places like Etowah, Nacoochee, and Stallings Island (Claflin 1931; Heye et al. 1918; Lyon 1996; Moorehead et al. 1932), and at Cahokia in the Illinois, where Warren K. Moorehead's (1923, 1929 [2000]) fieldwork and lobbying led to the preservation of parts of the site by the state. Moorehead's work spanned this era, and included investigations at the Hopewell type site, the Etowah mounds in Georgia, the Cahokia mounds in Illinois, and at the very end of his career, at the Chesterfield shell ring in South Carolina (Flannery 1943; Guthe 1939; Kelly 2000; Meltzer 1985).

Moorehead's lobbying in support of archaeological goals such as the preservation of portions of the Cahokia site reflects another long-standing tradition in the archaeology of the Southeast. Scholars like Charles R. McGimsey and Hester Davis (McGimsey and Davis 1977; McGimsey 1972), among many others, for example, helped usher in the modern era of cultural resource management (CRM) archaeology, and have worked tirelessly to maintain strong state archaeological research and resource management programs. The active involvement and frequent successes by archaeologists in the political process in the Southeast, which dates back at least as far as the Great Depression when the establishment of strong state relief programs required local support, cannot be too strongly emphasized (e.g., Lyon 1996; Watson 1990:46).

What is sometimes overlooked is the fact that Moorehead also sympathetically interacted with Native Americans, having been at the Pine Ridge Reservation at the time of the Wounded Knee massacre (Jenson 1997:261; Moorehead 1914:101), producing an account of the event. From 1909 to 1933 he served as a commissioner for the Bureau of Indian Affairs, where he worked actively to improve Indian living conditions on reservations, as well as expose fraud and corruption in the agency. His work *The American Indian in the United States Period 1850–1914* is subtitled "*A Plea for Justice*" (Moorehead 1914). Southeastern archaeologist's interactions with Native Americans, while unquestionably more regular and sustained in recent years due to the passage of the Native American Graves Protection and Repatriation Act (NAGPRA) in 1990, thus have a long if intermittent history. Until the past two decades this interaction was unfortunately fairly minimal, dependent on the actions of individuals interested in specific research topics or the requirements of specific legal proceedings, like cases with the Indian Claims Commission (e.g., Levy 2001:30–31; Pluckhahn et al. 2006:12–13; Sullivan 1994:114). Fortunately this behavior has changed, and consultation with Native American as well as other descendant populations is now becoming a routine aspect of archeological fieldwork in the region. The Native American Affairs Committee of the Southeastern Archaeological Conference (SEAC) has been particularly active at promoting relations between Native nations and the regional archaeological community in recent years, including hosting forums with Native American speakers and panelists at the annual meetings of the conference.

The individual whose work in the late nineteenth and early twentieth centuries had perhaps the greatest influence on contemporary practice in southeastern archaeology was Clarence Bloomfield "C. B." Moore, a wealthy Harvard-educated businessman who, after retiring from running the family business, the Jessup & Moore Paper Company, at about age 40, spent the next three decades visiting, mapping, and excavating at scores of shell and earthen mound sites across the Southeast. Moore traveled in his personal flat-bottomed paddle steamer, the *Gopher of Philadelphia*, a name countless students in southeastern archaeology courses have come to know, and one that makes clear his interest was in digging (Pearson et al. 2000). Most importantly, and the reason his work is known and well regarded to this day, Moore published the results of his investigations in a timely fashion, in lengthy and well-illustrated reports produced to the professional standards of the time. He wrote detailed field notes, and saw to the long-term curation of his maps and notebooks, and the major artifacts found during this work. Such practices, while now a routine part of modern archaeological research, were decidedly uncommon at the time. Between 1892 and 1918, Moore traveled up and down the major river drainages and coastlines of the Southeast visiting as many Native American mounds as he could obtain access to. In the winter he would scout ahead to find sites and to obtain the necessary permissions for conducting site visits and excavations, and he would return with his full crew later in the winter or in the spring to conduct excavations. On board his riverboat were a crew of trained excavators, and his friend, secretary, and physician, Dr. Milo G. Miller, who also served as the project osteologist. The excavation and description of human remains as well as artifacts was an important component of his investigations, a collaboration between archaeology and physical anthropology that is another long-standing tradition in southeastern archaeology (e.g., Powell et al. 1991; Smith 1993, 1996).

During the months of the year when Moore was not digging, he analyzed his finds and prepared reports of the past seasons of fieldwork for publication in the *Journal of the Academy of Natural Sciences of Philadelphia*, at his own expense (Knight 1996:1–4; Larson 1998:3–5). His reports were lavishly illustrated and contain a wealth of information about many sites that have since been damaged or lost. The University of Alabama Press reprinted the entire series, which had become expensive collectibles, from 1996 to 2002, with subsidies provided by SEAC and other donors. These comparatively low cost volumes include detailed introductions and modern interpretations of the sites by knowledgeable local archaeologists. Long after C. B. Moore's day, fieldwork, data analysis, and reporting, particularly the production of site reports, monographs, and books, continues to be highly regarded in the Southeast.

The second great period of federal support for southeastern archaeology occurred from 1933 to 1942, during the Great Depression, when New Deal era survey and excavation programs occurred in many states, resulting in the collection of vast quantities of data that "in some regions remain unsurpassed even today" (Steponaitis 1986:364). While a handful of archaeologists began to be permanently employed in the Southeast beginning in the 1920s and 1930s, large numbers now devote their entire careers to working within the region, a trend that began in earnest in the 1930s (Brown 1994; Stoltman 2004:22). Under the leadership of President Franklin D. Roosevelt

Box 1-1. The Southeastern Archaeological Conference

What binds many of the scholars working in the region together is the Southeastern Archaeological Conference, or SEAC, as it is fondly known to its members. Co-founded in 1938 by James B. Griffin and James A. Ford, who put out a call for a "Conference on Pottery Nomenclature for the Southeastern United States" (Ford and Griffin 1937), the first meeting was held in Ann Arbor, Michigan in May of 1938, with 13 archaeologists attending. Regular meetings were seen as a means of sharing, standardizing, and disseminating information about the massive amounts of archaeological materials, and specifically ceramic artifacts, then being collected under the auspices of New Deal era relief programs. A second meeting was held in Birmingham, Alabama in November 1938 and, while two meetings were also held in 1939, in Birmingham and Macon (Figure 1B-1), the conference has met annually since 1940, albeit with a break from 1942 to 1949, during World War II and the initial post-war period. Other than the first meeting in Ann Arbor, all of the subsequent meetings have been held in the Southeast. SEAC remained fairly small from the late 1930s to the mid-1960s, under one hundred members, and most of the early meetings during this period took place in a single room. From 1952 to 1971, in fact, the conference met nearly every other year at the visitor's center at Ocmulgee National Monument near Macon, Georgia, rotating to different cities in the South during intervening years. Since 1972 the annual meeting has moved from city to city, typically alternating from the eastern to the western, or the northern to the southern part of the region.

The rise of CRM archaeology in the 1970s, with its increased funding and employment opportunities, changed southeastern archaeology and SEAC dramatically. From a few dozen practitioners in the 1950s, by the late 1970s hundreds of people were working in the region, many on large reservoir, highway, or channelization projects that rivaled the work done in the 1930s in scale and available resources. State archaeologist offices were established in every state by the 1970s, and beginning about this time many archaeologists began to be employed by federal agencies operating in the region, including the U.S. Forest Service, the Army Corps of Engineers, various other branches of the military, and the National Park Service. The Southeastern Archaeological Conference, as a result, grew markedly in the 1970s and 1980s. SEAC has had about a thousand members since the late 1990s, and the annual meetings for the past two decades have regularly had 400 to 500 or more registrants, reaching as high as 800 when the meeting was held jointly with the Midwestern Archaeological Conference, as was the case in 1994 and 2004. SEAC's membership no longer fits in a single room, save at the largest of hotels or conference centers, and the meeting is in fact now restricted to larger southern cities for that reason.

Figure 1B-1. The 1939 Southeastern Archaeological Conference annual meeting participants in front of the earthlodge at Ocmulgee National Monument.

The conference has published a Newsletter since 1939, an Annual Bulletin started by Stephen Williams since 1964, and since 1982, a scholarly peer-reviewed journal, *Southeastern Archaeology* (Steponaitis et al. 2003). In honor of C. B. Moore's extensive fieldwork and reporting efforts in the Southeast, since 1990 archaeologists making up the Lower Mississippi Archaeological Survey or LMS (Steponaitis et al. 2002; Williams 2003) and the membership of SEAC have maintained an award in his name for excellence in southeastern archaeology by a young scholar. The presentation of the C. B. Moore Award, the Lifetime Achievement Award, and the Student Paper Prize, the latter consisting of donated books averaging several thousand dollars in value, is a highlight of the SEAC business meeting each year, an event followed by a dance. But the annual meeting is primarily about scholarship, with hundreds of papers and posters presented each year. For the 50th anniversary celebration of the first meeting of the conference, at the 1988 annual meeting a series of papers were produced discussing the role of the Southeast in American archaeology, and examining research trends (Dunnell 1990; Peebles 1990; Watson 1990). This SAA Press volume appears on the 75th anniversary of the founding of the Southeastern Archaeological Conference, and offers an update on those perspectives.

a number of federal relief programs were established to put people to work, and early on archaeology was recognized as an inexpensive means of employing large numbers of people (Haag 1985; Lyon 1996:28ff; Means 2012; Setzler and Strong 1936; Stoltman 1973, 2004:22–25; Sullivan et al. 2011; Watson 1990:46; Wauchope 1966). By the early 1930s the establishment of cultural sequences and relative chronologies was recognized as of critical importance at the National Research Council's Conference on Southern Prehistory in Birmingham in 1932, and New Deal era funding made it happen (O'Brien and Lyman 1999b; O'Brien et al. 1997). So much archaeological fieldwork occurred across the Southeast during the New Deal era that by the time federal funding ended with the onset of World War II, basic ceramic prehistoric and early historic period cultural sequences had been developed in many parts of the region (Dunnell 1990:18–19; Gibson 1993; Stoltman 2004:22–24; Webster 2008). The culture-historical research approach was, to some, "a Southeastern intellectual product" with the region considered "the intellectual center of American archaeology though closely connected to the Midwest and Southwest" until the 1960s (Dunnell 1990:19; see also Stoltman 2004:22–25)

The first relief-era excavations occurred from August through November 1933 in Marksville, Louisiana, directed by Frank Setzler, an archaeologist from the Smithsonian Institution, and James A. Ford, a native of Mississippi who went on to have a long and distinguished career in southeastern archaeology (Brown 1978; Fagette 1996; Lyon 1996:1–4; O'Brien and Lyman 1998). Projects proliferated throughout the region in following years, offering employment and supervisory opportunities for a generation of mostly younger archaeologists, in circumstances akin to a trial by fire given the large workforces and few supervisory personnel involved (Haag 1985; Jennings 1994; Means 2012; Setzler and Strong 1936; Stoltman 1973, 2004; Sullivan et al. 2011; Wauchope 1966). Many of the leaders of southeastern and indeed American archaeology for the next two generations were forged in this crucible, including Joseph R. Caldwell, Joffre L. Coe, David DeJarnette, Charles Fairbanks, James A. Ford, James B. Griffin, William G. Haag, Jesse D. Jennings, Arthur R. Kelly, Madeline D. Kneberg, Thomas M. N. Lewis, Robert S. Neitzel, Robert Wauchope, William S. Webb, and Gordon R. Willey, among many others. While initially the work was directed almost exclusively to excavation, analysis and reporting was increasingly recognized as important, something that led to the establishment of the Southeastern

Archaeological Conference in 1938. Toward the end of the era, separate artifact processing laboratories were in place in some states where women found employment, being otherwise commonly barred from fieldwork by the social norms of the time. These strictures were ignored or waived on occasion, such as when all-female and mostly African-American crews (albeit under a series of white male supervisors) excavated the Swift Creek site near Macon and the Irene mound site near Savannah (Claassen 1993, 1999; Marsh 1998; Whalen and Price 1998).

The amount of work varied across the region, for reasons that were only partially due to the presence of archaeological resources available for examination. After 1935, with the establishment of the Works Progress Administration, relief projects were under state and local control, with the result that in many states where archaeologists were able to work successfully with local citizens and politicians, a great deal of archaeological research occurred, although in a few states, lacking such leadership and in some cases any interested archaeologists to begin with, little or no work took place (Anderson 2002a; Lyon 1996:64; Stoltman 2004:24). The same lesson applies today, where states in the Southeast with large and well-funded archaeological programs are typically those where public and hence political support has been carefully maintained, in part through outreach efforts and the support of avocational groups. Some New Deal archaeology programs, like that by the Tennessee Valley Authority, were exceptional in the amount of fieldwork, analysis, and reporting that occurred in proposed reservoir areas. Some of this was due to the nature and scale of the construction occurring, of which archaeology could be considered a logical part, but much of it was due to the diligence in pursuing opportunities by local scholars like William S. Webb in Kentucky and Thomas M. N. Lewis and Madeline Kneberg in Tennessee (Pritchard and Ahlman 2009; Stoltman 2004:24).

Many New Deal-era archaeologists went on to establish research programs in their states and training programs at local universities, and into the 1970s their names were often considered synonymous with the archaeology of these states, about which they were clearly the preeminent authorities. Most archaeologists currently active in the Southeast over the age of fifty, in fact, grew up professionally under the guidance or at least the eye of these New Deal-era veterans, who were fixtures at SEAC as well as at state and national archaeological society meetings for many years. At these and other venues, these venerable elders served as sources of great inspiration to younger generations of specialists in Southeastern archaeology, and often, in relaxed settings, they shared colorful stories about their lives in archaeology, and the people and projects they had been involved with. Just as many older southeastern archaeologists were trained by individuals whose careers were shaped by the massive field programs of the New Deal era, younger generations have grown up during the CRM era and have likewise had great opportunities to conduct field and laboratory research. Indeed, southeastern archaeology has been shaped, arguably, perhaps to a greater degree than in any other part of the country, by the massive field projects that have occurred in the region, most the result of federal funding.

The New Deal era left other legacies, however, besides creating a first and in some ways "greatest generation" of local archaeologists. Much of the work was directed to excavation activity, not survey, and only rarely was analysis and reporting funded, with the result that the materials collected during many large projects were never analyzed or published, at least in much detail. Exceptional examples of analysis and reporting that did occur at the time include Caldwell and McCann's (1941) Irene Mound report, or the many volumes produced by William S. Webb (e.g., Webb 1938, 1939; see also Haag 1965; Lyon 1996:97–108) based on TVA reservoir projects as well as at other locations in the Midsouth, but these were atypical. Fortunately, the records and collections from many of the New Deal era projects were properly curated, allowing the original excavators as well as subsequent generations of archaeologists the opportunity to analyze and report on these collections (Sullivan et al. 2011). Most reporting, of necessity, was deferred until after World War II, when a number of New Deal or independent research projects initiated by organizations like the LMS in the prewar years were completed—following accepted professional archaeological practice as monograph-length reports—such as Lewis and Kneberg's *Hiwassee Island* (1946), Willey's (1949) *Archaeology of the Florida Gulf Coast*, and Phillips, Ford, and Griffin's (1951) *Archaeological Survey in the Lower Mississippi Alluvial Valley 1940–1947*. Reexamining and writing up earlier investigations has thus long been a major part of southeastern archaeology and, as noted when discussing nineteenth-century work, one that continues to this day. Much of this work is accomplished by graduate students as well as by more established professionals, particularly at universities or museums where extensive collections and records are curated (e.g., Schroeder 2009; Sullivan 2007, 2009; Sullivan et al. 1995). It is also done through contracts with federal agencies like the National Park Service, who manage properties like the Shiloh National Military Park where New Deal-era work was only minimally reported (e.g., Welch 2006), or through celebratory volumes like the one commemorating the fiftieth anniversary of the start of excavations at Ocmulgee National Monument (Hally, ed. 1994). Indeed, it has been argued that the reason southeastern archaeologists did not engage in the theoretical debates of the 1960s and after was because they "were either just keeping ahead of construction projects or still digging out from under collections made in the 1930s" (Peebles 1990:28). An alternate explanation, advanced by Ian W. Brown (personal communication 2011), may be related to the fact that the Southeast was in the vanguard of the cultural historical movement, that is, on the cutting edge of American archeology for many years, and its practitioners in the region may have been loath to give up that hard-won honor.

After World War II, the expanding national economy precluded the need for relief work, and funding for archaeology was far less than during the preceding decade. The River Basin Surveys of the Smithsonian Institution's Bureau of American Ethnology, which operated from 1945 to 1969, when responsibility for archaeological investigations conducted or funded by the federal government was transferred to the National Park Service, proved to be the major source of funding and the training ground for archaeologists during this period (Binkley 2007; Keel 1988; Stoltman 2004:28). Much of the work occurred in the Missouri River Basin, although several comparatively small reservoir survey and excavation projects were conducted in the Southeast, recounted in four of the 39 volumes of *River Basin Survey Papers* that were ultimately published (Stoltman 2004:28). Federal funding was greatly reduced compared to during the Depression, however, resulting in a shift to "smaller-scale, low budget operations" in the region from the later 1940s through the late 1960s (Steponaitis 1986:364). Indeed, the number of archaeologists trained during this interval that went on to work in the Southeast, some of whom still attend SEAC meetings and actively publish, albeit most now from retirement, was significantly lower than the numbers appearing before and especially after that time. Important research did occur, however, including the broad resolution of the regional Archaic-period cultural sequence—or more properly the Archaic projectile point sequence—at deeply stratified sites like Russell Cave in Alabama (Griffin 1974; Miller 1956), Hardaway and Doerschuk in North Carolina (Coe 1964), and St.

Albans in West Virginia (Broyles 1966, 1971). Increased attention to regional survey, and analyses of collections acquired from surface or limited test excavations also occurred, with the research and publications of members of the Lower Mississippi Archaeological Survey exemplars of this work (e.g., Ford 1963; Ford and Webb 1956; Neitzel 1966, 1983; Phillips 1970; Phillips et al. 1951; Williams 2003). Only limited survey had occurred during the New Deal era, primarily for logistical reasons—moving people around was more difficult than keeping them all in one place at an excavation (Wauchope's [1966] northern Georgia survey was a notable exception)—but in recent decades that has changed dramatically in the region.

With the rise of the New Archaeology in the 1960s and after, it has been argued that southeastern archaeologists played little role in its early development and that some were "actively hostile to" the approach (Dunnell 1990:19). Of course, this perspective overlooks the fact that both Lewis R. Binford and Stanley A. South, among the founders of the "New Archaeology" in prehistoric and historical archaeology, respectively, grew up in the south and both received their early training at the University of North Carolina under Joffre Coe (South 2005a, 2005b). Binford's (1964, 1967) dissertation, in fact, was on the archaeology and ethnohistory of the coastal North Carolina and Virginia region, and South's (2005b) master's thesis work on prehistoric settlement in the Roanoke River Valley contributed significantly to Coe's (1964) influential statement on the Archaic prehistoric sequence of the North Carolina Piedmont and the Southeast, more generally. Both Binford and South conducted important fieldwork in the region in the 1950s, and attended meetings of SEAC. Indeed, from 1960 to 1977 the Conference on Historic Sites Archaeology, which South (1977, 2005a) founded, met at the same venue as SEAC, on the day before SEAC events began. A different perspective might be that while New Archaeology's prophets were natives of the American south, their messages, or at least Binford's, perhaps were not honored in their own homeland until somewhat later than they were embraced elsewhere. Regardless of the region's role in shaping theoretical developments in American archaeology in the 1960s, as we show in following chapters, in recent decades the Southeast has once again moved to the forefront of theoretical and methodological developments in American archaeology. A major reason for this is the vast amount of fieldwork that has occurred in the region as a result of federal environmental legislation, and the research and employment opportunities that came with it.

The 1970s marked the start of the third great period of federal involvement in the archaeology of the Southeast, sometimes known as the modern or CRM era. More fieldwork and reporting on southeastern archaeology has occurred since 1970 than in all the years prior to this combined, the results of which in a very real sense form the subject of this volume. While the laws that prompted this resurgence were passed from the mid-1960s onward, it took about a decade before funds directed to archaeology began to appear in sustained large amounts. The most critical for archaeology was the National Historic Preservation Act of 1966, or NHPA, which has been amended and strengthened on several occasions since initial passage, and greatly reinforced by subsequent legislation like the National Environmental Policy Act of 1969 and the Archeological Recovery Act (also called the Moss-Bennett Act) of 1974. The major provisions and implications of this remarkable piece of legislation, more than any other, have shaped modern archaeological practice in the Southeast, and indeed, across the United States.

Section 101 of Title I of the NHPA established the National Register of Historic Places (NRHP), state and tribal historic preservation officers or SHPOs and THPOs as they are now known, survey and planning grant programs, and mandated the development of state historic preservation plans. Under Section 106, any federally funded or assisted undertaking is required to "take into account the effect of the undertaking on any district, site, building, structure, or object that is included in or eligible for inclusion in the National Register." Under Section 108, the Historic Preservation Fund was established to help carry out the provisions of the Act, including the survey and planning grants program that is a source of much local funding for archaeology in many southern states each year. Under Section 110, federal agencies are charged with establishing preservation programs "for the identification, evaluation, and nomination to the National Register of Historic Places, and protection of historic properties." This "inventory process," basically, mandated the survey of federal lands in the region, to locate and assess cultural resources, something that has led to literally millions of acres of land being examined, tens of millions of shovel tests being excavated, and thousands of sites being tested. Under Section 112, professional standards for those responsible for historic resources were established, coordination of provisions of the NHPA with NAGPRA was addressed, and the development of databases summarizing archaeological research activity was officially sanctioned.

Under Title II of the NHPA, the Advisory Council on Historic Preservation was created, an authority charged with promulgating rules and regulations for interpreting Section 106 of NHPA, providing advice and assistance in implementing the act, and reviewing operations conducted under it, at the state or agency level. Title IV, in 1992, created the National Center for Preservation Technology and Training, located in Natchitoches, Louisiana, another significant source of technical advice, training, and funding for archaeology. Subsequent federal legislation—such as the National Environmental Policy Act of 1970, the Archeological and Historic Preservation Act of 1974, the Archaeological Resource Protection Act of 1979, and the Native American Graves Protection and Repatriation Act of 1990, and 36 CR 79, providing standards for the Curation of Federally Owned and Administered Archeological Collections—reinforced and built on the foundation provided by the NHPA (T. King 2004).

The amount of archaeology conducted under the provisions of the NHPA in the Southeast has been staggering. The number of recorded sites in the region as has gone from under 10,000 in 1970 to 180,000 in 1994 (Anderson and Horak 1995), to upwards of 375,000 today (Table 1–2), with almost all of the increase the result of survey work mandated by sections 106 and 110 of the act. Thousands of these sites have been intensively tested to evaluate their NRHP significance, while hundreds have been subject to large scale data recovery excavations, to mitigate their loss when avoidance, always the preferred option in historic preservation, was not feasible. The vast amount of site-specific information collected in recent decades, while a challenge to maintain, access, analyze, and interpret, is increasingly being employed at local to state scales with great success, among other things in predictive modeling and resource management efforts, documenting where people lived in the past with increasingly detailed resolution (e.g., Anderson and Smith 2003; Johanson 2011; O'Donoughue 2008).

While modern field teams only rarely approach those of the New Deal era in terms of numbers of people, the quantity, diversity, and quality of the data collected is sometimes far better. Sites of all kinds and periods are being examined, with cultural resources now understood to encompass a wide range of historic, Contact era, and prehistoric property types, including not only traditional archeological sites, but also buildings, landscapes, and sacred and traditional use areas. This has resulted in greater attention to smaller sites in a wider array of settings, "the full range of settlement types that once existed, rather than only the large or deeply stratified sites" (Steponaitis 1986:365). A large number of technical specialists are commonly involved in modern archeological fieldwork, including ceramicists, dating specialists, dendroclimatologists, geoarchaeologists, lithic analysts, paleoethnobotanists, palynologists, physical anthropologists, remote sensing specialists, zooarchaeologists, and many more, contributing data about past environments, diet, health, and the age, function, and context of recovered archaeological materials. While modern excavations are less likely to examine large areas by hand, a typical procedure during the New Deal, the use of heavy equipment for trenching and stripping on threatened sites by imaginative and highly competent field supervisors has resulted in the discovery, mapping, and excavation of feature assemblages equal in scale and completeness to any produced during earlier periods. Before any earth is turned on sites where architectural features are likely, from Archaic-period hearths and pits to Mississippian structures and fortification lines, furthermore, remote sensing is now routinely conducted, and used to strategically guide the subsequent ground truthing of signals and larger scale excavations, as well as to shape site preservation and management strategies (e.g., King et al. 2011; Thompson and Pluckhahn 2010; Welch et al. 2006). All of this has led to a better understanding of past occupations in the region.

The past 20 to 30 years have also witnessed massive increases in the numbers of technical reports, papers, and publications on southeastern archaeology, as well as in collections and project records, and in site files. Records and collections are maintained at the state level, and by federal land holding agencies, and many site, locality/installation, or state level syntheses of this work have appeared, but attempts to organize and use this information beyond the state level have been limited. A National Archeological Bibliographic Database (NADB) was established by the National Park Service in the 1980s to compile information about the reporting that was occurring (Childs and Kinsey 2002; NADB-Reports 2011). While incomplete and about a decade out of date, it listed references to 44,217 documents, mostly CRM reports, as of 31 December 2011 from the ten states comprising the core of the Southeast as discussed in this volume (Table 1–2). The recent Southeast volume of the *Handbook of North American Indians* released in 2004, in contrast, had roughly 5,600 references, mostly to traditional academic publications (Fogelson 2004:772–999). We would estimate that somewhere in the neighborhood of 75,000 to 100,000 papers, monographs, and technical reports of all kinds have been produced on southeastern archaeology over the past 150 years, with most written in the past half century. A major challenge facing the profession is compiling this information, and associated site file and collections data, at and especially beyond the state level, so that it is useful for research and management purposes.

The Practice of Modern Southeastern Archaeology: Building on a Tradition of Hospitality, Fieldwork, and Publication

Ian W. Brown (1994:73) famously noted that southeastern archaeologists are "a relatively pleasant folk... [and] in general are not a cantankerous lot" able to tolerate diversity in thought and expression. Not that intellectual differences do not exist, for as we shall see, archaeology is practiced in many different ways in the region, with unreconstructed and unrepentant cultural historians working side by side with processualists, post-processualists, historical processualists, behavioral ecologists, and even a few Marxists, among other approaches. Much current work and reporting is guided by strong theoretical principles, but these are often implicit and unstated rather than explicitly delimited, something particularly apparent in many contemporary CRM reports—although Schiffer and House's (1975) Cache River Archaeological Project was an early exception. Understanding and reporting on the regional archaeological record, and only less so the development of or arguments about theory, is the primary goal of most practitioners, although as we shall see this attitude has been changing dramatically in recent years. About the only thing local archaeologists do not tolerate is sloppiness or incompetence in fieldwork or analysis. Profiles and floors had better be clean in photographs of fieldwork, and numbers had better add up in tables, or the offending party will likely be told privately—and at early SEAC meetings sometimes quite publically, as Stanley South (2005a:95–106) has humorously recounted—to get their act together. In many ways, however, contemporary southeastern archaeology reflects a blending of the positive from many theoretical approaches, and the advancement of new approaches set in solid archaeological examples. Thus earlier interests in artifact classification and broad processes of adaptation and response to climate and culture change remain, albeit wedded to an interest in resolving how people in different areas created their own specific histories and traditions, how gender dynamics shaped past societies in the region, and how landscapes were created and maintained. This ecumenical and tolerant, even catholic approach to the practice of archaeology locally was observed in the papers celebrating the fiftieth anniversary of the Southeastern Archaeological Conference (e.g., Peebles 1990; Watson 1990) where Dunnell (1990:19) famously opined "its scope and diversity can support almost all kinds of inquiry" leading him to "suspect that the Southeast will rise again." As we approach the 75th anniversary of SEAC, we argue herein that archaeologically it has done so indeed.

The evidence for the reemergence of the region as a major player in American archaeology is compelling. Southeastern archaeology is now practiced by hundreds of professional archaeologists, assisted in many states by large numbers of interested members of the general public. Archaeological societies have been in existence in most southeastern states for decades, most with regular publications and some with formal training programs teaching technical skills to better allow members to assist professionals. Every state in the region has a state archaeologist assisted by staff of varying sizes managing site files and collections, coordinating with SHPO staff, and engaging in research or rescue projects. Some states like Arkansas, Florida, and Louisiana have dispersed offices and research stations, while in most other states centrally-based organizations exist to oversee archaeological research and compliance. Nearly every major state or private university has one or more archaeologists on their faculty whose primary research is conducted within the region. Over 20 schools offer graduate training in prehistoric and historical archaeology at the MA and Ph.D. levels, and most have several archaeologists on the faculty, albeit in some cases people whose research is conducted in other parts of the world. For every teacher, furthermore, there are many more students. Employment in the academy, in teaching positions at colleges and universities, however, encompasses only a small minority of the practicing professionals. The vast majority of archaeologists working within the region are employed by state and federal agencies, in museums, or by university or private contracting operations. As of September 2011 there were 541 Registered Professional Archaeologists (RPA) in the Southeast (Table 1–2), about one quarter of the national total, and significantly above the numbers in most other regions, reflecting a strong commitment to professionalism and ethics and, presumably, increased employment opportunities. For every RPA, furthermore, there are many more experienced field and laboratory technicians, or "shovel bums" as the best proudly describe themselves, many of whom work on a project-by-project basis, and many of

Table 1-2. Characteristics of Southeastern Archaeology by State in 2011

State	NADB Reports	Archaeological Sites 1994	Archaeological Sites 2011	RPAs	SEAC Members	SAA Members
Alabama	9424	15,700	28,034	36	42	41
Arkansas	3611	27,581	45,500	22	31	54
Florida	9920	17,131	32,185	118	110	189
Georgia	3625	23,597	52,592	68	91	88
Kentucky	7154	16,775	27,395	37	65	77
Louisiana	2002	8,574	19,000	43	34	74
Mississippi	2063	14,645	29,385	19	68	27
North Carolina	1110	25,919	46,369	50	43	98
South Carolina	1037	16,769	29,000	32	38	40
Tennessee	3015	13,253	25,000	37	76	77
Virginia	1256	n/a	41,809	79	23	128
TOTALS	44,217	179,944	376,269	541	621	893

NADB Reports On Line, Numbers of Recorded Sites in 1994 and 2011, and RPA, SEAC, and SAA Membership Totals.

whom are great sources of practical knowledge that any serious archaeologist should be willing to consider (Kintz 1997).

Perhaps the most obvious and impressive measure of the re-emergence of southeastern archaeology on the national and international scene is the record of publication. Over the past forty years, hundreds of books and technical monographs on southeastern archaeology have been produced, through university presses and from CRM work. In every state these longer works are the foundations of knowledge that need to be read in order to practice archaeology competently, while the innumerable shorter papers and reports are essential when conducting work on specific topics or project areas. The book or monograph remains the principal research product of most professionals, even given university promotion policies rewarding the production of peer-reviewed journal articles. Southeastern archaeologists, happily, routinely produce both in impressive numbers. While arguably underrepresented in the pages of *American Antiquity* during the first decades of the New Archaeology, in the 1960s through the 1980s—at least when compared to the region's apparent dominance during the earlier cultural historical period (Gibson 1993:20)—nearly every issue of the journal now has a major article on the archaeology of the region. The journal *Southeastern Archaeology*, furthermore, publishes 15 to 20 significant articles each year, and state journals publish another 25 to 50 or more, and papers on the archaeology of the region are becoming more and more frequent in other regional, national, and international journals.

Increasingly, southeastern archaeologists are devoting effort to the production of research syntheses, something critically important given the pace and volume of current research. In addition to the production of overviews of evidence for past occupations in major river basins or from entire states already noted, regional syntheses have appeared, typically edited volumes but also including CRM monographs and theses and dissertations, encompassing broad time periods like the Paleoindian/Early Archaic (Anderson and Sassaman, eds. 1996; Gingerich, ed., 2012), Mid-Holocene (Sassaman and Anderson 1996), Late Archaic (Thomas and Sanger 2010), Archaic (Emerson et al. 2009; Gibson and Carr 2004; Phillips and Brown 1983; Sassaman 2010a), Woodland (Anderson and Mainfort 2002; Wright and Henry 2012), Early Woodland (Farnsworth and Emerson 1986), Middle Woodland (Brose and Greber 1979), Late Woodland (Emerson et al. 2000; Nassaney and Cobb 1991), Mississippian (e.g., Anderson 1994; A. Barker and Pauketat 1992; Butler and Welch 2006; Muller 1997; Pauketat 2004, 2007; Scarry 1996; Smith 1978, 1990), and Contact eras (e.g., Cobb, ed. 2003; Ethridge and Hudson 2002; Ethridge and Shuck-Hall 2009; Kwachka 1994; McEwan 2000; Pluckhahn and Ethridge 2006; Smith et al. 2002; Thomas 1990, 1993; Walthall and Emerson 1992; Waselkov et al. 2006; Wesson and Rees 2002). Overviews have also appeared summarizing archaeological cultures like Lamar (Hally 1994a; Williams and Shapiro 1990), Plaquemine (Rees and Livingood 2006), and Swift Creek (Williams and Elliott 1998; Wallis 2011); physiographic regions like the Appalachian highlands (Dickens 1976; Keel 1976; Sullivan and Prezanno 2001), the Gulf Coast (N. White 2005), the Central and Lower Mississippi Valley (Dye and Cox 1990; McNutt 1996; Morse and Morse 1983; O'Brien 1998; Rafferty and Peacock 2008), the Midsouth (Walthall 1980), the Middle Ohio River Valley (Applegate and Mainfort 2005; Jefferies 2009; Muller 1986) and portions of the Atlantic coastal sea islands (e.g., D. Thomas, ed. 2008). Technical and popular syntheses have also appeared of some of the massive CRM projects undertaken in recent years, like those in the Richard B. Russell (Anderson and Joseph 1988; Kane and Keaton 1994) and Tellico (Chapman 1995) reservoirs, and of the work in the Tennessee-Tombigbee Waterway (Brose 1991).

Other volumes have addressed research topics for specific periods, such as for the Mississippian on art and iconography (e.g., Galloway 1989; King

2007; Lankford et al. 2011; Reilly and Garber, eds. 2007; Townsend and Sharp 2004), community layout (e.g., Lewis and Stout 1998; Payne 1994; Rogers and Smith 1995), origins (e.g., Pauketat 2004, 2007; Smith 1990), hoe production (Cobb 2000), mortuary practices (Sullivan and Mainfort 2010), political organization (e.g., Muller 1997; Scarry 1996), and statuary (Smith and Miller 2009), to cite some but by no means all major works. Still other volumes cross-cut multiple periods or deal with specific research topics, such as bioarchaeology (e.g., Lambert 2000; Larsen 2001; Powell et al. 1991; Stojanowski 2010), caves and cave art (e.g., Carstens and Watson 1996; Dye 2008; Faulkner 1986), ceramics (e.g., Sassaman 1993; Saunders 2000; Saunders and Hays 2004), earthen enclosures (e.g., Mainfort and Sullivan 1998), ethnoastronomy (Lankford 2007), gender and gender relations (e.g., Claassen 1992, ed.; Eastman and Rodning 2001), interaction (Nassaney and Sassaman 1995); lithic analysis and sourcing (Banks 1990; Carr, Bradbury, and Price 2012; Ellis and Lothrop 1989; Ray 2007); mound building and monumentality (Gibson and Carr 2004; Milner 2004a; Prentice 2000; Thomas and Sanger 2010), paleoethnobotany (e.g., Gremillion 1997; Scarry 1993), shell middens and rings (e.g., Carstens and Watson 1996; Claassen 2010; Crothers 1999; Marquardt and Watson 2005; Russo 2006; Saunders 2002; Thomas and Sanger 2010; Thompson 2006, 2007), structures (e.g., Lacquement 2007; Lewis and Stout 1998; Rogers and Smith 1995; Steere 2011), traditions (Pauketat, ed. 2001), warfare (Dye 2009), and even the history of archaeology itself within the region or of specific agencies, individuals, and installations (e.g., Binkley 2007; Brain and Brown 1982; Browman and Williams 2002; Brown 1978; Brown and Steponaitis 2010; Johnson 1993; SRARP Staff 2003; Tushingham et al. 2002; Watson 2005; White et al. 1999).

Numerous books and literally hundreds of technical monographs have appeared in recent years focusing on work at specific sites or areas, such as Bottle Creek (I. Brown 2003), Cahokia and the American Bottom (Emerson 1997; Fowler 1997; Milner 1998; Pauketat 1991, 2004, 2007, 2009), Etowah (King 2003a), Fusihatchee (Waselkov et al. 1990; Wesson 2008), King (Hally 2008), Kolomoki (Pluckhahn 2003), Lubbub Creek (Blitz 1993a; Peebles 1983); Mill Branch (Ledbetter 1995), Moundville and the Black Warrior River (e.g., Knight 2010; Knight and Steponaitis 1998; Welch 1991; Wilson 2008), Ocmulgee (Hally, ed. 1994), Page-Ladson (Webb 2006), Shiloh (Anderson, Cornelison, and Sherwood 2012; Welch 2006); Sloan (Morse 1997), Spiro (Brown 1996), St. Catherines Island

(Thomas, ed. 2008), Topper (Miller 2010; Sain 2011), Townsend (Marcoux 2010), Windover (Doran 2002), and Zebree (Morse and Morse 1980), to name but a very few of the many fine reports that have been written. Thematic issues of *Southeastern Archaeology* have also appeared, encompassing such topics as Archaic mounds in the Southeast, Mississippian frontiers, transportation archaeology in the American Bottom, the spread of shell-tempered pottery, two issues on geophysical surveys and remote sensing techniques, the late prehistoric and protohistoric Cherokee settlement at the Coweeta Creek site in North Carolina, and essays primarily on North Carolina archaeology in honor of Trawick Ward and Bennie Keel and on Georgia archaeology in honor of Lewis Larson. Finally, dozens of overviews or historic preservation plans have been produced for federal installations in the region—such as national forests, military bases, national wildlife refuges, Department of Energy reservations, or national parks—that include descriptions and syntheses of the fieldwork and research that have occurred on these lands, often supplemented by massive compendiums of primary data (e.g., Anderson and Smith 2003; Benson et al. 2006; National Trust 2008; Sassaman et al. 1990). Our knowledge of southeastern archaeology, it is clear, is reflected by an increasing number of books and monographs, continuing a regional tradition of publishing dating back to the nineteenth century. Now for the details.

2

Pioneers and Colonists of the Late Pleistocene and Early Holocene

When people first entered the Southeast is not currently known, although debates about how they arrived and what they did the first few millennia after they got here remain lively. Humans are currently assumed to have arrived in the region sometime around or after the last glacial maximum, ca. 21,000 cal yr B.P., and many sites and artifact finds dating from the late Pleistocene have been reported from the region (e.g., Figure 2-1). Occupations dating to the Pleistocene, that is, older than ca. 11,500 cal yr B.P., the arbitrary date assigned to the beginning of the Holocene by geological convention, have been called Paleoindian since ca. 1940, when Frank H. H. Roberts coined the term. More recently the term "Paleoamerican" has been coming into vogue, partially in response to the morphological distinctiveness and uncertain origins of these peoples—particularly aspects of their skeletal biology (i.e., crania) that indicate a greater affiliation with southeastern than northeastern Asian peoples, although the samples are small (Jantz and Owsley 2005)—and, perhaps, partially to reduce the tensions the study of human remains has sometimes generated between archaeologists and Native peoples (e.g., Bonnichsen 2005; Schneider and Bonnichsen 2005).

Traditional perspectives have the first peoples entering the Southeast from the north and west, ultimately coming out from Beringia through the ice-free corridor and then down the Missouri, Platte, and other south and east flowing drainages, or if coming along the Pacific coast, by moving inland following drainages like the Columbia, eventually crossing the continental divide and reaching these same drainages on the central and northern Plains, and from there pressing on to the east (e.g., Anderson 1990; Goebel et al. 2008; Haynes 1964; Haynes 2002; Lepper and Funk 2006; Meltzer 2009).

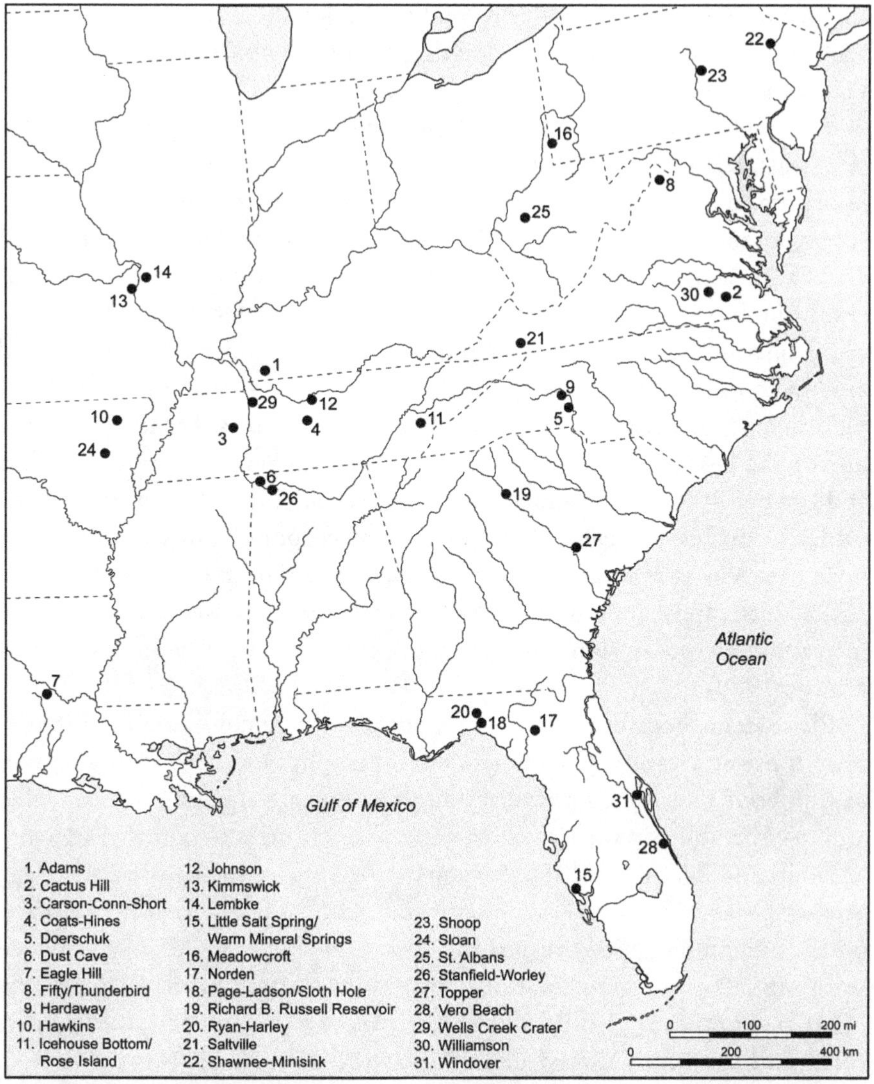

Figure 2-1. Locations of Late Pleistocene and Early Holocene sites mentioned in the text.

While these may indeed prove to be correct, in recent years alternative routes have been advanced, with entry into the Southeast occurring from the south or west, by people moving along the Gulf Coast after coming down the Pacific rim and crossing to the Gulf or Atlantic coast somewhere in Latin America, such as across southern Mexico, Panama, or northern South America, or possibly via Baja California and the Colorado and Gila rivers, which lead to the headwaters of rivers draining across the Southwest and southern Plains and into the Gulf of Mexico (Anderson 2012a; Anderson and Gillam 2000; Faught 2006; McElrath and Emerson 2012). Early populations in the Southeast, regardless of how they arrived, were thus either coastal or riverine in orientation, or both, and may well have been quite familiar with the construction and use of watercraft. Unfortunately no evidence for watercraft exists at present, at least not until later Paleoindian times, when the occurrence of adzes in a number of parts of the region suggests the possibility of canoe building (e.g., Engelbrecht and Seyfort 1994; Jodry 2005; Morse and Goodyear 1973). Perhaps the most controversial entry model has early people reaching the east coast from western Europe across the north Atlantic during the last glacial maximum (cf. Bradley and Stanford 2004; Stanford and Bradley 2002, 2012; Straus 2000; Straus et al. 2005). Given that genetic evidence makes it clear contemporary native populations arrived from northeast Asia (Kemp and Schurr 2010), this "Atlantic Ice-Edge hypothesis," if ultimately demonstrated correct, may be a classic case of a failed migration, a colonization attempt by people who died without issue (e.g., Meltzer 1989).

Pleistocene environments in the Southeast were considerably different from those at present, with climate, physiography, and biota changing rapidly, in ways that our own civilization, interestingly enough, may be facing and may be able to take lessons from in the centuries to come (Anderson, Maasch, and Sandweiss 2012; Sassaman 2012). The end of the last ice age actually began with a rapid rise in temperatures ca. 14,700 cal yr B.P. with the onset of the Bølling, and the next two thousand years was a time of extended warming, albeit with fluctuations and reversals, such as the Older Dryas (14,075–13,950 cal yr B.P.), the warmer Allerød (ca. 13,950–12,850 cal yr B.P.), and the Inter-Allerød Cold Period (ca. 13,400–13,100 cal yr B.P.) (Alley 2000; Rasmussen et al. 2006). The cold reversals each played out differently in different regions, and it is difficult to detect biotic signatures of the shorter ones in the Southeast (Williams et al. 2004). The last major cold reversal of the glacial era was the Younger Dryas (ca. 12,850–11,650 cal yr B.P.), characterized by a rapid onset and highly variable as well as cooler climate, and the close of which was characterized by rapid warming (Grafenstein 1999; Steffensen et al. 2008). The end of the Younger Dryas marks the onset of Holocene climatic conditions, although as noted that epoch does not "officially" begin until some two centuries later. The Early Archaic period in southeastern culture sequences, dating from 11,500 to 8900 cal yr B.P., is roughly coeval with the Boreal climatic period from ca. 11,650 to 8900 cal yr B.P., a cool but more stable climatic interval between the Younger Dryas and the much warmer Atlantic, or Mid-Holocene warm period (e.g., Anderson 2001; Anderson and Sassaman 2004; McElrath et al. 2009).

The Southeast was unglaciated during the glacial maximum, although whether small glaciers or other permanent ice masses or snow caps were present in the southern Appalachians or elsewhere during the Late Pleistocene is unknown. The major river system flowing through the region, however, the Mississippi and its tributary the Ohio, carried vast amounts of glacial meltwater during warming intervals. Braided stream channels were present in the central and Lower Mississippi Valley, which were replaced by a meander regime once meltwater discharge ceased (Saucier 1994:45, 93–98). With lowered sea levels, many late Pleistocene river systems may have been much narrower and more deeply incised than at present. With post-glacial warming and increased moisture, rivers in the Atlantic and Gulf Coastal Plains switched from braided to meandering patterns after ca. 16,000 cal B.P. (Leigh 2006, 2008; Leigh et al. 2004). With post-glacial sea level rise, silting would have occurred along many channels, burying potential locations for early Pre-Clovis and later Paleoindian sites, which in the larger river systems may have subsequently been lost to meander scouring (Goodyear 1999; Knox 1983; Leigh et al. 2004).

With the onset of the Bølling warming, Paleoindian inhabitants along the coast, if any were present, would have experienced rising seas, with shorelines perceptibly shifting inland within individual lifetimes. Minor to more pronounced fluctuations occurred, however, rather than a pattern of steady rise, such as the ca. 20 m rise known as Meltwater pulse 1A that occurred over several centuries in the Bølling, or the apparent plateaus or periods of decreased rise during cold reversals (Lambeck, Estat, and Potter 2002:204; Weaver et al. 2003). Shorelines were at ca. -140m at 20,000 cal B.P. and ca. -120m, -100m, -75m, -68m, -55m, and -45m at 16,000, 14,000, 13,000, 12,000, 11,000, and 10,000 cal B.P., respectively, with a possible plateau, when sea level may have been fairly stable, roughly coeval with the later Younger Dryas from ca. 12,500 to 11,500 cal yr B.P. Sea level rise was ca. 3.3 mm/yr from 19,000 to 16,000 cal yr B.P., and 16.7 mm/yr over the next 3,500 years, to ca. 12,500 cal yr B.P., comparable to the rate predicted at present for the twenty-first century (Allison et al. 2009; Lambeck, Yokoyama, and Purcell 2002:358). At the time of the last glacial maximum the southeastern Coastal Plain was almost twice its present size, with shorelines 200 km beyond their present positions in many areas, and from the late Pleistocene to the Mid-Holocene ca. 6,000 years ago when sea levels reached close to their present stand, these now-flooded areas would have been vegetated for thousands of years and hence been attractive for settlement (e.g., Anderson, Yerka, and Gillam 2010; Dunbar 2006a; Faught 1996, 2004a, 2004b; Gillam et al. 2006). Widespread evidence for human occupation of the Southeast in the form of Clovis artifacts and assemblages appears about 13,000 years ago and, given the presence of these sites in large numbers in the portions of the Atlantic Coastal Plain and the Florida peninsula that survived post-glacial sea-level rise, these peoples would have certainly exploited those areas now flooded, and probably would have been well aware of the changes occurring along the coast. This vast submerged landscape, we are coming to realize, holds a major and significant part of the early southeastern archaeological record.

Biotic communities also underwent profound changes during the Late Pleistocene in the Southeast, and included mixtures of species not seen in the Holocene (e.g., Stafford et al. 1999; Williams et al. 2004:324–326). Many large mammals went extinct during this period, such as giant beavers, camels, dire wolves, giant ground sloths, horses, mammoths, mastodons, and saber-toothed tigers, to name a few of the ca. 35 genera affected, most of which were present in the Southeast. Localities where examples of these taxa have been found in the region are documented online in FAUNMAP (Graham and Lundelius 1994), and appreciable debate revolves around whether humans had much if any role in the extinctions, at least at the continental scale (e.g., Fiedel 2005; Fiedel and Haynes 2004; Grayson 1991, 2007; Grayson and Meltzer 2002, 2003, 2004; Haynes 2009). Whether the presence of humans on the landscape contributed to these extinctions in the Southeast is unknown, although the hunting of some extinct species like mastodon clearly occurred, as evident at the Kimmswick site in Missouri (Graham et al. 1981). Possible kill sites found in the Southeast in recent years include the disarticulated remains of a young male mastodon at the Coats-Hines site in central Tennessee, together with a number of stone tools, and a bone from a canine (Breitburg et al. 1996). Additional mastodon remains were found nearby in 2010, and plans are underway for an excavation beginning in the summer of 2012 (Broster et al. 2012; Deter-Wolf et al. 2011). When domestic dogs arrived in the Americas is currently unknown, but they would have provided valuable assistance to early colonizing peoples, just as they did in later millennia (e.g., Fiedel 2005; Morey 2010). A *Bison antiquus* skull was found in the Wacissa River of Florida with a nondiagnostic projectile point fragment embedded in the frontal bone, providing just about the clearest association between humans and extinct fauna possible (Webb et al. 1984). Whether the animal actually died of this wound and was consumed by Paleoindians is unknown, but the association is unequivocal, and certainly indicates the species was targeted. The wound itself had not healed, indicating the animal died at or soon after the time of injury, possibly from blows to other parts of the body.

Bone and ivory from extinct species has been found at a number of submerged sites in Florida that was worked when fresh, or green, into abraders, anvils, awls, digging tools, points, and presumed point foreshafts, suggesting acquisition through either hunting or scavenging (Dunbar and Webb 1996; Dunbar et al. 1989; Hemmings 2004; Hemmings et al. 2004). Some formerly secure associations have proven to be more ambiguous, however, such as the giant land tortoise (*Geochelone crassiscutata*) found at Little Salt Spring in Florida that appeared to have been speared with a wooden stake (Clausen et al. 1979:609–610); the dark staining on the shell originally attributed to cooking is instead due to differential oxidation, and whether the spear was directly associated is unknown (Dunbar and Webb 1996:352). The late Pleistocene extinctions were apparently complete by the early part of the Younger Dryas (Haynes 2009), although faunal remains found at Suwannee sites in Florida like Ryan-Harley and Norden suggests that some species may have survived slightly later in this area or, alternatively, that Suwannee is older than we currently think, coeval with Clovis or even earlier (Dunbar and Vojnovski 2007:197, 201; Dunbar et al. 2005:92–94; Stanford 1991:9).

Late Pleistocene fauna in the Southeast, of course, also included species known to have been exploited by later populations such as brown and black bears, opossum, rabbit, raccoon, and white-tailed deer, as well as a wide range of amphibians, fish, and turtles and other reptiles. Secure evidence for Paleoindian subsistence is restricted almost exclusively to the post-Clovis era, when it is clear a wide range of plant and animal species were being exploited, with fruits and nuts, migratory birds, a range of small mammals, and white-tailed deer apparently receiving particular attention (e.g., Dunbar

Box 2-1. Postglacial Sea Level Rise and Underwater Archaeology on the Continental Shelf

Archaeological investigations directed to documenting past human occupation of the now submerged continental shelf in the Southeast have been underway at an increased level in recent years. This has included the work of terrestrial archaeologists examining materials dredged from the ocean bottom by fishermen, which has a long if erratic history (e.g., Blanton 1996), and more recently by teams of underwater archaeologists. Sites and assemblages dating from the Middle Holocene back to Late Pleistocene times have been found along the submerged channel of the Aucilla River in the northeastern Gulf of Mexico, by targeting promising locations like stream confluences and chert outcrops, and using remote sensing as well as hands on exploration (e.g., Faught 1996, 2004a, 2004b) (Figure 2B-1). The discoveries to date have been in comparatively shallow water, under ca. 10 to 15 meters, and hence are on landscapes submerged in the early to mid-Holocene, but efforts are currently being directed to older surfaces in much deeper waters, at and beyond the Clovis shorelines on the continental shelf in the eastern Gulf of Mexico, in waters >70m in depth (Adovasio and Hemmings 2011). This work is logistically challenging, but our understanding of prehistoric settlement systems in the Southeast will never be complete until we can document what was occurring in the vast areas lost to sea-level rise. This includes understanding the effects of fluctuations within the past few thousand years, that while on the order of no more than 1 to 2 m and seemingly minor compared to those occurring during the late Pleistocene and early Holocene, nonetheless appear to have profoundly influenced local settlement (e.g., Marquardt 2010a, 2010b; Sanger 2010; Sassaman 2010a, 2012; Thomas 2008; Thompson and Turck 2009, 2010). For Paleoindian research, the discovery of sites beyond the Clovis shoreline would be a compelling means of identifying and dating Pre-Clovis occupations. Underwater archaeology may also be the only means of determining whether early populations in the region had a significant interest in estuarine and maritime resources.

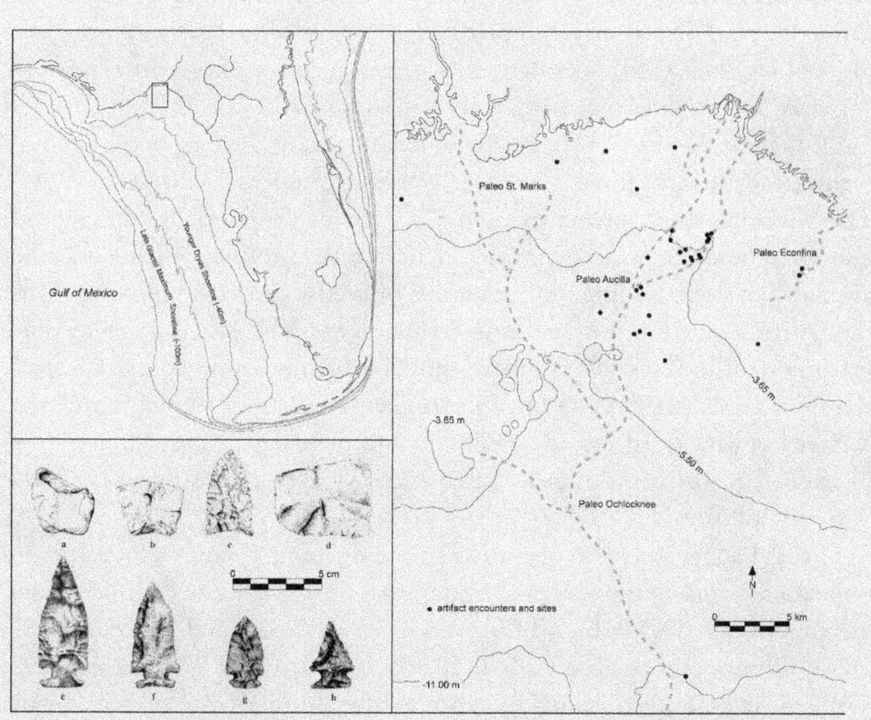

Figure 2B-1. The exploration of the PaleoAucilla River in the eastern Gulf of Mexico: submerged Paleoindian and Archaic sites and artifacts. Images from Faught 2004a, courtesy Society for American Archaeology.

and Vojnovski 2007; Hollenbach 2007, 2009; Walker 2007; Walker and Driskell 2007). These early peoples had also developed sophisticated means for cooking their food, as evidenced by the occurrence of prepared fired clay surfaces, formal hearths, and small charcoal pits in late Paleoindian and Early Archaic contexts at Dust Cave and in the Early Archaic occupations at Icehouse Bottom (Homsey et al. 2010; Sherwood and Chapman 2005). These features were apparently used not only for regular daily cooking, but also for processing on a large scale, including the broiling of fish and other animals, and the boiling and parching of seeds, primarily nuts, both for immediate consumption and long-term storage. The distribution of these features within sites also suggests possible gender-specific use of space (Homsey et al. 2010:190–193). Paleoindian populations were not just male hunters, but included women, children, and the elderly, whose archaeological record is just beginning to be considered (e.g., Adovasio et al. 2004; Surovell 2000).

Great changes were also occurring in the distribution and composition of vegetational communities over the Southeast during the late Pleistocene and early Holocene (Delcourt and Delcourt 1985, Delcourt and Delcourt 1987, 2004; Grimm and Jacobson 2004; Jacobson et al. 1987; Webb et al. 1993; Williams et al. 2004). An oak-hickory hardwood forest was present during the glacial maximum in the southern part of the region, while cold adapted northern species like spruce were present in the interior and as far south as central South Carolina on the Atlantic seaboard. As the climate warmed, plant species spread latitudinally to the north or to higher elevations, or died out locally, much the same way modern species are dealing with rapidly changing climate. Boreal conifers like spruce and jack-pine dominated southeastern forests during the full glacial north of latitude 33 degrees, from about the vicinity of central South Carolina west to the Arkansas-Louisiana state line. With the onset of rapid deglaciation in the Bølling, mixed hardwood forests began to move northward from refugia in the lower Southeast. These movements, like sea level rise, were not steady, but varied. During the Younger Dryas, for example, replacements of spruce with hardwoods and back again occurred in the Midsouth and Midwest, reflecting the highly variable climatic conditions of the period (Grafenstein et al. 1999; Grimm and Jacobson 2004:390–392; Meeks and Anderson 2012). By 11,500 cal yr B.P., hardwood and mixed hardwood-pine forests were present over much of the region, communities that remained in place until pine forests began to replace the mixed hardwood forest in the Coastal Plain in the early Mid-Holocene (Delcourt and Delcourt 1985:19; Delcourt and Delcourt 1987, 2004; Jacobson et al. 1987; Watts et al. 1996; Webb et al. 1993; Williams et al. 2004).

Evidence for Early Paleoindian Pre-Clovis human occupation in the Southeast is sparse, at least when compared with Middle Paleoindian Clovis assemblages, which appear widely during or immediately following the Inter-Allerød Cold Period, and had diversified into a number of subregional variants by shortly after the start of the Younger Dryas. Sites determined by absolute dating to be of Pre-Clovis age in the Southeast and that range from a few hundred to a few thousand years prior to Clovis include Cactus Hill and Saltville in Virginia (McAvoy and McAvoy 1997; McDonald 2000), Coats-Hines in Tennessee (Breitburg et al. 1996; Broster et al. 2012), Little Salt Spring and Page-Ladson in Florida (Clausen et al. 1979; Dunbar et al. 1988; Webb 2006), and Topper in South Carolina, where dates back to 50,000 years ago have been reported (Goodyear 1999, 2005:107–111). While some of these sites are well reported, notably Cactus Hill and Page-Ladson, and most appear to have plausible artifacts, none are universally accepted by the professional community at present, primarily because the assemblages are either sparse or in some cases in uncertain context (Anderson 2005; Fiedel 2012; G. Haynes 2002:33–35; Wheat 2012). Unlike later periods in the region, where an array of distinctive artifact types can be used to identify components to particular periods or areas, nothing comparable has been recognized yet for Pre-Clovis occupations. Small lanceolate and triangular unfluted bifaces described as the Early Triangular, Miller Lanceolate, and Page-Ladson types have been found at Cactus Hill, Meadowcroft Rockshelter (located just outside the region in Pennsylvania), and at Page-Ladson and other sites in Florida, respectively, however, and these may ultimately prove to be useful diagnostic indicators of Pre-Clovis occupations (Adovasio et al. 1999:427–428; Anderson 2005:32; Dunbar and Hemmings 2004; Thulman 2008) (Figure 2–2). Other well-dated and reported sites with Pre-Clovis assemblages from nearby areas include Debra L. Friedkin in Texas and Big Eddy in Missouri (Lopinot et al. 1998, 2000; Ray and Lopinot 2000; Waters et al. 2011), suggesting humans were present with low population levels across the region, although our present site and assemblage sample is so small that we have little idea how such groups were organized and what they were doing on the landscape.

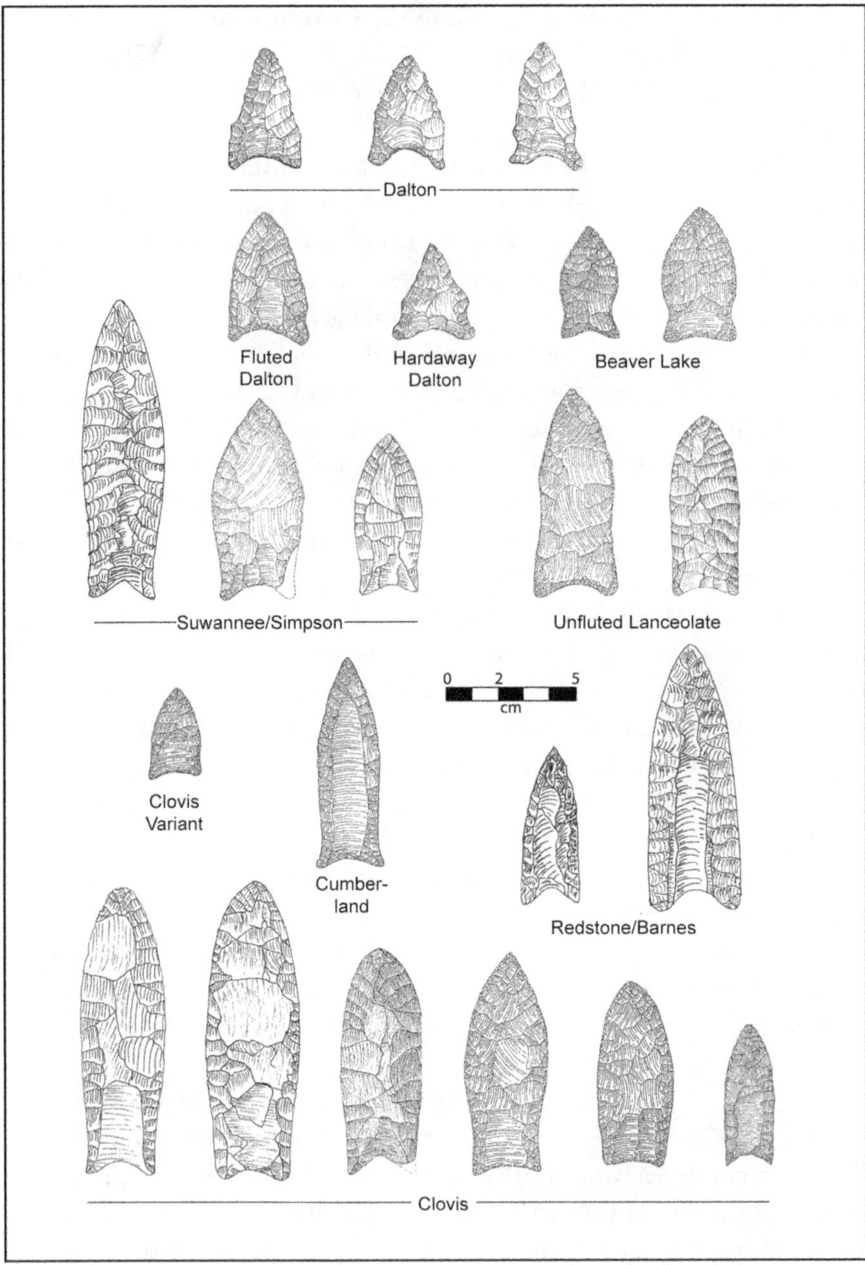

Figure 2-2. Examples of Paleoindian and Early Archaic diagnostic projectile points found in the Southeast. Artifacts drawn by R. Jerald Ledbetter, used with permission of the artist.

The First Widespread Settlement

The picture changes dramatically about 13,000 years ago, when sites and assemblages characterized by fluted projectile points occur seemingly suddenly and nearly everywhere on the southeastern landscape (Box 2-2). Rapid population growth or in-migration is suggested, or, alternatively, the first appearance of a readily identifiable diagnostic artifact category among preexisting populations whose assemblages go unremarked amid 13,000 years of later land use. Fluting involves the removal of flakes from the base up along the blade using direct percussion or indirect instrument-assisted pressure flaking, a distinctive and readily recognizable procedure that, curiously, occurred commonly only once in all of prehistory, at the end of the Pleistocene in portions of the New World. The procedure was used to make Clovis points, currently assumed to be the earliest fluted point type, and a number of related forms presumably made by descendant populations, such as the Cumberland, Folsom, and Redstone types (Figure 2-2). Clovis points have parallel to slightly expanding blades, and were made using a distinctive manufacturing procedure employing overshot flaking and yielding characteristic debitage and preforms (e.g., Morrow 1995, 1996). They occur as isolated finds over the landscape—perhaps reflecting individual hunting episodes or prey that got away—and in a variety of site types with other artifacts, such as debitage, bifaces and preforms, blades and blade cores, scraping and engraving tools, and bone and ivory points and other implements, and less commonly paleosubsistence remains, although the occurrence of each varies over the region depending on site function and preservation conditions (e.g., Tankersley 2004; Walker and Driskell 2007).

Clovis, currently the earliest known fluted point type, has been dated at a number of sites across North America to between ca. 13,150 and 12,850 cal yr B.P. (Waters and Stafford 2007). Within the Southeast proper, dates for Clovis assemblages falling around 13,000 years ago have been reported from the Cactus Hill site in Virginia, Sloth Hole in Florida, and Topper in South Carolina, at the latter site from OSL rather than AMS determinations (Goodyear 2005; Hemmings 2005:47; McAvoy and McAvoy 1997:124, 167, 169; Waters et al. 2009). Dates on fluted points resembling Clovis that fall within the narrow temporal range documented by Waters and Stafford have also been reported at sites just outside the boundaries of the region, including at Big Eddy and Kimmswick in Missouri (Graham et al. 1981;

Box 2-2. Documenting Paleoindian Occupations in the Southeast: State Artifact Recording Projects and PIDBA

Paleoindian archaeology comprises the primary research focus of at least one archaeologist in just about every state in the Southeast. For the past two decades artifact recording projects have been underway in most of these states, and while early on were directed to documenting fluted points, in recent years these efforts have expanded to include other point and artifact types. As a result a great deal of primary attribute and image data has been systematically recorded for early points (Table 2B-1), and is starting to be systematically compiled for preforms, blades and blade cores, and other artifact categories. Avocational archaeologists supply the vast bulk of the information, and this kind of data recording, curating, and sharing helps instill the kind of ethical behavior that the practice of archaeology requires, for both amateurs and professionals alike. Since the late 1990s much of the primary information collected from the Southeast has been compiled and posted online on the Paleoindian Database of the Americas (PIDBA) website through the voluntary efforts of a number of researchers (Anderson, Miller, Yerka et al. 2010; see http://pidba.utk.edu/). The information in PIDBA has been widely used to determine sources of bias in the data (e.g., Miller 2011; O'Donoghue 2007; Prasciunas 2011; Shott 2005), to infer where people were concentrated on the landscape, and to determine temporal changes in range mobility based on the occurrence of arti-

Table 2B-1. Southeastern Paleoindian Projectile Points with Detailed Attribute Data Recorded in PIDBA, September 2011.

	STATE								Sample
Point Type	TN	MS	AL	GA	FL	SC	NC	VA	Total
Clovis	1232	107	494	378	12	295	136	785	3439
Clovis Variant	0	0	0	19	0	5	58	0	82
Ross County	0	2	0	0	0	0	9	0	11
Gainey	6	0	0	0	0	0	0	15	21
Redstone	45	3	51	25	0	58	32	31	245
Cumberland	264	10	378	6	0	0	6	0	664
Barnes	69	0	0	0	0	0	0	0	69
Wheeler	9	1	28	21	0	0	0	0	59
Simpson	0	0	0	98	12	18	0	0	128
Suwannee	0	0	0	77	74	62	0	0	213
Quad	220	70	195	41	0	0	2	0	528
Beaver Lake	316	10	214	36	1	2	0	0	579
Coldwater	0	116	0	0	0	0	0	0	116
Dalton, Type unspecified	903	193	0	917	0	0	0	0	2013
Dalton, Fluted	46	4	0	58	0	0	0	0	108
Dalton, Hardaway	13	0	0	13	0	0	0	0	26
Dalton, Side Notched	0	310	0	0	0	0	0	0	310
Dalton, Lanceolate	0	79	0	0	0	0	0	0	79
Harpeth River	152	0	0	0	0	0	0	0	152
Agate Basin/Misc. Plano	22	1	0	0	0	0	0	0	23
Arkabutla	0	8	0	0	0	0	0	0	8
Hinds	0	56	0	0	0	0	0	0	56
Totals	3297	970	1360	1689	99	440	243	831	8929

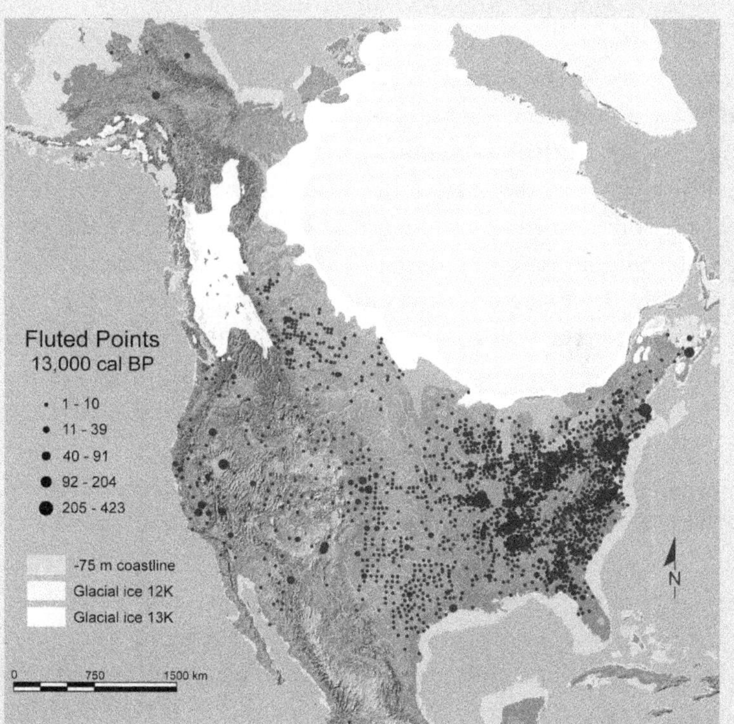

Figure 2B-2. The distribution of fluted points in North America based on data from PIDBA (Paleoindian Database of the Americas). The map includes all Clovis and Clovis variants, plus all untyped fluted forms that have not been assigned to a later type like Folsom, Barnes, Cumberland, etc., in the database.

facts away from raw material sources (e.g., Anderson et al. 2010a:74–75, 78) (Figure 2B-2). Most effort to date in the state-level recording projects has been directed to fluted or immediate post-fluted lanceolate point types, however, with the result that comparatively little detailed attribute data has been collected for later Paleoindian Dalton or side-notched forms (Table 2B-1). This needs to be corrected, because these point forms and associated assemblages appear to be widespread within the region (e.g., Anderson, Miller, Yerka et al. 2010; McElrath and Emerson 2009, 2012; McElrath et al. 2009; Morse and Morse 1983; Sherwood et al. 2004; Walthall and Koldehoff 1998). Until coverage is more uniform and systematic, however, exactly how common these later Paleoindian, non-fluted point forms, artifacts, and assemblages are will remain unknown. Like FAUNMAP, another online database detailing the occurrence of animal species over the region (Graham and Lundelius 1994), PIDBA plays an important role in educating the general public about scientific research and the importance of making data available.

Ray et al. 1998:77, 80), and Shawnee-Minisink in Pennsylvania (Dent 2002, 2007; Gingerich 2007, 2011, 2012; Waters and Stafford 2007). The evidence suggests Clovis spread very quickly, but given the few dates from the Southeast, the region where these points occur in greatest abundance, this range may be subject to change, particularly at the early end. That is, Clovis technology may originate somewhat earlier either within the Southeast or in the southern Plains, as suggested by dates of ca. 13,500 cal yr B.P. at the Aubrey site in Texas (Ferring 1995) and ca. 14,000 cal yr B.P. at the Johnson site in Tennessee. Of the three dates obtained at Johnson, two unfortunately have very large standard deviations, causing the excavators to believe that further corroboration of the dating is in order (Barker and Broster 1996; Broster and Norton 1996:292–294). Few post-Clovis age dates are available from the Southeast until towards the end of the period, in Dalton times (e.g., Goodyear 1982; Martin-Siebert 2004; Miller and Gingerich 2012; Sherwood et al. 2004), making finding and securely dating Paleoindian assemblages within the region, ideally in stratified context, a critical research priority (Anderson et al. 1996; Miller and Gingerich 2012).

The distribution of Clovis artifacts and sites is not uniform, but characterized by concentrations indicating parts of the region were highly favored, particularly terrain along and near the major rivers of the midcontinent, including the Ohio, Cumberland, and Tennessee, as well as portions of Florida and the Atlantic Coastal Plain. The Gulf Coastal Plain and the Appalachian Summit, in contrast, apparently saw far less use. Settings rich in exploitable resources, such as plants, animals, and high-quality toolstone, have been hypothesized to have been staging areas, where initial populations settled and grew, albeit still employing high-range mobility, and providing a stable social environment from which the exploration and settlement of the larger region could occur, and groups return to in the event they lost members or were unable to find mates or other critical resources (Anderson 1990:187, 1996a:36–39; see also Dincauze 1993 who calls such settings "marshaling areas"). This "place-oriented" model is an alternative to the "technology-oriented" perspective that views Clovis populations as highly mobile, dependent on their technology rather than settling into particular places (cf. Anderson 1990:202–205; Kelly and Todd 1988). The staging area model was based on fluted point distributions and general landscape characteristics, the evaluation of which has been superseded by more sophisticated GIS-based analyses. Shane Miller (2011), for example, has shown that large

Paleoindian sites in the Southeast, possible aggregation loci, tend to occur at the intersection of major rivers, macro-ecotones at physiographic and biome boundaries, and sources of toolstone. Smallwood (2011, 2012), in a test of the staging area model, demonstrated differences in Clovis projectile point manufacturing in different parts of the region, an expectation of the model, although she noted that more precise dating will be needed to determine whether this reflects a temporal distinction or diversity due to drift.

More comparative analyses among Clovis assemblages are needed, but the work undertaken to date indicates appreciable intersite and even intrasite variation exists, related to whether initial quarrying, subsequent reduction and manufacturing, presumed habitation, or special activities were occurring, as well as probable seasonal or longer-term factors in play (e.g., Carr, Adovasio, and Vento 2012; Carr, Stewart, Stanford, and Frank 2012; Gardner 1989; McAvoy 1992; Miller and Smallwood 2012; Sanders 1990; Smallwood 2010, 2011; Smallwood et al. 2012). The occurrence of endscrapers, for example, appears to be determined in part by environmental factors, such as winter temperatures and the need for hides for clothing and shelter, since endscrapers appear to be more prevalent in eastern Paleoindian sites at higher latitudes (Cable 1996; Loebel 2012; Miller and Goodyear 2008). Another group of tools whose occurrence at a few Paleoindian and Early Archaic sites suggests heavy-duty woodworking are choppers, adzes, and blocky adzes, which have been noted at Topper and in the northern Middle Atlantic at Fifty, Thunderbird, and Shoop (Carr, Adovasio, and Vento 2012; Carr, Stewart, Stanford, and Frank 2012; Smallwood et al. 2012), and widely in the central Mississippi River Valley in Dalton times (Koldehoff and Walthall 2009; McElrath and Emerson 2012; Morse 1997; Morse and Goodyear 1973). These tools may have been used to produce watercraft and possibly structures, both of which would have been useful in late Pleistocene environments, particularly given the extent groups may have had to travel to meet other people. With the greatly expanded Coastal Plain, regular exploitation of the coast from sites like Topper and Thunderbird, which would have been far inland at the time they were occupied, would have been greatly facilitated. Given the climate in the late Pleistocene, which was characterized by more pronounced seasonality than at present, durable shelters would be expected. An apparent post-in-ground structure was found at Thunderbird measuring 6 by 10 m, or ca. 330 square feet, associated with multipurpose tools, bifaces, and utilized flakes (Carr, Stewart, Stanford, and

Frank 2012; Gardner 1974, 1989). Although the identified postholes were found at the base of the plowzone, and hence are not in secure context, no later artifacts were found in the area, leading the discoverers to argue that the structure they delimited was built in Clovis or immediate post-Clovis times, perhaps during the Younger Dryas. Resembling a small longhouse with internal partitions, if accurately identified, it is the only Paleoindian period structure found to date in the Southeast.

Social organization throughout the Paleoindian period is thought to have been by band level groups characterized by a high degree of residential mobility, fluid group membership, and periodic multi-band aggregation. The basic unit is thought to have been the extended family or band, based on the size of artifact clusters noted at several Eastern Clovis sites like Bull Brook, Thunderbird, and Shoop, ca. 20 to 30 m in diameter, and the possible structure found at Thunderbird (Carr, Adovasio, and Vento 2012; Carr, Stewart, Stanford, and Frank 2012; Robinson et al. 2009). While most of the time people lived in small groups, periodic larger gatherings are inferred, at times and places capable of supporting large numbers of people, probably a few weeks at most. Such gatherings are assumed to have continued to occur throughout all of later prehistory in the region, at least until people began to live in larger, permanent communities. These aggregation events would have been critical for forming and maintaining social and kinship/mating networks, exchanging information about resources and conditions over large areas (including the locations of other people), and reinforcing social ties through feasting, ceremony and ritual, perhaps incorporating specialized crafting, such as the manufacture and caching of challenging stone implements, or their destruction (e.g., Anderson 1990, 1995; Deller et al. 2009; Ellis and Deller 2002; Meltzer 2002, 2004; Robinson and Ort 2011). While common in the west, caches of elaborate or hypertrophic stone tools are unknown in the southeastern United States until Dalton times, although presumably utilitarian caches of raw material and tools are fairly common on Clovis and later Paleoindian sites.

A question to be asked, of course, is where are the ceremonial sites and aggregation sites, if they were settings for regular and important events in Paleoindian life? Have they been lost to rising sea levels or meandering river channels? Large artifact-rich Paleoindian and Early Archaic period sites have been observed at macroecotones like the Fall Line between the Coastal Plain and Piedmont on the Gulf and Atlantic slopes, or at chert quarry sites like

Topper and Thunderbird, but documenting actual aggregation requires an immense amount of excavation and analysis, particularly to determine the location and contemporaneity of associated habitation areas. Other than the kind of temporary situational complexity aggregation would require, there is little evidence for social inequality anywhere in the region save for later in the period, when cemetery behavior appears in the Dalton culture in the Central Mississippi Valley (Morse 1997; Walthall and Koldehoff 1998).

Clovis points, the icon of Paleoindian culture, have been traditionally thought to be fairly uniform in shape and manufacture across the continent, albeit with broad geographic trends in certain aspects of their morphology and appreciable idiosyncratic variation produced by knappers of differing skill levels (e.g., Buchanan and Hamilton 2009; Morrow and Morrow 1999). Work within the Southeast in recent years, however, has shown that appreciable variation exists within Clovis points at regional and subregional scales, and within fluted forms in general. An analysis of biface assemblages from three major Paleoindian sites, Carson-Conn-Short in Tennessee, Topper in South Carolina, and Williamson in Virginia, found that aspects of early stage Clovis manufacturing were shared between the three sites, and hence presumably across the Southeast and perhaps beyond, but that later stages in each area had distinctive morphologies and manufacturing signatures (Smallwood 2011:166–172, 2012). This appears to be due to the isolation and divergence of discrete populations within a larger Clovis technological tradition, but whether this involved drift in the cultural transmission of technological procedures within a pre-existing population or to temporal differences brought about by the movement of people away from initial staging areas could not be determined. Thulman (2006) found a similar pattern of microstylistic variation in Clovis and immediate post-Clovis points in different portions of north-central Florida that he thought represented discrete group ranges or territories, and possibly change over time. The differences between areas arose in part, he argued, to small copying errors in the transmission of manufacturing procedures among populations somewhat isolated from one another by the irregular occurrence of surface water. Water availability, in addition to access to knappable stone (Dunbar 1991; Dunbar and Waller 1983; Thulman 2006, 2009), appears to have been a major factor shaping prehistoric settlement in the xeric interior uplands of late Pleistocene Florida.

The role of knappable stone has, of course, long played a role in the interpretation of Paleoindian and Early Archaic settlement and mobility in the

Southeast, beginning with William Gardner's (1974, 1989) work at the Flint Run complex of sites in Virginia, including at Fifty and Thunderbird, where he argued that quarry areas were central places in early settlement systems that people radiated out from and returned to in a cyclical pattern, a view that has been widely if perhaps somewhat uncritically accepted (cf. Anderson and Hanson 1988; Anderson and Sassaman 1996:24; Daniel 1998, 2001; Goodyear 1999, 2005; Kimball 1996; Speth et al. 2010). Gardner (1977:258–259; Carr, Stewart, Stanford, and Frank 2012) identified six site types, three associated with quarries and three away from them: (1) quarries, where primary raw material extraction took place; (2) quarry/lithic reduction stations, where initial reduction prior to transport occurred; (3) quarry-related base camps, where a wide range of activities including extended habitation occurred; (4) periodically revisited non-quarry related hunting/gathering camps; (5) sporadically visited non-quarry related hunting/gathering camps; and (6) isolated point finds. Many Paleoindian sites in the region are described using these or similar categories.

In a related argument, Goodyear (1979) proposed that Paleoindian groups made use of the highest-quality stone they could find whenever possible, since the predictable knapping characteristics would facilitate efficient raw material use and toolkit curation among groups moving widely over the landscape (see also Kelly and Todd 1988). Indeed, Clovis points in the Southeast are commonly found hundreds of kilometers from known source areas, and are frequently made on high-quality materials (e.g., Goodyear et al. 1990; Tankersley 1990). Fluting required great knapping ability, something that would additionally ensure that people ranging far from quarry areas could maximize the lifespan of the material they were carrying. The technology may have helped create a sense of shared identity between peoples, facilitating interaction, and perhaps was demonstrated or performed under special and possibly public and ceremonial circumstances. This has been suggested at Bull Brook, a possible multiband aggregation loci in the Northeast, where fluting took place primarily in a few central parts of the site (Robinson and Ort 2011; Robinson et al. 2009).

There has been some questioning and refinement of these arguments, which have perhaps uncharitably been called "lithic determinism" (Anderson and Sassaman 1996b:23), such as the idea that a number of quarries could be used successively, in a serial or cyclical pattern rather than one primary source (e.g., Custer et al. 1983; McAvoy 1992). Another critique has been that the use of high versus low quality and local versus extralocal lithic raw materials may be characteristics of the availability of these materials on the landscape, or earlier versus later occupations in the Paleoindian era, before and after people had determined where knappable stone occurred on the landscape, or range mobility had decreased to the point where distant sources were no longer considered or were no longer accessible (Anderson, Miller, Yerka et al. 2010; Blong 2012; Lowery 2002; Speth et al. 2010). Increased use of locally available lithic raw materials does, in fact, characterize later Paleoindian and Early Archaic assemblages over much of the Southeast, something attributed to decreasing range mobility and less use of highly curated tools (Anderson 1990:202, 1995:9; Ellis et al. 1998; Morse et al. 1996), perhaps brought about as well by changes in the practices peoples used to define themselves in relation to others.

Several major Clovis sites in the Southeast have been reported in detail in recent years. At the Adams site in Kentucky, Sanders (1990) showed how basic description and illustration of materials from Paleoindian sites, coupled with comparative analyses of these materials between sites, is important to providing a baseline of information about what is present in a given area, and variation between sites over a larger region. Monograph length treatments, in the form of MA theses and doctoral dissertations, are appearing on the decade-long investigation of the Clovis assemblages at the Topper site (Miller 2010; Sain 2011; Smallwood 2011), and are also underway on the Pre-Clovis materials, which should help resolve the status of this controversial assemblage (Hoak 2012). Comparable work involving students occurred at the Flint Run complex in Virginia under the leadership of William Gardner, demonstrating the role graduate student research can play in ensuring large, complex excavation and analysis projects are thoroughly reported (e.g., Gardner 1974, 1989; Carr, Stewart, Stanford, and Frank 2012). Tune's (2010) reanalysis of the Wells Creek Crater assemblage, demonstrating that much of it actually dated to Post-Clovis times, highlights the importance of properly curating records and producing detailed site reports detailing what was found and in what context, and how it was analyzed (cf. Dragoo 1973; Tune 2010).

Clovis and later Paleoindian and Early Archaic quarrying behavior has been explored in some detail at both Flint Run and Topper. Gardner's major quarry-related site types, noted previously, were assumed to be discrete locations separated from one another by at least some distance, but research at Topper has shown significant differences in assemblage composition can occur within a few meters of outcrops, such as extent of biface manufacture or the occurrence of various tool forms suggesting specialized activities or habitation (Miller and Smallwood 2012; Smallwood et al. 2012). Work in both areas is also helping to refine the basic cultural sequence for early occupations in the region, complementing and refining sequences developed at Hardaway and Doerschuk in North Carolina, at St. Albans in West Virginia, and at sites like Icehouse Bottom and Rose Island in the Little Tennessee River Valley (Broyles 1971; Chapman 1985; Coe 1964). Investigations in settings that until recently have received very little research attention, such as Carolina Bays, have shown that far greater use of interriverine areas occurred than assumed in earlier models (Brooks et al. 2010; Moore et al. 2010). Finally, new analyses have been conducted or excavations resumed at sites where classic early work was accomplished, such as at Hardaway and other locations in North Carolina (cf. Coe 1964; Daniel 1998, 2001), or at early rockshelter sites in the central Tennessee River Valley of northern Alabama (cf. DeJarnette et al. 1962; Hollenbach 2009; Sherwood et al. 2004).

Culture Change during the Younger Dryas

Clovis culture, or at least the Clovis projectile point horizon, ends about the same time as the onset of the Younger Dryas climate episode about 12,850 cal yr B.P., although whether the two are related is the subject of appreciable debate at present. A series of successive projectile point styles and broader horizons characterize the Late Paleoindian period, with the earliest consisting of what are called "instrument assisted" or fully fluted forms like the Barnes, Cumberland, Folsom, Gainey, and Redstone types (Anderson et al. 1996; Anderson, Miller, Yerka et al. 2010; Goodyear 2010). These are assumed to have been made by Clovis descendants, and each occur with greatest incidence in different parts of the Southeast—or in the case of Folsom and Gainey at the margins of their greatest occurrence in the Plains or Midwest—suggesting local cultural traditions were present. These are replaced by unfluted forms like the Beaver Lake, Dalton, Quad, Suwannee, and Simpson types, again occurring widely but with discrete centers or areas of greatest incidence (Figure 2-2). Sometime in the later Younger Dryas, Dalton points become common over much of the region, with a number of distinct named subtypes or varieties in specific areas, such as the Colbert, Greenbrier, Hardaway, and Nuckolls Dalton types and the related San Patrice varieties *Hope* and *St. Johns* in the western part of the region (Jennings 2008a, 2008b; Morse 1997). Dalton points are rare in the Northeast and upper Midwest, although they are present in low incidence (Justice 1987), and they are decidedly uncommon in Florida, where the Suwannee point has been suggested as a local equivalent (Dunbar 2006b:408). Dalton points were replaced at the end of the Younger Dryas and in the initial Holocene by side-notched and corner-notched forms, which occur widely throughout eastern North America during the Early Archaic period. Many later Paleoindian and Early Archaic point forms exhibit extensive reworking, suggesting they saw repeated use, probably as multipurpose hunting/butchering tools. In the western part of the Southeast and Midwest, classic Plains forms are present in low numbers, including Agate Basin, Angostura, Folsom, and Scottsbluff points; indeed, unfluted lanceolates occur more widely across the east, although care must be taken to avoid confusing them with later forms like the Guilford Lanceolate (e.g., J. Bradley et al. 2008; Coe 1964:43; Justice 1987; Munson 1990). Interaction or movement between peoples over large areas is clearly indicated, although the nature of this behavior is not well understood at present (Anderson 1995; Jennings 2008a, 2008b; Johnson 1989).

The number and diversity of fluted and nonfluted forms in the Southeast is remarkable, leading some to suggest that Clovis technology may have originated locally. Whether this morphological variation is due to significant differences in adaptation or stylistic drift related to how cultural transmission occurred is unknown. Unfortunately, few well-dated deeply stratified sites spanning the Middle Paleoindian through Early Archaic periods and Clovis through side- and corner-notched forms have been found in the region, making determining the age of assemblages and hence the study of change over time difficult (Anderson et al. 1996; Miller and Gingerich 2012). Dust Cave in Alabama and Thunderbird and Fifty in Virginia are three significant exceptions, but significant gaps still exist, particularly in the time immediately following Clovis. Dating of many southeastern Paleoindian point forms, accordingly, is tentative, and relies on comparisons with morphologically similar forms more securely dated in other parts of the continent, which is admittedly problematic (e.g., Goodyear 2010; Meltzer 1988, 2009; Meltzer and Holliday 2010). Indeed, in the absence of secure chronologies, arguments suggesting the Cumberland type or forms like it may be Pre-Clovis in age must be considered possible (e.g., Gramly 2009; O'Brien et al. 2001).

Resolving later Paleoindian chronology and occupations in the Southeast will be important to exploring the impact of climate change on human culture. The Younger Dryas marked a return to colder conditions that appears to have occurred rapidly, within no more than a few years to decades, and perhaps even more rapidly if it was caused by massive outflows from periglacial lakes, the current prevailing hypothesis or, more controversially, the impacts of extra-terrestrial objects like a comet or meteorites (cf. Alley 2000; Broecker et al. 2010; Firestone et al. 2007). Great changes in climate, culture, and biota occurred around this time, although the causal relationships among them, if any, remain to be determined. The replacement of weakly fluted Clovis by instrument-assisted full-fluted forms involved the adoption of a more difficult manufacturing procedure, suggesting increased concern with knapping ability and maximizing the use life of stone tools and materials. If fluting was a means of promoting a sense of shared identity among far-flung peoples, and as a means of dealing with uncertainty in the surrounding world, this may be far more than the simple stylistic change. The initial centuries of the Younger Dryas, when this form of full or instrument assisted fluting technology apparently appears, may have been a time of increased subsistence stress. A decline in population or reorganization in settlement from Clovis to immediate post-Clovis times is suggested by four lines of evidence. First, there is a decline in the numbers of identifiable diagnostics. Second, there is a decline in the numbers of radiocarbon dates. Third, there is evidence for reduced use of quarries in some areas. Finally, group range mobility appears to have decreased, as indicated by the distribution of utilized raw materials over the landscape (Anderson, Miller, Yerka et al. 2010; Anderson et al. 2011; McAvoy 1992). These changes were apparently not the same everywhere, however, and may not even have occurred at all in some areas, such as on the Great Plains or in parts of the Midsouth (e.g., Holliday and Meltzer 2010; Meltzer and Holliday 2010; Miller and Gingerich 2012). If the major river systems of the Midsouth were ideal staging areas for Clovis populations, for example, they likely continued to be favored during the early Younger Dryas, and indeed much larger numbers of full-fluted forms are found in this part of the region than on the margins (cf. Broster et al. 2012; Goodyear 2006; Miller and Gingerich 2012).

Given the biotic extinctions and relocations that were occurring, Paleoindian and certainly post-Clovis populations had a changing and probably much narrower array of subsistence resources from which to choose. These may have led to changes in and perhaps an expansion of diet breadth. The extinction of large animals, if these had been highly ranked resources previously, may have led to the exploitation of a wider range of smaller animal species, and to increased use of plant foods (e.g., Anderson 1995, 2001; Kelly and Todd 1988; Waguespack and Surovell 2003). Such a pattern is certainly indicated in the regional archaeological record. Well preserved later Paleoindian age floral and faunal remains have been found in a number of rock shelters in the Midsouth, at sites like Dust Cave and Stanfield-Worley in northern Alabama, and at submerged sites in Florida (Dunbar and Vojnovski 2007; Hollenbach 2007, 2009; Walker 2007; Walker and Driskell 2007). The assemblages from these sites typically encompass a wide range of species from a variety of environments, and include small mammals, reptiles, fish, and birds, as well as seeds from fruits and nut mast, indicating subsistence was diversified and not restricted to large game animals. At Dust Cave, in fact, birds were extremely common in the Dalton assemblage, and it has been suggested that they were in earlier periods in the Southeast as well, during Clovis times if not before. Observing and following migratory birds, it has been suggested, may have prompted and facilitated group movement and even colonizing behavior, and offered a source of food on the journey (e.g., Dincauze and Jacobson 2001; Fiedel 2007). White-tailed deer were traditionally assumed to have been a major food source to later Paleoindian populations in the Southeast, and the Dalton toolkit was even interpreted in terms of its utility for the bulk processing of deer meat and hides (Goodyear 1974:14; Morse 1973). The animal may well have been important, as it clearly was in later times, but the evidence suggests instead that Late Paleoindian populations had a highly diversified subsistence economy, in which small game played an important role (Driskell and Walker 2007; Walker 2007; Walker et al. 2001; Walker and Driskell 2007). An awareness of the exploitable subsistence resources of the Southeast thus appears to have developed early on and perhaps fairly quickly, and possibly in the uncertain environmental conditions of the Younger Dryas if not before, contrary to earlier views that this took thousands of years (e.g., Caldwell 1958).

Ritual, Ceremony, and Social Complexity in the Late Pleistocene Southeast

Southeastern Paleoindian peoples were undoubtedly living within and constructing the sacred landscape recognized by their descendants thousands of years later. Prominent locations appear to have held a particular attraction for Paleoindian populations, such as major shoals, river fords, river confluences, sinkholes, outcrops of high-quality stone, and mountain peaks or other unusual geological features like Wells Creek Crater in Tennessee or Eagle Hill in Louisiana (e.g., Gunn and Brown 1982; Tune 2010). Did these easily relocated places facilitate group rendezvous and aggregation, and at what point were any of them considered sacred places in the landscape? Unfortunately, no obvious permanent markers of ritual or ceremonial behavior dating to the Paleoindian period, like rock or cave art, are currently known from the Southeast, although their existence cannot be ruled out. Likewise, portable art, or *arte mobiliére,* dating to the Paleoindian period is currently extremely rare, with only one recently reported example from Vero Beach Florida, of an incised mammoth or mastodon on a fossil longbone fragment from a large mammal (Purdy et al. 2011). While seemingly carefully documented, extreme caution is warranted when such finds are reported, given how the profession has been fooled in the past by early "artwork" (e.g., Griffin et al. 1988), especially if such materials are subsequently offered for sale at high prices. Just outside the Southeast, several small cobbles were found at the Gault site in Texas with incised designs, including one of a possible plant (Collins et al. 1992). This is an interesting alternative to possible hunting-related imagery, and certainly plausible, given the arguments about the importance of generalized foraging adaptations that have been advanced for Paleoindian populations in the region in recent years (e.g., Hollenbach 2009; Walker and Driskell 2007).

Of course, what is actually meant by art warrants consideration. Aesthetic or ceremonial/ritualistic qualities could be attached to many of the elaborately carved ivory and bone points, foreshafts, and other tools found in Florida, as well as to large or well-made flaked stone tools, such as some of the Clovis, Cumberland, Redstone, or Sloan Dalton points that have been found in the region (e.g., Morse 1997; Sassaman 2005a:82–85; Walthall and Koldehoff 1998). The workmanship on many of these tools is superb, reflecting cultural values and a level of expertise rarely attained by knappers in subsequent periods. The production of oversized or hypertrophic artifacts, however, is a characteristic of southeastern ceremonialism throughout prehistory, and can be seen during the Archaic period in the production of at least some bannerstones, Benton points, soapstone bowls, and ground stone axes, and in the Mississippian period in the production of chert swords depicted in Mississippian artwork (Marceaux and Dye 2007; Sassaman 2005a, 2010a). It appears this form of ceremonialism has great antiquity in the region, dating to the Late Pleistocene.

The Dalton culture in the Central Mississippi Valley demonstrates that elaborate ceremonial behavior was not just present in the Southeast during the later Paleoindian and Early Archaic periods, but was shared over a fairly large area. Dalton projectile points are known from across the region, but are extremely common in the Central Mississippi Valley, where hundreds of Dalton sites have been reported (e.g., Gillam 1996a, 1996b; Morse 1973; Redfield 1971). Most of these sites are characterized by normal-sized tools that are worn-out or broken, and are assumed to represent habitation or special activity areas created by generalized foragers. A major debate in the 1970s, in fact, addressed the nature of Dalton settlement in the area of northeast Arkansas and southeast Missouri, focusing on identifying the range of sites used by these peoples, and whether they lived along single drainages or cross-cut several watersheds in their use of resources (e.g., D. Morse 1973, 1975a, 1975b, 1977; Schiffer 1975a, 1975b). This presaged a similar debate about Early Archaic site types and mobility patterns on the south Atlantic slope two decades later (e.g., Anderson and Hanson 1988; Daniel 1998, 2001). In both areas settlement appears to have been oriented along drainages, but with some cross-drainage movement also clearly occurring (Brooks et al. 2010; Gillam 1996a, 1996b, 1999).

The Dalton culture in the Central Mississippi Valley is unusual, and indeed unique to date in the Southeast during the Paleoindian period in that cemeteries and ceremonial caches of tools also appear to have been present, including oversized or hypertrophic bifaces known as Sloan points, after the site in northeast Arkansas where they were found. At Sloan, which was excavated by Dan F. Morse in 1974, 439 artifacts were found in shallow deposits in some twenty discrete clusters, covering an area of about 14 by 14 meters in extent and located in a sand dune (D. Morse 1975a, 1997). The tools included Sloan points, as well as a wide range of utilitarian items such as points, preforms, adzes, scrapers, and abraders. Most had been buried in pristine condition, with working edges that were either freshly resharpened or unused (Gaertner 1994; Yerkes and Gaertner 1997:69–71). Some 200 small fragments of highly weathered bone were found in and among these clusters, some of which positively identified as human and the rest unidentifiable (Condon and Rose 1997). The absence of overlapping clusters suggests a cemetery with marked graves, the earliest one known in the Americas. Such formal mortuary behavior is not seen again until later in the Early Archaic period, with the occurrence of submerged burials in ponds and sinkholes in Florida, such as at the Windover site (e.g., Doran 2002). Sloan was located well away from typical Dalton occupation or special activity sites, on an unusual landform, a sand dune. Its placement on the Dalton landscape raises the possibility that other early ceremonial sites may be present in the Southeast, in areas not typically examined.

Sloan points have been found at more than 30 locations in the Central Mississippi Valley, from northeast Arkansas to the American Bottom (Koldehoff and Walthall 2009; Walthall and Koldehoff 1998), unfortunately only rarely in excavation context. Two other intact caches of Dalton tools have been found in this area, at the Hawkins site in northeast Arkansas, and the Lembke site in Illinois, about 20 km east of the American Bottom. The former was dominated by points and stoneworking tools and the other by endscrapers, although at least one point and adze were found in each; no evidence for burials was found, and the possibility that they were gender specific toolkits, for Hawkins typical of that for males and Lembke females, was suggested (Morse 1971; Walthall and Holley 1997:159–160). Dalton adzes are also fairly common in this area, suggesting that watercraft or other large objects or structures of wood were being made; the archaeology of the Pacific Northwest offers a parallel about the things that could have been present, as do the remarkable utilitarian and ceremonial objects found in waterlogged deposits at Key Marco by Cushing (1897). An analysis of edge wear on Dalton adzes from Sloan indicates that these tools were likely used to work charred wood, one means by which dugout canoes were observed being made in the early Contact era (Yerkes and Gaertner 1997:63–66). Dalton adzes are decidedly uncommon over much of the remainder of the Southeast, however, and if other tool forms served as substitutes they are not as ubiquitous, a distribution that remains unexplained at present.

The incidence of Dalton sites and cemeteries, hypertrophic bifaces, and adzes in a relatively restricted section of the Central Mississippi Valley has led to the suggestion that these people were in regular contact, bound together by water traffic and through ritual and ceremony in a "Cult of the Long Blade" (Walthall and Koldehoff 1998:260–261). Given the unusual nature and extent of Dalton culture in this region, it may have been a comparatively short-lived precursor to the more complex tribal-level organizational forms that became common in the Mid-Holocene across the region (Anderson 2002b:250–251; Bender 1985; Sassaman 2005a:83–85). That Dalton culture in the Central Mississippi Valley is unusual compared to sites where these points are found in the rest of the region is clear (Koldehoff and Walthall 2004:63–64; 2009). McElrath and Emerson (2012:455) have further argued that, since the use of cemeteries and watercraft are foreign to Clovis, derivation of Dalton culture from that source is unlikely, and that we should perhaps look to earlier unspecified coastal and riverine societies for their origins. Given the similarities between Clovis and Dalton in biface manufacture, toolkit form and diversity, and the use of hypertrophic objects, coupled with the dating of Dalton (at least so far) as post-Clovis and the co-occurrence of both forms across the Central Mississippi Valley, and the absence of a identifiable alternative precursor culture, such a scenario, while plausible, is less parsimonious then assuming a local development from pre-existing Clovis and Clovis-related descendant populations (Anderson and Sassaman, ed. 1996; Anderson and Sassaman 2004; Bradley 1997; Morse 1997; Sassaman 2010a). Regardless of their origins, soon after the start of the Holocene, the precocious Dalton culture disappeared from the Central Mississippi Valley, leaving no successors, for reasons not currently understood in what has been called the "Dalton collapse" (Morse and Morse 1983; Morse et al. 1996). Initial Holocene climatic conditions were less varied than those of the Late Pleistocene, perhaps making more complex organizational forms unnecessary for a time—at least until regional population levels grew appreciably larger—if one of their purposes was risk minimization (Braun and Plog 1982).

Use of marked cemeteries began in other parts of the Southeast about this time, notably in Florida, where burials have been found submerged in bogs and ponds, sometimes in large numbers. The Windover site is the best known example of such a "subaqueous cemetery," and several others are known from Florida, with most dating to the early Holocene, from ca. 10,000 to 7000 cal yr B.P. (Doran 2002). The earliest submerged human remains from the region at present have been dated from ca. 11,500 to 10,200 cal yr B.P. at the Warm

Mineral Springs site in Florida, found on a ledge ca. 12 to 14 m below the surface (Clausen et al. 1975a, 1975b; Goodyear 1999:445). Whether they were intentional burials or drowning victims of people who fell into the cenote and were unable to climb out is unknown. Associated artifacts included Greenbrier/Bolen projectile points, suggesting a late Dalton/Early Side-Notched cultural affiliation. These cemeteries may have marked group territories, and they at least point to the possibility that territorial claims were being made by at least some groups in the late Pleistocene/Early Holocene Southeast. The presence of subaqueous cemeteries additionally suggests that the concept of a watery underworld, a theme common in later southeastern cultures (Mooney 1900:239), like the use of hypertrophic artifacts, has great antiquity in the region, apparently dating back to the Pleistocene (Hudson 1976:131–168; Sassaman 2005a, 2010a).

The Transition to the Holocene

As discussed in the next chapter, sophisticated research is demonstrating significant continuity in the settlement patterns and material culture of the Late Paleoindian and Early Archaic period residents of the Southeast, blurring the boundary between these somewhat arbitrary periods. Excavations have occurred at many sites in recent years, thanks in large part to CRM funding as well as the presence of many more academic and museum positions in the region. The multi-decade-long effort at the deeply stratified Dust Cave site in Alabama by Boyce Driskell and a number of younger scholars exemplifies current research efforts covering this time period, incorporating sophisticated geoarchaeological, zooarchaeological, paleoethnobotanical, and lithic analyses with materials and matrix from the site. Numerous masters theses, doctoral dissertations, papers, and books have come from the work (Sherwood et al. 2004; Walker and Driskell 2007). Hollenbach's (2009) insightful analyses of physiographic, paleosubsistence, and gender-linked foraging behavior around Dust Cave, for example—guided by behavioral ecology—offers an arguably more nuanced and complete model of Early Archaic settlement than seen in earlier efforts based largely on traditional lithic artifact categories. Given how few archaeologists in the Southeast work on late Pleistocene and early Holocene archaeology, at least compared to the efforts directed to later periods (Claassen 1999:91–92; Sassaman 2010a:5–7), it is remarkable how much we have learned in recent years. Much remains to be done, however, not the least of which includes better sequence definition in many areas, particularly before and after Clovis. The period spans several thousand years, and over this interval it is clear that human cultures in the Southeast were more varied than traditionally assumed, and were continually changing and reinventing themselves. The same, as we shall see, applies to peoples in all subsequent periods in the Southeast.

3

Archaic Diversity

The Archaic period encompasses more than eight millennia of Native American experience in the southeastern U.S. In radiocarbon years, the Archaic is known generally as the period from 10,000–3000 B.P., which is actually a good bit longer and older in calibrated years, ca. 11,500–3200 cal yr B.P. (see Sassaman 2010a:14–21). The period is usually divided into three subperiods—Early (11,500–8900 cal yr B.P.), Middle (8900–5800 cal yr B.P.), and Late (5800–3200 cal yr B.P.)—taxonomically on the basis of changes in subsistence technology, notably hafted bifaces, and interpretatively on the basis of large-scale environmental and demographic change. The applicability of this tripartite division is not universal in the Southeast, but no matter the particular archaeological units of time and form employed locally, the Archaic is generally regarded as a long period of transition between the initial colonization of North America and the subsequent Woodland and Mississippian periods whose relatively higher levels of organizational complexity were attended by more permanent settlement and larger populations than in the Archaic. In the widely influential treatise on Eastern U.S. prehistory, Caldwell (1958) portrayed the Archaic period as a time of gradual change—a slow, progressive trend toward increased efficiency in the exploitation of emerging new forest niches of the postglacial era, leading to larger populations and greater permanence, demand for better technologies, and, eventually, the networks of interaction and cultural diffusion that accounted for the spread of pottery, food production, and institutions of politics and religion of post-Archaic times.

Recent fieldwork and collections research have taken our understanding of the Archaic period well past the narrative famously scripted by Caldwell. Although the broad contours of Archaic experience may have been shaped by the trends Caldwell identified (Dye and Watson 2010), recent work reveals a greater level of organizational and structural diversity than ever imagined. Many of the shifts in subsistence and technology thought to develop in sync with a maturing eastern Woodlands environment (including coastal zones) actually occurred early in the period. There is also good evidence for rapid, eventful change (i.e., significant change within a human lifetime) at times, stimulated in many cases by abrupt environmental change but manifested socially in the demographic realignments attending abandonment and resettlement. Growing evidence for connections among Archaic communities across vast geographies means that the fate of numerous small-scale societies were to a large extent interdependent. As Caldwell (1958:17) himself anticipated, the Eastern Archaic was to become "an interconnected historical structure." Current data show that the sort of sociohistorical structures Caldwell (1958, 1964) envisioned—exemplified by the "interaction sphere" of Hopewell, for instance—did not have to await a slow, gradual process of incremental change to culminate in the elaborate cultures of the terminal Archaic, but instead arose much earlier under a variety of circumstances and in varied settings.

In this chapter we focus on all that is new in our archaeological understanding of the Archaic period (Figure 3–1), dividing recent work into five topics. To begin, we suggest that an improved understanding of the Archaic has turned on new discoveries, and arguably the most influential of these has been the discovery of earthen mounds in the Lower Mississippi Valley dating to the Middle Archaic period, from ca. 5650 cal. B.P. The surprisingly early age of these mounds is an unassailable archaeological fact, but their significance is a matter of great debate and uncertainty. Without question, research stimulated by the discovery of Archaic mounds has been a defining aspect of regional archaeology for the past 15 years (e.g., Russo 1994, 1996; Saunders et al. 1994, 1997, 2005; papers in Gibson and Carr 2004), especially if we include controversial new work on shell deposits, which is spawning productive debate about the intentionality and significance of mounding (cf. Anderson 2010:287–289, 297–298; Marquardt 2010a, 2010b; Russo 2006, 2010; Sassaman and Randall 2012; Thompson and Worth 2011).

A second major advance in Archaic archaeology has been the development of data on alliance and exchange. Building on the pioneering work of Howard Winters (1968, 1969), archaeologists have documented evidence for the transfer of raw materials and goods since the beginning of the Archaic. Such investigations have operated at two related levels: (1) recon-

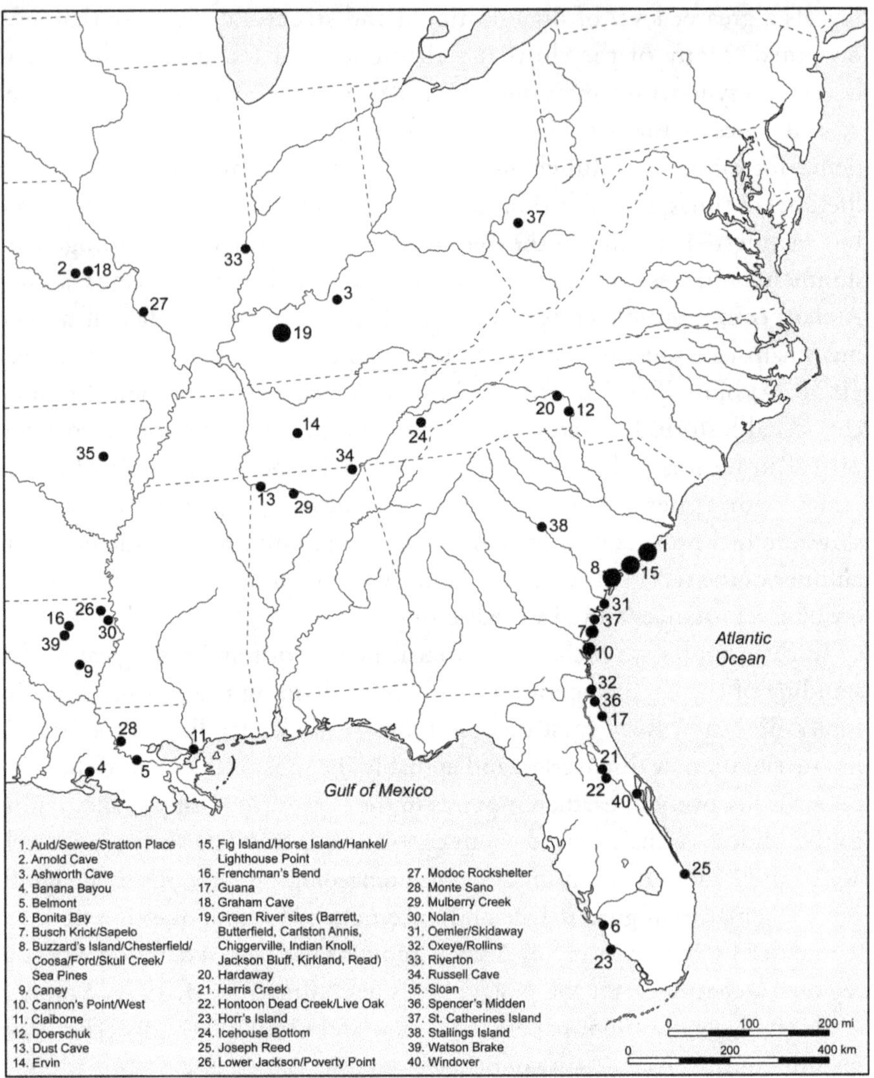

Figure 3-1. Locations of Archaic period sites mentioned in the text.

structing the identity and organization of particular groups of people, and (2) reconstructing the networks of interaction among such groups that would account for the movement of objects and materials. Practitioners today appreciate the mutuality of group identity and intergroup alliance, finding good evidence for practices that involved both local and nonlocal elements of public ritual. All such work has benefited immensely from ongoing development of regional databases on site distributions and chronology (e.g., Anderson 1996b), data directly informing our perception of population distributions and their change over time. Government-sponsored archaeology and the agencies charged with state site file management have been essential to the development of such data.

A third area of recent inquiry has centered on mortuary practices of the Archaic period. For decades, Archaic skeletal populations of the lower Midwest and Midsouth formed the comparative baseline for hunter-gatherer biology relative to farming peoples of the Woodland and Mississippian periods (e.g., Bridges 1989, 1991; Haskins and Hermann 1996; Smith 1996). Biological research continues today in these and other subregions with new analytical tools such as stable isotopes and ancient DNA, as well as renewed interest in morphometrics. Added to this has been growing interest in the cultural and social dimensions of mortuary practice, well beyond the enduring efforts to infer social differentiation from variations in treatment and health. Death was perhaps never a trifling affair for any Archaic community, and recent work has documented tremendous variation in the style and context of burial, ranging from the late Paleoindian period Dalton cemeteries of the Central Mississippi Valley discussed in the preceding chapter, to the pond burials of Florida, to the shell mounds of Alabama, Tennessee, and Kentucky.

We next take a look at recent advances in the study of subsistence economies and ecologies of the Archaic. Here the application of theory from the natural sciences—such as behavioral ecology—has been most productive when based on the long-term study of particular locales, such as St. Catherines Island on the Georgia Coast (Thomas, ed. 2008), and Dust Cave in Alabama (Carmody 2009, 2010; Hollenbach 2009; Sherwood et al. 2004). The investment of long-term, interdisciplinary engagements with archaeological evidence from particular locales has paid off in highly nuanced understandings about local ecology coupled with robust samples of materials needed to characterize human choices. Put into comparative context, microeconomic approaches have enhanced our ability to assess the efficiency of explanations for change seen in macroevolutionary narratives, such as that of Caldwell (1958). Ancillary to this line of research has been the development of much new data on plant domestication in the Archaic, processes involving cucurbits and a variety of seed-bearing plants that were underway early in some locales but apparently did not coalesce into a "horticultural complex" until the twilight of the Archaic period (B. D. Smith 1992, 2006; Smith and Yarnell 2009). Still, the management of mast-bearing trees throughout the Archaic may have paved the way for processes of plant domestication and eventual agricultural economies (Gardner 1997; Moore and Dekle 2010).

The "transition" from the Archaic to the Woodland period is the subject of our fifth and final theme of this chapter. When the outlines of Eastern Woodlands culture-history took shape in the middle part of the last century, the Woodland was distinguished from the preceding Archaic period by the adoption of pottery, village life, food production, exchange alliances, and monument construction. We know now that all such features have expression in Archaic traditions dating hundreds, if not thousands, of years before the onset of the Woodland period at ca. 3200 cal. B.P. Attention has turned away from a trait-list approach and towards close examination of the environmental and social circumstances that led to the abandonment of certain areas of the Southeast at the close of the Archaic (Kidder 2006, 2010; Thomas and Sanger 2010). Brought to the fore by this work is keen appreciation for eventful environmental change, such as flooding, coastal transgression, and drought. At the same time, coincident cultural changes crosscutting ecological regimes go to show, as noted earlier, that existing sociohistorical structures of the Archaic meant that the fate of a local group experiencing say, massive flooding, indirectly affected many others in the patterns of abandonment and resettlement precipitated by such dramatic events.

The five topics we choose to highlight in this chapter transcend the usual culture-historical divisions of the Archaic period and thus may impose a bit of confusion to the reader with little or no prior knowledge of regional archaeology. Thus, before delving into the themes that, in our estimation, define the freshest and most interesting work in the Southeast, we review in brief some basic knowledge about Archaic archaeology within the traditional tripartite scheme noted earlier. For further details, we direct the reader to some of the regional syntheses of Archaic archaeology that have been issued in the past two decades (Anderson and Sassaman, ed. 1996; Anderson and Sassaman 2004; Jefferies 2009; Kidder and Sassaman 2009; Sassaman 2010a; Sassaman and Anderson, eds. 1996; Sassaman and Anderson 2004).

Archaic Basics

The way Southeastern archaeologists have divided the Archaic period into subperiods has changed over time with improvements in chronology and regional survey. The Southeast boasts a large number of deeply stratified sequences in floodplains, terraces, rockshelters, and caves, as well as anthropogenic accumulations of shell and other media in coastal and riverine settings. It is in these contexts that the framework of Archaic taxonomy was established, often through public-funded field studies starting with those of Depression-era relief programs. Coupled with an ever-growing array of paleoenvironmental data from stratified contexts, sequential changes in artifact forms afforded not only a means to monitor time, but also a basis for investigating the effects of environmental change on Archaic communities. The tripartite scheme of Early, Middle, and Late Archaic subperiods has long been recognized to coincide with broad climatic trends of the postglacial era and it remains the primary basis for both describing and explaining Archaic variation across most of the region.

Early Archaic

A sharp increase in global temperature at the end of the Younger Dryas marks the onset of the Holocene era and with it the Early Archaic period, ca. 11,500 cal yr B.P. Hardwood forests dominated by oaks and hickory expanded northward quickly from late Pleistocene refugia in the lower Southeast (Delcourt and Delcourt 1987; Jacobson et al. 1987; Webb et al. 1993; J. W. Williams et al. 2001; Williams et al. 2004). Fairly dense human populations existed across much of the region during the Early Archaic period, as evidenced by the presence of large numbers of sites and artifacts, particularly when compared with the preceding Paleoindian era (Anderson 1990:198–201, 1996b:158). Irrespective of environmental change at this time, continuity with late Paleoindian traditions is evident in certain aspects of flaked stone technologies of the Early Archaic. At the same time, changes in land use, including the first extensive use of cave and rockshelter sites (Walthall 1998a), signify adjustments to environments appreciably different than those of the late Pleistocene. One major exception may be the coast, which was some 30 m below modern elevation at the onset of the Early Archaic. Evidence for early coastal settlement is being actively sought (e.g., Adovasio and Hemmings 2011; Faught 2004a, 2004b), but remains elusive.

Early Archaic occupations in the Southeast are recognized by successive side- and corner-notched and bifurcate-based hafted bifaces (e.g., Anderson et al. 1996; Bense 1994:62–68; Chapman 1985:147–149; Coe 1964:67–70). Some late Paleoindian period forms and associated tools, such as Dalton and its affines (Goodyear 1982; Justice 1987:35–43; Morse 1997), extended into the Early Archaic period, but as early as 11,800 cal yr B.P., side-notched point forms had appeared in Alabama and Florida and within a few centuries variants of this form are found in large numbers across the Southeast (Justice 1987:60–71). By 10,800 cal yr B.P., corner-notched types such as the Palmer and Kirk became pervasive, followed in limited areas by bifurcate forms, including the MacCorkle, St. Albans, LeCroy, and Kanawha types, dating from ca. 10,000 to 8700 cal yr B.P. (Broyles 1966, 1971; Chapman 1985; Justice 1987:91–96).

A fundamental reorganization of culture and technological organization took place during the later Paleoindian era, following Clovis, that continued into the Early Archaic. The change in point forms from lanceolate to serrated and notched types, for example, is thought by some to reflect a change from the occasional procurement of very large animals, such as mammoth and mastodon, to the regular killing and processing of smaller game, of which deer soon assumed a primary role. In addition, Early Archaic assemblages demonstrate an increased reliance through time on local raw materials and a decline in the use of formalized tools. The marked increase in sites over the Paleoindian period is thought to reflect increasing population levels and decreasing group ranges (Anderson 1990:198–201, 1996b:160–163; Dunbar and Webb 1996:352; Walthall 1998a, 1998b). Groups are believed at this time to be organized into mobile bands oriented to either particular physiographic ranges (e.g., drainage basins [Anderson and Hanson 1988]), or tethered to certain raw material sources (Daniel 1998, 2001), and, in Florida, to sinks that offered good sources of potable water in an otherwise dry landscape (Dunbar 1991). These bands in turn appear to have been loosely tied into larger networks of affiliation, or macrobands, to facilitate mating and information exchange (Anderson 1996a:39–45; Anderson and Hanson 1988). Overall, organizational changes since the Paleoindian period are thought to have been brought about, in large measure, by the increasing importance of generalist foraging strategies over the region in response to post-glacial warming, increasing human population levels, and the replacement of Late Pleistocene floral and faunal communities by essentially modern ones.

Middle Archaic

The Middle Archaic period of 8900–5800 cal B.P. is synonymous with the Mid-Holocene climatic interval known variously as the Hypsithermal, Altithermal, Atlantic, or Climatic Optimum. Once thought to be a prolonged era of higher-than-present temperatures across the globe, regional climates actually varied wildly. Without delving too deeply into such variations, we can say simply that Middle Holocene climate in the Southeast was not like that of today, even at comparable temperatures (Anderson et al. 2007b). Seasonal extremes in precipitation and temperature were greater than today in many areas. Mid-Holocene climate at times in the lower Midwest and Midsouth was hotter and dryer than at present, leading to a reduction in upland vegetation, increased surface erosion, and aggrading floodplains (Knox 1983:32–34; Schuldenrein 1996:9–10, 26–27; Wright 1992), as well as occasional eastward expansion of prairie into Illinois and Indiana. In river systems of the central interior, formation of backwater slough habitat enhanced floodplain productivity, and shoal environments promoted freshwater shellfish. Pine forests began to re-expand, replacing oak, and cypress swamps began to develop along the slowing and flooding river systems of the lower Southeast (Delcourt and Delcourt 1987; Jacobson et al. 1987; Watts et al. 1996:32–36; Webb et al. 1993:448–450; Williams et al. 2004). Such warming and drying trends may have rendered riverine areas more favorable, and upland areas less favorable, to human populations (J. Brown 1985:219–221; Brown and Vierra 1983:167–168; Dye 1996). Along the Gulf Coast and across peninsular Florida, rising sea levels supported wetland development and a burgeoning of habitat for aquatic flora and fauna. Except for limited sites of coastal occupation situated on elevated landforms of stranded estuaries (e.g., Mikell and Saunders 2007; Ricklis 1988), the Middle Archaic coastal record is inundated, but apparently still preserved in places (Faught 2004a, 2004b).

The onset of the Middle Archaic period is known to archaeologists across much of the Southeast by the introduction of stemmed biface technology. Certain stemmed forms are believed to be historically derived from Early Archaic ancestry, as in the Carolina Piedmont sequence established by Joffre Coe (1964) from sites in North Carolina. In other subregions of the Southeast, however, continuity with the previous period is difficult to track, owing, in part, to hiatuses of varying length during the millennium of ca.

9500–8500 cal yr B.P. (e.g., various bifurcate traditions that occupy this interval had limited distribution across the region [Anderson 1991a]). This pattern no doubt reflects the sorts of organizational shifts attending climatic and demographic change, but to what extent did it include the influx of immigrants from outside the region, as Coe (1964) once opined about the widespread Morrow Mountain type (see also Sassaman 2010a)?

Whether or not change in the Middle Archaic cultural landscape involved newcomers, the changes were relatively dramatic. It is during this period that (1) freshwater shellfish began to be collected and deposited in large piles along rivers of the Midsouth and Florida; (2) earthen mounds were erected in the Lower Mississippi Valley and later in northeast Florida; (3) long-distance exchange networks flourished in several subregions; (4) innovations such as bannerstones appeared and were drafted into ritual uses; and (5) instances of interpersonal violence or warfare become evident. All of these factors indicate local cultures were growing in scale and organizational complexity. While fairly simply organized foraging groups are still present, they increasingly became circumscribed in areas such as in the South Atlantic Piedmont of the Carolinas and Georgia and in western Louisiana (Anderson 1996b:164–165; Sassaman 1995:191). Elsewhere, in varied contexts of cultural elaboration in mound building and exchange, social formations akin to ethnographic tribes appear to have developed (Anderson 2002b, 2004).

Late Archaic

Largely modern climatic conditions were established by the onset of the Late Archaic period at 5800 cal yr B.P. and thus sites of the period are located in contemporary zones of inhabitable land and favorable resources. Site frequencies across the Southeast register a 40 percent increase over those of the Middle Archaic period, a trend almost certainly attributable to widespread population growth (Anderson 1996b; Steponaitis 1986:373). These same data show no major geographic gaps in the distribution of sites across the region. Locations underutilized or abandoned during the Mid-Holocene, notably portions of the Gulf and Atlantic Coastal Plains, had once again become populated, and coastal zones throughout the region became major centers of settlement.

Perhaps the most defining environmental factor of the Late Archaic period was the expansion of wetland habitat throughout the region. This process occurred in riverine zones as floodplains adjusted to increased precipitation and lowered channel gradients compared to the Middle Holocene (Schuldenrein 1996); and in coastal zones, where the diminishing rate of sea level rise after ca. 5000 cal. B.P. enabled the establishment of estuarine habitat in the generally modern configuration.

Archaeological recognition of Late Archaic cultures centers again on variations in stone tool technology, but added to inventories after ca. 5000 cal yr B.P. were pottery vessels in the south Atlantic Slope, and slightly later in the lower Midsouth, Gulf Coast, and Lower Mississippi Valley (Saunders and Hayes 2004). Once thought to predate pottery across much of the Southeast, vessels carved out of soapstone generally postdate 4200 cal yr B.P., but they were to become one of the major items of exchange from quarries in the southern Appalachians and Piedmont. An array of hafted biface forms across the region share a common theme for broad-blades and large, robust stems, classic examples being the Savannah River Stemmed of the Carolina Piedmont and Ledbetter Stemmed of the Interior Plateau. However, subregional variations are many and tend to be downplayed by the use of typologies developed elsewhere. Many analysts would agree that demographic and environmental conditions during the Late Archaic were conducive to cultural diversification. Maturing floodplain habitats and diminished rates of sea-level rise, coupled with overall moist climate, enabled certain Late Archaic groups to maintain more-or-less permanent settlement in increasingly circumscribed areas (Thompson and Turck 2009, 2010; Turck 2011). Coastal sites have provided the best direct evidence for year-round occupation, beginning well before the Late Archaic period (Russo 1996b; Thompson and Andrus 2011). Interior groups may have been relatively more mobile, responsive to the rhythms of spring floods or occasional droughts, but no matter the frequency and distance of movement, a pattern of land-use redundancy is indicated by the accumulation of dense middens along rivers of the Deep South, lower Midwest, Midsouth, and south Atlantic Slope (Claassen 1996, 2010; Dye 1996; Marquardt and Watson 2005). Cross-cutting the development of innumerable local communities were networks of exchange that were at times as structured and redundant as patterns of land use. The grandest expression of such a network was the terminal Archaic Poverty Point culture of northeast Louisiana. After a local hiatus in mound building lasting over a millennium (Saunders 2010), a public works project was started at Poverty Point that would materialize in earth a set of beliefs and social relationships involving the importation of objects and materials from across the entire Southeast and beyond, such as the aforementioned soapstone vessels. In its mound building and long-distance exchange, Poverty Point was once believed to be without precedence in the culture history of the Archaic period (Gibson 1996, 2000). To some extent this remains true today, but as we have seen in this short synopsis of Archaic cultural and environmental history, mounds and networks have a deeper past than ever before imagined, providing Southeast Archaic specialists much new data to contemplate.

Mounds and Monuments

In a 1994 issue of the journal *Southeastern Archaeology* (Russo 1994), nine authors introduced to its readership an assemblage of sites stretching across the lower Southeast that contained mounds up to 2,000 years older than the hitherto oldest known mounds. Three years later one of those mound sites—Watson Brake in Louisiana—garnered the attention of the premiere journal *Science* (Saunders et al. 1997) and with it an international audience. More than simply pushing back the onset of monument construction, Watson Brake showed at once that relatively small-scale hunter-gatherer groups had mobilized considerable labor in public works projects rivaling those of larger, more "settled" populations, and that they had materialized in enduring form, through mound architecture, core metaphors of society and the cosmos.

We have known this to be the case for the Poverty Point site of Louisiana, long ago regarded as an anomaly (Figure 3-2). When brought to archaeological light in the middle twentieth century, Poverty Point was thought to be the work of Mesoamerican colonists or the influence of Adena and Hopewell cultures of the American Midwest (Gibson 2000:18–19, 24). Just as the recent announcement of even older mounds in the region touched off debate and skepticism, claims that Poverty Point was Archaic in age did not find unanimous acceptance. For archaeologists of the day, the construction of monumental landscapes involving planning and labor coordination was just not something expected of people unable to produce their own food. We now know this to be unremarkable for several hunter-gatherer traditions of the Southeast.

As of 2010, 13 mound sites in Louisiana and two in Mississippi have been dated to between 5650 and 4750 cal yr B.P. (Saunders 2010). Many other mounds in the Lower Mississippi Valley are believed to be Archaic in

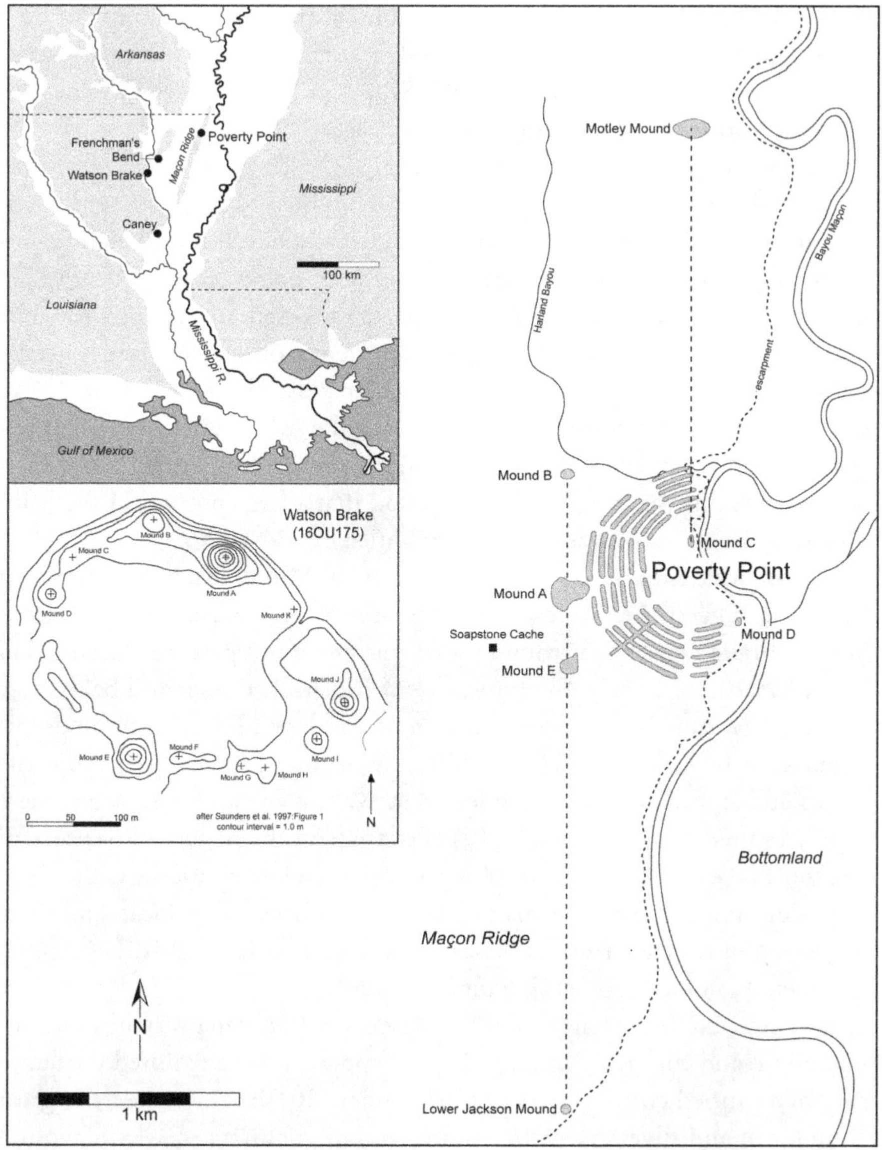

Figure 3-2. Plan map of Poverty Point with insets for the location of select Middle Archaic mounds in the region (upper left) and plan map of Watson Brake (left).

age but have not been confirmed. All mounds in this area were constructed of earth, and those investigated through coring or excavation show that construction was usually staged. At some sites, mounds were erected over occupation surfaces or buildings. However, none of the mounds appear to have been built as platforms for houses or other constructions. With the exception of Monte Sano (C. Kuttruff 1997; Saunders 1994), none of the mound sites has produced evidence for human burials.

Mound complexes in the Lower Mississippi Valley range in size from the 11-mound array at Watson Brake (Figure 3-2) to isolated single-mound examples at Banana Bayou, Lower Jackson, and Belmont. Mound height varies from 1 to 7.5 m and most mounds are conical or dome shaped. Low earthen ridges connect individual mounds at several of the sites, forming plaza-like enclosures at Watson Brake, Caney, and apparently others. Sites are generally located along upland terraces overlooking wetlands. The four-mound Nolan site, however, was found on a relict channel of the Arkansas River in the modern floodplain of the Mississippi River (Arco et al. 2006). Buried by 3–4 m of recent alluvium, Nolan raises the likelihood that a large portion of the Mid-Holocene moundscape was destroyed or buried by alluviation.

The high density of artifacts found at many Middle Archaic mounds in Louisiana suggest they were places of residence, and subsistence data from Watson Brake suggest year-round use of this site, if not perennial occupation (Saunders 2010:71–72). An abundance of fire-cracked rock and baked clay blocks at Watson Brake accompany an assemblage of animal bone dominated by fish (Jackson and Scott 2001). Workshops for making projectile points and stone beads were also found at Watson Brake. Remarkably, there is only limited evidence for long-distance trade in the material inventory of Watson Brake and other mounds in the region (Johnson 2000); with minor exception, raw materials for making bifaces and beads were local, and there is nothing in the organization or scale of production to suggest that mound sites were economic centers (J. Saunders 2004).

Because Middle Archaic mound complexes in Louisiana vary in size, configuration, and composition, they do not "appear to have required the adoption of a unified cultural tradition" (Saunders 2010:73). Rather, the great abundance and diversity of freshwater aquatic habitats to which mound complexes seem to be oriented enabled relatively autonomous local economies, circumscribed in places of sustained production and participating in only limited, if any, extralocal exchanges. That is the view of Joe Saunders (2010:73–74), as well as many other archaeologists who rightfully point out the material basis for stability and autonomy. Others have pointed to temporal variations in Mid-Holocene climate as a stimulus for mound building (Hamilton 1999; Peacock et al. 2010), relating cultural elaboration to a bet-hedging strategy for reducing the risks of variations on biological fitness. The more typical strategy for reducing risks among hunter-gatherers worldwide is to participate in networks of reciprocal exchange that crosscut environmental regimes to ensure access to resources when local sources are inadequate, often by relocating. That little connection is seen among the Louisiana mound communities is thus especially curious.

Cultural connections among the various mound complexes may not be evident in the objects or raw materials they house, but perhaps in the geometry and layout of the mounds themselves. Three of the multi-mound sites (Watson Brake, Caney, Frenchman's Bend) were laid out using similar geometric principles and units of measure (Clark 2004; Sassaman and Heckenberger 2004). Geometric and proportional regularities among these complexes do not seem to be tied into any sort of astronomical alignments, and complexes vary in their orientation to cardinal directions. While these complexes seem to have been independent of one another within a broadly shared belief system, there is tantalizing, albeit inconclusive evidence that complexes were parts of an integrated whole (Sassaman and Heckenberger 2004). This would suggest the existence of pathways or circuits of movement among complexes, something akin perhaps to the intersite alignments of Hopewell (Bernardini 2004; Lepper 2006). Arguably, the regional complex of mounds symbolized cosmogeny, somewhat like those of later traditions (e.g., Knight 1986, 2006), but with its symbolic referents (mounds) distributed widely across a regional landscape. It follows that each place was enchained with others in webs of reference, all perhaps subject to alternative interpretation by those who drew symbolic resources from these places. That interaction such as this did not leave material traces in the form of nonlocal goods or materials is indeed problematic, although absence of such exchange does not eliminate the possibility that ritual participation that enhanced each community's capacity to remain economically autonomous was in place.

A second major venue for early mounding is in the middle St. Johns valley of northeast Florida. Ridges and mounds dating from ca. 7200 cal yr B.P. vary in size, shape, and composition, and they numbered in the score if not hundreds before the early twentieth century, when most were mined for shell (Figure 3-3). Because mounds typically contain the inedible remains of freshwater shellfish (chief among them *Viviparus georgianus*), regional specialists have generally assumed that they formed through the gradual accu-

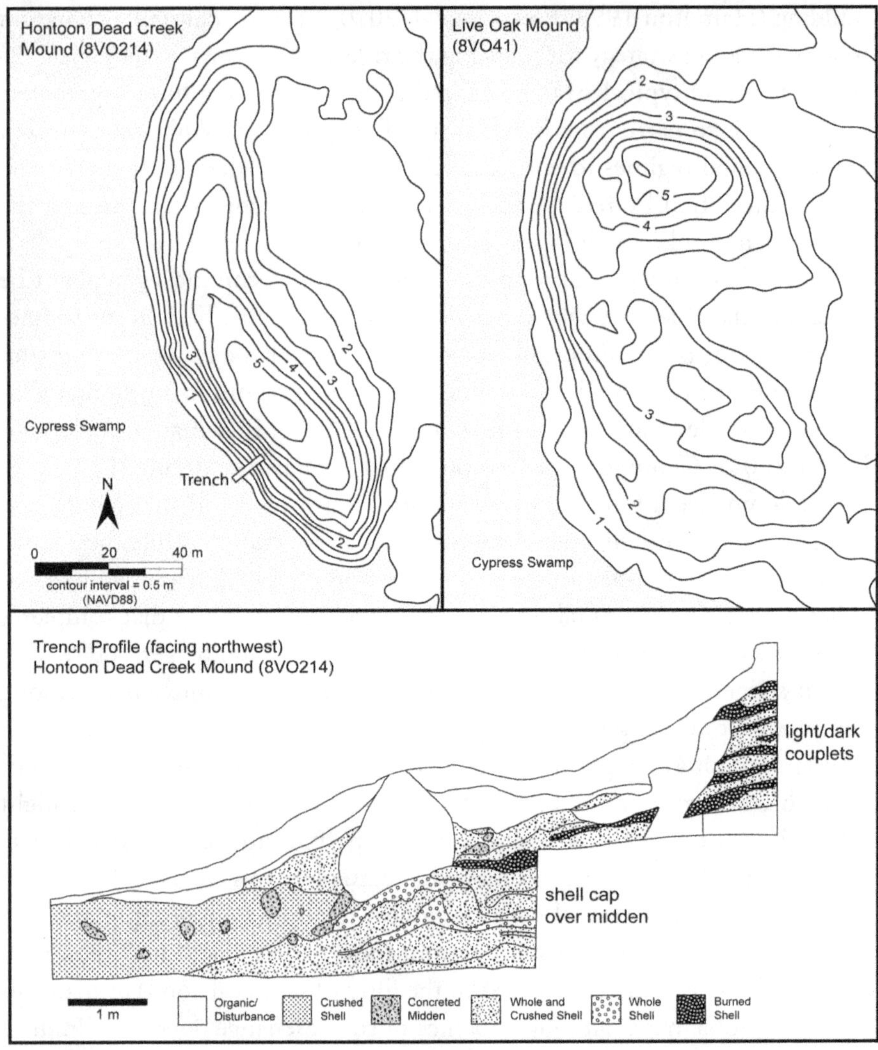

Figure 3-3. Plan maps of two early shell mounds in middle St. Johns valley of Florida (top), and cross-section of trench into Hontoon Dead Creek Mound (bottom).

mulation of domestic refuse, with the shells discarded after the meat was consumed (Milanich 1994:90–92). Water levels in Florida at this time were rising rapidly, supporting emergent wetland habitat within a low-gradient river with innumerable impoundments in lakes, lagoons, and backwater sloughs (Miller 1998). As in Louisiana, these very conditions are thought to have encouraged repeated use of particular locations and presumably a level of local economic autonomy stemming from bounties of fish, turtle, and other aquatic resources, including shellfish. Moreover, newly formed aquatic adaptations in northeast Florida appear to have been highly sustainable judging from the continuity of land use and lack of dietary change for thousands of years (Milanich 1994:86).

One ongoing program of fieldwork in the region has shown that the history of mounding was actually highly eventful, with several major disjunctures in practice and tradition, arguably tied to changes in local environment and demographic realignments (Randall 2010, 2011; Randall and Sassaman 2010; Sassaman and Randall 2012). Many accumulations of shell and associated materials (artifacts, vertebrate fauna, plant remains) were evidently locations of dwelling, with strata of stacked living surfaces and midden, often interspersed with mantles of clean shell or sand. But some of the oldest show that former locations of dwelling were capped with shell and then received multiple layers of structured deposition intermittently over the next century or two (Sassaman and Randall 2012). Simultaneously, the first mortuary mounds were established in the region, which, in addition to shell, involved the emplacement of white sand and black swamp muck over burial clusters (Aten 1999). At about 5600 cal yr B.P. the mounding of earth over shell ridges ushered in a twist on tradition (the Thornhill Lake phase), coincident with an influx of nonlocal goods (Beasley 2008; Endonino 2008, 2010). At about 4500 cal yr B.P. another major shift occurred when some mounds were reconfigured into massive U-shaped or multi-ridge structures, forms highly reminiscent of some of the larger shell rings of the Florida coast (Russo and Heide 2001; Russo 2006) (Box 3–1). Coincident with this final shift in mounding was the first pottery in the region, an innovation also with coastal origins (Sassaman 1993, 2002, 2004a).

Debate on shell mounds and shell rings has turned on the intentionality of accumulations that arguably consisted of the remains of everyday living (cf. Marquardt 2010a, 2010b; Russo 2004, 2010). Considering recent observations on mound stratigraphy, one would be hard pressed to separate the mundane from the ceremonial in Archaic mounds. There are clear parallels between the acts of mounding that encased the dead in shell and sand on the one hand, and the alternating sequences of living surfaces, midden and emplaced shell/sand on the other. Whether involving burials or not, Florida Archaic mounds routinely express structured deposits that juxtapose light matrix (unburned shell, white sand) with dark matrix (burned shell, muck,

Box 3-1. Shell Rings of the Atlantic and Gulf Coasts

Among the Southeast's most vexing sites are the arcuate or circular accumulations of shell and associated remains known generically as "shell rings" (Figure 3B-1). With few exceptions, shell rings are coastal sites, ranging widely in shape and size (Russo and Heide 2001; Russo 2006), and dating mostly to the Late Archaic period. The roots of a shell ring tradition may be seen in the arcuate shell deposits at Spencers Midden in northeast Florida, dating as early as 6200 cal yr B.P. (Russo 1996b; Russo and Saunders 1999), but full-fledged rings date from ca. 4600 to 3200 cal yr B.P., coincident with the first pottery traditions of North America (Russo 2006; Sanger 2010). The ravages of sea-level rise likely erased sites older than 4,600 years, when slowing in the rate of rise attended the establishment of modern estuarine systems of the south Atlantic and Gulf coasts. Rings are distributed from central Florida to South Carolina on the Eastern Seaboard, and from southwest Florida to Mississippi along the Gulf. The relatively greater age of Atlantic rings may be more apparent than real, because Gulf coastal sites have been especially vulnerable to inundation.

Florida rings in general are about three times larger on average than those to the north along the Atlantic coast (Russo and Heide 2001). Examples on both the Atlantic and Gulf coasts, as well as freshwater sites on the St. Johns River, reach up to 300 m in length in U-shaped configurations. South Carolina and Georgia rings are generally less than 100 m wide, often enclosed completely, and occasionally grouped or enchained with others. Reasons for these geographic differences are unknown, but may be related to the size or organizational complexity of the groups creating these structures.

As the name implies, shell rings consist mostly of shell, usually those of oyster, with coquina, various other clam species, and gastropods forming minority species. Stratigraphic sections include sequences of crushed shell and debris indicative of living surfaces, but also massive layers of whole shell from episodes of rapid accumulation. Direct evidence of architecture is lacking, but cooking pits are common within and along the edges of rings. At one site on St. Catherines Island in Georgia, massive pits are dis-

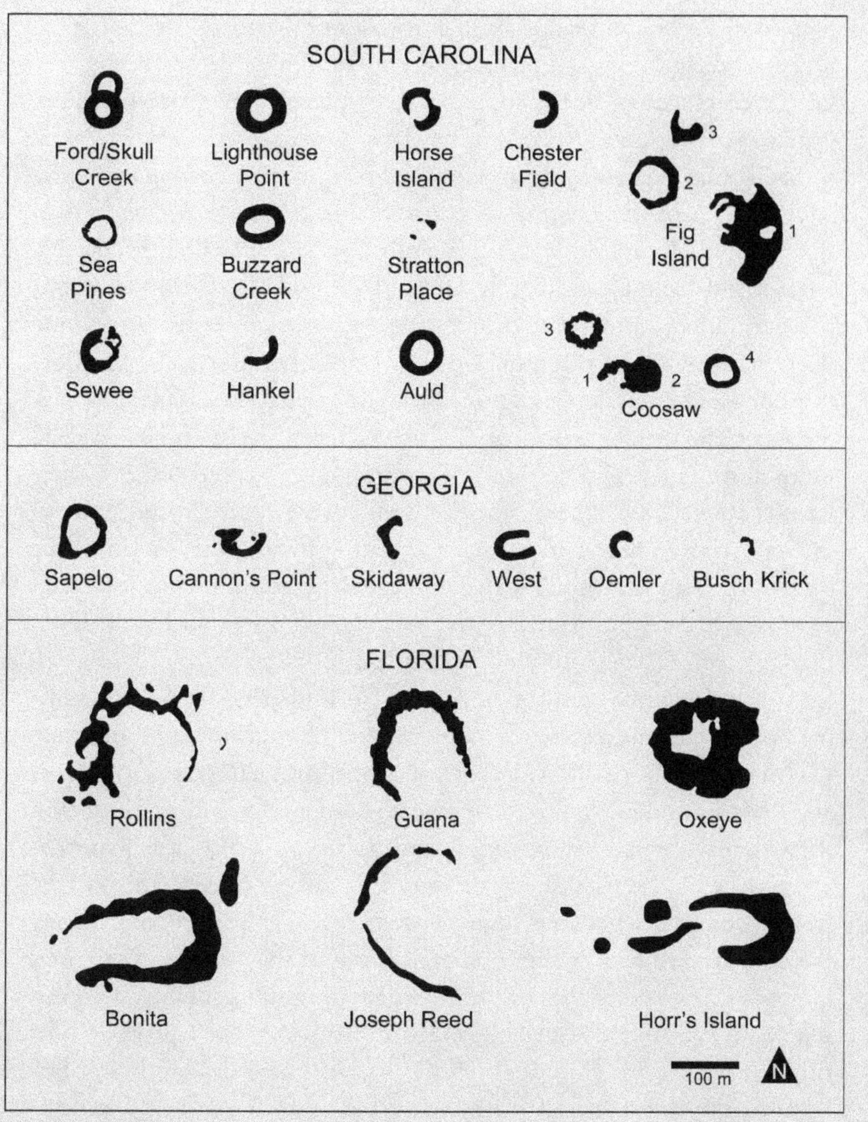

Figure 3B-1. Composite plan of shell rings along the Atlantic and Gulf coasts. Image adapted from illustration provided courtesy of Michael Russo.

tributed across the center of the ring (Sanger and Thomas 2010), an exception, along with Sapelo Island (Thompson 2007), to an apparent pattern of generally clean plaza-like interiors. Apart from sizeable pottery assemblages, rings in general do not contain dense or diverse artifact assemblages (save for some on the western Gulf Coast, notably Claiborne [Bruseth 1991]), and they lack human interments.

Shell rings have long stimulated the imagination of archaeologists and thus have been a source of considerable debate, particularly over their function. Archaeologists generally concede that shell rings were locations of habitation, literally life in the round. They disagree about the permanence and scale of occupations, and about less mundane matters, such as the ceremonial uses of rings and the social implications of differential deposition of shell (e.g., asymmetrical plans or segments of enhanced elevation). A flurry of recent research has resulted in an abundance of new data informing on these and other topics: Russo (2004, 2006, 2010) and R. Saunders (2002, 2004) have documented stratigraphic and formal patterning to support the inference that rings were locations of ritual feasting by communities or social groups with differing status or ranking; Thomas and colleagues (Sanger and Thomas 2010; Thomas, ed. 2008) have conducted an intensive program of testing on rings at St. Catherines Island to examine both social and ecological change; and Thompson and colleagues (Thompson 2006, 2007; Thompson and Andrus 2011; Thompson et al. 2004) have deployed remote sensing and stable isotope studies to show that the functions of rings changed over time. Whereas hypotheses about practical uses of rings continue to appear (Marquardt 2010a, 2010b), most practitioners appreciate that shell rings were not merely the de facto result of living in a circle, even as they caution that rings may have never been thrown up in an act of monumentality. Thompson (2007, 2010) may have hit on the most reasonable explanation for rings: namely, that they started off as places of everyday living but became, through persistent use, historically significant and occasionally the locus of ritual activities, such as feasting, that resulted in large accumulations of shell. In this sense, shell rings were not all that much different than the monuments seen elsewhere insofar as they took their significance from a history of prior use.

brown sand). Among later mound builders, color contrasts such as these indexed a variety of relationships, such as direction, earth and sky, or birth and death (Buikstra et al. 1998; DeBoer 2005), while the capping of mounds was an expression of rebirth (Knight 1986). But in this earlier context, water may have been among the core symbolic referents, an outcome of living through a period of rapidly rising water levels (Sassaman 2012).

The Poverty Point site of northeast Louisiana provides perhaps the best example of materializing the cosmos and society in earth during the Archaic period. Emerging after ca. 3700 cal yr B.P. and developing over several ensuing centuries, Poverty Point culture involved unprecedented levels of mound construction and interregional exchange centered on the type site, Poverty Point, a 3-sq-km complex of nearly one million cubic yards of mounded earth in six nested, elliptical half-rings, two massive effigy mounds, and several conical and flat-topped mounds (Ford and Webb 1956; Gibson 2000). A gap of over 1,000 years separates the latest Middle Archaic mound from the first construction at Poverty Point (Saunders 2010). However, at least one Middle Archaic mound south of the main complex at Poverty Point—the Lower Jackson Mound (Saunders et al. 2001)—was used by Poverty Point architects to establish a baseline from which all other mounds and the nested rings were sited, apparently using the same measurement system of Middle Archaic mound builders (Clark 2004).

Recent work at Poverty Point has established good detail on the sequence of construction events spanning about four centuries (Gibson 2000, 2004; Kidder 2011; Kidder et al. 2008; Kidder et al. 2009; Ortmann 2010). Midden beneath the rings shows that people were living in a semi-circular village with a central plaza for a short while before the first earth was mounded. According to Gibson (2010:88), the inner ring was erected first, and each of the five other rings in sequence from inside out. As for the various mounds, Ortmann (2007, 2010) has established that Mound B came first, followed in order by Mound E (Ballcourt) and Mound C (Dunbar), and finally the massive Mound A and Motley Mound. Additional detail on the construction of Mound A provides testament to the scale and organization of labor. Second in size in North America to only Monks Mound at Cahokia—the bulk of Mound A was thrown up in less than three months and it was constructed as an enactment of an origin myth (e.g., Earth Diver myth). This is the inference of Kidder (2011) after recent stratigraphic excavation, demonstrating the mound was built directly over a marsh or pond, and his case is compelling. Putting this act into its own historical context, Poverty Point communities were always in a dialogue with their past. In addition to citing mounds of the Middle Archaic tradition long since past, the objects of Poverty Point exchange indexed other places and times materially, through acquisition of all sorts of nonlocal materials, and metaphorically in its six-ridge earthworks, which, when the dimensions are scaled upwards in multiples of six, appears to capture successively greater arrays of social interaction and history (Sassaman 2005b).

Archaeologists will continue to debate the intended actions of Poverty Point moundbuilders, but even greater disagreement stems from inferences about the size, permanence, and identity of the resident population. Gibson (2004) has estimated that the labor pool necessary to construct the mounds and rings was 700–800 workers drawn from a population of at least 2,000 individuals. To him, Poverty Point was a large town occupied by local residents he has dubbed the *Tamaroha,* a Tunica term for "Mound Cave People." Undeniably, people dwelled at Poverty Point throughout its four-century history, but was it the largest town at that time in native North America, as Clark et al. (2010) suggest? Alternatively, was Poverty Point a trade fair that attracted people from across the greater Southeast and beyond (Jackson 1991)? Or, was it the *axis mundi* for a variety of peoples of distinct language and ancestry who converged occasionally to participate in mounding and other collective actions (Sassaman 2005b)? One glaring contradiction in the totality that is Poverty Point is that it is simultaneously a one-of-a-kind place, replicated nowhere else in the region in even remotely similar form and scale, and it was the recipient of nonlocal goods and materials that, by necessity, must have involved at least some contact with people of distinct disposition and identity (but see Arco and Ortmann [2010], who suggest the Poverty Point site plan may derive, in part, from natural and constructed landscapes at the Jaketown site). As we will see in Chapter 4, so many of the subsequent mounds of the Woodland period appear to have been points of articulation between two or more communities, rather than the outcomes and symbols of corporate identity that invokes a sense of territoriality and competition. Evidence for long-distance exchange pervades all such instances, and we can see that like mounding, such exchange patterns extend far back into Archaic times to link together people across vast geographies.

Population Nodes and Alliances

Culture history in the Southeast, as elsewhere, was predicated on the logic that Archaic societies consisted of self-organizing, self-sufficient, and self-replicating units of consanguinity and affinity. In the taxonomy of culture history, such units were conceived of as archaeological *phases*, the ancient equivalent to ethnographic "bands" or "tribes" (Willey and Phillips 1958). To define a phase was to locate in a limited range of time and space a series of attributes that distinguish it from other phases. Differences between phases of the same age were tacitly accepted as the consequence of relative isolation, just as similarities between phases was taken as evidence of interaction or historical affinity.

Several decades of critical self-reflection in anthropology has exposed the biases of traditional culture history and opened up alternative ways of organizing observations on cultural variation and change. For instance, rather than assuming Archaic societies were discrete, functioning units, we can instead consider how they were nodes in networks of affiliation and interaction. The archaeological phase is still a useful taxonomic unit for this way of thinking, but now in relational, not essential, terms. A corollary to this perspective is the recognition that cultural difference may be an outcome of interaction, rather than isolation. It follows that detailed reconstructions of the distribution of social nodes and the interactions connecting them poses great challenges to an archaeology built on a foundation of normative culture history.

As we saw in the previous chapter, efforts to reconstruct the distribution of populations across the study area depends on the recognition of artifact forms with discrete time-space distributions, in that case distinctive Paleoindian projectile point types or varieties. The Archaic period in general, compared to its predecessor, was an era of increased cultural diversity, coupled with apparent growth in population and greater geographic circumscription of particular groups. Acknowledging the biases of a normative approach to culture history, we remain confident that the broad patterns of group affiliation and distribution can be inferred from diagnostic artifacts, which, during the Archaic period, expanded to include items other than flaked stone tools.

In an effort to characterize the "big picture" of Archaic settlement, Anderson (1996b) compiled data on over 32,000 records in the site files of ten southeastern states. These data evince a clear trend for increasing site frequency from the Early Archaic through the Late Archaic, but they also show that demographic expansion was neither uniform nor pervasive (see also Milner 2004a, 2004b). When standardized for differential time, the Middle Archaic period actually shows a slight decrease in site counts before growing dramatically in the Late Archaic period. Although biases of site preservation and recognition abound, this apparent decrease (or at least stabilization) in site frequency during the early Middle Archaic coincides with abandonment or limited use of large tracts of land that were utilized regularly during the Early Archaic period. Most notable is reduced site frequency in the Atlantic and Gulf Coastal Plain, a region whose expanding pine forests may have diminished the potential for sustained human settlement; this may have begun during the period when bifurcate points were in vogue (Anderson 1991a, 1996b:165; Chapman 1975; Sassaman 1995). The province was not entirely abandoned, however, as ongoing work at Carolina Bays in the Atlantic Coastal Plain documents routine use of upland wetlands throughout the Mid-Holocene (Brooks et al. 2010). Likewise, coastal records of Middle Archaic settlement remain spotty but continue to reveal themselves occasionally in both terrestrial and underwater contexts (Faught 2004a, 2004b; Mikell and Saunders 2007; Russo 1996b).

Where Middle Archaic sites do occur with great frequency we find stark contrasts in demographics on either side of the Appalachian divide. Sites with diagnostic artifacts of the Morrow Mountain tradition (Coe 1964) are ubiquitous in the Georgia-Carolina Piedmont, distributed widely across landforms with seemingly little intersite variation and a nearly compete reliance on local raw materials for stone tools (Blanton and Sassaman 1989). West of the divide, in the Interior Low Plateau of the lower Midwest and Midsouth, Middle Archaic sites tend to cluster along major rivers, separated from one another by areas of limited settlement. This is the pattern of an emergent riverine tradition known as the Shell Mound Archaic that apparently had one ancestral root in the Morrow Mountain tradition (Dye 1996), but quickly diverged into a series of formations with apparently redundant land-use practices at select locations and perhaps distinct territories (Anderson 1996b; Sassaman 2010a, 2010b).

Expressions of group identity and alliances among Middle Archaic communities of the Interior Low Plateau are evident in a number of traditions. Among them is the Benton Interaction Sphere that linked communities of the Shell Mound Archaic with the Gulf Coastal Plain through the transport

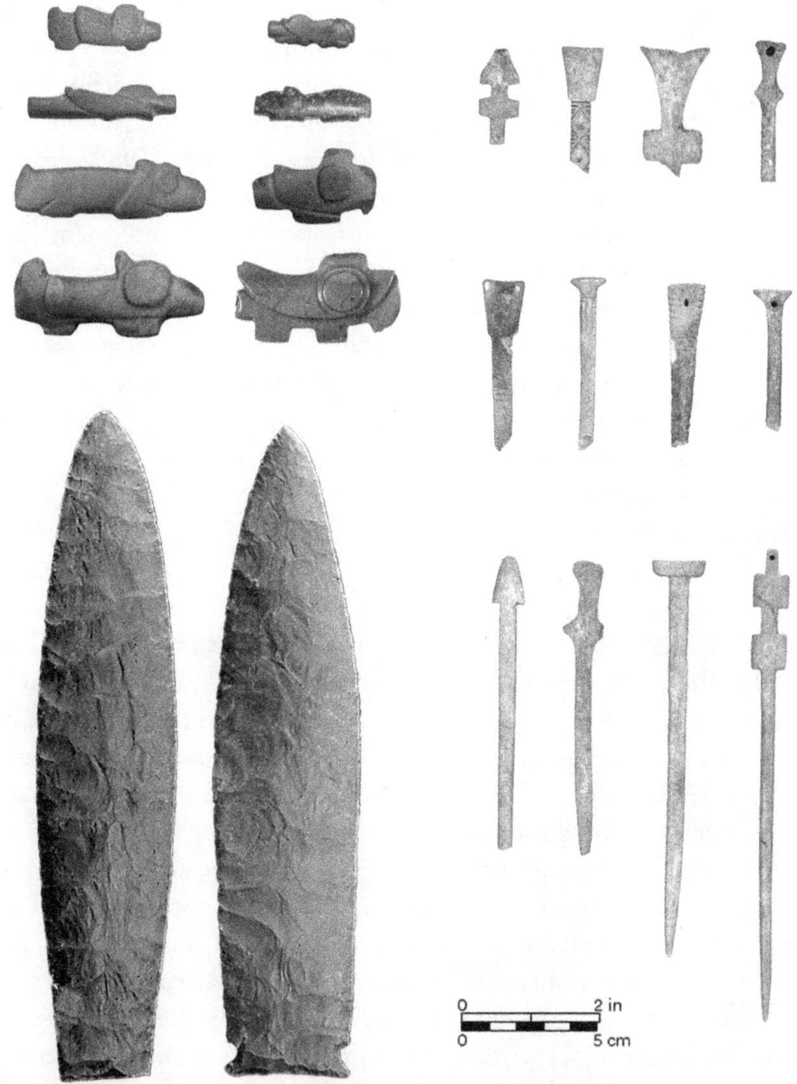

Figure 3-4. Items of Middle Archaic exchange: stone effigy beads (upper left); oversized Benton points (lower left), and bone pins (right). Image adapted from Crawford 2003; Jefferies 2009; Johnson and Brookes 1989.

and caching of well-made, oversized bifaces (Figure 3–4). More than a dozen such caches have been found along the Upper Tombigbee River of Mississippi and in adjoining areas of Tennessee and northern Alabama (Johnson and Brookes 1989; McNutt 2008; Meeks 1999, 2000). Up to 26 cm in length, bifaces in Benton caches were made from blue-gray Fort Payne chert of the middle Tennessee River area of northwest Alabama. Caches typically contain both oversized bifaces and smaller, mundane forms. Although none of the caches documented by Johnson and Brookes (1989) from the Tombigbee River were expressly mortuary, sites on the Tennessee, Harpeth, and Duck rivers provide good association with human interment (Dowd 1989; Hofman 1985; McNutt 2008:50; Webb and DeJarnette 1942), including cremations, which appear to involve the most elaborate caches (Futato 2004). Poor preservation outside of shell deposition may account for the lack of human bone at some caches, although it appears certain that refined or oversized Benton bifaces made from nonlocal materials were sometimes cached in nonmortuary contexts (Futato 2004).

Included in graves or not, Benton caches do not conform to the expectations of down-the-line exchange or any manner of displacement that was gradual or incremental. This is the implication of metric data provided by Johnson and Brookes (1989). With distance from the geological sources of Fort Payne chert, Benton points found outside of caches decrease in length, as well as frequency, eventually being replaced by local raw materials at locations greater than 60 km from the source area. Cached bifaces, on the other hand, whether oversized or not, do not exhibit attrition with displacement, even at distances of over 160 km from the source area. Details remain sketchy on the intent of caching and the identity of participating communities, but it would appear safe to infer that certain Benton bifaces were produced to be exchanged and cached, and that, based on the overall distribution of Benton caches, alliances involving Benton exchanges linked communities along a north-south corridor from central Tennessee to south Alabama.

Coeval with, but apparently independent of, the Benton Interaction Sphere was a network centered in Mississippi involving the production and distribution of stone beads (Figure 3–4). Tubular forms were most common, but also produced was a series of zoomorphic effigy beads (Crawford 2003). A few locations of bead production have been documented (e.g., Connaway 1977, 1981; McGahey 2005) and the final products have shown up as far away as east Texas and northeast Florida. Thus, unlike the north-south orientation of Benton exchange, Middle Archaic stone bead exchange linked nodes along an east-west corridor, paralleling and likely including the Gulf

Coast, and anticipating similar networks of interaction during the Late Archaic period.

Another expansive network of alliances linking communities east and west is evident in the production of ornate bone pins in the lower Midwest (Figure 3–4). Jefferies (1996, 2004a, 2009:183–186) has compiled a database on hundreds of bone pins to infer patterns of affiliation and alliance. The actual function of pins is uncertain although the ornate design of some forms evokes a sense of expressive style. During the late Middle Archaic (ca. 6900–5800 cal yr B.P.), bone pins across a 500-km stretch of the lower Midwest shared a panoply of styles, expressed most clearly in the shape of the heads of pins. These various designs did not, however, cross southward over the Ohio River and into the well-populated subregion of Shell Mound Archaic communities. The river itself was not likely an impassable boundary, as the east-west network of interaction crossed the Mississippi channel with no trouble (Jefferies 2004a:80). Rather, the Lower Ohio River appears to have delimited the boundary between two major "ethnic cores," to borrow a phrase from Emerson and McElrath (2001). Other classes of material culture—bannerstones (Burdin 2004), fish hooks (Moore 2010), and plummets (Goldstein 2004)—mirror the bone pin data in delimiting the Ohio River as a major cultural boundary. A similar boundary condition has been inferred for the Early Woodland Adena traditions centuries later (see Chapter 4).

Similarities between groups north and south of the Ohio River may actually outweigh any differences throughout the Archaic era, and we of course do not have archaeological purchase on numerous other measures of identity and alliance, such as language, performance, and myth. However, the material evidence we do have for differences among groups who are otherwise similar in disposition and ecological niche goes to suggest that cultural boundaries were asserted and reproduced as a means of rendering intergroup interactions more predictable, and likely more formalized, than chance encounters might entail. At the same time, skeletal data from the "borderlands" show that interactions were occasionally violent and likely ritualized (e.g., Schmidt et al. 2010). More specifically, Claassen (2010) has argued that intercultural violence (i.e., captive taking) was linked to the consecration of ritual places along the Green River and ultimately the formation of Shell Mound Archaic communities.

Other examples of the interplay between group identity and intergroup alliance are found in the Late Archaic period, when the density of sites doubles and virtually no major area of the Southeast was unoccupied (Anderson 1996b; Milner 2004a). One of the better-documented examples comes from the Savannah River Valley of Georgia and South Carolina. During the Mid-Holocene, the inferred valley-wide pattern of seasonal mobility present during the Early Archaic period (Anderson and Hanson 1988) was replaced by more circumscribed settlement, and for the Late Archaic period we can infer from the distribution of material culture the existence of distinct Piedmont and Coastal Plain/coastal populations (Sassaman et al. 1988). The use of the region's first pottery by the latter communities at ca. 4800 cal yr B.P. and its absence for centuries among the former were among the vast differences between these populations (Sassaman 1993, 2006a). As distinct as they may seem archaeologically, these groups engaged in practices that resulted in the transfer of province-specific items, notably Piedmont soapstone and occasional bannerstones to the Coastal Plain, and marine shell, usually in the form of beads, to the Piedmont (e.g., Sassaman and Randall 2007). As one history would have it, these interprovincial practices led eventually to a coalescent community know to archaeologists as the Stallings tradition (Sassaman 1993, 2006a). Accompanying this process among Piedmont groups, perhaps out of resistance to change, was an exaggeration of some items of "traditional" material culture and a staunch resistance to innovation, namely pottery (Sassaman 2001a, 2001b).

In cases like that of the Savannah River, existing alliances seem to have enabled the relocation of one group into the "home land" of another group. And yet, despite prior history, contradictions were not unexpected when people of two or more distinct traditions were drawn together more permanently. It is under these conditions that social life appears to have become more formalized or structured, with expected attention to ritual protocol, bodily orientation, and other symbolic action. In its circular village, plaza cemetery, and structured deposition, Classic Stallings culture at the namesake site exemplifies the sort of formality we have in mind (Sassaman et al. 2006). A much grander example is of course the Poverty Point site of northeast Louisiana. Arguably the most formalized built environment of the Archaic period, Poverty Point is also the region's grandest example of extralocal connections. Literally tons of raw materials and goods were delivered to Poverty Point from as far away as the upper Midwest, eastern Plains, and Appalachians (Gibson 2000). Because most of the nonlocal materials were drafted into apparently mundane uses (e.g., soapstone for cooking vessels;

granite, basalt, and greenstone for celts; hematite and magnetite for plummets; and various cherts for projectiles and cutting tools, among others), Poverty Points imports may very well have been a practical solution to settled life in a relatively stone-less land. This may partly explain the one-way quality of Poverty Point exchange: that is, diverse and abundant materials were imported in but nothing of any real archaeological consequence (i.e., preserved, observable form) was exported out. However, some items of import went beyond practical concern. Soapstone vessels from the southern Appalachians, for example, were extraneous as container technology given that Poverty Point residents were familiar with pottery (Gibson and Melancon 2004). The importation of soapstone vessels to Poverty Point was hardly trivial, as it involved hundreds of items transported hundreds of kilometers from source areas. Rather than assess the value of this exchange in practical terms, it may be useful to consider how the reproduction of Poverty Point culture was dependent on long-distance connections like those involving soapstone (Sassaman 2005b, 2010a).

An enduring theme in the interpretation of long-distance exchange in the Southeast is that material conditions at times were such that groups sought out and maintained connections to far-flung groups as a way of reducing risk against local failure (Bissett 2010; Brose 1994; Brown 1985; Jefferies 1995, 1996). According to James Brown (1985), this strategy was encouraged by environmental and demographic conditions of increasing sedentism and geographic circumscription, which precluded the use of mobility to buffer risk (see also Carmody 2010). To this we can add the wholesale movement of groups in response to time-transgressive ecological trends that shifted zones of inhabitability and primary production, such as those of the Early Archaic, and resulted in partial or complete abandonment of large tracts of land in places like the Atlantic Coastal Plain. Moreover, we have several examples of intergroup exchange or interaction that defy the expectations for down-the-line exchange or the logic of practical needs. Finally, the intensity of intergroup exchange correlates roughly with growing populations, increased sedentism, and geographic circumscription, but it did not have to await those conditions in the Southeast. Rather, since at least the Dalton era, ritual involving the acquisition of nonlocal materials appears to have been central to group identity, and, since this founding time, much of this ritual centered on treatment of the dead.

Mortuary Traditions

If disposal of the dead is dissociated from the material conditions of life, as Alfred Kroeber (1927) once suggested, then we may find in mortuary practices of the Southeast Archaic some of the best evidence for cultural continuity and change independent of the sways of climate and energy budgets. However, not all archaeologists would agree with Kroeber (e.g., Binford 1971), as mortuary practices were also influenced by the pragmatics of living off the land. Certainly the mortuary practices of the Archaic period were diverse, with some existing but a short time and seemingly incidental, others persisting in highly formalized regimes for millennia. Archaic mortuary practices included dedicated cemeteries, in-flesh inhumation and cremation, and traditions of mortuary caching. Many programs were combinations of in-flesh inhumation and cremation, both primary and secondary, although cremation is totally absent in the Green River region, which boasts the largest skeletal populations in the Southeast.

Much of the discussion of Archaic mortuary practice in the Southeast centers on the recognition of formal cemeteries, which, like mounds, has been assumed to signal a level of cultural complexity unexpected of small-scale, mobile hunter-gatherer societies. Arguably, as noted in the previous chapter, the oldest known cemetery in the Southeast is the Sloan site of northeast Arkansas, dating to the Dalton horizon of ca. 12,500–11,300 cal yr B.P. (Morse 1997). Situated on a sand ridge in the Mississippi Valley lowlands, the site contained in an area 14 by 14 m nearly 300 bifaces and adzes and additional flaked stone items of distinctively Dalton design. Bone preservation was extremely poor, but enough bone was recovered from clusters accompanying caches of artifacts to suggest the site was the formal cemetery of an estimated 30 individuals, adults and subadults alike, none of which apparently were cremated. Among the grave lots were bifaces made from cherts of the Crescent Quarries near the American Bottom, several of exaggerated proportions that Dan F. Morse (1997) refers to as Sloan points.

Several other locations dating to the early Holocene parallel the formalized and elaborate qualities of the Sloan cemetery, while others involve simple inhumations or cremations at sites of habitation. In a thorough review of early Holocene mortuary behavior, Walthall (1999) explains these variations as a consequence of varying land-use patterns. He draws a distinction between expedient and special-place disposal, the former expected of mobile groups lacking routinized land-use practices, the latter indicative of predictable, redundant movements of dispersed groups that share nodes of ritual significance. The marked variation seen in Dalton mortuary treatment continues into subsequent Early Archaic phases. Rockshelter and cave burials dating to the Early Archaic have been documented at Graham Cave (Logan 1952) and Arnold Cave (Shippee 1966) in Missouri, Modoc Rockshelter in Illinois (Fowler 1959), Ashworth Cave in Kentucky (DiBlasi 1981), and Dust Cave in Alabama (Hogue 1994). Five open-air sites reviewed by Walthall (1999) include sites of inhumation and cremation, but never a mix of the two. Cremations of Early Archaic age are restricted in the Southeast to two isolated examples from the Icehouse Bottom site of eastern Tennessee (Chapman 1973).

Walthall (1999) predicts that expedient disposal would have been the mode of burial among the late Pleistocene populations of the Paleoindian era, as these are expected to be highly mobile populations with limited or no ties to particular places (e.g., Kelly and Todd 1988; cf. Anderson 1990; Dincauze 1993). In contrast, later groups, having established territories and routine rounds, are expected to practice special-place disposal. Walthall's model is thus diachronic, as it outlines the sorts of changes expected as pioneer groups moving into the Eastern Woodlands at the end of the Ice Age carved out habitual use areas and established their rights over them. Cemeteries in this sense were corporate markers underwritten by assertions of ancestry (e.g., Buikstra and Charles 1999; Charles and Buikstra 1983). Walthall makes the argument that this change occurred early in the Holocene, marked dramatically by the Dalton adaptation to temperate forests and its time-transgressive trend northward (Walthall 1998a, 1998b). He thus concludes that early Holocene burial practices were more similar to those of later periods than to the immediately preceding Paleoindian period, reflecting, again, fundamentally different land-use practices than what came before. A similar line of argumentation is proffered by Hofman (1985) in his explanation of Benton-period burial diversity at the Ervin site in Tennessee.

When put into broader comparative perspective (i.e., the entire Eastern Woodlands), the models of Hofman and Walthall cannot explain all of the variability of Archaic mortuary traditions (see Sassaman 2010a:78–91). Northern traditions suggest that cremations were not always a logistical matter, as they were sometimes prepared in crematories within eyeshot of cemeteries. Conversely, entire programs of human interment in the Southeast

Figure 3-5. Excavation of the Mulberry Creek site in advance of the flooding of the Pickwick Basin on the Tennessee River in north Alabama (Webb and DeJarnette 1942).

apparently precluded cremation, even in cases where patterns of land use match the expectations set forth by Walthall and Hofman. For instance, shell-bearing sites in the Green River valley of Kentucky were locations of intensive seasonal habitation and often large skeletal populations, but not a single cremation has ever been documented (Hensley 1994:249). The point here is that cultural disposition over burials cannot be reduced to patterns of mobility or the logistics of transporting bodies to locations of interment. Factoring into the equation are ancestral practices and the representations of "idealized" culture that ritual often embodies. No archaeological phenomenon illustrates this point better than the Shell Mound Archaic of the lower Midwest and Midsouth (Figure 3-5).

The Green River Valley sites of the Shell Mound Archaic have produced some of the largest skeletal populations of hunter-gatherers worldwide and they have long been looked to as a baseline for hunter-gatherer biology and demography across the greater Eastern Woodlands. Over 3,000 burials from Green River sites date to the Archaic period, with nearly 1,200 individuals excavated from Indian Knoll alone (Haskins and Herrmann 1996). Other shell-bearing sites with sizable burial populations include Carlston Annis, Read, Chiggerville, Barrett, and Butterfield. We can add to the list 433 burials from Ward, a site with virtually no shell, and 70 from Kirkland, a shell-free midden (Hensley 1994). Small burial populations have been recovered from several other sites, both with and without shell. The number of burials does not appear to be correlated with shell density. Among those sites Hensley (1994:231) ranks as having "high" shell density, the ratio of interments to area excavated ranges from 1:5 burials/m^2 (Carlston Annis) to 1:176/m^2 (Jackson Bluff). A similar range can be found among sites with low shell density, while the shell-free site, Kirkland, has a ratio of 1:15/m^2. That burials do occur at relatively high density at locations lacking shell midden underscores the fact that the overall high density of burials in the area is not merely an artifact of the preservation shell affords.

Irrespective of the amount of shell involved, Green River burials are exclusively inhumations. The vast majority are tightly flexed individuals placed in shallow, round graves when found in soil below or apart from shell middens, or, if in shell midden, often placed in a shallow depression and covered with loose fill. The proportions of submidden and midden burials vary across sites. For instance, 55 percent of the 880 burials excavated by William S. Webb (1946) at Indian Knoll were found in submidden sands, but only 16 percent of burials at Carlston Annis were below the shell (Hensley 1994:234). In locations where shell deposits are discrete, such as Read (Milner and Jefferies 1998), burials were often placed in areas lacking shell. Across contexts, flexing of the bodies was frequently so tight that individuals must have been wrapped or bound upon death. Irrespectively, it was common for bodies to be placed in holes barely large enough to contain them, which resulted in contorted postures in some instances. Minority treatments included semi-flexed and "seated" burials, and rare examples of extended burials. Again, cremation and other sorts of secondary treatments (e.g., bundle burials) are virtually nonexistent. Graves with multiple individuals, embedded projectiles, and dismemberment (decapitation and removed limbs) occur with sufficient frequency to suggest Green River denizens were occasionally engaged in intergroup conflicts.

Most individuals buried at Green River sites had unadorned graves, but the proportion of those with accoutrements is remarkably consistent across sites, at least those with shell. Roughly 25–30 percent of all individuals were buried with some sort of artifact, most commonly shell beads. Much fewer interments included grave goods at sites lacking shell. Both local and nonlocal sources of shell were used, with the latter dominated by marine gastropods (whelk and conch) whose sources could be no closer than the Gulf of Mexico. It is noteworthy that Green River sites have produced more marine shell beads (at least 23,000 [Marquardt and Watson 2005]) than any other subregion of the Eastern Woodlands. Complete or broken spearthrowers, marine shell "cups" or pendants, turtle-shell rattles, bone implements and ornaments, and various stone tools were occasionally included in graves. The red ochre so common to burials to the north and east is but a minor addition to Green River graves. Various attempts to locate nonrandom patterning in the distribution of grave goods by age and sex have disclosed little patterning other than the disproportionate occurrence of shell beads with children (Claassen 1996).

Dogs were often buried at Green River sites (Morey 2010:168–176). They were usually treated like humans, tucked into graves in a somewhat flexed position, but never with grave goods. The ratio of human to dog burials ranges from a low of 4:1 to as much as 42:1. Usually about half of the dogs buried at sites were included with humans, but curiously never at Read, the site with the largest dog population (n = 65).

Recent research into the mortuary practices of the Green River Archaic have centered on the question of whether so-called shell mounds were in fact burial mounds, as hypothesized by Claassen (1991a, 1991b, 1992b, 2010). That the Green River sites were locations of human interment is unequivocal, and most analysts agree that the "shell mounds" were neither mounded nor dominated by shell (Crothers 1999, 2004; Hensley 1994; Marquardt and Watson 2005; Milner and Jefferies 1998). As noted above, burial density varies independently of shell density, with some dense shell deposits lacking burials and some large burial populations located in nonshell middens. Researchers of late have also emphasized, as William S. Webb (1946) did long ago, that Green River sites with burials were habitations, not dedicated places for the dead. Because burials were included in "pile(s) of occupational refuse," some modern analysts have dismissed any claims for more formalized programs of interment (Milner and Jefferies 1998:130).

Claassen's (2010) most recent thinking on the Shell Mound Archaic extends her initial hypothesis about burial mounds to a broader realm of rituality. She dismisses entirely the notion that Shell Mound Archaic sites were places of habitation, but instead nodes of ritual practice for geographically dispersed groups. Such locations were positioned with reference to an unspecified cosmology involving places materialized by the mounding of underworld substances (in this case shellfish) and the interment of sacrificial persons. Food remains at these sites are interpreted by Claassen as the output of feasting, and objects left as offerings to ancestral deities. In this sense, shell mounds were places of renewal, as well as hubs of social interaction in which community identity was negotiated.

Claassen's (2010) argument is perhaps the most original and provocative model of the Shell Mound Archaic ever conceived. It follows logically from the premise that Archaic life was shaped foremost by belief, but it will require much more data to know how such beliefs were materialized in actual human experiences. Despite a long history of research in the Green River region, including large, multidisciplinary projects (e.g., Marquardt and Watson 2005), basic issues like chronology remain elusive. As Claassen (2010:219–220) notes, with better chronology in the Green River region, many of the intersite variations in mortuary treatment may prove to be historical, not simply structural or functional. Some advances along these lines have been seen recently in the other major venue of the Shell Mound Archaic, the middle Tennessee Valley. Using correspondence analysis of grave good content from a Shell Mound Archaic site in Alabama, Shields (2010) was able to distinguish practices that he argues reflect community identity, and he was able to posit changes in identities over time. The palimpsest effects of centuries of intensive ritual activity and inhabitation clearly obscure variability in mortuary practices that only careful re-analyses such as those by Shields can reveal.

Geographically distant from the goings-on of the Shell Mound Archaic were the mortuary traditions of peninsular Florida. Earlier in this chapter we introduced the shell mounds of the middle St. Johns region, noting a series of historical transformations in the scale, configuration, and siting of mounds. Although not all shell deposits were demonstrably mortuary, shell was clearly employed in the interment of humans, as was sand, swamp muck, and other substances. The oldest known mortuary mound in Florida is the Harris Creek site on Tick Island (Aten 1999). The 175 burials salvaged by Ripley Bullen in 1961 were emplaced on two successive platforms atop a shell ridge, the first capped with white sand, the second with additional shell midden. Recent analysis of the assemblage included four new AMS assays on human teeth, ranging from ca. 7000–6600 cal yr B.P., placing the assemblage early in the Mount Taylor phase (Quinn et al. 2008; Tucker 2009). Moreover, stable isotopic data on tooth enamel enabled Tucker (2009) to infer that shellfish were unlikely a major contributor to the diet, and he located a few individuals in the assemblage who apparently spent their formative years at locations as distant as Virginia. By the late Mount Taylor period, known as the Thornhill Lake phase, mortuary practices included conical sand mounds sited on older shell deposits and included in the graves of some individuals were objects from as far afield as Mississippi and South Carolina (Endonino 2010).

The shift from shell to sand burial was not the first major transformation in mortuary practice in Florida. Long before the first burial mound was erected, Early and Middle Archaic communities interred their dead in shallow ponds. Several mortuary ponds have been documented across the peninsula, but only the Windover pond, near Cape Canaveral, has seen serious study (Doran 2002). Salvaged in the 1980s by a team headed by Glen Doran were 168 individuals, most dating from 8100 to 7900 cal yr B.P. Burials tended to occur in clusters that were apparently marked by stakes anchored to peat (Dickel 2002:80). Whether the area surrounding Windover was also a place of habitation cannot be inferred from modern data, but biological data suggest that this population and the mortuary tradition of pond burials in general were widespread during the Early Archaic period (Wentz and Gifford 2007). None of the known pond burials post-dates ca. 5800 cal yr B.P., when burial mounds of sand first appeared. The transformations from pond to shell and then from shell to sand burials appear to coincide with changes in water levels attending sea-level rise, suggesting that each change was underwritten by a cognitive shift attending changing land-use patterns and the demographic realignments associated with abandonment and relocation (Sassaman 2012).

Outstripping in number all the mortuary traditions discussed above were many others that did not leave behind conspicuous evidence for the treatment of human remains. It is hardly inconsequential that the oldest earthen mounds in the Southeast provide no insight on mortuary practice, or that the elaborate Poverty Point site has yet to produce a single interment. It follows that mounds were not uniformly erected to inter the dead, but it does not follow that mound building and beliefs about life and death were dissociated among those that did not inter their dead in mounds. Issues of preservation aside, the lack of formal cemeteries amongst any Archaic community should not be accepted uncritically as a lack of cultural complexity, however that is defined. Relational properties amongst human bodies, objects, and the built environment do not require that all co-occur in spaces Westerners recognize as cemeteries. Enough evidence exists for formalized mortuary programs among varied Archaic societies in the Southeast to consider the lack of such evidence problematical.

Archaic Subsistence

As we discussed at the outset of this chapter, archaeologists originally conceived the Archaic Period as an era of increasingly intensive foraging in the postglacial environs of the Eastern Woodlands. Although modern practitioners acknowledge a high degree of diversity in Archaic foraging practices, and many have expanded inquiry into realms other than subsistence, a sizeable portion of research on the Southeastern Archaic remains focused on the food quest. Materialist approaches of all ilk, and most notably those of an ecological bent, privilege subsistence over other aspects of cultural variation because of the undeniable need of all humans to ensure an adequate supply of energy for both biological and social reproduction. Until recently, emphasis on Archaic subsistence focused almost exclusively on the biological, and an enduring assumption in such work was that over time Archaic diets diversified to include foods that were otherwise inaccessible or simply too costly to use. Through some combination of environmental, technological, and demographic change, the cost-benefit ratios of foods such as fish, shellfish, acorns, and small seeds improved over time, leading to greater dietary diversity, the capacity to generate food surpluses, and, eventually, the conditions for food production. Modern data challenge these notions and bring us closer to detailing the actual histories of Archaic subsistence and its connection to other aspects of culture and society.

Among the more interesting new studies are those seeking to illuminate the relationship between traditional foraging and emergent agriculture (Box 3-2). Long before corn was enfolded into the domestic and political economies of Southeastern populations, a variety of starchy and oily seed species and members of the squash family were altered through exploitation to beget the Eastern Agricultural Complex. Although the use of these native plants appears to have remained "low-level" throughout the Archaic and Woodland periods (Gremillion 1998, 2002; B. D. Smith 1992, 2001a,

Box 3-2. Hickory Silviculture and Early Horticulture

Use of nuts and nut-processing technology extends far back in the Archaic, but judging from the technology alone, use of mast resources grew markedly during the Late Archaic period. Groundstone mortars and pestles, fire-cracked rock, clay and stone vessels, and occasional storage pits are among the accoutrements of intensive nut processing during the Late Archaic. A variety of nuts and acorns were harvested, but most often recovered is hickory, whose thick hulls were sometimes charred in fires—perhaps as fuel—and thus rendered more-or-less invulnerable to rapid decay.

For Caldwell (1958), intensified use of acorns and nuts signaled greater efficiency in the exploitation of temperature forest environments, enabled, in part, by innovations such as pottery. Influenced by ecological theory, modern analysts look to the relative costs of exploiting all available resources to infer how and why certain foods were added to the diet. In the logic of optimal foraging known as the "diet breadth" model, foragers are expected to select resources that provide the greatest net return on energy expenditure. The relative worth of edible resources in any environment varies with nutritional value, taste, abundance, and reliability, as well as the costs of pursuing or harvesting, and processing. Diets become specialized when high-ranking resources remain productive, and they diversify when top-ranked resources are depleted and lower-ranked foods are added. The macroevolutionary model that Caldwell scripted—essentially an unbroken, gradual trend toward diversified diets—does not hold up to modern data because the relative costs of food resources changed in nonlinear fashion with shifts in ecology, technology, and demographics (e.g., Carmody 2010; Fritz 1990; Gremillion 2002, 2004b; Hollenbach 2009).

From a broader perspective, the increased use of hickory nuts during the Late Archaic, like the addition of shellfish, was not merely a consequence of diversified diet, but also a possible cause of ecological and cultural change. Moore and Dekle (2010), for instance, point out that the use of stationary resources such as shellfish entailed changes in social relations that promoted the adoption of bulk processing technologies (Figure 3B-2) and thus an increased net value for resources that otherwise may have been too costly to exploit. Many of the riverine sites of the Midsouth contain fire-clayed floors that Carmody (2010) interprets as nut roasting or parching surfaces (see also Hollenbach 2005:77; Sherwood and Chapman 2005). Large assemblages of pestles, mortars, and nutting stones at these sites lend further testimony to a reliance on mast for groups who apparently made regular forays or seasonal moves into upland zones, where mast-bearing trees were concentrated. As communities intensified the use of mast they may have engaged in practices that enhanced the productivity and predictability of nut and acorn harvests. Controlled burning, girdling, and tree felling were among the options avail-

Figure 3B-2. Groundstone technology presumed to be used in processing of seeds and nuts: bell-shaped pestles (upper left); grinding basin (lower left); and "nutting" stones (right).

able to promote mast forests and to remove its competitors. Silvicultural practices such as this do not usually lead to domestication and we would be pushing interpretation beyond reasonable evidence to suggest Archaic people "cultivated" hickory or oak trees (but see Delcourt and Delcourt 2004; Gardner 1997; Munson 1986). Nonetheless, a recent review of broad-scale ecological patterns in the Eastern Woodlands by Abrams and Nowacki (2008) concluded that the land-use practices of Native Americans, particularly but not just limited to firing, not only promoted mast, but also the entire historical development of eastern oak and pine forests, savannas, and tall-grass prairies. Moreover, modifications to forested habitat—intentional or not—likely enhanced encounters with and the utility of weedy species that would eventually form the core of the Eastern Agricultural Complex (Delcourt et al. 1998; Moore and Dekle 2010). In this sense we can imagine how the use of wild resources besides those that were actually domesticated indirectly affected the pathway and pace of plant domestication (Gremillion 1998, 2004b). We can also see from this example how models such as diet breadth require detailed information on not only the costs and benefits of available foods, but also data on land-use patterns, technology, and social relations.

2006), the long road to domestication enveloped a variety of changes in technology, settlement, and society that arguably anticipated the emergence and florescence of full-blown agricultural economies. Even the exploitation of mast resources—a hallmark of Archaic subsistence in the Eastern woodlands—may have contributed indirectly to the domestication of certain native plants.

The long-term research of Bruce Smith (e.g., 1992, 2001a, 2001b, 2006) and colleagues on the domestication of native plants in eastern North America shows that processes leading to cultivation were predicated on preexisting hunting and gathering economies in the river valleys of the lower Midwest and Midsouth, and did not involve any sort of revolutionary change attending population packing or environmental stress (Smith and Yarnell 2009). Over the interval from ca. 5000 to 3800 cal yr B.P., at least four indigenous seed-bearing plants were domesticated: squash, sunflower, marshelder, and chenopod. Sunflower was thought to have been domesticated in both Mesoamerica and the Eastern Woodlands; we now know from genetic sequencing analyses that there was only one center, in Eastern North America (Blackman et al. 2011). Three other native plants (erect knotweed, little barley, maygrass) do not show the morphological changes (i.e., increased seed size and reduced thickness of seed coat) of the domesticated species, but they were likely cultivated. The earliest indications of cultivation are scattered at sites across the region where preservation allows (generally caves and saturated deposits), but the first indication of the coalescence of various plants into a horticultural complex has been documented by Bruce Smith and Richard Yarnell (2009) at the Riverton site in southeastern Illinois (Winters 1968). Dating to ca. 3800 cal yr B.P., Riverton was a locus of relatively permanent village settlements, supported by a diverse diet of shellfish, fish, deer, smaller game, mast resources, and the aforementioned cultivars. Defying explanations for domestication that privilege environmental or demographic stress, Late Archaic diet expansion at the Riverton sites appears to have taken place within the context of stable, long-term habitation in resource-rich biomes, namely the river valleys of the Midcontinent.

Throughout the Southeast, the trend toward plant cultivation did not come quickly because it was not likely to present immediate benefits in a Darwinian sense. In a study of the cost-effectiveness of small grain use, Gremillion (2004b) concludes that these foods were not profitable if other, less costly resources, such as hickory nut, were available. Her analysis of eastern Kentucky sites (where rockshelters have produced evidence for small grain use) shows that better alternatives in the Late Archaic period were not only available, but were, in fact, on the rise due to increased fire frequency. It follows that the diet-breadth model does not account for the use of small grains, at least not without qualification. Gremillion (2004b) points out that by deferring the benefits and the costs of small-grain use to times when other subsistence pursuits were minimal enhanced their marginal utility. The greatest costs of using small grains resided in the processing needed to remove the inedible portions of seeds, notably the coating. Winter may have been an ideal time to invest in seed processing given the low opportunity costs and availability of rockshelter sites for both storage and overwintering. This perspective broadens the pathways towards domestication beyond floodplains—which Bruce Smith (1987, 1992) has long pointed to as a primary disturbance regime for weedy annuals—and towards upland locales whose roles in Late Archaic settlement were most likely seasonal or perhaps specialized (see section on rockshelter and cave use in Chapter 4).

Modern studies of terrestrial game are also bringing greater focus on subsistence variations attending environmental and demographic change. In research involving the well-stratified vertebrate fauna remains of caves, rockshelters, and open-air sites in the Midwest and Midsouth, an overall trend is seen for increased use of white-tailed deer from the early to middle Holocene (Styles and Klippel 1996). A parallel decrease in the use of smaller mammals, notably squirrel, reflects both diminished forest cover in places like the Midwest, as well as a trend toward more focused deer hunting in locations of aquatic settlement in the Midsouth. Small terrestrial game never disappeared from the repertoire of hunting, but the fish, turtles, and shellfish of rivers and other aquatic biomes appear to have been more-or-less equivalent resources for small game over at least part of the year. Throughout this time, deer procurement intensified in many parts of the Southeast, but when the climatic optimum of the Mid-Holocene abated after ca. 6000 cal yr B.P., causing acorn productivity in upland settings to drop in uplands of the Midsouth, deer procurement was on the wane compared to other resources (Bissett 2010).

As alluded to earlier, the addition and expansion of shellfish in Archaic diets has long been problematized in ways that assume shellfish were more of a fall-back resource rather than a preferred staple (Binford 1968). Worldwide, the procurement and consumption of shellfish, both freshwater and marine, intensified in the Holocene (Claassen 1998:1–2). The extent to which this pattern reflects global-scale trends in the balance between food supply and demand is uncertain, in part because sea-level rise has truncated most of the record of coastal living prior to ca. 4500 cal yr B.P., and also because conditions along rivers of the mid-latitudes may not have been conducive to productive freshwater shellfish habitat until the Mid-Holocene. The most recent perspectives on shellfishing tend to downplay the limits of supply and focus instead on matters of demand. Claassen (2010), for instance, characterizes the onset, burgeoning, and eventual demise in freshwater shellfishing in the middle Ohio valley as a matter of cultural choice that in fact had less to do with diet and more to do with ritual feasting that involved the procurement and consumption of large quantities of mussels. Similarly, Russo (2004, 2010), R. Saunders (2004), and others attribute at least some of the large deposits of shell at coastal shell rings to ritual feasting, while acknowledging that shellfish, along with small fish, comprised the bulk of Archaic daily fare.

Ongoing research along the coasts of the Southeast continues to add greater detail on the composition and structure of Archaic subsistence. The conclusion that coastal settlements by at least the Late Archaic were perennial has been strengthened in recent years (Marrinan 2010; Russo 1996b; Thompson and Andrus 2011). Oyster was instrumental in enabling year-round settlement, comprising in at least one case more than a diet breadth model would predict (Thomas, ed. 2008). Many other resources were of importance too, and perhaps encouraged coastal denizens to position settlements in locations affording access to a variety of habitats, including maritime forests. White-tailed deer were taken by coastal Archaic hunters apparently whenever encountered, even though the size of these populations and the individuals within them were small compared to counterparts in the hardwood forests of the interior Southeast. However, coastal deer populations were just as dynamic as the seas, resulting in wide shifts in density and size over time, as well as marked inter-island variations. At St. Catherines Island on the Georgia coast, for instance, Thomas (ed., 2008) documented a relatively high level of deer exploitation when its two shell rings formed ca. 4850–4450 cal yr B.P., coincident with rising seas and the isolation of the island from the mainland. The exceptional research of Thomas and colleagues on the Georgia coast goes to show how important it is to develop data specific to particular islands, both spatial and temporal, and at multiple scales of observation (see also Thompson 2007, 2010; Thompson and Turck

2009). As we will see in the closing section of this chapter, long-term trends in sea-level fluctuations, as well as events such as floods, droughts, and storms, contributed to dramatic change in the disposition of Archaic communities throughout the region, changes of sufficient magnitude to warrant recognition as the end of an era.

The End of the Archaic

The appearance of pottery (Figure 3-6), villages, monuments, and domesticated plants no longer marks the end of the Archaic and the beginning of the Woodland period, as it once did, because all such attributes appeared long before the Archaic-Woodland "transition" some 3,000 years ago (Anderson and Mainfort 2002; Kidder and Sassaman 2009; Sassaman 2005a, 2010a; Sassaman and Anderson 2004). Instead, modern analysts have replaced these presumed marks of difference with a more interesting puzzle, namely the region-wide restructuring of the cultural landscape involving the abandonment of many sites and even entire subregions (see papers in Thomas and Sanger 2010). In contemplating this puzzle, archaeologists in recent years have focused their attention on two closely related themes: (1) climate-induced events that disrupted human settlement; and (2) the consequences that displacement and resettlement had on group identity and alliance. Because hunter-gatherers worldwide rely on intergroup alliances to ameliorate the risks of uncertainty and failure, disruptions in the environmental and social realities of Archaic life were mutually consequential. In framing this problem, we find it useful to distinguish between change and variation, following Gamble (2007:26). *Change* in this sense is the appearance of new organization based on novel social premises, whereas *variation* is the accommodation of novel circumstances within existing social premises. In many parts of the Southeast, the transition from the Late Archaic to the Early Woodland appears to have involved real social change.

Kidder (2006) provides a detailed account of major climatic changes documented at the turn of the third millennium. A large body of high-resolution climatic data shows that the period from about 3200–2600 cal yr B.P. was generally cooler and wetter than centuries immediately before and after. Storms increased in magnitude and frequency, as did flooding in the major river valleys of region. All of the Mississippi River Valley, for example, experi-

Figure 3-6. Examples of sherds from some of the oldest pottery traditions in the Southeast: Stallings Drag and Jab Punctate (top two rows); Orange Incised (third row); Tick Island Incised (bottom row).

enced floods of historically unprecedented scale and duration. The Northeast U.S. appears to have experienced similar conditions at this time (Fiedel 2001).

Changes in the distribution and organization of Late Archaic populations in many parts of the Southeast were many. Poverty Point ceased to operate as a locus of nonlocal import and the site was apparently abandoned at ca. 3100–3000 cal yr B.P. Although the inhabitants of Poverty Point experienced severe flooding before and occupied a position on Macon Ridge that was far above even the highest flood stages (Gibson 2010), a movement of the river channel fronting the site may have been intolerable as it may have cut-off Poverty Point from navigable water. If Poverty Point was home to thousands of residents as Gibson and others have surmised (Clark et al. 2010; Gibson 2010), the patterns of resettlement would likely be conspicuous archaeologically, but they are not. We can be virtually certain that Poverty Point was not reconstituted in another place, the way that Chacoan towns in the Southwest were relocated after intolerable periods of drought. That archaeologists in the Deep South have trouble locating post-Poverty Point settlements would suggest that (1) the resident population of Poverty Point at the time of abandonment was not especially large; (2) that post-abandonment settlement patterns were highly dispersed, meaning that sites of occupation were small and transient; and/or (3) the evidence of post-abandonment consequences are not apparent to us because natural (taphonomic) and cultural (identity) factors have conspired to render such evidence inconspicuous, even if abundant. Elsewhere across the Southeast we find multiple other cases of abandonment of riverine sites and apparent dispersal of displaced communities into adjacent upland zones, where they assumed patterns of residential mobility that left only faint archaeological traces (e.g., Sassaman 2006a). Sites of the Shell Mound Archaic were largely abandoned at this time in multiple locations, although we hasten to note that many such sites were abandoned at various times prior. More to the point, the Shell Mound Archaic tradition more-or-less terminated at about 3000 cal yr B.P. Although climatic events no doubt factored into the particular occupational histories of specific sites and locales, Claassen (2010; see also Russo 2010) characterizes the demise of the Shell Mound Archaic as a transformation in ritual beliefs, from communal feasting to individual and in some cases mounded burial treatment.

Coastal living at the close of the Archaic period likewise registered some dramatic change. The tradition of shell rings came to a close at ca. 3000 cal yr B.P., although in some locations, such as panhandle and north Gulf coastal Florida, circular settlements involving shell deposition continued or reappeared in the Woodland era (Russo 2010; Sassaman et al. 2010; Stephenson et al. 2002). With fluctuations in global temperature, sea levels rose and fell within an overall post-glacial trend towards rising levels. Unfortunately, the resolution of sea-level curves for the Southeast is not especially fine, and some efforts to infer changes below the century scale have drawn on data from as far away as Denmark (Marquardt 2010a, 2010b), although the need to develop local sea-level reconstructions has been recognized by some researchers (e.g., Sanger and Thomas 2010). Irrespective of the appropriateness of such far-reaching extrapolations, fine-grained data suggest that sea-level change was at times eventful, most likely accompanied by storm surges and other abrupt changes (e.g., overwash of oyster reefs) that would have caused immediate effects on the ability of coastal dwellers to sustain settlement. Abandonment of Late Archaic coastal shell rings has been attributed to changes in sea level that compromised the sustainability of settlement by either drowning sites (rising seas) or stranding them (falling seas) from productive habitat and navigable water (e.g., DePratter and Howard 1980; Russo 2010; Sanger 2010; Thomas 2008; Thompson and Turck 2009). However, during a span of close to 1,000 years, shell rings across the Southeast were largely abandoned. With data on more than 50 shell rings in the region, Sanger (2010) documents three phases of abandonment: (1) one at about 4230 cal yr B.P. that coincides with a high sea-level stand; (2) another at about 3970 cal yr B.P. during a lower stand; and (3) a third at about 3670 cal yr B.P. that does not correlate with a either a high or low stand. Sanger points to a variety of topographic and ecological factors that rendered distinct each of these abandonment phases, but also notes that historically situated decision-making accounted for diverse trajectories. By way of contrast, Russo's (2010) reading of the archaeological record of coastal dwelling in south Florida reveals a higher level of settlement continuity on the coast before, during, and after fluctuations in sea level that apparently caused site abandonment farther north. Future research may benefit from considering not only how changes in coastal settlement were affected by climatic events, but also how much variation in sea level could be tolerated within any given adaptive regime.

Climate change may be the ultimate cause of settlement change at the end of the Archaic period, but causes for cultural change can be found in the realignments between people and the places from which they drew practical experience and symbolic meaning. If one accepts that phenomena like Poverty Point, the Shell Mound Archaic, and coastal shell rings were predicated on social arrangements (alliances, exchange networks, etc.) that ensured the necessary resources for sustaining traditions—some of which involved at least temporary aggregation of personnel—then disruption locally would have had reverberations across networks of affiliation (Anderson 2010:284–287; Sassaman 2010a). Archaeologists who recently convened at St. Catherines Island to contemplate the Archaic–Woodland transition disagreed on the causes and consequences of such change (see papers in Thomas and Sanger 2010), but no one disputed that dramatic change indeed occurred. On balance, the regional picture shows an abandonment of many of the places and practices that were materialized in things like mounds, or actualized in rituals involving nonlocal objects or large quantities of food. Tracing directly the descendants of Archaic communities may be futile, especially if large-scale migrations were more common than ever imagined. Still, the abandonment of sites, some subregions, and entire ways of life, even if it resulted in settlement systems lacking large-scale aggregations of people, did not entirely sever the legacy of mound building, long-distance exchange, and mortuary ritual established in the Archaic era. Not long after what was arguably one of the more significant changes in culture history, Woodland communities would arise again in networks of connectivity centered on the construction of mounds, interment of the dead, acquisition and manipulation of foreign objects, and ritual feasting. Given the interval of dispersed settlement between the Archaic and Woodland "crescendos" of cultural connection, one would be hard-pressed to find evidence of direct historical linkages. On the other hand, no one has ever suggested that the denizens of the Southeast at the onset of the Woodland era were not direct descendents of indigenous Archaic communities. Making such linkages, no matter how indirectly, remains a pressing archaeological problem.

4

Woodland Regionalism

For roughly two millennia after the Archaic Period, cultural developments in the American Southeast followed divergent pathways that resulted in distinctive regional traditions. Intermittently over this time span, communities of diverse disposition participated in panregional religious movements involving mound construction, elaborate mortuary ceremonialism, animal effigies, and the acquisition of nonlocal materials. One such movement—known to archaeologists as Hopewell, with origins in the Midwest—stretched across the Southeast to become adopted and adapted by communities in the Lower Mississippi Valley, Midsouth, Gulf Coast and Coastal Plain, north Florida, and the Appalachians. Smaller-scale religious traditions also arose in these and other locales, some arguably rooted in indigenous, Archaic practices. Many communities at various times apparently had little direct involvement with institutions that integrated diverse people through collective ritual, leading instead dispersed, mobile lifestyles of political and economic autonomy. The mosaic of cultural diversity in the millennia following the Archaic period can be likened to the patterns in a kaleidoscope, in which elements of difference aligned, disengaged, and realigned as integrated structures with each turn of a century. Because participation in panregional religion did not usually result in the permanent aggregation of participating communities, but instead took place at so-called "vacant" ceremonial centers, archaeologically conspicuous elements of "everyday" living (subsistence technology, diet, domestic architecture) reflect greater regional diversity than do the material remains of collective ritual (i.e., mounds, tombs, and ceremonial objects).

The Woodland Period (ca. 3200–1000 cal B.P. or 1200 B.C.–A.D. 1000)[1] is typically portrayed by archaeologists as an era of *regionalism* (Figure 4-1). The sense of regionalism intended, explicitly or not, is the process of cultural

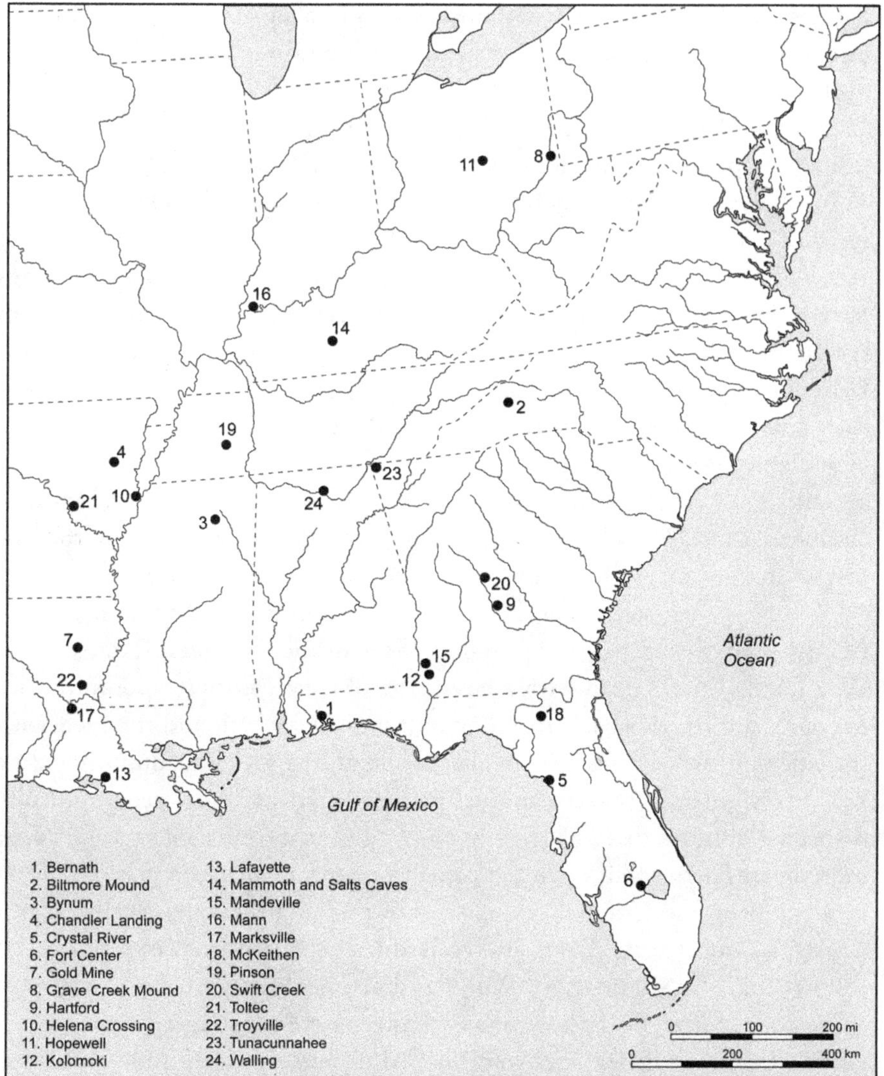

Figure 4-1. Locations of Woodland period sites mentioned in the text.

differentiation leading to partially autonomous communities and distinct traditions across subregions of the Southeast. The Southeast volume of the *Handbook of North American Indians* (Fogelson 2004), for instance, divides treatment of the period into seven subregions: Florida, the south Atlantic coast, eastern interior, western interior, the Gulf Coastal Plain, the Lower

Mississippi Valley, and the Central Mississippi Valley. Archaeologists are certainly justified in dividing Woodland histories along geographic lines for multiple reasons, not the least being variations in pottery (e.g., Bense 1994:114–119; Caldwell 1958). However, much of the cultural differentiation of the period appears to have roots in the Archaic, as we saw in Chapter 3. It follows that there may be nothing uniquely regional about Woodland regionalism.

An alternative approach to Woodland archaeology is to focus on long-term trends that contributed to the eventual rise of Mississippian societies of the last millennium, those known for hereditary inequality, intensive corn farming, and civic-ceremonial centers (see Chapter 5). In his contribution to the *Handbook*, Richard Jefferies (2004b) identifies four major trends of the Woodland Period: (1) increased dietary importance of seeds; (2) increased sedentism; (3) more elaborate mortuary ceremonialism and burial mound complexes; and (4) widespread adoption of pottery. Acknowledging the historical precedence of all four traits in the Archaic Period, Jefferies (2004b:115) suggests "it was during the following two millennia that [these trends] precipitated major cultural changes in the Southeast." Indeed, the Woodland Period began with a landscape of small, scattered communities networked through ritual sites they occasionally visited, and it ended with the emergence of compact, hierarchically organized societies administered by hereditary elite in civic-ceremonial centers. Why and how geographically dispersed communities physically converged in certain places to become more-or-less permanent townspeople is an enduring archaeological puzzle. It is apparent to modern archaeologists that this trend was neither linear nor pervasive, and that its causes and consequences varied from case to case. It follows that any summary of Woodland archaeology must be attentive to subregional variations in how major changes were experienced without forgetting that such differences were shaped in part by larger-scale processes, such as the panregional religious movements noted earlier.

We thus take a topical approach to Woodland archaeology in the Southeast, bringing attention to the most current research projects that help us to understand how life was differentially experienced during the period while also shedding light on processes and forces beyond one's experience and perception. As in Chapter 3, however, we begin with brief summaries of the usual culture-historical taxa of the Woodland period, to again enable readers with limited background in Southeast archaeology to relate this to a well-established literature on the subject. In addition to the chapter-length synthesis of Woodland archaeology by Jefferies (2004b) noted above, other chapters in the *Handbook* provide excellent reviews of subregional archaeology (I. Brown 2004; Early 2004; Hally and Mainfort 2004; Kidder 2004a; Milanich 2004a, 2004b; Rolingson 2004), and the edited volume by Anderson and Mainfort (2002) remains the most comprehensive collection for the entire Southeast. Other recent collections deal with particular subperiods (Nassaney and Cobb 1991), taxonomies (Applegate and Mainfort 2005), cultures (Williams and Elliott 1998), or ritual features (Mainfort and Sullivan 1998). Woodland period archaeology of the lower Midwest is also well represented in two major collections (Emerson et al. 2000; Farnsworth and Emerson 1986).

Woodland Basics

By convention, the Woodland Period began at the close of the Archaic Period, ca. 1200 B.C., and ended with the onset of the Mississippian Period, ca. A.D. 1000. The beginning and end points of the Woodland Period, and how these are defined, varies across the Southeast. Likewise, a tripartite division of the ca. 2,200-year-long Woodland period is widely acknowledged throughout the region, but the specific timing of each subperiod varies across subregions. Brief summaries of the culture history of the Early, Middle, and Late Woodland periods follow.

Early Woodland (1200–100 B.C.)

If we are to mark the onset of the Early Woodland period with the broad-scale changes that brought an end to the Archaic at ca. 1200 B.C., then the period begins at a point of diminished archaeological resolution. As we discussed at the close of Chapter 3, several subregions of the Southeast experienced dramatic changes in land-use practices at this time, many apparently precipitated by climatic events, others affected collaterally by disruptions in social networks. Either way, the archaeological visibility of land-use and settlement patterns over the next few centuries was reduced. Many sites and localities were abandoned, to be sure, but perhaps not entire subregions. Rather, mobile, dispersed settlement precluded the accumulation of dense middens and other evidence of redundant land-use practices that made so many Late Archaic records conspicuous.

Countervailing the conditions that rendered Early Woodland sites less conspicuous than Late Archaic precursors was the widespread adoption of pottery. Not long after 1200 B.C., pottery that was formerly restricted in distribution became much more widespread. Ironically, dispersed settlement patterns may have enabled the diffusion of pottery among neighboring groups (Sassaman 1993), and, in turn, the use of durable vessels may have enhanced the ability of small groups to sustain themselves (Muller 1986).

By 700 B.C. pottery had become widespread in the Southeast and variations in the form and surface treatment of pottery vessels signal distinct traditions (Box 4-1). Several major traditions are evident at this time, those located in the Gulf Coastal Plain, the interior Midsouth, the South Appalachian area, and the middle Atlantic seaboard (e.g., Bense 1994:114–19; Caldwell 1958); peninsular Florida had its own, unique traditions, with roots in the Late Archaic (Milanich 2004a:191). Cord or fabric impressions applied with a wrapped paddle characterize the ceramic traditions of the Middle Atlantic and Midsouth; those of the South Appalachian and Gulf coastal areas include more elaborate designs applied with carved wooden paddles in the former area and characterized by dentate and rocker stamping and incising in the latter area. In all locations surface treatments encompass considerable variation within traditions, as do technological and functional attributes, although these tend to be underappreciated as significant emblems of cultural choice. The burgeoning use of pottery during the Early Woodland has long been seen as an indication of greater reliance on seeds and/or acorns (Caldwell 1958; B. D. Smith 1992). The same has been said about soapstone vessels (Truncer 2004), although this innovation appears to have actually postdated the adoption of pottery in most areas of the Southeast (Sassaman 2006b).

After a relatively quiet beginning, the Early Woodland period witnessed new efforts at mound construction. From about 700 B.C. in several locales, earthen mounds were erected for disposal of the dead. In the Lower Mississippi Valley, for instance, during the Tchula period of ca. 800 B.C.–A.D. 1, communities of the Tchefuncte cultural tradition erected conical earthen mounds as much as 5 m tall, but more often less than 2 m tall and 20 m in diameter (Hays and Weinstein 2010:107–109; Kidder et al. 2010). The largest of three mounds at the Layfayette Mound complex in southern Louisiana contained 30 burials placed on a premound floor and on two successive layers of earth, all capped by a thick mantle of soil (Weinstein 1986). Graves were consistently unadorned. More typical than mounds were the primary and secondary interments of the dead in midden deposits, likewise generally unadorned, but occasionally with nonlocal goods (Morse 1986a:75–76).

While the acquisition of nonlocal goods during the Tchula period (e.g., novaculite, quartz crystal, galena), limited as it was, hints at the continuation of Poverty Point culture (Gibson 1994), the mortuary program, whether in mounds or middens, is entirely novel to the Lower Mississippi Valley. Irrespective of the lineal relationship between communities of these times, Tchefuncte pottery assemblages bear technical and stylistic affinity to traditions spanning the Gulf Coastal Plain and north Florida, notably, Wheeler, Alexander, and St. Johns (Hays and Weinstein 2010:102, 111). Sand mounds were also occasionally erected for mortuary purposes in several local communities along this expanse as early as 600 B.C. (Jefferies 2004b:118). A few centuries later, sand burial mounds were erected along the Atlantic coast of Georgia by makers of Deptford pottery (Larsen and Thomas 1979; Milanich 1994:141).

On the northern margin of the Southeast, in Kentucky, West Virginia, and farther north into the lower Midwest, the Adena tradition of the first millennium B.C. foreshadowed the elaborate mortuary ritual of Hopewell, which overlapped and followed it in time, from ca. 200 B.C. to A.D. 300 in this area, and extending somewhat later in time in the Southeast. Conical earthen mounds of the Adena tradition were accretional deposits resulting from repeated mortuary events (Clay 1998). Graves often contained ritual objects made from nonlocal materials (e.g., copper, mica, marine shell), and mounds do not appear to be sited in the vicinity of habitations. The same can be said for Adena "sacred circles," low-relief embankments of encircled earth, ranging from but a few meters to hundreds of meters in diameter, and generally with exterior ditches. Clay (1998) interprets these elements as part of integrated ritual landscapes, with mounds and circles emplaced in locations between areas of settlement. Objects of Adena affinity turn up occasionally in the Southeast, but there is no clear indication that the mortuary mound practices of the Gulf Coast and south Atlantic were influenced by this more northern tradition.

Little is known about Early Woodland settlement across much of the region other than that sites are generally small and dispersed, as noted earlier. Some Early Woodland cultures, such as the Kellogg phase of northwest Georgia (Bowen 1989; Caldwell 1958:23–25; Wood and Bowen 1995),

Box 4-1. Changing Views on Changes in Pottery

As one of the hotbeds of methods for constructing culture-histories, the Southeast boasts a deep and enduring legacy in the analysis of ancient pottery. It is a legacy that reaches back over a century (e.g., Holmes 1903), bolstered by the Depression-era fieldwork that provided excellent stratigraphic contexts for monitoring changes in pottery over time. And it was the effort of Phillips, Ford, and Griffin (1951) in the Lower Mississippi Valley that led to widespread use locally of *seriation*, a method for ordering chronological variation in the relative frequency of pottery types under the assumption that changes in pottery were gradual, incremental, and more-or-less continuous. Attributes of pottery that varied over time (e.g., paste, form, surface treatment) were tacitly assumed to be normative attributes, that is, indicative of a particular peoples' tradition for making pottery at a particular time and place, hence amenable to the construction of culture history (Figure 4B-1).

With the rise of processual archaeology in the 1960s, Southeastern archaeologists questioned the normative approach to pottery analysis and began to explore alternatives to culture history. Inspired by Braun's (1983) call to treat "pots as tools," regional specialists began to develop data on the technology and function of ceramic vessels to address issues as diverse as subsistence intensification (Braun 1983), labor organization (J. Brown 1989), ethnogenesis (Sassaman 1993, 2004a), and ritual (Cordell 1984). Technofunctional perspectives opened up insight on broad-scale changes in the uses of durable containers through time, such as the shift from indirect-heat ("stone boiling") to direct-heat cooking (Sassaman 2002), the increased thermal efficiency of direct-heat cooking with greater dependence on cultivars like goosefoot and marshelder (Braun 1989), and the increasing role of pottery in contexts of large-scale public consumption (Knight 2001). Also revealed in modern studies of pottery was the lack of concordance between culture-historical types useful for chronological purposes and attributes that crosscut such types. For instance, the technology of pottery manufacture is known to vary within types based on surface treatment alone, and the uses to which vessels are put likewise vary within technological groupings. In a comprehensive

Figure 4B-1. An assortment of Woodland vessel forms from across the Southeast: Weeden Island effigy vessels (a, b); Weeden Island Incised (c); Carabelle Punctate (d) Carabelle Incised (e); Tucker Ridge Pinched (f); Swift Creek (g); Marksville Incised (h); Marksville Stamped (i); Marksville Plain (j, k); Tchefuncte Stamped (l); Badin Fabric Impressed (m); Deptford Check Stamped and Linear Check Stamped (n); Mossy Oak Simple Stamped (o). Image adapted from Caldwell 1958; Griffin, ed., 1952; Willey 1949.

study of variation in Woodland pottery from the North Carolina coast, Herbert (2009) shows how the manufacture and use of pottery crosscut the taxa of culture history, implicating a greater level of complexity to community formation than ever assumed. He is able to infer from patterned variation that "communities of practice" were constituted at multiple scales of social interaction, resulting in the nonlinear transmission of technical skill and knowledge. Precluding any direct, linear trend in technical transmission (e.g., mother to daughter only, with no geographic displacement), traditional culture historical taxa mask consideration of variation essential to the reconstruction of networks of social alliance and interaction. The growing use of chemical sourcing and petrographic methods to determine the provenance of pottery adds quantitative rigor to such reconstructions (e.g., Wallis 2011).

Having developed a nuanced sense of the complexity between pottery and people hitherto obscured by culture-historical types, archaeologists expectedly returned to the drawing board to ask how existing types inhibit research (see, for instance, papers in Applegate and Mainfort 2005). In so doing, some have refined methods of seriation to distinguish attributes that vary over time from those that register variations in social status, ritual, and other dimensions independent of time. Karen Smith and Fraser Neiman (2007), for example, apply correspondence analysis to distinguish temporal from nontemporal variation in Middle and Late Woodland pottery of the Gulf Coastal Plain and north Florida. This is a region of marked interregional interaction during the Woodland era, leading to the formation of pottery assemblages containing both locally made and acquired vessels, and, throughout much of the Middle Woodland, pottery traditions that attained the level of high art for purposes of mortuary ceremonialism. Indeed, caches consisting of numerous animal and human effigies, eccentric forms, and vessels with lavish decoration (e.g., Milanich et al. 1984; Pluckhahn 2003; Sears 1956; Steinen 2006) provide not-so-subtle reminders that pots were far more than tools and the calling cards of particular traditions, but also powerful media for asserting social prerogatives in public ritual.

consisted of seemingly stationary communities with well-defined structures, large subterranean storage pits, and dense occupational middens. Colbert-phase settlement in the Middle Tennessee River valley emphasized shell middens along the banks of the river, and rockshelters in the adjacent uplands were utilized intensively (Knight 1990; Walthall 1980:114–115). In the Duck River drainage of Tennessee, Long Branch-phase occupations exhibit single or small isolated clusters of features (storage pits, shallow processing basins, earth ovens), suggesting short-term, occasional occupation by isolated domestic units (Faulkner and McCollough 1974:192, 1982:292–300). Sites of the Watts Bar phase of the Little Tennessee River are concentrated along the edges of alluvial terraces, but with lesser feature and midden accumulations compared to preceding Iddins phase sites of the Late Archaic (Davis 1990:227–230). Tchefuncte settlement along the Gulf Coast involved both large and small communities at shell-bearing sites, some apparently carrying forward the shell ring tradition of the Late Archaic period (Hays and Weinstein 2010).

Gardening in small plots became significant for some groups of the interior Southeast and lower Midwest. Species of the Eastern Agricultural Complex (B. D. Smith 1987, 1992, 2006) were already domesticated by the Late Archaic period (see Chapter 3), and by 500 B.C., starchy and oily seeds were deposited with appreciable frequency at upland sites, rockshelters, and caves of the Midsouth (Gremillion 1998, 2002, 2004b; B. D. Smith 1992, 2006; Watson 1985). Elsewhere in the Southeast, seed-bearing plants and other members of the Eastern Agricultural Complex do not appear to have had much of a role in local diets, although increased use of nuts and acorns at this time likely signals a similar intensification of plant food collection, storage, and consumption, as Caldwell (1958) surmised.

Middle Woodland (100 B.C.–A.D. 500)

Many of the established subregional traditions of the Early Woodland period persisted in modified form for the next several centuries, during the Middle Woodland period. Pottery continues to be the primary trait archaeologists have used for distinguishing among subregional traditions, and among them some elaborate expressions in form and surface treatment are evident. In north Florida and southern Georgia, the Deptford tradition of simple- and check-stamped pottery gave way to complicated stamped pottery of the Swift Creek tradition by 100 B.C. This in turn was superseded after A.D. 200 by the Weeden Island tradition, while Swift Creek continued to be made alongside check-stamped (Cartersville) and brushed or simple-stamped (Connestee/Vining) pottery in north Georgia and adjoining areas through ca. A.D. 750 (Anderson 1998; Milanich 2002; Williams and Elliott 1998). In the Lower Mississippi Valley, Tchefuncte pottery was replaced by Marksville pottery after A.D. 1, with its Hopewell-related repertoire of incised, dentate, and rocker stamping expressed most elaborately on vessels placed in burials (McGimsey 2010). Although Middle Woodland pottery traditions in the Appalachians (Connestee), Tennessee River Valley (McFarland, Candy Creek), upper Gulf Coastal Plain (Miller I and II) and elsewhere appear far less elaborate than those of Swift Creek, Weeden Island, and Marksville, widespread participation in mound ceremonialism signals greater panregional influence than the diversity of pottery types might suggest.

Arguably, the defining feature of the Middle Woodland period in the Southeast is the rise and spread of mortuary mound ceremonialism rooted in the Hopewell tradition of the Midwest (Bense 1994:162; Chapman and Keel 1979; B. D. Smith 1986). Inferred connections between Hopewell and various ceremonial complexes of the Southeast usually hinge on the presence of Hopewellian ritual objects, such as copper and ceramic earspools, quartz crystals, flint blades, mica cutouts, shell and pearl beads, and other exotic materials (galena, serpentine, obsidian) (Figure 4-2). Multimound complexes with apparent Hopewell affinity appear in several areas of the region. The largest and most complex of these was Pinson mounds in southwest Tennessee (Mainfort 1986). Dating from 100 B.C. to A.D. 350, Pinson included 12 mounds, a geometric enclosure, and other ritual features distributed over an area of 160 ha. Other major ceremonial centers include Mandeville (B. A. Smith 1979), Kolomoki (Pluckhahn 2003; Sears 1956), and Tunacunnahee (Jefferies 1976) in Georgia; Walling (Knight 1990) in Alabama; Helena Crossing (Ford 1963; Giles et al. 2010) in Arkansas; Marksville in Louisiana (McGimsey 2010); Bynum in Mississippi (Cotter and Corbett 1951); and McKeithen (Milanich et al. 1984) and Crystal River (Pluckhahn et al. 2010) in Florida. A variety of other mound sites are distributed widely across the Southeast. Not all ceremonial complexes in the Southeast incorporating Hopewellian objects included mortuary mounds, but nearly all occurrences of such objects are in mortuary contexts.

Middle Woodland mound complexes in the Southeast typically include conical mounds, and these are typically mortuary features with central

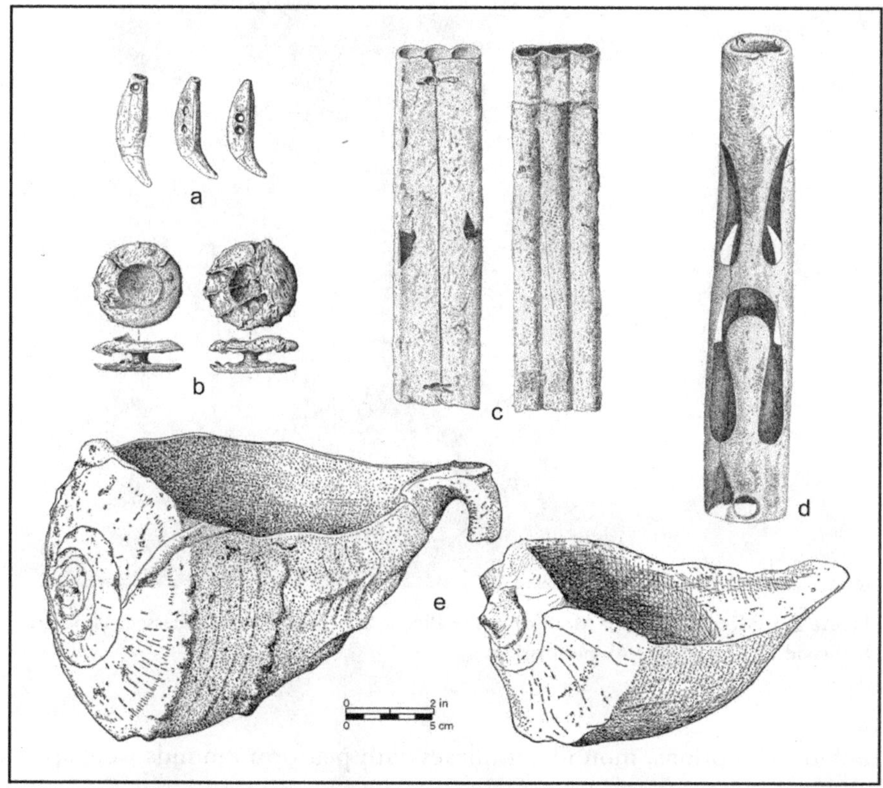

Figure 4-2. Items of Hopewell affinity recovered from the Helena Crossing site in Arkansas: perforated red wolf canines (a); copper earspools (b); copper panpipe (c, front and back views); copper tube with cutout design (d); conch shell drinking cups (e). Adapted from images in Ford 1963.

tombs, like those of Hopewell. However, complexes sometimes include platform mounds with limited parallel in the Hopewell Midwest (Figure 4-3), but not unlike those of the later Mississippian era (see Chapter 5). In fact, platform mounds were once routinely assumed to be Mississippian (Sears 1992), but in the past few decades, archaeologists have substantiated a Middle Woodland affiliation for sites stretching from the Lower Mississippi Valley to the Appalachian Summit (Dickens 1975; Jefferies 1994; Kimball et al. 2010; Knight 1990; Lindauer and Blitz 1997; Mainfort 1996; Morse 1986b; Pluckhahn 1996, 2003). Excavations around platform mounds have not revealed evidence that they were used for domestic purposes, or to house elite persons atop, as they did during the Mississippian era. Rather, with

Figure 4-3. Mound 5 (Ozier Mound) at the Pinson Site in western Tennessee. Photograph by David H. Dye, used with permission.

notable exceptions, mound complexes with platform mounds were apparently ritual centers for dispersed populations who aggregated for mortuary rituals, including feasting (Knight 2001). Architecture atop mounds also appears to have been associated with mortuary ritual (but apparently not many, if any, charnel houses). Individuals buried in submound tombs were likely of privileged status, acquired perhaps through their participation in long-distance exchange and public ceremony.

Settlement patterns of the Middle Woodland period are diverse, but consist mainly of dispersed hamlets and small villages, many likely relocated frequently, but perhaps commonly reoccupied over many generations. With notable exceptions (see below), there is little to suggest that mound complexes and other ritual facilities were located at the center of settlement clusters, so mounds were not likely to be the territorial markers of corporate groups, as we discuss further below. To the extent that mounds and cemeteries were the facilities of particular lineages or clans, archaeologists are challenged to determine how structures of descent and affinity articulated with each other to form networks of ceremonial practice. This is a central focus of ongoing research, involving new investigations in and around mound centers (Pluckhahn 2003; Pluckhahn et al. 2010), as well as provenance studies of pottery and other material culture (e.g., Wallis 2011).

Some Middle Woodland communities of the interior Southeast appear to have grown rather quickly or moved toward more consolidated settlement over a short span of time. McFarland-phase settlement of the Duck River in Tennessee witnessed a six-fold increase in sites from 200 B.C. to A.D. 200, resulting in large villages with substantial architecture (Faulkner 2002). Villages of the succeeding Owl Hollow phase (post A.D. 300) became even more formalized and permanent, with large oval winter houses and oval or square summer pole houses, sometimes arranged in a circle around debris-free plazas (Faulkner 2002:196). Hopewell influences actually waxed and waned over this span, with interaction northward rekindled in the Owl Hollow phase after diminishing during the McFarland phase.

As noted in Chapter 3, activities resulting in circular or arcuate arrangements of shell seem to have persisted beyond the Late Archaic period on the northern Gulf Coast and Panhandle of Florida, where sites of the Deptford tradition abound. Dating to as early as 800 B.C. on the Atlantic coast and spreading across much of the South Atlantic Slope and northwest Florida over the ensuing few centuries, the Deptford tradition was once considered a largely coastal tradition (Milanich 1971). Although no longer regarded as exclusively coastal (Anderson 1975; Stephenson et al. 2002), the Deptford subtraditions along both the Atlantic and Gulf coasts entailed large, complex settlements, some circular in array. Most Deptford shell middens of the Atlantic coast are amorphous or linear in plan, but one ring of shell and earth about 67 m in diameter is described by Milanich (1971) as possibly Deptford. On the northern Gulf Coast and Panhandle of Florida, Deptford ring middens are more numerous, even if the majority of sites of this age are small, amorphous middens along eroded shorelines. For instance, arcuate, raised oyster middens some 60–75 m in diameter are common in the Cedar Key area of northern Gulf coastal Florida (Sassaman et al. 2010), some forming conglomerates of rings and ringlets not unlike compound Late Archaic shell rings (e.g., Fig Island, S.C.). After about A.D. 100 on the Gulf Coast, burial mounds and associated mortuary goods of the so-called Yent complex ushered in the region's most remote Hopewellian influences. The multimound Crystal River site on the northern Gulf Coast of Florida is perhaps the most famous of the coastal mound centers (Pluckhahn et al. 2010).

The conveyance of ritual traditions of the lower Midwest to the coast most likely involved Deptford-related communities of the interior Coastal Plain and lower Piedmont. Archaeologists disagree on where to draw boundaries around quintessential Deptford traits, such as Liner Check-Stamped pottery, but most would agree that Deptford communities made more than transient use of the interior Coastal Plain (Stephenson et al. 2002). Some sites along the Savannah, Ocmulgee, and Oconee rivers, for instance, attest to large circular arrays of presumably household middens, some as large as 300 m in diameter.

None of the developments of the Middle Woodland period were associated with a reliance on maize (Fritz 1993; Gremillion 2002), even though the cultigen may have been grown in Tennessee as early as A.D. 200 (Chapman and Crites 1987). Wild plant and animal foods were increasingly supplemented by crops of the Eastern Agricultural Complex, but food production was apparently not a primary pursuit among any Southeastern community until the full-blown cultivation of maize after ca. A.D. 900.

Late Woodland (A.D. 500–1000)

The Middle Woodland comes to close at ca. A.D. 500 when the center of panregional influence shifted away from the Midwest and toward the Lower Mississippi Valley and Gulf Coast. The Hopewell tradition actually came to an end in the Midwest at about A.D. 350, but some of its cognates in the Southeast continued for another century or two. The Late Woodland period started off with rather uneven social and cultural developments, some of which appear to mark a "devolution" of the Hopewellian-inspired networks of the Middle Woodland (Bense 1994:181), a change not unlike the transition between the Late Archaic and Early Woodland periods discussed in Chapter 3. Networks of interaction were disrupted, much as they were earlier with the abandonment of Poverty Point, but this was hardly an era of social isolation (Cobb and Nassaney 1991, 2002), and not long after the landscape was rearranged by demographic shifts, populations grew, settlements consolidated, warfare erupted, and new mound traditions appeared, including the first civic-ceremonial centers. Emphasis on interregional connections and rituality shifting southward may have had as much to do with the relative invulnerability of the Deep South to climate changes that affected ecologies to the north as much as it did the greater degree of continuity evident in the culture history of the Gulf Coast. Elsewhere, the apparent decline in interconnectivity was a possible consequence of greater local autonomy afforded by the adoption of increasingly effective pottery technology, as well as the bow and arrow after A.D. 600 (Blitz 1988; Nassaney and Pyle 1999).

Middle-Late Woodland mound traditions and the emergence of civic-ceremonial centers are seen in the Weeden Island tradition of eastern Gulf Coastal Plain and Coast, and the Coles Creek tradition of the Lower Mississippi Valley. Beginning in the Middle Woodland period A.D. 200 and lasting until about A.D. 1000, Weeden Island culture had antecedents in the Deptford and Swift Creek traditions of the Gulf Coastal Plain and Coast (Milanich 2004a). Pottery of the Weeden Island tradition includes elaborate forms, notably animal and human effigy vessels, along with ornate incised, punctuated, and painted surface treatments. Caches of elaborate vessels in burial mounds continue the Middle Woodland rituality of Swift Creek and its Hopewell affines and contrast sharply with the largely simple and unadorned vessels of domestic contexts. Sites with domestic Weeden Island wares are distributed more widely than are locations of mounds, but none of the mound centers are "vacant" in the sense of Early and Middle Woodland complexes. Rather, Weeden Island mound complexes or single-mound sites also housed large arcuate or horse-shaped ring middens that formed from households arranged around a central plaza. At the early Weeden Island McKeithen site in north Florida, three mounds were emplaced at the ends and central position of a horseshoe-shaped midden 450 by 500 m in plan (Milanich et al. 1984, 1997:54). The mounds were erected over three platforms that housed variously a charnel house, a mortuary, and an elite residence.

At about the same time at the Kolomoki site in southwest Georgia, some eight mounds were erected both within and outside a massive horseshoe-shaped midden (Pluckhahn 2003). Elaborate mortuary assemblages were emplaced on platforms beneath two of its domed mounds. At Kolomoki and McKeithen, as elsewhere in the early Weeden Island world, civic-ceremonial centers are thought to have grown up around an emerging leader and his or her kin group. The death of this individual appears to have prompted a ritual process that involved burning the charnel house, emplacing pottery caches and the cremated and bundled remains of other deceased kin on platforms, and constructing an earthen mound over the platform. After A.D. 750, elaborate mortuary and mound ceremonialism dissipated, even as the Weeden Island tradition persisted in other dimensions of culture. Some of the late Weeden Island communities of Florida contributed to the local development of Mississippian culture and its civic-ceremonial centers, but others returned to a more dispersed settlement pattern, with smaller, less elaborate mounds serving as cemeteries for related, scattered communities.

A parallel but seemingly separate trend towards civic-ceremonial centers is seen in the Lower Mississippi Valley. The Late Woodland period of this subregion is divided into early (Baytown) and later (Coles Creek) subperiods (Kidder 2002:80). A great deal of variability characterizes early, Baytown settlement. Mounds are generally absent in the northern reaches of the tradition (Yazoo Basin and eastern Arkansas), save at the type site, and mortuary data are few. In contrast, Baytown period sites in the valley between Vicksburg and Baton Rouge (including the lower Red River Valley) include multimound complexes with plazas (Kidder 2002:82–85). Mounds at several sites were arranged in oval patterns with adjoining midden and open, enclosed spaces virtually devoid of midden or other debris (Figure 4-4). Not all multimound complexes housed sizeable and more-or-less permanent communities, but clearly they were not categorically "vacant" ceremonial centers. Mortuary practices of the Baytown tradition ranged from mounds with simple extended burials lacking grave goods, such as Bluff Mound at Troyville (Walker 1936), to the varied mortuary program at a single low mound at the Gold Mine site in Richland Parish, Louisiana (Belmont 1984), with defleshed but re-articulated extended interments, bundle burials, skull piles, collections of long bones, and dog burials.

At about A.D. 700 in the Lower Mississippi Valley, the subregional variation of Baytown traditions was subsumed by a more unified cultural regime known as Coles Creek (Kidder 2002; Roe and Schilling 2010; Rees 2012). As summarized by Kidder (2002:85–86), the Coles Creek period ushered in the use of distinctive pottery, flat-topped platform mounds arranged in formal plaza groups, and a shift from the use of mounds as mass mortuaries to elevated structures for individuals of distinct status. Open plazas became a defining feature of multimound centers (Kidder 2004b), with mounds placed along the edges of plazas and extensive middens beyond the mounds, often encircling them. Village-mound-plaza complexes such as these, as well as other novel attributes, anticipate some of the defining elements of Mississippian culture. In fact, Kidder (2002:90) argues that Coles Creek architecture, site layout, and political organization align it more closely with Mississippian than with Late Woodland, as traditionally defined. In cases such as

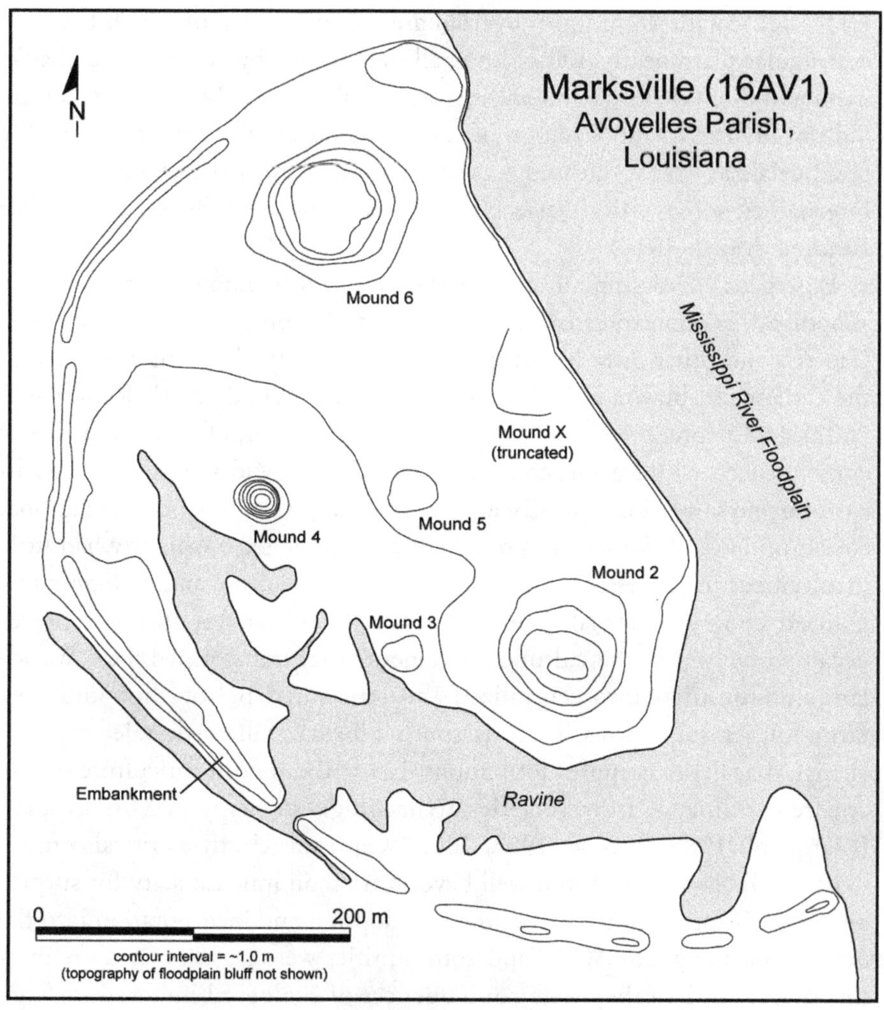

Figure 4-4. The Marksville Mound Complex in Louisiana.

these, the term "Emergent Mississippian" is sometimes used. Although it never gained much importance until the end of the period, corn has been recovered from several Coles Creek sites (Fritz and Kidder 1993).

Other instances of "Emergent Mississippian" are seen northward along the Mississippi Valley (Rolingson and Mainfort 2002) and into the American Bottom of the Midwest (Kelly 2002). Toltec Mounds in Arkansas was the largest of three multimound complexes of the Plum Bayou culture (A.D.

700–1050), with 18 mounds over an area of 40 ha, ten of which border a rectangular plaza nearly 400 m long, all surrounded by an earthen embankment and ditch (Rolingson 2002). As with Coles Creek, Plum Bayou culture did not involve the importation of "exotic" goods, and there are remarkably few burials at Toltec, although other mound sites in the vicinity housed interments, some with diverse assemblages of grave goods (e.g., Chandler Landing; Moore 1910).

Emergent Mississippian, or as it is coming to be known, terminal Late Woodland, is also expressed in the American Bottom, the eventual locus of Cahokia and other early Mississippian civic-ceremonial centers and some of the earliest full-blown agriculture (Fortier and McElrath 2002; Kelly 1990, 2002). In Chapter 5 we take a closer look at the advent of Mississippian as a consequence of antecedent conditions both in the Midwest and the Southeast. For now we close this discussion by noting that some of the regional communities and the societies to which they belonged apparently had little involvement in processes leading to Mississippian culture and its highly formalized civic-ceremonial centers. Coastal Carolina, for instance, never became involved in the cultural movements that transformed local Woodland communities into centralized and structured polities, nor did they farm. Other subregions, such as south Florida, followed trajectories of change that led to complex formations, but without corn agriculture or any apparent influence from societies archaeologists classify as Mississippian (Marquardt 1988; Widmer 1988, 2002). Corn was clearly a critical component in Mississippianization, well beyond its economic capacity for surplus and intensification, and thus its uneven adoption and incorporation into the cultures of many Late Woodland communities were perhaps far more matters of choice than they were consequences of ecological imperatives (e.g., Schroedl et al. 1990; Welch 1990).

This brief summary of Woodland culture history goes well beyond the "basics" of typology and chronology to introduce a number of topical issues and problems that we explore in greater detail in the balance of this chapter.

Woodland Problems

Research on the Woodland period in the Southeast is a thriving enterprise of creative theorizing, an ever-accumulating body of new field observations, and many innovative projects using extant collections. Long-standing, familiar questions endure alongside new problems. Archaeologists of all theoretical stripes contribute to basic research in chronology, subsistence, and settlement. Each of these subjects takes on added significance in research programs that address topics such as landscape, memory, symbolism, and ritual (e.g., Carr and Case 2005; Mainfort and Sullivan 1998; Wallis 2008, 2009, 2011). Recent surveys and excavations supply information on life away from ceremonial centers (e.g., Rafferty and Peacock 2008), and recent work at ceremonial centers supply information on life apart from mounds and burials (e.g., Pluckhahn 2003). Much of the research on the Woodland Southeast is situated at the interface of ritual and daily practice, public and private experiences, or, as Sears (1973) famously dichotomized, the "sacred" and the "secular." Such research necessarily traces back to Hopewell of the Midwest and its traditions of mounding, ancestor veneration, animal symbolism, and display goods. However, the bearers of Hopewell religion in the Midwest were probably no more proselytizers who canvassed the Southeast for converts (cf. Carr and Case 2005:25) than were indigenous Southeast natives passive recipients of a foreign, yet irresistible belief system. The Woodland Southeast had much going on before, during, and after Hopewell in the Midwest that evidently affected the way that Hopewell religion was locally engaged.

Hopewell in the Southeast

Decades of archaeological research support the inference that Hopewell religion originated or at least became most spectacularly materialized in present-day Ohio, specifically the Scioto River Valley of south-central Ohio, from whence it spread. Of course, how one delimits Hopewell influence outside of Ohio is determined by the attributes one chooses to map. Based on the distribution of its signature forms of material culture—mica and copper cutouts, panpipes, dentate rocker-stamped pottery, stone platform pipes with animal effigy forms, among other items—Hopewell extends from the Great Lakes to the Gulf of Mexico, and from the eastern Plains to the Appalachians. All such items are portable and thus subject to not only geographic displacement but also temporal attenuation as heirloom items, although most were ultimately deposited in caches or in burials. Greater circumscription is found in the nonportable attributes of Ohio Hopewell, namely its mounds and other earthworks, especially its geometric earthworks (Bernardini 2004).

Recent compendia on Hopewell archaeology in the Midwest showcase an enormous wealth of new information and insight (Byers and Wymer 2010; Carr and Case 2005; Case and Carr 2008; Charles and Buikstra 2006; Dancey and Pacheco 1997). Work in the Ohio heartland has been dominated lately by analyses of community organization and settlement, particularly the relationship between earthworks and domestic life. Enabling such work is a conceptual shift away from Hopewell as primarily an integrated cluster of religious symbols and practices that operated socially at the *interregional* scale (e.g., Caldwell 1964) and towards the *local* experiences of constituent communities, what Christopher Carr (2005:67) calls "personalized reconstructions of local societies and cultures." A corollary to this shift is growing emphasis on how participation in Hopewell religion was motivated by local needs and rationalized by local logics. It is now widely expected that "being" Hopewell meant different things to different people. Although the symbols of Hopewell religion may have served as a sort of "lingua franca" for people of diverse language and culture (Seeman 1995), the interactions or intergroup activities they facilitated varied with local contexts and personal histories.

When considering Hopewell experiences in the Southeast, it bears repeating that mound construction in the region predated any such practice in the Midwest by several millennia. This is not to suggest that Hopewell mounds originated in the Southeast, but merely to underscore that Hopewellian practices involving structured deposition and mortuary ritual may not have appeared all that foreign to some recipient communities. Added to the repertoire of mound traditions in the Southeast during Hopewell times were flat-topped, platform mounds, constructions with few direct counterparts in the Midwest. Moreover, none of the heartland Hopewell mound centers were truly both "civic" and "ceremonial" centers, like the civic-ceremonial centers of the Mississippian Southeast, but by the time Hopewell dissipated in the Midwest, some mound centers in the Southeast were occupied more-or-less permanently by relatively large resident populations, such as Kolomoki, in Georgia. Arguably, Hopewell experiences in the Southeast did more to anticipate the Mississippian cultural revolution yet to come than did it merely mimic the ontology and practice of the Ohio Hopewell.

From Ceremonial to Civic-Ceremonial Centers

Hopewell specialists remain fully engaged in a long-standing debate about the relationship of mound centers to places of dwelling (see chapters in Byers and

Wyman [2010] for recent examples). Lacking strong evidence for habitation at sites of geometric earthworks and multimound complexes, some specialists have concluded that ceremonial centers were vacant (e.g., Dancey and Pacheco 1997), much as they seem to have been during the preceding Adena era (Clay 1998). Few residential sites have been found in and around ceremonial centers, and those that have been found are generally small, ephemeral sites. Despite the lack of better settlement data, Hopewell archaeologists generally view ceremonial centers as gathering points for geographically dispersed communities. In this sense, centers served as symbolic or "surrogate" villages to integrate communities that were otherwise economically and politically autonomous. Judging from the labor involved in the construction of some of the largest earthworks—geometric earthworks up to 300 m in diameter—the geographic (and social) range of participating communities appears to have been well beyond the local (Bernardini 2004).

Occupational histories at mound centers in the Southeast provide better evidence for resident populations, some apparently permanently settled at places of ritual activity. One of the more detailed histories of a Middle Woodland mound center in the Southeast is seen in the work of Pluckhahn (2003) at Kolomoki in southwest Georgia (Figure 4-5). Kolomoki was established as a multimound center ca. A.D. 350–450, just as the Hopewell traditions of Ohio were on the wane. In the centuries immediately preceding the founding of Kolomoki, Middle Woodland settlements were distributed along a 250-km stretch of the Chattahoochee River. Among a cluster of sites to the northwest of Kolomoki was Mandeville, the locus of two mounds (conical and platform) adjacent to a village midden indicative of intensive, perhaps permanent settlement. With its inventory of copper, mica, and ceramic objects, Mandeville was one of the few locations with clear connections to Hopewell, but it was also one of the first locations of a platform mound. After Mandeville was abandoned at ca. A.D. 300, major restructuring of the regional landscape ensued, with Kolomoki emerging as a primary center of population and ceremony.

The abandonment of Mandeville coincided with a general shift toward settlement clustering at either end of the middle Chattahoochee Valley. Equidistant from each of these clusters and placed back off the river 12 km, Kolomoki was established in a flurry of construction along an east-west axis with mounds at either end, a central plaza, and a massive earthen enclosure, coupled with permanent settlement along the inside of the enclosure. Pluck-

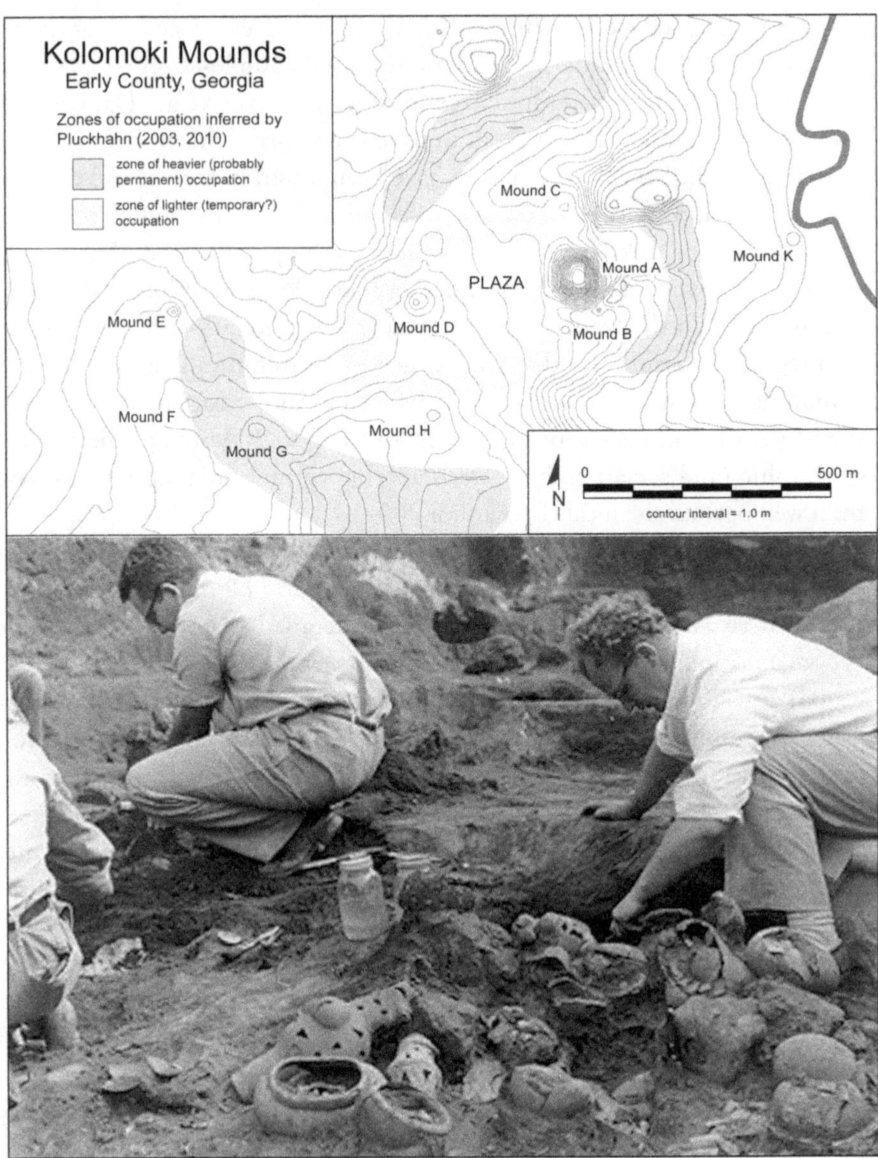

Figure 4-5. Plan map of the Kolomoki site, Georgia (top), and photograph of the excavation of a vessel cache at base of Mound D (bottom). Map adapted from Pluckhahn 2003, 2010; photograph courtesy of Thomas J. Pluckhahn.

hahn (2003:190) estimates that the resident population during the first century of Kolomoki's history (ca. A.D. 350–250) ranged between 225 and 405 people, although it may have occasionally ballooned to 525 people with transient residents. Compared to other early civic-ceremonial centers in the Southeast, Kolomoki's founding population was quite large. Given the equally large plaza established at the outset, Kolomoki was equipped for large social gatherings, but its scale of mounding this early on was modest, leading Pluckhahn (2003:196) to suggest the site was both the home of a sizeable resident population and a locus of gathering for regional allies.

In the ensuing century, the resident population of Kolomoki seems to have remained steady in numbers, but the frequency of temporary residents grew. This is most evident in the shared attributes of pottery stamped with Swift Creek designs (see below). A 17-m-tall platform mound was erected and other earth-moving projects intensified. Throughout this phase and the preceding one, mortuary treatment and associated ritual appears to have been inclusive and group oriented, with no clear evidence for ceremony emphasizing particular persons or personae. Pluckhahn (2003:207) interprets this phase as a gradual trend toward greater regional interaction, involving both competition and cooperation, but largely within an ethos of egalitarianism. Communal feasting was among the public ceremonies that appear to have included all residents and nonlocal guests. A few generations later the resident population declined, as did mounding, and Kolomoki lost its central position in a network that appears to have shifted southward with Weeden Island influences. As with its genesis 200 years earlier, the decline of Kolomoki is understood by Pluckhahn (2003) as a historical process of contested traditions, the interplay between structure and practice. He resists the temptation to pigeonhole Kolomoki into a cultural evolutionary type (e.g., tribe, chiefdom), or attribute its evolution to the aggrandizing behaviors of a few big men, or women.

Pluckhahn and colleagues (2010) are now working on the Crystal River site of the north Florida Gulf Coast, adding to a body of archaeological evidence for early civic-ceremonial centers, in this case involving shell mounds, including platform mounds. Geophysical survey, low-impact coring, and new radiocarbon dates indicate that the Crystal River earthworks were built as early as 300 B.C., with a higher degree of planning and complexity than ever imagined. Like Kolomoki, Crystal River has produced objects of Hopewell affinity, but it clearly had pre-existing traditions of mounding and interregional interactions, and it persisted as much as 300 years past the demise of Hopewell in Ohio.

Looking beyond the similarities of Middle and Late Woodland mound centers in the Southeast we find a great deal of variation in the scale, structure, and organization of subregional communities. The cases of Crystal River and Kolomoki underscore the importance of historical contingency in the rise of particular centers, and how all such local events were embedded in larger-scale histories, spatially and temporally. In other cases, established villagers constructed mounds and mortuary facilities without any obvious nonlocal input (e.g., Knight 2001; Milanich et al. 1984), occasionally emplacing mounds directly over habitation areas, as with the Biltmore Mound in Asheville, North Carolina (Kimball et al. 2010). Along the northern Gulf Coast and Panhandle of Florida, Swift Creek and Santa Rosa–Swift Creek mounds were located proximate to circular or arcuate villages (Willey 1949), while in northeast Florida mortuary mounds were often located several hundred meters from locations of habitation (Ashley and Wallis 2006; Wallis 2008). In the former subregion, occasional sites lacking mounds housed large cemeteries in the plaza of circular villages (e.g., Bernath in the western panhandle [Bense 1998]). Other locales such as north Georgia seem to recapitulate the Adena and Hopewell pattern of "vacant" ceremonial centers (Williams and Freer 1998), perhaps serving as gateways of exchange linking the Coastal Plain to the interior Southeast (Anderson 1998). Other subregional variations on the basic Swift Creek model of circular village-plaza-and-mound complexes abound (see papers in Williams and Elliott 1998). With so much variation in how panregional influences were experienced and materialized in villages and ceremonial structures, it stands to reason that interconnections among communities would emerge as a major research topic.

Networks of Interaction

The Southeast has a long history of research on interregional interaction but generally this has focused on the "exotica" of religious objects such as those of Hopewell, made on materials, such as galena, mica, and copper, whose geological provenance is generally known (Goad 1979). With growing access to sophisticated and relatively inexpensive sourcing techniques (e.g., instrumental neutron activation analysis [INAA], X-ray diffraction, and XRF), analysts are turning to other classes of material culture to reconstruct the networks of human movement and material exchange that underwrote the panregional distribution of particular cultural traits, notably pottery.

In the repertoire of Swift Creek Complicated Stamped pottery, geochemical insights on the composition of clay and temper have been coupled with forensic-like data on decorative elements that afford unprecedented detail on patterns of interaction. Building on the pioneering work of Broyles (1968), Snow (1975, 1998; Snow and Stephenson 1998) has amassed a database of scores of designs that were carved into wooden paddles by Swift Creek potters to impress the exterior surfaces of vessels before they were fired (Figure 4-6). A variety of geometric and concentric lines were used to create abstract images resembling birds, mammals, flowers, insects, and mask-like faces (Snow 1998). Shared designs among regional sites imply some manner of cultural affinity, but Snow has collected data on minute attributes that enable him to identify pots made from the exact same paddle, sometimes on pots deposited at sites hundreds of kilometers apart. A large inventory of so-called "paddle matches" have been documented by Snow, providing direct evidence for the movement of pots, paddles, or both (Snow and Stephenson 1998). Petrographic analysis of Swift Creek sherds from 11 sites in Georgia provided good evidence for the movement of pots from the Piedmont into the Coastal Plain, as well as evidence for paddles being exchanged for local production (Stoltman and Snow 1998). Swift Creek sherds found at more distant locales (e.g., Pinson Mounds in western Tennessee, and the Mann site in Indiana) came from vessels made locally (Mainfort et al. 1997; Ruby and Shriner 2005), suggesting that paddles but not pots were distributed outside the core area of Swift Creek traditions.

In a recent study of Swift Creek pottery from northeast Florida and southeast Georgia, Wallis (2011) combines geochemical, petrographic, and technofunctional data to infer the structure of Woodland interaction and its change over time. According to Wallis, Swift Creek pottery exchange was structured by a gift economy of reciprocal relationships among people both near and far. The iconic complicated stamping first appeared in the study area via connections to the Gulf Coast at about A.D. 200. The simple vessel forms of an existing Deptford tradition did not change when Swift Creek paddle designs were first applied, but coincident with this change was the use of a novel, locally distinctive temper, crushed charcoal. Earthen mounds were erected in several locations, and human bodies, exotic materials and objects, specialized pottery forms (jars, beakers, multi-compartment trays,

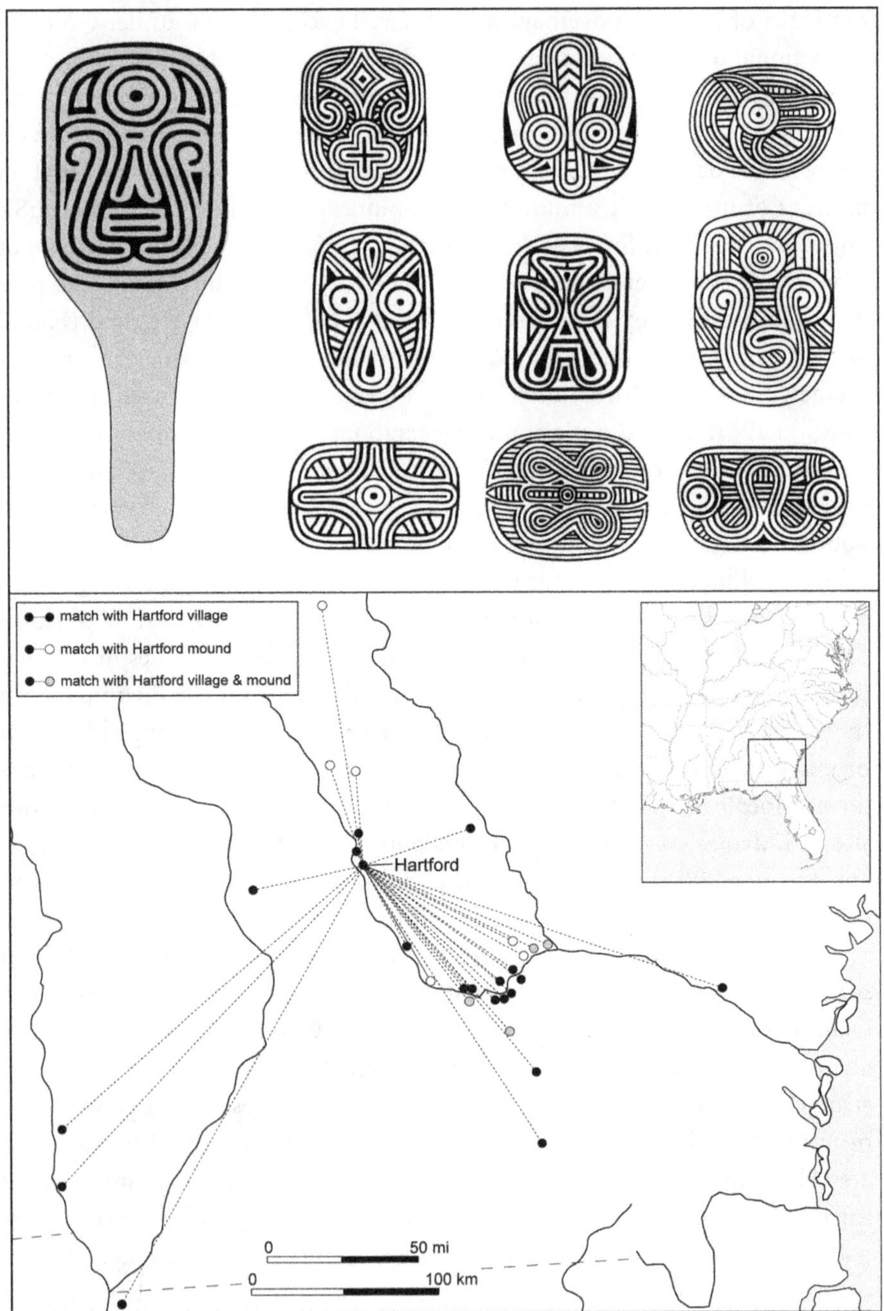

Figure 4-6. Swift Creek paddle designs (top) and paddle matches (bottom) between Hartford site and other sites in the region (adapted from images in Snow 1998).

cups), and mundane pottery vessels were interred in those mounds. Most of the mound vessels, both the mundane and the exotic, were tempered with charcoal and thus locally made, a conclusion confirmed by Instrumental Neutron Activation Analysis (INNA) and petrography.

By about A.D. 500, changes in material culture and its distribution signal a restructuring of the social landscape, most evident in connections between the Lower St. Johns River and a cluster of Swift Creek sites on the Altamaha River, 200+ km to the northwest. Nearly one-fifth of all vessels from two Lower St. Johns mounds were made along the Altamaha River and paddle matches link three of these vessels to specific sites. Wallis (2011:196) expects a reciprocal figure for St. Johns vessels in Altamaha River mounds, although such data have yet to be developed. In any case, across-the-board changes in the technology and stylistic expression of Swift Creek pottery register region-wide influence. One sweeping change came in the appearance of thick, folded rims, another in an enhanced tradition of paddle stamping. Before about A.D. 500, Swift Creek paddles were used to stamp vessels, but often in ways that obscured designs. Whether paddle impressions were legible or not, stamping compressed the clay body, enabling potters to achieve uniform thickness and hence greater performance in both firing and use. But Wallis (2011:195) suggests further that paddle stamping early on was never intended to convey in literal form the design of paddles, even though paddles themselves were highly distinctive. That changed after A.D. 500 when paddle execution became precise, enabling the design of paddles to be transferred literally, if in negative form, to multiple other objects, some of which were transported great distances and interred in mounds. Remarkably, the nine vessels demonstrated to be from the Altamaha region in the two mounds noted above were not ceremonial forms, but rather domestic forms, all with evidence of having been used for cooking purposes (see also Wallis 2007).

As Wallis (2011:29) notes, Swift Creek Complicated Stamped pots, like Hopewell objects, were exchanged among distinct societies and thus do not signify the existence of a unified "culture" or "tradition," even if those terms remain useful to describe their translocal qualities (see also Williams and Elliott 1998). Unlike Hopewell exchange, however, Swift Creek vessel exchange involved both nonutilitarian and utilitarian items, offering insight into the relationship between social identities forged in daily practice and those negotiated in public. The presumed dichotomy between "sacred" and "secular" life may not apply in this case. Wallis (2007, 2008, 2011) goes further to suggest that spatial relationships among mounds, objects of ritual importance, places of dwelling, and mobile human bodies contributed to relational identities that cannot be reduced to particular locations, times, or things. It follows that networks may have defined Woodland identities in the Southeast more so than discrete places or persons. Thus, carved vessel designs were effective in inducing memories of associations among objects distributed across the landscape, such as pots made from the same paddle (Wallis 2011:198). Inasmuch as the imagery of Swift Creek designs includes animate beings, some Swift Creek vessels may have been the embodiment of personhood, or more precisely, according to Wallis (2011:198–199), and following Gell (1998), of "distributed" persons—constructs of social identity spread out over time and space, as in the ancestral beliefs we can infer from Swift Creek mortuary practice (see also Giles [2010] for an example involving Hopewell mortuary ritual). At a time when vessel exchange or gifting began to involve the interment of objects from distant sources, Swift Creek potters were careful to execute paddle designs so that the bibliographies and geographies they embodied could be transferred unambiguously.

Symbols of Objects and Earth

The Swift Creek repertoire of complicated stamping is among the better sources of information on the spiritual beliefs and cosmology of ancient Southeasterners. Aside from the zoomorphic beads of the Lower Mississippi Valley (Crawford 2003; Gibson 2000) and occasional decorated bone, shell, and pottery, Archaic material culture was not often adorned with representations of apparent symbolic import. That all changed with the Middle Woodland inventory of effigy pipes and pots, copper and mica cut-outs, necklaces, masks, fetishes and charms, and a rich array of anthropomorphic and zoomorphic imagery stamped, incised, punctated, and painted on the surfaces of pottery vessels. Missing from most inventories of any age are the carvings, engravings, and paintings of wood (e.g., Gilliland 1975; Sears 1982); the plaited and woven designs of textiles, the painting of hides and tattooing of human skin; and the arrangements of feathers, hair, and fur that surely existed beside more durable items. In these fleeting forms of material culture, certain Archaic traditions may have foreshadowed those of the Woodland era, but judging from the more durable media alone, the Middle Woodland witnessed a true explosion of symbolic expression, much of it coincident with the religious movements of Hopewell and its cognates.

Animal symbolism was as prominent in Swift Creek and Weeden Island rituality as it was in any of the Hopewell traditions of the Midwest. In a classic study of McKeithen Weeden Island effigy vessels, Knight (in Milanich et al. 1984) explored the social implications of animals materialized in clay by looking at the relationships between social and natural systems of classification. Through the interpretive lens of structuralism, Knight identifies a tripartite division among symbols of propriety (deer), counterparts in impropriety (turkey vulture and dog), and mediators (roseate spoonbill, wood ibis, nocturnal carnivores, opossum). The edibility of these classes of animals mirrors their signification for appropriate behavior, with one class edible, another inedible, and the third ambiguous. Taking this one step further, Knight suggests that this division likely mirrored rules about social distance and alliance, such as marriage and residency. DeBoer (1997) provides a similar analysis of Hopewell symbolism involving both animal effigies (in the form of platform pipes) and the built environment, all in the service of reproducing—in this case expanding—the social network from which suitable mates were drawn.

With the rise in post-structuralist theory, Southeastern archaeologists have begun to consider how symbolism went beyond *representing* social categories to *actively generating* social relations in situated practice. Pluckhahn (2007) and Wallis (2011), for example, each look at the design symmetry of Swift Creek paddles to infer processes of social reproduction. In a study of over 200 paddle designs, Pluckhahn (2007) documents a concern for various forms of symmetry (mirror and/or rotational), most consistently expressed on vessels from village deposits at Kolomoki, and less so on those from mounds. Through a concatenation of other data on social life at Kolomoki, Pluckhahn is able to infer that design symmetry was among the symbolic resources actively manipulated to enforce an ethos of social inclusion.

Wallis (2011:46–52) takes a somewhat different approach. Focusing on paddle designs that appear to represent plants, animals, and humans (see Snow 1998), Wallis finds evidence for decorative styles that use a technique called "split representation." Many designs seem to depict faces, both human and nonhuman, that are rendered two-dimensional by "splitting" the face along the vertical axis. Occasionally depictions of whole bodies, such as birds, were treated this way too. Following Levi-Strauss (1963) and Gell (1998), Wallis (2011:48) argues that split representation was used exclusively when artwork was meant to constitute a person, not merely symbolize one, as noted earlier. In short, Swift Creek decorative style was "inextricable from the constitution of social persons and, therefore, often correspond[ed] with prestige struggles and rivalry among ranked lineages as ancestral identity [wa]s understood as embodied in living persons" (Wallis 2011:50–51). It is not clear how this played out in archaeologically observable social practices such as feasting, mound building, caching, and human interment, but it would appear to involve a greater level of differentiation and exclusivity than Pluckhahn (2003, 2007) sees in the Kolomoki data.

Human effigy vessels in the Swift Creek and Weeden Island worlds provide tantalizing evidence for the existence of religious specialists (Milanich et al. 1984; Pluckhahn 2010), as they do in Hopewell (Carr and Case 2005). An inventory of 17 vessels from 15 sites in Georgia and Florida show a great deal of consistency in overall form and style. As summarized by Pluckhahn (2010:62), the figures in all the vessels are kneeling or squatting, with clenched fists on their chests or legs, eyes shut or hollow, and most mouths closed with pursed lips. Animal vessel effigies include forms that may have paralleled human forms in their connection to spiritual realms. Although many types of animals are represented, birds comprise a commanding fraction, and constitute the only type of animal represented in 14 of the region's 39 mound caches with animal effigies (Pluckhahn 2010:62). As animals of the Upper World in the tripartite cosmos known from ethnohistory (Grantham 2002), birds may have accompanied religious specialists in travels from the Middle World of human dwelling. Elevated above the Middle World, mounds themselves may have materialized the Upper World, or at least access to it. Although religious specialists likely presided over the caching of vessels and burial of humans in mounds, the visibility of these acts to places where groups could gather (i.e., central plazas) may have affirmed the social inclusiveness Pluckhahn (2003, 2010) envisions.

The symbolism of Woodland mounds and other earthworks has not received as much attention in the Southeast as it has in the heartland of Hopewell. The geometry and scale of Hopewell enclosures and mound complexes are indeed evocative. Enormous earthen enclosures of conjoined circles and squares common in the Scioto Valley have been interpreted as village surrogates (Dancey and Pacheco 1997) or "big houses" (DeBoer 1997), places of ritual gathering for communities otherwise dispersed across the landscape. Other research on Hopewell earthworks has examined astronomical alignments (Lepper 1998; Marshall 1996; Romain 2000), the significance of colors and soil composition in depositional sequences (Charles et al. 2004; Greber 2006; Van Nest et al. 2001), and regional integration of dispersed sites (Dancey and Pacheco 1997). New theoretical perspectives have turned attention away from the mounds as referentially meaningful to Hopewell people and towards an experiential approach that examines the relationship between symbol and action (Bernandini 2004). In one particularly far-ranging interpretation, Giles (2010, 2011) argues that Hopewell enclosures were liminal places where rituals of world renewal took place. In this sense, enclosures were instruments of social action whose engagement may have been routinized in religious practice, but whose material effects were seen in the mobilization of large social bodies.

Programs of research on the symbolic dimensions of Woodland mounds and mound complexes of the Southeast follow similar lines of inquiry as those of Hopewell (see papers in Mainfort and Sullivan 1998). As we have noted repeatedly, the existence of civic-ceremonial centers in the Southeast adds a dimension to public ritual that clearly had the potential to institutionize differences among social bodies and the spaces they habituated. Thus, efforts to elucidate social meaning in the symbolic expressions of Woodland communities include comparisons of pottery styles across households or household clusters (e.g., Pluckhahn 2003; Saunders 1998) to infer the existence of lineages, clans, moieties, or some such social divisions. No matter how such patterning is conceived, researchers have not found compelling evidence for institutionalized inequalities such as those known for the Mississippian era, underscoring the likelihood that intensified food production in a corn-based economy was a truly transformational social experience.

The Role of Farming

Knowledge on the patterns and processes of food production in the Woodland Southeast has grown by leaps and bounds in recent decades thanks to a dedicated cadre of archaeobotanists who have brought much new evidence to light and theorized about it in innovative ways. We introduced in Chapter 3 the work of Bruce Smith and colleagues in elucidating the domestication of early cultivars of the Eastern Woodlands. Various species of oily and starchy seed-bearing plants and indigenous varieties of squashes had been collected in wild form throughout the Holocene, but after about 4,500 years ago, morphological changes in several plant species signal trends toward cultivar status. Bruce Smith (1987, 1992) pointed out long ago that most of the species in question are fast-growing weeds, species that would thrive in places disturbed by natural or human agents. He surmised that floodplains of major rivers in the region would be ideal habitat for colonizing weeds due to floods that periodically disturbed old surfaces. Given that later Mississippian farmers often selected floodplain locales for settlement, it seemed reasonable to propose that Woodland precursors got the process started earlier with the exploitation and eventual cultivation of weedy annuals.

Research on the origins of food production in the Southeast in recent decades has shifted the focus away from the floodplains of major rivers and towards the rugged uplands of the Ozarks and Cumberland Plateau. Building on the pioneering work of Volney Jones (1936), archaeologists armed with the modern recovery techniques of flotation have targeted rockshelters and caves because of superb organic preservation and have found abundant evidence for the collection, storage, and consumption of a suite of plants, including species that were manipulated in ways that led to morphological changes (large seeds, thinner hulls) beneficial for human use (e.g., Cowan 1985; Cowan et al. 1981; Fritz 1990, 1993, 1997; Gremillion 1998, 2004b; Ison 1988). The deep recesses of caves, of course, were never conducive to human habitation or even food storage, but they have provided abundant evidence for plant cultivation in the paleofeces left by ancient explorers, artists, and miners (Box 4-2). Rockshelters of the Southeast, on the other hand, offered not only protection from the elements and commanding views of lowland terrain, but also strategic places for the settlement of small, dispersed communities. As we discussed in Chapter 3, the dispersal of Late Archaic populations after about 1200 B.C. led to increased use of interriverine zones and possibly greater anthropogenic disturbances conducive to weed propagation, as well as promotion of mast resources (Abrams and Nowacki 2008; Gremillion 1998). Increased flood severity and frequency likely contributed to this pattern, making floodplains locales risky places to dwell and to farm. The narrow, densely vegetated floodplains of interriverine zones may have been especially prone to flash flooding during periods of increased precipitation (Gremillion et al. 2008). Although the soils of upland ridge and slopes were not as productive for farming as those of lowland terrain, they were likely more stable and also in close proximity to rockshelter locations of storage and consumption (Gremillion 2006).

Only the subregion of the Southeast north of the Lower Mississippi Valley and west of the Appalachians appears to have been involved in the development of a native seed crop economy (Fritz 1993; Fritz and Kidder 1993). Even within this core area of the continent, food production before the adoption of maize some 1,000 years ago was never very intensive (C. Scarry 1993; Smith 2001b). In a series of papers, Gremillion (2002, 2004b; Gremillion et al. 2008) has applied models of behavioral and evolutionary ecology to explain the uneven distribution of early food production. Her approach is based on the principle that involvement with native seed crops depended on the costs and benefits of farming under particular environmental circumstances. The benefits of adopting seed crops, for example, are outweighed by the high processing costs involved when alternatives, such hickory nuts, are widely available (Gremillion 2004b). However, when intra-annual variations in the availability of alternative foods are considered, seed crops offer a good return on its costs. Rockshelters of the Cumberland Plateau have been interpreted as cold-weather habitation sites, at which seed caches were stored for consumption during the winter. Because winter poses less demand on food-collecting budgets than does the growing season, the relative costs of processing seeds is lowered and thus the benefits raised. Gremillion (2002:497) compared the broader distribution of pre-maize farming in the Eastern Woodlands against average climate and found reasonable correspondence between zones with 60 or more below-freezing days per year and dependence of seed crops. In contrast, zones with fewer than 50 below-freezing days per year have produced virtually no evidence of pre-maize farming (see also Fritz 1990). It would appear that the primary role of seed crops in the Southeast was to alleviate the risks of plant food shortages during winters; from this perspective rockshelters were granaries of food security. Additionally, of course, they also likely served as temporary or extended occupation areas, places where ceremony and ritual may have occurred, and retreats for both male and female members of society, identified by specific categories of artifacts and artwork (e.g., Claassen 2011; Franklin and Bow 2009; Simek and Cressler 2004, 2008; Simek et al. 2001).

Cost-benefit analyses of plant food alternatives tend to support Caldwell's (1958) explanation for the limited role of pre-maize farming in the Southeast, namely, that resources of greater economic value (mast resources) precluded the adoption of more costly foods. Dubbed the "Caldwell Effect" by Gremillion (2002:494), this would also explain the lack of food production in coastal zones, where the abundance of fish and shellfish appears to have precluded the cultivation of native seed crops. Of course, historical factors

Box 4-2. Cave Explorers

Jutting up from the ground to heights as great as 21 m and containing lavish material culture and burials, mounds have garnered more attention by archaeologists and the public than have other Woodland-period sites, for several generations. But beneath the surface of the earth, deep in the caves of Kentucky and Tennessee, Woodland explorers left a record of ritual activity that archaeologists have only begun to investigate (Figure 4B–2). Cave archaeology actually began in earnest about 50 years ago with work in Salts Cave, Kentucky. Joseph Caldwell, then Curator of Anthropology at the Illinois State Museum, directed the research, but Robert Hall and Patty Jo Watson carried out the fieldwork, and it was Watson (1969) who authored the report (Dye 2008). Watson would go on to develop an enduring and multifaceted research program in many of the region's caves, mentoring dozens of students in the highly specialized—and somewhat dangerous—pursuit of deep cave exploration. From the outset of this research Watson and colleagues were able to show that Woodland cavers traveled deep into the recesses of underground worlds consisting of narrow passes, steep inclines, low ceilings, muddy flats, jagged rock piles, and other impediments to human entry. This was not every-person's archaeological pursuit; after just one trip into a Kentucky cave, Caldwell himself declared he would never do it again (Dye 2008:2).

Along with repeated expeditions through the 370 miles of passage in the Mammoth Cave system (Watson 1974), the very first trips into Salts Cave revealed evidence that ancient cavers had mined minerals and crystals, some of obvious practical value, such as speleothem salts (mirabilite, epsomite), which are effective food preservatives (Tankersley 1996). They also mined gypsum, selenite, and satinspar, as well as chert for making stone tools (Franklin 2008; Simek et al. 1998). Although cave exploration began as early as 4,500 years ago, it was during the Early Woodland period that mining operations began in earnest (Crothers et al. 2002). Because the burgeoning of mining activity coincided with increased use of seed-bearing plants of the Eastern Agricultural Complex, it stands to reason that substances useful in the processing and preserving of plant foods would be sought. Paleofeces left deep in caves indeed contain evidence for the consumption of goosefoot, maygrass, knotweed, marsh elder, and sunflower, among other cultivars (Yarnell 1974; Yarnell and Black 1985).

Figure 4B-2. Patty Jo Watson in chimneying position returning an ancient climbing pole to the ledge where it had been kept since Euroamerican cavers discovered this Lower Salts cave passage in 1954. Paleoethnobotanist Lee Newsom (foreground) identified the wooden pole as red/black oak, and a small sample of the wood returned an uncalibrated AMS age estimate of 2760 ± 40 B.P. (Crothers et al. 2002:507). Cave Research Foundation photo (1995) by Charles Swedlund courtesy of Patty Jo Watson and used with permission of the Cave Research Foundation.

However, caves were visited for purposes other than mining minerals, and not all uses of cave minerals were necessarily practical. Caves were repositories for the dead since at least the Archaic period, and they were visited by ancient artists who expressed themselves in glyphs carved into mud and rock, a practice that also began in the Archaic and persisted well into the Mississippian era (Faulkner 1986; Simek and Cressler 2004, 2008; Simek et al. 2001). And some caves or portions of caves were what Watson called "footprint" caves: deep passages where exploration itself was the primary activity. The ostensibly ritual aspects of caving (burials, art) raise alterative explanations for the mining of minerals and other substances. Speleothem salts are also cathartic substances, whose ingestion accelerates defecation (Tankersley 1996). Bodily purging may have been part of a larger program of ritual practice involving passage into an underworld charged with symbolic power and meaning. In Creek and indeed apparently in the cosmology of many southeastern peoples, the world was divided into Upper, Middle, and Lower realms (see Grantham 2002; Hudson 1976). Opposed to the forces of an Upper World characterized by order, clarity, and permanence, the Lower World consisted of powers inducing chaos, creativity, and reversals. Unlike the world inhabited by humans (the Middle World), access to the Upper and Lower Worlds was privileged, requiring ritual proscriptions that may have been a source of social and political power. Crothers (2001), in fact, views the advent of gypsum mining as indicative of broader changes in society, including perhaps the emergence of property rights. In this respect, paleofeces from caves add an interesting twist on inferences about social change. To date, all analyzed specimens have been found to contain male hormones (Solobik et al. 1996). If caving was indeed exclusively the purview of men, we can imagine that access to the spiritual forces of the Lower World may likewise have become gender-specific, and with it a powerful force of societal change at a time of subsistence change that was arguably promoted by women (Watson and Kennedy 1991). Ironically, the chief person to develop the archaeology leading to such knowledge was not the man who preferred the Middle World over the Lower World, but a woman, Patty Jo Watson, whose vision of things out of sight and out of reach to most humans sparked a tradition of cave archaeology throughout the Midwest and Southeast that continues to thrive today (see papers in Dye 2008).

must be considered too (Gremillion 2002:498–500). The species of seed-bearing plants and squashes that were ultimately domesticated in the Eastern Woodlands did not necessarily occur naturally in all locations, particularly in coastal zones. Dispersal by human agents is a relevant factor, of course, and distribution outside of "natural" ranges is among the criteria used to determine the cultivar status of any species. The extent to which the limited range of seed crops in the Southeast is an accurate reflection of human plant use and not a bias of preservation or recovery remains a nagging problem for archaeologists. It seems reasonable to conclude, however, that the degree of interconnection among regional populations was far greater than the distribution of seed crops, so the limited range of seed crops is not likely to be due to limited knowledge of or access to such plants.

This brings us to the question of maize and its role in Woodland subsistence economies. We have known for a long time that corn farming was central to the Mississippian economies of the past millennium. And we have known for several decades that corn actually shows up in the Eastern Woodlands about 1,000 years before the advent of Mississippian at ca. A.D. 900. However, none of the admittedly scant occurrences of maize kernels before A.D. 900 appears to come from contexts of full-blown cultivation, and one of the locations of purportedly early corn—Fort Center in south Florida (Sears 1982; Sears and Sears 1976)—has been recently re-dated to the Euroamerican era (Thompson et al. 2012). Unlike the slow, gradual process of domestication that characterized the history of indigenous seed-bearing plants and squash, corn entered the Southeast from parts elsewhere and was spread to locations lacking pre-maize farming as an entire cultural package (Jenkins and Krause 2009). Many of the elements of Mississippian culture may have been foreshadowed by the mound and ritual traditions of the Deep South, but apparently few, if any, of the communities with these precocious traits had much prior experience with farming native seed crops, let alone corn.

Cultural Revolutions in the Making

Just as the Early Woodland Southeast had experienced traditions of mounding, mortuary practice, and object display long before Hopewell religion infiltrated the region, the Late Woodland communities of the greater Southeast had experienced many of the elements of ritual and daily living that would come to characterize Mississippian cultures of the last half millennium prior to European contact. We stated earlier that the Middle Woodland traditions of platforms mounds and civic-ceremonial centers did more to anticipate the Mississippian cultural revolution to come than they did to emulate Hopewell. Because of the half-millennium gap separating Middle Woodland and Mississippian across most of the region, archaeologists are loathe to draw direct historical linkages among practices like flat-topped mound building. However, discontinuities at one scale of observation become continuities at larger scales, reminding us that cultural expressions that appeared in bursts of elaboration and great fanfare were never entirely novel. What may be novel in the Woodland experiences of the Southeast are the civic-ceremonial centers that not only focused the interests of a large group of people, but also situated them more-or-less permanently in relation to one another.

Cultural revolutions involving complex built environments and civic-ceremonial centers in the Woodland Southeast were not underwritten by agricultural food production, so we are reluctant to argue that changes in the region are directly analogous to those of, say, Neolithic Europe, where a subjective revolution accompanied colonies of farmers across the continent, permanently transforming the cultural and physical landscape (Bradley 1998; Hodder 1990). Woodland traditions involving mounds, plazas, domestic zones, and other "planned" architecture evoke a similar sense of social discipline, even though they never seem to have escalated into full-blown agricultural chiefdoms but instead dissipated after a few generations. Variations in the instances of mounding over time are regarded by Cobb and Nassaney (2002) as cultural traditions that oscillated between ritual and domestic experiences. Consistent with the Neolithic model, Cobb and Nassaney draw a distinction between hunter-gatherers who envision land as an *object* of labor, and farmers who see land as an *instrument* of labor. But they also recognize that many of the Woodland traditions of the Southeast fit neither of these categories by virtue of both deep histories of materializing beliefs and histories in the form of earthworks, shellworks, and other constructions, as well as experimentation with native plants in select subregions. They thus suggest a third type of worldview during the Woodland period, namely that land was viewed as the *subject* of labor. It was a social discipline more rigid perhaps than most Archaic predecessors and those Woodland communities that never participated in mound building, elaborate mortuary ritual, and the like, but significantly less than that of the Mississippian period, to which we now turn.

Note

1. Commencing with this chapter, age estimates are reported in the familiar B.C./A.D. framework. The deviation between any given radiocarbon assay and its calibrated age over the span of the Woodland period is usually less than a century, and, for a short time around 2000 years ago, radiocarbon assays actually overestimate actual years by a few decades. The rationale for converting time referents to the B.C./A.D. convention is simply that virtually all the extant literature on late-period archaeology in the Southeast makes use of this system. Because radiocarbon and calibrated ages do not deviate all that much—at least not compared to the late Pleistocene or early to Mid-Holocene—researchers do not always make note of the dating conventions followed. In this and the following chapter, we strive to standardize the reporting of dates and date ranges, using calibrated C14 ages throughout, but now with reference to the Common or Christian era.

5

Mississippian Complexity and Contact Coalescence

Complex societies by some definitions of the term were present in parts of the Southeast from the Archaic period onward, and during the Mississippian and Contact periods, after ca. A.D. 1000, remarkable societies were scattered widely over the landscape. Many were what have been traditionally described as chiefdom-level societies, and in one area, in the American Bottom, a state was arguably present. After European contact, Native American populations were initially heavily reduced by disease and later by warfare and the Indian slave trade, and in the 1830s suffered the tragedy, and for the United States, the national disgrace of Removal. Up to then, however, and in some places long after, resilient societies, many coalescent in nature, were present and adjusting to the new circumstances. In terms of chronology, the Mississippian period extends from ca. A.D. 1000 to the period of intermittent European contact in the sixteenth century, at least until the time when the De Soto expedition passed through the region from 1539 to 1543. The accounts of this expedition, particularly in the interior, provide a detailed first look at Mississippian societies in "pristine" condition, save in the eastern part of the region in Florida and along the lower south Atlantic slope, where the effects of contact were already present in the form of disease-induced depopulation and the occurrence of people familiar with European languages and artifacts (Clayton et al. 1993; Hudson and Tesser 1994).

Like the definition of the Southeast itself, what is meant by the term "Mississippian" has changed over the years, from a culture defined by specific items of material culture like shell-tempered pottery, wall trench houses, and flat-topped pyramidal mounds; a subsistence adaptation heavily reliant on maize agriculture or oxbow lake/riverine/floodplain environments; a characteristic form of the social organization, specifically the presence of herditary inequality between people and groups; by the nature of the religious/ceremonial/iconographic systems in use; and most recently, by a constellation of material, organizational, and religious practices given initial form at and near Cahokia and whose precepts if not peoples spread widedly throughout the region over the next two centuries (e.g., Alt and Pauketat 2011; Anderson 1994; Dye 2012; Griffin 1967, 1985; Knight 1986; Muller 1997; Pauketat 2007; Smith 1986, 1990; Steponaitis 1986:387–388). Here we use the term as a time period, since there is great variation among the societies present in the region with regard to the presence, onset, and importance of all of the definitional categories noted above. Just as the beginning of the Mississippian period depends on the definitional characteristics chosen, so too the ending of the period is hard to pin down, blurring as it does into a "protohistoric" or "Contact" era. Accordingly, we combine and discuss both the late prehistoric Mississippian and early historic Contact period occupations of the Southeast together in this chapter. In many ways the people and processes were the same. Just as Mississippian societies rose and fell, or coalesced and collapsed, so too did Contact period societies. While by the mid-eighteenth century hereditary elites may have been gone from across the region, they were unquestionably present no more than a century earlier in some areas, as archaeological evidence and historical accounts about the Calusa, Cofitachequi, and the Natchez chiefdoms make clear (e.g., Barnett 2007; I. Brown 1985; DePratter 1994; Hudson et al. 2008; Lorenz 2000; Neitzel 1966, 1983; Widmer 1988) (Figure 5-1).

While an entire volume could be written about the late prehistoric and historic Native American occcupations of the Southeast, and indeed many already have been, here we focus on major themes and high points in research rather than attempting an exhaustive treatment. The Mississippian and Contact periods in the Southeast have received tremendous research attention in recent years, something made abundantly clear by an examination of the number of papers published by time period in the two major journals covering the field, *American Antiquity* and *Southeastern Archaeology* from 1982 to 2011, the interval over which both journals were being produced (Table 5-1). Many more articles have been published about these time periods over the past 30 years in these two journals, in fact, than the totals for the preceding Paleoindian, Archaic, and Woodland periods in the region combined. Examining the catalogs of the major university presses in the region that publish extensively on local archaeology—such as Alabama,

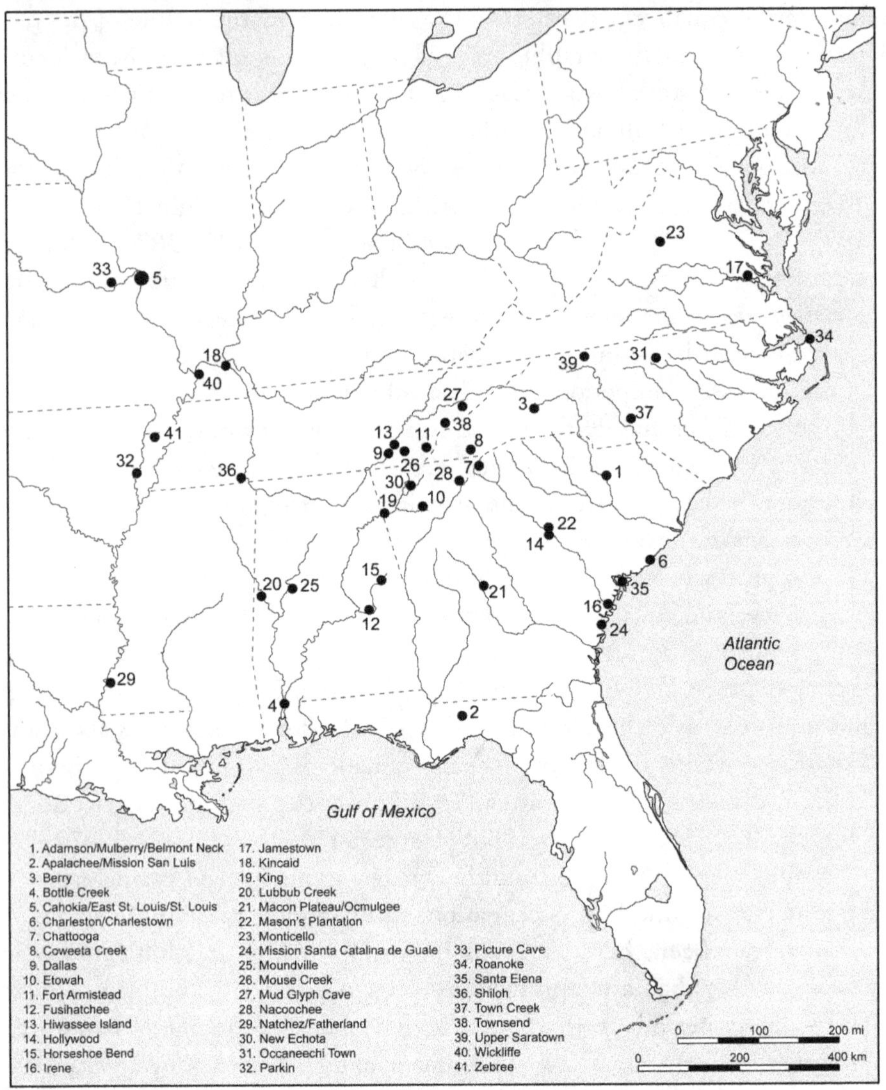

Figure 5-1. Locations of Mississippian and Contact period sites mentioned in the text.

Florida, and Tennessee—the same pattern holds and is in fact even more pronounced. Earlier periods of southeastern prehistory until recently have not been the subject of much research effort and publication; the later periods have a comparatively vast abundance. There is far more archaeological research and reporting on subjects like the historical trajectories of specific

Table 5-1. Articles on Southeastern Archaeology by Major Time Period in the Journals *Southeastern Archaeology* and *American Antiquity* 1982–2011

	Southeastern Archaeology		*American Antiquity*	
Paleoindian	6	1.3%	9	5.2%
Archaic	50	11.2%	36	20.8%
Woodland	54	12.1%	17	9.2%
Mississippian	139	31.1%	61	35.3%
Contact	69	15.4%	16	9.2%
Historic	32	7.2%	11	6.4%
Other*	97	21.7%	24	13.9%
Totals**	447	100.0%	174	100.0%

* Category includes articles that cannot be assigned to a specific period and consists primary of papers on methods or the history of archaeology in the region.

** Totals exclude book reviews. In all, a total of 1410 articles were published in *American Antiquity* over this interval.

Mississippian centers and societies; the effects of agricultural intensification and environmental change on late prehistoric and early historic Native peoples; the emergence, maintenance, and collapse of complex society in the region in general, and Mississippian organizational forms in particular; and the relationships between European settlement and encroachment and the attenuation and coalescence, and dissolution and reemergence of Native American tribal societies and confederations.

Mississippian Origins

After ca. A.D. 900, societies characterized by central communities with temple/mortuary mounds arranged around plazas, hereditary inequality between people and groups, and a reliance on intensive maize agriculture began to appear in the Southeast, perhaps first in the Coles Creek area of the Central and Lower Mississippi Valley, and slightly later in the Bootheel of Missouri and the American Bottom region (e.g., Kidder 2002; Pauketat 2007; Roe and Schilling 2010; Rolingson 2002). (Box 5–1). Over the next several centuries similar societies appeared across much of region, albeit with a great deal of local variation, and generally in a time-transgressive fashion from west to east (Anderson 1999; Pauketat 2007; Smith 1990) (Figure 5-2). Specific artifact categories, subsistence adaptations, or organizational forms are no longer considered useful in delimiting whether a southeastern society is "Mississippian" or not. Shell-tempered pottery became widespread after ca.

Box 5-1. The Remote Sensing Revolution

For those of us old enough to remember when we had to dig to know what was beneath the ground surface, the widespread adoption of remote sensing in southeastern archaeology is unquestionably a revolution. We are now able to see, at least where soil conditions are acceptable, subsurface features ranging from individual pits and structures to groups of structures, as well as ditch and stockade lines, up to entire village plans—all without the need for large area excavation (Figure 5B-1). At sites that are protected, furthermore, such as Etowah or Kincaid, both state parks, remote sensing precludes the need to excavate large areas, and facilitates the identification and protection of features that, in the absence of excavation, would have previously been unknown (Bigman et al. 2011; Butler et al. 2011; King et al. 2011). In cases where sites are threatened, furthermore, remote sensing allows archaeologists to target particular areas or features without the need for large-area hand or machine stripping, expensive or destructive procedures that would have likely occurred in the past. Finally, the remote sensing revolution has expanded not only the scale but also the character of fieldwork at many sites, with less emphasis on the excavation of small block units and the accumulation of primarily stratigraphic data about assemblage change over time, to the increased examination of large areas and the reconstruction of activity areas, and the documentation of household, community, and landscape use. Remote sensing is now regarded as an essential early if not first step in field research, and an important independent source of data. Of course, large-scale excavations are also continuing in the Southeast, complementing remote sensing data, and offering opportunities for "ground truthing" or evaluating the effectiveness of various procedures (e.g., Hammerstedt et al. 2010; Lydick 2008; Maki and Fields 2010).

A.D. 900, for example, but it was present centuries prior to this in both the western and eastern parts of the region, in the Ozarks and along the Middle Atlantic Seaboard (Feathers 2009; Feathers and Peacock 2008; Herbert 2009). Instead, history and tradition is implicated in the definition. A pronounced crystalization of ideology, iconography, and religion, as well as

Figure 5B-1. Structures on the summit of Mound A at the Etowah as revealed by magnetic gradiometry. Images from King et al. 2011, courtesy Society for American Archaeology. Etowah Mound A photograph by David H. Dye, used with permission.

aspects of material culture and community organization apparently took place in the American Bottom in the decades after ca. A.D. 1000, and the resulting constellation of features is what many now think of as Mississippian culture, and what is assumed to have spread (Anderson 1997b, 1999; J. Brown 2004a; Pauketat and Emerson 1997a; Pauketat 2004, 2007, 2009).

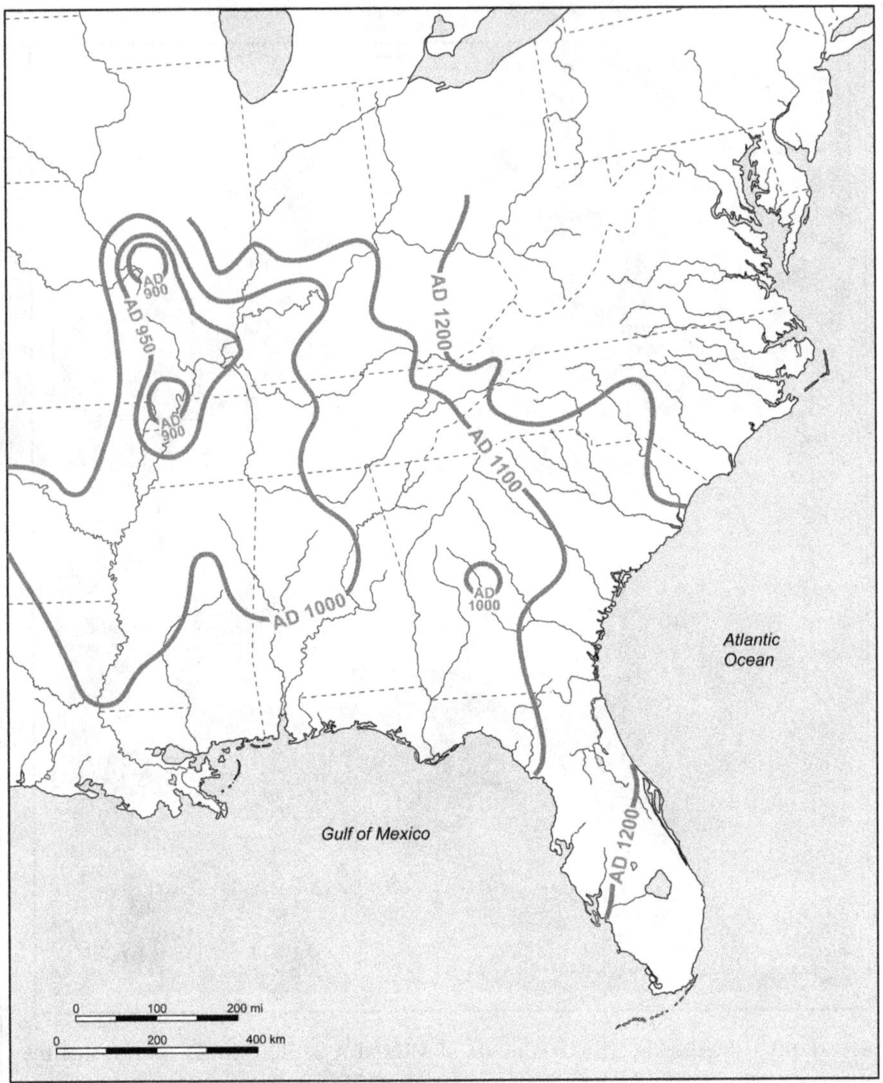

Figure 5-2. Inferred spread of complex "chiefdom" organizational forms in the southeastern United States. Image adapted from Anderson 1999:226).

Major questions southeastern archaeologists have wrestled with for decades are how and why these societies emerged and changed over time, why egalitarian or transegalitarian organizational forms in place for millennia were replaced by systems of pronounced and institutionalized inequality. The intensive cultivation of maize appears to have played an important role, by providing a reliable and storable food source, which not only could have led to population growth, but also supported the production of surpluses that could be used for a number of purposes, including risk management, the support of craft specialists, and the advancement of personal/elite agendas. Maize was present in the east by Middle Woodland times in the American Bottom and eastern Tennessee, and possibly much earlier, at the end of the Late Archaic on the Gulf Coast, although that determination is based on somewhat controversial pollen evidence (Chapman and Crites 1987; Eubanks 1997; Fearn and Lui 1995, 1997; Riley et al. 1994). Stable isotope analyses indicate the widespread adoption of intensive maize agriculture did not occur until after ca. A.D. 900 in the Southeast (Hutchinson et al. 1998; Lynott et al. 1986). In some parts of the region, notably those rich in wild resources such as in the Lower Mississippi Valley and southern Florida, it was not adopted until somewhat later or only after European contact (Fritz 1990; Fritz and Kidder 1993; Hutchinson 2004; Hutchinson et al. 1998). The switch to intensive maize agriculture, where it occurred, typically happened quickly, something documented by analyses of macrofossils and pollen from the plants, as well as stable isotope signatures in the bones of the people themselves (Steponaitis 1986:388). The spread of maize agriculture over the region in some ways mimics and appears to be coeval with or occur slightly in advance of the spread of Mississippian culture itself.

Traditional explanations for the "Mississippian emergence" over the region have taken two forms, including those emphasizing (1) a spread from a single source of ideas, ideology, and people through processes like migration and population replacement (e.g., Smith 1984); or (2) simultaneous development or independent invention in a number of areas, facilitated by interaction and competitive emulation but primarily influenced by shared underlying conditions, such as growing local and region population levels and the adoption of new subsistence adaptations (Milner 2004a; Muller 1997; Smith 1978, 1990). Both are now assumed to have happened, but how the Mississippian emergence occurred on a case by case basis, in different parts of the region, remains the subject of appreciable debate (cf. Cobb and Butler 2004; Pauketat 2007; Smith 1984, 1990; Williams 1994). Warfare has been advanced as a possible factor in the emergence and development of complex societies traditionally classified as chiefdoms and states, given that organizationally complex and populous societies will tend to have a distinct military advantage over smaller and simpler forms (Carniero 1970, 1981; Redmond and Spencer

2012). Warfare unquestionably played a major role in Mississippian life. Evidence for conflict is widespread in the form of weapons trauma on skeletal remains, fortifications, and iconographic representations of trophy taking, and the early historic accounts are rife with instances of warfare within and between Native societies (e.g., Brown and Dye 2007; Cobb and Drake 2008; Cobb and Giles 2009; Dye 2004, 2006, 2007, 2009; Dye and King 2008; Hudson 1997; Milner 1999; Wilson 2012). The role of conflict in the emergence and spread of Mississippian culture is uncertain, but it clearly played a critical role in shaping the behavior, and long-term survival, of people as well as larger communities and entire societies.

Complex organizational forms, like the adoption of intensive maize agriculture, however, appeared in some areas perhaps a century or more before classic Mississippian culture. Appreciable debate has thus attended what happened during this period, and how to describe the societies in question. In some areas terminal Late Woodland societies have been described as "Emergent Mississippian" because they are characterized by some, but not all, of the characteristics of what came later (e.g., Kelly 1987, 1990; Kelly et al. 1984). The term has fallen out of favor, however, because of its teleological implications, and because it emphasizes what came after, and not what was occurring during this critical period (Fortier and McElrath 2002). In recent years the uncritical use of neoevolutionary taxa in general—terms like band, tribe chiefdom, or state—has been challenged, since their use can mask or prevent consideration of the variability and events actually present. A recent highly influential synthesis and critique of southeastern archaeological research focusing on later prehistoric societies, and emphasizing the need to avoid terminological straightjackets, in fact, is entitled *Chiefdoms and Other Archaeological Delusions* (Pauketat 2007), a volume that has generated considerable interest and debate among local scholars (e.g., see papers in the 2009 issue of *Native South* compiled by Anderson and Ethridge). Current research increasingly focuses on reconstructing fine-grained descriptive histories of sites and localities, and seeking commonalities and differences among them in the pursuit of explanations or factors shaping these historical trajectories. Such "historical processual" approaches—for which Timothy R. Pauketat and his colleagues are the leading voices in the region—are routinely being employed in southeastern Mississippian and Contact period research, and increasingly in the study of earlier periods as well (e.g., Blitz 2009, 2012; Cobb, ed. 2003; Marcoux and Wilson 2010;

Pauketat 2001, 2007, 2012; Pauketat, ed. 2012; Pluckhahn 2003; Sassaman 2010a, 2010b). Neoevolutionary classifications, that is, determining whether a society was a "tribe" or a "chiefdom" or some subcategory thereof (i.e., apical/constituent, corporate/network, simple/complex) are no longer considered satisfying explanations nor, we would like to add, were they likely ever considered as such among serious researchers, especially those who applied these terms in the study of social and political dynamics in specific Mississippian societies (e.g., Anderson 1994; Beck 2003; King 2003a, 2003b; Marcoux and Wilson 2010; Steponaitis 1978; Wilson et al. 2006). Now heuristic devices employed in teaching and in broad general description, neoevolutionary terminology is losing its force in shaping research and thinking, as concerns about historical trajectories and human agency, and ritual economy as opposed to political economy, decision-making, and power structures become more prevalent in southeastern as well as Americanist archaeology in general (e.g., Hegmon 2003; Marcoux and Wilson 2010; Pauketat 2007; Pauketat, ed. 2012; Wilson 2010).

Cahokia appears to have played a crucial role in the emergence of Mississippian culture in the Southeast and lower Midwest. During the terminal Late Woodland considerable population growth occurred in the Central Mississippi Valley, and in the decades after A.D. 1000 at Cahokia and nearby centers a dramatic transformation of the social and physical landscape occurred, what has been described as the "Big Bang" by Pauketat (1997). The emergence of Cahokia, we now know, is actually part of a much larger story of the emergence and relationships between three closely spaced centers, the St. Louis, East St. Louis, and Cahokia mound groups—what Pauketat and Emerson (1997:9) call the "Central Political-Administrative Complex" (Figure 5-3)—as well as numerous outlying smaller centers, villages, and hamlets over the surrounding landscape in and near the American Bottom. The rapid appearance and growth of this society appears due to a coalescence or resettlement of peoples and cultures both locally and from across the region, perhaps from as far away as the lower Ohio and Mississippi river valleys, a "Big Crunch" that soon thereafter led to the "Big Bang," a cultural fluorescence that subsumes far more than its primary archaeological manifestation, the site of Cahokia (Alt 2002, 2006, 2008, 2010, 2012; Anderson 1997b; Emerson 1997, 2002; Milner 1998, 2004a, 2012; Pauketat 1997, 2003, 2004, 2007; Pauketat and Alt 2003, 2004; Pauketat and Emerson, eds. 1997). Cahokia and its affiliated sites was the most impressive

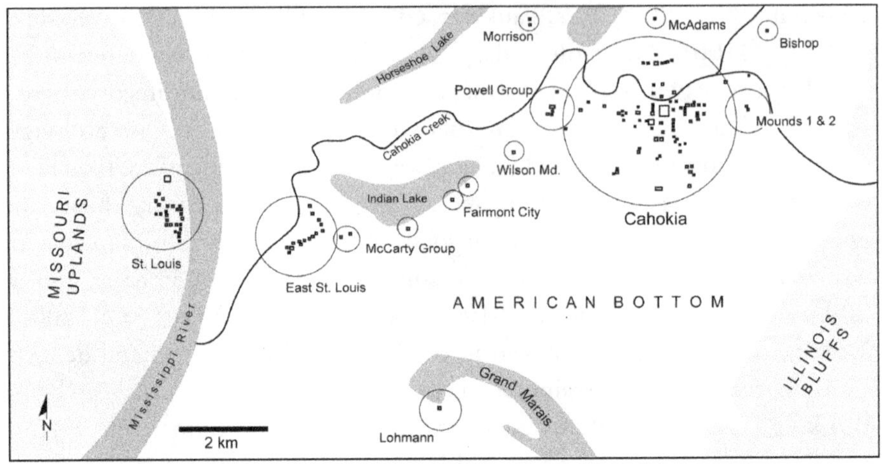

Figure 5-3. Mounds in and around Cahokia: the "Central Political-Administrative Complex." Image adapted from Pauketat and Emerson 1997:9.

and politically centralized prehistoric society ever to emerge in the Eastern Woodlands in terms of size, population, and organizational complexity as reflected in the extent of its monumental architecture. It was also the earliest full-blown expression of what we think of as Mississippian culture, and as such it undoubtedly influenced the behavior of contemporary societies, and those that came after, through its ceremony and ritual, its location astride the major communications artery of the continent, the Mississippi River, and, for its time, its unrivaled monumentality (Anderson 1997b; Pauketat and Emerson, eds. 1997; Pauketat and Emerson 1997; Pauketat 2004, 2007, 2009). A similar argument has been made for the extent of influence Poverty Point and other early singularly precocious centers had on regional developments, both in the Southeast and elsewhere in the Americas and beyond, with people "the desired resource and object of competition" whose presence and organization simultaneously came about through and led to the construction of monuments, both physical and spiritual, including networks of interaction and belief (Clark et al. 2010:238–240).

Described recently as a theater state—a pilgrimage center of ritual and drama on the landscape modeled after Geertz's (1980) Negara—it has been suggested that Cahokia's power and certainly its impact may have lain more in its ceremonialism, ideology, and iconography, and its monumental constructions, rather than in its military might (Holt 2009:232; Kehoe 1998;

Pauketat and Emerson, eds. 1997). Indeed, fortifications and the full extent of monuments like Monks Mound—when completed the second-largest earthen mound in the Americas behind only the Great Pyramid of Cholula—occurred only late in the center's history, suggesting its people had little need for them early on. Given the pronounced militaristic aspect to Cahokian iconography, even if other-wordly combat is sometimes what is being referenced (e.g., Dye 2004; Knight et al. 2001), the numbers of weapons and human sacrifices associated with presumed leaders at Mound 72 provide one of the most impressive and theatrical displays of power and legitimacy known from the archaeological record of the Americas (e.g., J. Brown 2003, 2004a, 2006; Fowler et al. 1999). The use of force, clearly, was not a foreign concept to these people. As an early, dramatic, and impressive example of what could be, Cahokia undoubtedly influenced subsequent developments, to the point where it might well be that "much of what we think of Mississippian across the region appears to be the idea of Cahokia writ large" (Anderson 1997b:263). In exploring the appearance and development of Mississippian societies across the region, we of course need to look at local and regional histories at multiple scales of analysis (Anderson 1999; Cobb and Garrow 1996; Pauketat 2007). There is no one simple explanation for the Mississippian emergence over time across the region (B. D. Smith 1990:2). Cahokia provided the spark, but local peoples built their own fires, which continued long after the original hearth had grown cold.

Agricultural Intensification and Environmental Change

The rise of intensive maize agriculture in the Southeast after A.D. 900 occurred during the Medieval Warm Period from ca. A.D. 800 to 1200, a time of global temperatures slightly warmer than average for the Holocene, and similar to those of today, with conditions thought to be favorable for agriculture in the Southeast, perhaps facilitating its rapid spread and adoption in many areas (Broecker 2001; Crowley 2000; B. D. Smith 1992). After about A.D. 1300 a cooling trend known as the Little Ice Age set in, which continued to about A.D. 1850, and the late prehistoric period in the Eastern Woodlands seems to have been a time of increased warfare and greater fortification of communities, settlement nucleation, and in some areas a decrease in monumental construction (Anderson 2001:165–167; Dye 2009:153–154; J. B. Griffin 1961:711–713; Livingood 2010:14–16; Milner 1999:125,

2012:445). For societies dependent upon agricultural food production, variation in climate would have assumed great importance. Successful harvests would have been essential not only to feed people, but to finance the social structure, through tribute mobilization and storage, and ensure stability through the alleviation of shortfalls. The potential of dendroarchaeology in the Southeast is being increasingly realized, not only for fine-scale dating purposes, but in the exploration of relationships between past climates and cultures (Anderson 1994; Anderson et al. 1995; Blanton 2000; Blanton and Thomas 2008; Grissino-Mayer 2009; Koerner et al. 2009; Stahle et al. 1985; Stahle et al. 1998; Stahle et al. 2007). Bald cypress and eastern red cedar growth rings are being used to reconstruct rainfall patterns over the past two millennia in parts of the region, with exceptional coverage now available over the past thousand years, encompassing the period when intensive maize agriculture was important in local life (Cook et al. 2007; Stahle et al. 2007). These reconstructions are being used with great effect to examine the influence of periods of increased, average, or decreased rainfall on local societies; not surprisingly, strong associations between climate and culture are noted (Anderson 1994; Anderson et al. 1995; Benson et al. 2009; Blanton 2000; Blanton and Thomas 2008; Blitz and Lorenz 2006; Meeks 2009; Meeks and Anderson 2012; Nolan and Cook 2010; Stahle et al. 1998).

Large areal "abandonments" or more properly population relocation, resettlement, and reorganization are common across the region during the late prehistoric and Contact era (Anderson 1991b, 1996c; Milner et al. 2001). The movements of historic Native peoples are well documented in the region, and similar processes were occurring in the late prehistoric era (and perhaps well back into the past, if the "Dalton collapse" or the abandonment of numerous coastal Archaic sites due to sea-level fluctuations are any indication), albeit for somewhat different reasons. Portions of major drainages like the Chattahoochee, Savannah, or the Tennessee valleys were depopulated during the later Mississippian period, for example (Anderson 1991b, 1994, 1996; Blitz and Lorenz 2006; Meeks 2009; Meeks and Anderson 2012; Milner et al. 2001), but the most famous example is the "Vacant Quarter hypothesis" first advanced by Stephen Williams (1983, 1990, 2001), the observation that significant depopulation, if not outright abandonment of sites and centers, occurred in the central Mississippi Valley and adjoining areas of the lower Midwest and Midsouth in the late prehistoric era. The abandonment of the Cahokia site, following a century-long period of increasing fortification and declining population, is perhaps the exemplar of what was occurring, but the effects were more widespread, encompassing occupations in portions of the central Mississippi, lower Ohio, and lower Tennessee River drainages (Benson et al. 2009; Cobb and Butler 2002; Mainfort 2001; Meeks 2009; Meeks and Anderson 2012). While originally thought to be linked to regional political conditions and specifically threats of or actual warfare, these abandonments are now thought to have also been caused, at least in part, by climate change, and specifically extended periods of decreased precipitation, or "megadroughts" (e.g., Stahle et al. 2007). Climate-induced political instability contributing to subsequent abandonment was first proposed for the Savannah River basin and adjoining areas during the late Mississippian and early Spanish colonial period about twenty years ago (Anderson 1994; Anderson et al. 1995). This argument has subsequently been tied to crises during the initial English settlements at Roanoke and Jamestown (Blanton 2000; Stahle et al. 1998), and to other late prehistoric depopulations, along the lower Chattahoochee River, and across the Vacant Quarter itself (e.g., Benson et al. 2009; Blitz and Lorenz 2006; Meeks and Anderson 2012; Nolan and Cook 2010). While the causes of abandonments and resettlements in the late prehistoric and early historic Southeast were undoubtedly complex and involved multiple factors, including warfare and the formation of alliances and buffer zones, coalescence among scattered groups, and the effects of disease induced depopulation, the role climate played is receiving increasing attention, something undoubtedly because of the importance it has for our own civilization (e.g., Anderson, Maasch, Sandweiss, and Mayewki 2007; Anderson, Maasch, and Sandweiss 2012; Sassaman 2012).

Characteristics of Mississippian Complexity

During the Mississippian period individual societies of varying size and complexity were widespread across the Southeast. Recognizing and determining the size, spatial extent, and temporal duration of these societies has received considerable research attention, including a long tradition of determining the extent of ceramic, gorget, or other artifact style zones within the region (e.g., Griffin 1967; Hally 1993, 1994b, 2006; Smith 2000). Population estimates for individual Mississippian societies have been advanced and debated, based on measures of house size and duration or the extent and fertility of arable agricultural land, and while estimates vary, they are not wildly far apart, at least among archaeologists (cf. Milner 1998; Muller 1997; Pauketat and Lopinot 1997). Most societies appear to have had from a few hundred to few thousand people, with perhaps 15,000 or so living at and near Cahokia at its peak about A.D. 1100. Population estimates at a larger scale, for all of Eastern North America, have also been variously proposed for the late prehistoric/early historic era, based on historic accounts and where archaeological sites were located on the landscape (e.g., Muller 1997; Ubelaker 2006). A recently published analysis ranges from between .5 to 2.6 million people, with a best estimate somewhere in the middle (Milner and Chaplin 2010), comparable to Ubelaker's (2006) estimate of about a million for eastern populations. These are well below estimates advanced by other scholars based primarily on historic accounts (e.g., Dobyns 1983), but probably more realistic given their literal grounding. The archaeological evidence still indicates large numbers of people, probably upwards of half a million, were living in the Southeast at Contact in about A.D. 1500, and that a significant decline in their numbers occurred in the centuries that immediately followed (Milner and Chaplin 2010; Milner et al. 2001).

Individual Mississippian societies emerged and declined across the landscape, rarely existing for more than a century or two, with the expansion of one typically at the expense of others elsewhere in the surrounding region, in processes variously described as cycling or fission-fusion, with individual cases shaped by a multiplicity of factors (e.g., Anderson 1994, 1996c; Blitz 1999). Regional-scale maps at century or longer intervals are becoming fairly common in local syntheses, and they show these societies appearing and disappearing in a pattern comparable to the blinking lights on a Christmas tree (e.g., Anderson 1991b; Hally 1999, 2006; Milner et al. 2001). The actual recognition of such societies has proven challenging, with the distribution of distinctive artifacts and sites and centers on the landscape receiving considerable attention in recent decades (e.g., Lipo et al. 2005; Mainfort 2001, 2003; B. D. Smith 1978; Steponaitis 1978). David Hally (1993), in a classic study, examined the spacing and duration of mound centers in northern Georgia, documenting two major groupings, those within 18 km of one another that he argued were within the same polity if contemporaneous, and a grouping greater than ca. 32 km apart that he argued were in different polities. The polities Hally identified were to some extent reflected in ceramic style zones or phases, work he has continued to refine (Hally 1993,

1996, 1999, 2006). Subsequent work by Livingood (2012), focusing on least-cost pathways as opposed to straight line distances and including water as well as overland travel, shows essentially the same groupings, with travel time (less than six hours and beyond this distance) providing the significant difference. Hally (1993, 1996) also examined the duration of these societies, by determining the numbers of and periodicity of construction episodes or stages in the mounds at centers. Major periods of construction tended to occur at about 25- to 50-year intervals, with most societies rarely lasting longer than a century or two (Hally 1993:145, 1996:112, 124, see also Anderson 1994:126–129; Blitz and Livingood 2004:295–299). Blitz and Livingood (2004:298–299), in a follow-up study, found that these patterns were less obvious at the largest Mississippian centers, where mound volume was much greater, requiring the cooperative activity of much larger numbers of people and presumably multiple social groups. At the largest sites, they suggest, construction episodes were more likely to be subject to "unpredictable or volatile sociopolitical events directed by powerful chiefs and less by regular or predictable social rules such as periodic renewal ceremonies" (Blitz and Livingood 2004:299). The duration of the largest centers, interestingly, was not obviously different (i.e., longer or shorter) than smaller sites in both studies, indicating these societies were fairly unstable, regardless of size (cf. Gavrilets et al. 2010).

The location of Mississippian sites and centers on the landscape has been used to construct models of political organization and tribute flow, from the movement of subsistence and craft goods to regional patterning in settlements. A classic example used by regional specialists is that of simple and complex chiefdoms, to which paramount chiefdoms were later added, that are differentiated on the basis of apparent levels in regional settlement hierarchies. This framework has been used to examine the flow of subsistence as well as other goods between sites or levels (e.g., Barker 1999; Steponaitis 1978, 1981; Welch 1991), as well as to advance models to explain the emergence, collapse, and re-emergence of complex and paramount chiefdoms across a regional landscape, or cycling (Anderson 1994, 1996c), a process first described archaeologically in ancient Mesopotamia by Henry Wright (1984), and by Sahlins (1963:298–299) based on Polynesian history and ethnography. Careful examination of site distributions suggests other processes were also operating, of which Blitz's (1999) fission-fusion model—the aggregation and dispersal of populations at and away from centers—is an important alternative that reflects events observed commonly in the historic period, and one that appears to also accommodate greater variability in prehistoric site distributions, at least in areas where these alternatives have been carefully examined (e.g., Blitz 1999; see also Beck 2003; Hally 1996:126; King 2012). While there is no question that elite provisioning by commoners occurred in at least some local societies, based on historic accounts as well as archaeological analyses of subsistence remains (e.g., Jackson and Scott 2003; Welch and Scarry 1995), whether most tributary economies were anywhere near as formal as those in state-level societies is highly debatable, especially given the diversity in size of Mississippian polities in the region. Economic and political relationships were more typically situational and transitory, reflecting "alliance more than true hegemony... [and] constantly subject to fragmentation and realignment as political and military fortunes changed" (Steponaitis 1986:391). Increasingly, research directed to Mississippian organization privileges the ritual and sacred as well as the political or secular economy, and avoids reifying assumptions behind rigid typological constructs like the chiefdom (e.g., J. Brown 2004a, 2006; Dye 2012; A. King 2004; Marcoux and Wilson 2010; Pauketat 2007, 2009).

One characteristic all scholars can agree on when considering Mississippian societies in the region is that many were characterized by impressive monumental architecture. Mounds and structures arranged around plazas are a common theme, with surrounding fortification ditches and palisades in many cases. That there was a detailed architectural grammar—a standardized community plan reflecting an approved way to lay out sites—appears unlikely given the variation evident from site to site, except at the most general level of mounds or ceremonial buildings fronting on plazas (cf. Gougeon 2007; Holley 1999; Lewis et al. 1998; Pauketat 2007; Rees 2012; Williams 1995). Indeed, arrangements of people and architecture around open spaces appear to have great antiquity in the region, dating back to the Mid-Holocene and possibly much further. While the effort used to build mounds has long been appreciated, in recent years it has been realized that in some cases it was even more involved and ritually charged than once thought, with great care given the selection and processing of fills, some of which were colored and mixed and cleaned before deposition (Pursell 2004; Sherwood and Kidder 2011) (Box 5-2). Mound building and use varied over the region and over time, with the largest multimound groups occurring in the western part of the region and overall construction peaking around A.D. 1200 to 1300

Box 5-2. Monument Construction as Ceremonial Behavior

How mounds were built from both practical engineering and ritual/ceremonial perspectives has received increased attention in the Southeast in recent years, thanks to combinations of meticulous excavation, specialized geoarchaeological analyses, and the recognition that the process of monument creation was as important, if not more important, than the finished product. While religious structures and symbols have long been identified on top of or under mounds, in the form of temples, charnel houses, burials, or tombs, only comparatively recently has it been recognized that the process of building the mounds was, in most if not all cases, a ritually charged and in some cases highly structured communal activity (e.g., Knight 1986). Evidence for specialized disposal patterns, of ceramic or feasting debris, down particular sides or corners of mounds was first recognized by Marvin Smith and Mark Williams (1994). Work at Cahokia's Monks Mound, Poverty Point, and Shiloh over the past decade has shown the high level of skill and ceremony involved in their creation, making southeastern mound builders true "DaVinci's of Dirt" (Sherwood and Kidder 2011) (Figure 5B-2). The recognition that some mound fills were unusual in color or texture has, of course, been long known, but research only rarely focused on how mound construction took place and the symbolic and ritual aspects of that behavior. The discovery of elaborately colored and processed fills at the principal mound at the Shiloh site in 2001 helped change the assumption that southeastern mound construction was an uncomplicated, simply conceived exercise in earthmoving, and that upon completion of a new stage the mound was maintained in green, closely cropped grass, a stereotype reinforced in many popular paintings and museum displays of Mississippian mound groups (Anderson 2012b; Anderson and Cornelison 2002; Anderson, Cornelison, and Sherwood 2012; Pauketat 2007; Sherwood and Kidder 2011; Welch 2006). Vegetation cover would reduce erosion of mound faces (e.g., Van Nest et al. 2001), but so too would clay caps, which could probably be more easily maintained by peoples lacking lawnmowers and weed wackers; the clay caps could also be colored, reinforcing the sym-

Figure 5B-2. Complex fill deposits at Shiloh Mound A. Image courtesy Southeast Archeological Center, National Park Service.

bolic message conveyed by the mound. Similar unusually colored and elaborately processed fills were subsequently recognized at many other late prehistoric mound sites in the region, and at other mounds at Shiloh itself, making the discovery less aberrant than the excavators originally thought (e.g., Pauketat 2007:98–99; Pursell 2004; Sherwood and Kidder 2011; Welch 2006:257–258). Given the widespread occurrence of color symbolism in the region—of which the red/war and white/peace towns of the Creeks are perhaps the most famous example (DeBoer 2005; Hudson 1976:235; Lankford 1987; Rodning 2010:63–66)—that it was applied to mound fills and surfaces is not at all surprising, at least in retrospect. Specialized geoarchaeological analyses of the Shiloh Mound A deposits by Sarah Sherwood (2006; Sherwood and Kidder 2011), one of the project directors, revealed how unusual these fills were, reflecting appreciable labor in collection and processing. Some were mixtures of materials of different colors and textures, and had been carefully selected and cleaned before being laid down in deposits ranging from thin veneers to massive loads. Subsequent work later in the decade at Poverty Point and at Cahokia reinforced the view that mound building was a sophisticated and likely ritually significant activity, requiring skills in ceremony, soils engineering, and labor management (e.g., Kidder 2011, 2012; Kidder et al. 2008; Kidder et al. 2009; Sherwood and Kidder 2011). These studies indicate that traditional labor estimates based simply on moving fill from one point to another considerably underestimate the effort involved (cf. Anderson 2012b; Milner 1998; Muller 1997; Sherwood and Kidder 2011). Mound stages where nearby midden or unprocessed fills were used required far less labor to build, and probably were created with far less ceremony, than stages built from carefully selected and processed deposits. Comparisons between centers need to consider more than just the size of mounds in the resolution of political hierarchies or relationships, but also must take into consideration the way they were constructed.

and declining thereafter (Livingood 2010:14–16), suggesting changes in authority structures and ceremony, although mounds continued to be built into the early historic era. In recent years it has also been recognized that large amounts of labor went into the construction of plazas, involving the cutting and filling of terrain to create a level surface (Alt et al. 2010; Dalan 1997; Dalan et al. 2003; Holley 1999; Holley et al. 1993; Kidder 2001, 2004b; Pauketat 2007:93–96). Plazas, and where present surrounding ditch and palisade lines, served to anchor and demarcate communities (e.g., Milner 1998:147–148; Pauketat 2007:99–101). Traditional comparisons between centers based on mound volume alone, in an attempt to determine their relative power and importance, thus likely seriously underestimate or misrepresent the actual labor involved; size mattered, but so too did the effort involved in creating these public landscapes (e.g., Anderson 2012b; Hammerstedt 2005; Pauketat 2007; Sherwood and Kidder 2011).

The location, size, and arrangement of monuments and other architectural features like screening walls, houses, and storage, cooking, and crafting areas within Mississippian (and earlier) communities reflected and reinforced the social order, the spatial distribution of peoples by status, kin group, and gender (e.g., DeBoer 1988; Gougeon 2006, 2007; Knight 1998; Steponaitis 1986:390; Sullivan 1987, 2006; Sullivan and Rodning 2001, 2011; Vanderwarker and Detwiler 2002; Wilson 2008). Knight (1998, 2010) has suggested that the occurrence of paired mounds at the Moundville site represented the residence and mortuary/burial areas of ranked clans, whose status or power was reflected in their size and placement on the plaza and with regard to principal mounds. Such arguments have been applied to earlier monuments of earth and shell in the region, and may reflect a pattern dating well back into the Archaic (Russo 2004). Building monuments, while likely an important part of religious life and ritual among southeastern peoples (Knight 1986) was not the only form of public ceremony. Plazas were apparently the scene of games like chunky as well as of large scale communal feasting and ceremonies like the historic busk or green corn festival, types of activities that probably had a long tradition in the region. Public feasting in or near the central plaza was clearly occurring on a monumental scale at early Cahokia, and "may encapsulate the process by which people accepted or accommodated (or even resisted) a Cahokian organization, identity, or way of life" (Pauketat et al. 2002:275).

Personal status was indicated a number of ways in Mississippian society. Mortuary ritual indicated the relative social positions of the living as well as the deceased by the nature of associated grave goods, as well as the use of space, specifically the location of graves in mound or mortuary as opposed to village contexts (e.g., Peebles and Kus 1977; Sullivan and Mainfort 2010). Status was signaled by dress in the historic period, a pattern also evident in the prehistoric era as well, as indicated by textile color and manufacturing complexity at sites like Bottle Creek, Spiro, and Wickliffe (Drooker 1992, 2003; Hudson 1976; Kuttruff 1993). Elites and commoners also differed in the foods they ate and the vessels these were served in, at least in some societies and in public as opposed to private settings (e.g., Blitz 1993b; Hally 1986; Pauketat and Emerson 1991). Special cuts of meat and maize were sometimes received as tribute, and consumed in special serving vessels as opposed to more utilitarian cooking vessels (e.g., Blitz 1993b; Jackson and Scott 2003; Welch and Scarry 1995). While there were differences in diet and health between individuals and groups, status was to some extent malleable, and was related to abilities in crafting, warfare, ceremony, or community affairs, for both men and women (Dye 2009; Sullivan 2006; Wilson 2008).

Exchange and Iconography

During the Mississippian period elaborate finely crafted objects of copper, pottery, shell, stone, wood, and other materials circulated throughout the Southeast, many characterized by distinctive artistic styles and motifs that have come to be associated with specific sites, areas, or time periods (Figures 5-4, 5-5). The similar nature of the artwork found at a number of major centers led to the inference that they were of symbolic and religious significance, representing a "Southern Cult" that had occurred widely across the region in the immediate Pre-Contact era (Waring and Holder 1945). Since renamed the Southeastern Ceremonial Complex, or SECC (Galloway 1989; King 2007), and most recently characterized as the Mississippian Ideological Interaction Sphere (MIIS; Lankford et al. 2011; Reilly and Garber 2007:3), the diversity of styles, motifs, and materials lumped under this complex is now widely acknowledged, to the point where SECC has come to refer to almost any object or depiction of symbolic art produced during the Mississippian period. Knight (2006) has, in fact, noted that the SECC concept is problematic and needs to be discarded, because it is not a complex, it is not

Figure 5-4. Mississippian iconographic art: (top left) seated female figurine from Desha County, Arkansas; (top right) kneeling male figurine from Shiloh, Tennessee; (center left) Birdman gorget from Etowah, Georgia; (center right) headpot from Shawnee Village, Arkansas; (bottom) and Dover "sword" from Humphreys, County, Tennessee. Artifact photographs by David H. Dye, used with permission.

Figure 5-5. Mississippian iconographic art: (top left) Great serpent/underwater panther pottery vessel from Mississippi County, Arkansas; (top right) pottery vessel with hand and eye motif from Moundville, Alabama; (center) palette with hand and eye motif surrounded by intertwined serpents from Moundville, Alabama; (bottom) and presumed mortuary temple statuary from Etowah, Georgia, and Sellars Mound, Tennessee. Artifact photographs by David H. Dye, used with permission.

exclusively southeastern, nor is it entirely ceremonial in nature. Instead, Knight (2006:2) calls for the careful evaluation of the variability in "the separate domains of art style, iconographic context, ritual practice, and exchange" present in the region. Such an approach, in fact, characterizes current research. A revolution in the study of Mississippian art, iconography, and religion has occurred in southeastern archaeology in recent years, which includes the recognition of distinctive styles and their areas of origin, such as Braden at early Cahokia or Craig at Spiro (e.g., J. Brown 2004a, 2011; Kelly 2006; Phillips and Brown 1978). The production of these objects entailed the use of distinctive motifs and religious beliefs in the creation and maintenance of a Mississippian identity.

The growing literature about Mississippian symbolic artwork includes several truly magnificent scholarly as well as visually stimulating compilations (e.g., Brose et al. 1985; Phillips and Brown 1976; Townsend and Sharp 2004) as well as an impressive body of specific scholarly analyses addressing the meaning behind the art and objects (e.g., I. Brown 1989, 2006; J. Brown 1997, 2004a, 2006, 2011; Diaz-Granádos et al. 2001; Dye 2004, 2007; Emerson 1989, 1997; Emerson et al. 2003; Hall 1997; Lankford 2004, 2007; Lankford et al. 2011; Pauketat and Emerson 1991; Prentice 1986; Reilly 2004; Reilly and Garber, eds. 2007; Reilly and Garber 2007; Smith and Miller 2009; to cite but a few of the many recent studies that have appeared). Effort has been directed to specific portable artifact categories, such as figurines or paint palettes, the latter of which are now thought to be part of bundled ritual gear or portable altars (e.g., Steponaitis and Knight 2004:174–175; Steponaitis et al. 2011) (Figure 5–5). Not all elaborate Mississippian artifacts, we now recognize, were "prestige goods" demarcating elite status; many figured in both private and public ritual and ceremony (Marcoux and Wilson 2010; Steponaitis et al. 2011; Wilson 2008). Research has also focused on fixed artwork, including designs drawn into mud deposits in caves, as well as petroglyphs and pictographs in a range of settings, such as caves, rock shelters, cliff faces, or open surfaces (Crothers et al. 2002; Diaz-Granádos 2004; Diaz-Granádos and Duncan 2000, 2004; Faulkner 1986, 1997; Simek and Cressler 2004, 2008; Simek et al. 1997, 2001). Much of this artwork is quite late, dating to the Late Archaic, Woodland, Mississippian, and Contact eras. This late temporal placement may be subject to change, since the existence of cave art of any kind in the region was unknown as recently as a quarter of a century ago, and new discoveries are being made every year. Spectacular examples of cave art are now known to exist in the region, of which perhaps the most dramatic are Mud Glyph Cave in Tennessee (Faulkner 1986) and Picture Cave in Missouri. At the latter site, the dating of the impressive artwork to about A.D. 1000—with its detailed images of people using bows and arrows and maces, as well as bird man/falcon warrior, Long-Nosed God, and concentric circle shoulder iconography of the Braden style—further supports the idea that Cahokia was a center for the emergence of Mississippian religion and iconography (J. Brown 2004a:113; Diaz-Granádos 2004:142–147; Diaz-Granádos et al. 2001).

Southeastern archaeologists have long had an interest in tracing exchange through studies of the occurrence of artifacts of local as opposed to extralocal origin, for which a vast literature exists encompassing every period (e.g., Brown et al. 1990; Gibson 1994; J. Johnson 1994; Lafferty 1994; Steponaitis 1983, 1986). Studies of exchange have received a tremendous boost in recent years through the use of a variety of sophisticated techniques for sourcing materials. Such research has encompassed Cahokian effigy pipes, now known to have been made from nearby Missouri flint clay (Emerson and Hughes 2000; Emerson et al. 2003), and that circulated widely in the lower Southeast. Limestone effigy pipes found over the lower Mississippi River valley are now known to have been made from the Glendon Limestone near Vicksburg, Mississippi, based on the identification of distinctive marker fossils (Steponaitis and Dockery 2011). Analyses of *Busycon* shells using atomic absorption spectroscopy have resolved approximate source areas along the Atlantic and Gulf coasts (Claassen and Sigmann 1993). Similar studies with pottery using instrumental neutron activation analysis have revealed four large clay mineral subregions with fairly distinctive signatures over the Southeast; more specific source areas for clays used in vessel manufacture have also been documented (e.g., Lynott et al. 2000; Steponaitis et al. 1996). Perishable goods were of course also widely circulated, such as salt, feathers, wooden objects, and no doubt many other materials as indicated by Contact-era sources, but resolution of this exchange remains difficult, save in settings where unusual preservation occurs (e.g., Brown 1980, 1999a; Hudson 1976; Krech 2009).

Exchange with peoples outside of the Southeast proper was probably a good deal more extensive than we currently recognize during the Mississippian era. Clear ties with source areas in the upper Midwest are demonstrated in the occurrence of copper and other materials, whose movement over large areas of the East dates back to the Middle Archaic period (J. Brown 2004b; Brown et al. 1990; Sassaman 2010a). Contact with the Plains and perhaps more indirectly with the Southwest are also indicated by the presence of *Olivella* shells from the Gulf of California at Spiro (Kozuch 2002), as well as other artifacts from agricultural crops to aspects of ceremonialism (I. Brown 1999b; J. Brown 2004b; N. White 2005; N. White and Weinstein 2008). *Olivella* shells are thought to have come from the Southwest onto the Plains, where they are fairly common in late prehistoric sites, and moved from there into the Mississippian world through gateway communities like Spiro (Hoard and Chaney 2010; Kozuch 2002). An obsidian scraper from the Great Mortuary at Craig Mound at Spiro was found to have come from a source near Pachuca, Hidalgo, some 100 km northeast of Mexico City, representing the first securely documented example of an artifact from Mesoamerica in Mississippian context (Barker et al. 2002). Some scholars see these interregional connections as more significant and enduring throughout prehistory than currently assumed, and argue that the comparative study of the large-scale processes common to and possibly shared between these regions is worthy of far more research than they receive at present (e.g., Lekson and Peregrine 2004; Neitzel 1999; Peregrine and Lekson 2006, 2012).

Contact Period Changes: Collapse and Coalescence

Native peoples had been living in the Southeast for upwards of 13,000 years when European contact occurred, and while they had experienced significant changes in climate and environment, and brought about great changes on the landscape and in their cultures, the centuries that followed were a time of great challenge and dramatic, transformative events. European contact was intermittent and largely restricted to coastal areas initially, but in the mid-sixteenth century a series of entradas penetrated well into the interior, including expeditions led by Hernando de Soto (1539–1543), Tristran de Luna (1559–1561), and Juan Pardo (1566–1568), whose legacies were significant and in many ways catastrophic (e.g., Clayton et al. 1993; Hudson 1990, 1997; Thomas 1990) (Figure 5–6). Perhaps the most immediate consequence of European contact, and one that persisted for centuries, was widespread death due to diseases to which the Native peoples had no resistance. While the rates and routes of depopulation that occurred in the six-

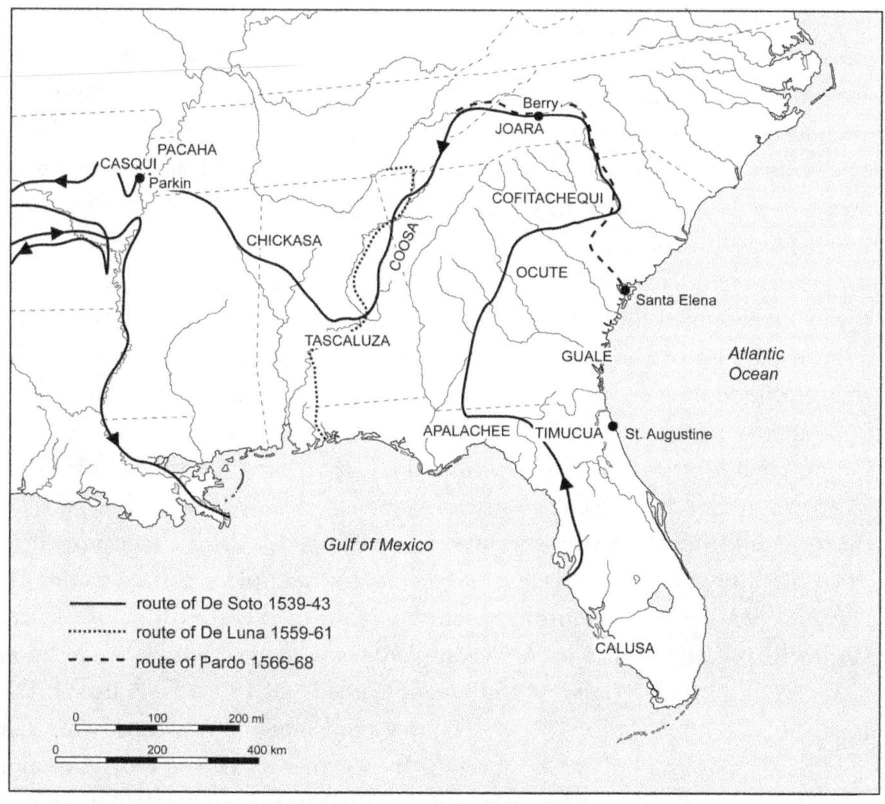

Figure 5-6. Sixteenth-century Spanish expeditions in the southeastern United States.

teenth and seventeenth centuries and after have been the subject of appreciable scholarly debate, there is unanimity that it was substantial, especially in areas visited or frequented by Europeans (e.g., Dobyns 1983; Smith 1994; Milner et al. 2001).

Reconstructing the routes of early explorers in the region and identifying the locations of early Native settlements and societies has received considerable attention in recent years, thanks in great measure to the work of Charles Hudson and his colleagues (e.g., Hudson 1990, 1997; Hudson et al. 1985; Milanich and Hudson 1993), albeit not without appreciable debate and refinement (e.g., Boyd and Schroedl 1987; Galloway 2005; Young and Hoffman 1993). The routes of the De Soto and Pardo expeditions in particular have been examined in such detail that where they traversed is now thought to be known with a high degree of confidence in some, but by no means all, parts of the region. Earlier reconstructions of the route (e.g., Jones 1873; Swanton 1939), as a result, are now known to have been significantly in error, particularly in the eastern part of the region, where the province of Cofitachequi is now known to be along the Wateree River and not the Savannah, over 100 miles to the east of where it was traditionally located (cf. DePratter 1994; Hudson et al. 2008; Jones 1873; Swanton 1939). Most important for the study of the Native American Southeast, these expeditions provide eyewitness accounts of flourishing late Mississippian societies, albeit many in the eastern part of the region near the coast were already undergoing rapid change due to contact, primarily disease-induced depopulation. Many of the individual societies or provinces encountered by De Soto, complex or paramount chiefdoms in traditional terminology, have been the subject of intensive archaeological examination in recent years, fieldwork inspired in part, by the renewed interest in the accounts. De Soto's 1539–1540 encampment at the central town of the Apalachee in Florida, for example, has been examined (Ewan 1998), as have a number of Indian sites in the provinces of Ocute, Cofitachequi, and Coosa in the South Appalachian area, which the entrada traversed and briefly visited in 1540 (e.g., Cable et al. 1999; DePratter 1994; Hudson et al. 2008; Smith 2000). The town of Mabila in Alabama, where an epic battle was fought in October 1540, remains undiscovered, although plausible locations have been recently identified (cf. Hudson 1997; Knight 2009). Likewise, the fortified town of Casqui in Arkansas, where the expedition became caught up in the rivalries between local societies in the late spring and summer of 1541, has been fairly conclusively identified as the Parkin site, now a state park (Morse 1993; Morse and Morse 1990; Young and Hoffman 1993); in addition to a number of mid-sixteenth-century Spanish artifacts, the possible remains of the wooden cross De Soto erected atop the main mound have been found at the site (Mitchem 1996). The archaeological research directed to the routes of these early expeditions has focused, understandably, almost exclusively on Native American sites, markedly expanding our understanding of life in these societies, including about their subsistence practices, health and diet, political organization, the roles of women and men, the effects of warfare, and the uses to which European goods were put (e.g., DePratter 1991; Dye 2009; Hudson 1990, 1997; Smith 2000; Trocolli 2002). These provinces may not have had great time depth or internal homogeneity, but appear instead, a least in some cases, to reflect alliances or short-term confederations between otherwise essentially autonomous societies. The sixteenth-century province of Coosa, for example, although described by the early sources as one of the most extensive and powerful in the region (e.g., Hudson 1997; Hudson et al. 1985; Smith 2000), appears to have been made up of groups characterized by differences in material cultural and mortuary practices in northern Georgia and eastern Tennessee (Sullivan and Harle 2010; Sullivan and Rodning 2011), with little evidence for biological interaction between the peoples in these areas (Harle 2010). The identification and dating of some of the sites remains controversial or equivocal, as do some of the interpretations that have been made about the assemblages recovered, such as whether Spanish weapons trauma was present among Native burials at the King Site in northern Georgia (cf. Blakely and Mathews 1990; Milner et al. 2000).

Spanish interest in the interior Southeast waned in the later sixteenth century, after repeated failures in colonization and exploration, and after this time there was little Spanish contact, and hence minimal written records about interior groups (Box 5-3). The capital of the Spanish colonial province of *La Florida* was relocated from Santa Elena in coastal South Carolina to St. Augustine in northern coastal Florida after 1587, although an extensive series of missions occupied for varying lengths of time were maintained in the lower Atlantic and Gulf coastal portions of northern Florida and Georgia over the next century and a quarter. These were increasingly encroached upon by the English following the settlement of Jamestown in 1607 and especially Charleston in 1670, and most had been abandoned or destroyed by the early eighteenth century (McEwan 1993; Milanich 1999). Appreciable archival and archaeological research on these Spanish mission sites has been undertaken in recent decades, bringing to light a wealth of information about Native groups like the Apalachee, the Guale, and the Timucua, and their relations with each other and the Spanish (e.g., Hann 1988; Hann and McEwan 1998; Worth 1997, 1998a, 1998b, 2004). The missions of Santa Catalina de Guale on St. Catherines Island and San Luis among the Apalachee in particular have been the subject of sustained research, generating a wealth of archeological, bioarchaeological, and archival information, documenting the potential of such sites (e.g., Blair et al. 2009; Hann and McEwan 1998; Larsen 1990, 2001; Scarry and McEwan 1995; Shapiro and Hann 1990; Shapiro and McEwan 1992; Thomas 1987, 1993).

Box 5-3. The Discovery of Joara and 1567–1568 Fort San Juan

One of the most exciting discoveries in recent years in southeastern archaeology has been the recognition that the Berry site in western North Carolina is the location of the town of Joara, a major polity visited by the De Soto and Pardo expeditions in the mid-sixteenth century, and where the Spanish established and briefly maintained a garrison, Fort San Juan (Beck 1997; Hudson 1990). The remnants of this outpost on the Spanish colonial frontier, found at the site of the principal town in the powerful chiefdom and province of Joara, represent the earliest Spanish occupation found to date deep in the interior of the Southeast. The fieldwork is conducted by an array of students and specialists, and led by Rob Beck, David Moore, and Chris Rodning (Beck et al. 2006, 2011; Beck and Moore 2002; Moore et al. 2005; Rodning et al. 2012), whose excavation techniques are second to none. The project fieldwork is multidisciplinary in the truest sense of the word, with scholars in dendrochronology, geoarchaeology, paleoethnobotany, and zooarchaeology among other disciplines involved in the excavations and subsequent analyses. A group of five burned rectangular structures representing a Spanish compound were found at the northern edge of a Native American settlement, which, at five hectares in size, represents one of the largest early Contact era Native American towns in western North Carolina (Figure 5B-3).

The burned structures and associated pit features found at the Berry site comprise the remains of the 1567–1568 Spanish Fort San Juan, a garrison of 30 soldiers. The fort was established by the explorer Juan Pardo, who had been sent out from Santa Elena—then the capitol of the Spanish colonial province of *La Florida*, and located on the South Carolina coast near Beaufort on Parris Island, and itself the subject of extensive archaeological and historical research in recent decades by Stanley South and his colleagues (e.g., South 1980; South and DePratter 1996)—to find an overland path to Mexico and, most importantly, obtain food for the men, which was in short supply (Hudson 1990). Fort San Juan was occupied for 18 months and it, along with five other garrisons in the northern borderlands of *La Florida*, was destroyed when the native peoples rose up suddenly. The archaeological investigations have examined both the

Figure 5B-3. Structure 3, a Spanish building in Fort San Juan/ Joara, at the Berry Site, North Carolina. Image from Beck et al. 2006:73, courtesy Warren Wilson College.

Spanish and Native occupations, and one surprising finding has been that the inhabitants of Joara thrived for decades after the fort was destroyed. They covered the area where Fort San Juan was located with fill, simultaneously effacing and commemorating their triumph over the garrison. The descendants of the people of Joara—who not merely endured but prevailed—may have been one of the peoples who a century later coalesced to form the Catawba (Beck 2009; Davis and Riggs 2004; Moore 2002; Rudes et al. 2004).

Sustained English settlement in the Southeast began early in the seventeenth century in Virginia and somewhat later in South Carolina, in 1670, while sustained French settlement in the western part of the region did not begin until the very end of the seventeenth century (Saunt 2004). Following the early Spanish expeditions of the mid-sixteenth century, contact with interior groups was so infrequent in many parts of the region that the sixteenth and seventeenth centuries have been described as "The Forgotten Centuries" by some scholars (Hudson and Tesser 1994; see also Wesson and Rees 2002). For many of the large, populous, and complex Native societies of the interior, the Spanish expeditions of the mid-sixteenth century were the first and last to see them and leave written accounts behind. The European and Native sites and artifacts from this period, fortunately, have been the subject a great deal of research attention in recent years, which, when coupled with precise dating procedures, is permitting a better and better understanding of this crucial formative period in the history of the Native peoples of the region (e.g., Blair et al. 2009; Deagan and Thomas 2009; M. T. Smith 1987; Smith and Good 1982; Sullivan and Rodning 2010; Waselkov 2009)

The European colonial and capitalist agendas, and particularly the devastating effects of disease, slave trading, and the deerskin trade, transformed the entire Southeast into what Robbie Ethridge has called a *shatter zone* characterized by "political turmoil, cultural upheaval, dislocation, and social transformation" (Ethridge 2006:208; Ethridge and Shuck-Hall 2009; see also Thomas 1990; Waselkov 2004). Native populations were both a source of hides and furs as well as slaves for Europeans, and obtaining these resources were activities that often went hand in hand. Comparable in its devastating effects on local communities as introduced diseases, the Indian slave trade, which operated with greatest intensity from ca. 1640 to 1716—when the aftermath of the Yamasee War appears to have caused some reconsideration of the wisdom of using Indians as slaves—is receiving increased scholarly attention in recent years from historians and archaeologists alike (e.g., Dye 2009:159–160; Ethridge 2006; Ethridge and Shuck-Hall 2009; Gallay 2003, 2009; Marcoux 2010; Saunt 2004:134–136). Slavery caught up everybody in the region, as either as participants in militaristic slaving societies or as victims, and over time, often both (Ethridge 2006:208; Gallay 2003, 2009; Waselkov 2004:688–689). Likewise, archaeologists and historians have recently concentrated on the dynamics of the deerskin trade, which was coeval and extended later in time than the slave trade in the seventeenth and eighteenth centuries, with skins in great demand in English, Spanish, and French markets. This gave Native populations opportunities to play the colonists off against each other, as the Chickasaw and Creeks sometimes did, or to favor one colonial trading partner, such as the Spanish in the case of the Apalachee or the French in the case of the Tunica (Brain 1970; Brain et al. 1988; Braund 1996; Lapham 2005; Johnson et al. 2008; Marcoux 2010; Saunt 2004:132–134; Worth 2002).

The Contact era was a time of great tragedy for Native Americans in the region, but another story that emerges is their remarkable resiliency. As chiefdoms and their successor societies dissolved or collapsed due to depopulation and conflict as the ripple effects of sustained European contact radiated across the region, Native groups repeatedly coalesced and confederated into new entities (e.g., Ethridge 2006; Ethridge and Hudson 2002; Ethridge and Shuck-Hall 2009; Galloway 1994, 2005; Hahn 2004; Marcoux 2010; Pluckhahn and Ethridge 2006; Smith 2000; Wesson and Rees 2002). An extensive literature has developed in recent years linking the historical and archeological records of these societies, particularly those present when sustained settlement and travel into the interior began anew under the English and French. This work has encompassed groups from the Middle Atlantic like the Powhatan or the Monacan, the largest of which were paramountcies or confederacies (e.g., Gallivan 2003, 2007; Hantman 2001; Potter 1993), as well as many southeastern tribes like the Caddo, Choctaw, Cherokee, and Creek, to name a few of the many groups studied (e.g., Galloway 1995; Knight 1994; Marcoux 2010; Rodning 2009; Rogers and Sabo 2004; Schroedl 2000; Waselkov 2004; Waselkov and Smith 2000).

New methods were developed by Native peoples to bring about political integration and create a sense of ethnic identity, or old ones assumed increased importance, such as the replacement of mound residential and temple complexes by the town square with its four surrounding buildings among the Creeks or council/town houses among the Cherokee (Hahn 2004:20–21; Schroedl 2000; Waselkov 1993). Post-Contact era public architecture served many functions, but above all anchored and promoted a sense of identity among the people of a community, in a process called emplacement (Marcoux 2008, 2010:136–144; Rodning 2009, 2010), much as earlier mound architecture and before that cemeteries were used to represent people's claims to the land in what Wilson (2010:14) aptly calls "place-based identity politics." The integration of disparate Native peoples, which was happening throughout the early historic period, would have been facilitated by more open meetings and decision-making activities bringing together people in regular face-to-face interaction.

Communal buildings or council houses, what are sometimes called nodal structures, did not appear only following European contact, of course, but were present in the late prehistoric period in some areas (e.g., Anderson 1994:119–120; DePratter 1991:163–165; Emerson 1997:161–176; Sullivan 1987). In the early Mississippian period submound earthlodges like the famous one at Macon are found across the South Appalachian area, and are thought to have served as places of communal meeting and ceremony (e.g., Fairbanks 1946; Larson 1994; Rodning 2010:60–61; Rudolph 1984). Changes in public architecture and in the use of centers occurred throughout the Mississippian period, when sites such as Cahokia, Etowah, Moundville, Town Creek, and Wickliffe shifted from densely occupied residential communities to either lightly populated mortuary necropolises or were abandoned altogether (e.g., Boudreaux 2007; King 2003a; Knight 2010; Knight and Steponaitis 1998; Milner 1998; Pauketat 2009; Wesler and Fortner 2001).

While in some areas townhouses were repeatedly rebuilt, as at the Coweeta Creek site in southwestern North Carolina (Rodning 2009, 2010) and the Chattooga site in northwestern South Carolina (Schroedl 2000, 2001), their maintenance over the long term appears to have been tied to patterns of community stability and group mobility, and the impact these had on permanence of site occupation. Among Cherokee and Creek populations that became increasingly mobile, investment in large-scale fixed public architecture apparently declined, contributing to societal instability through a resulting diminution or loss of activities and features that symbolized group identity (Rodning 2009:655, 2010). Although townhouses continued to be built well into the nineteenth century among the Cherokee and other groups, community plans changed dramatically as a result, as nucleated towns gave way to dispersed settlements in some areas of the Appalachian Summit (Marcoux 2010; Rodning 2009; Schroedl 2000, 2001).

Changes in domestic architecture also varied over the Southeast following European contact. In eastern Tennessee, for example, late prehistoric and early historic Dallas and Mouse Creek phase houses included examples that were much larger than domestic structures among the Overhill Cherokee of the eighteenth and early nineteenth century, something thought linked to status differences between these groups, with the later peoples less hierarchical and more egalitarian in nature (Sullivan 1995; Wilson 2010:14–15). Creek and Cherokee domestic architecture also changed in response to the slave and deerskin trades, both of which helped to scatter and isolate households and disrupt communities, and bring about an increased preoccupation with defense (e.g., Marcoux 2010; Rodning 2007; Sullivan 1995; Waselkov 1993; Waselkov et al. 1990; Wesson 2008; Wilson 2010:14–15). Marcoux (2010:137) has argued that investment in Cherokee household construction and repair, and in the length of time these structures were occupied, declined following contact, and suggests that "the seventeenth century heralded the disintegration of the physical house as a material 'anchor' for the social group." In contrast, seventeenth-century Apalachee domestic architecture in northern Florida changed very little, with circular as opposed to rectangular residences continuing to be built, even where Native peoples were living in close proximity with the Spanish at missions. The same was true of community buildings, as illustrated at Mission San Luis located in what is now Tallahassee, where the Apalachee maintained a massive council house into the early eighteenth century instead of adopting European style public architecture like the church or friary, which were nearby on the landscape (e.g., Hann and McEwan 1998; Scarry and McEwan 1995; Shapiro and Hann 1990; Shapiro and McEwan 1992). The reconstructed council house at the state park at Mission San Luis gives visitors an appreciation for the size and seating capacity of these buildings, which could accommodate hundreds of people.

Subsistence practices and preferences likewise varied over the region among Natives and colonists, with both similarities and differences apparent. In early colonial St. Augustine, for example, Spanish populations consumed more and larger sharks than Native peoples, which appears be related to differences in fishing techniques, watercraft, and areas exploited (Reitz 2004). At the late seventeenth- and early eighteenth-century Upper Saratown community in North Carolina, group identity was maintained, in part, through the continued intensive use of traditional wild and domesticated plant foods and game, which were sometimes prepared in large earth ovens in public areas, presumably for large-scale communal feasting and ritual activities (Vanderwarker et al. 2007; Ward and Davis 1999:248). Public preparation of food, presumably by women, has also been documented in the open areas around the Contact era council house, a traditional male domain, at the Coweeta Creek site in North Carolina, suggesting that gender roles related to the use of public spaces in these societies were not as rigid as has sometimes been inferred (cf. Hudson 1976:260; Perdue 1998; Rodning 1999; Sullivan 2006; Sullivan and Rodning 2011; Vanderwarker and Detwiler 2002). Men and women had different but complementary and sometimes overlapping spheres of influence.

The deerskin trade brought about changes in Native hunting practices and toolkits, and apparently in portions of the southeastern landscape itself. Zooarchaeological examination of hunting preferences associated with deer skin trade have, for example, documented a replacement of small mammals like rabbit and squirrel with fur-bearing animals among the later seventeenth-century Chickasaw (Johnson et al. 2008:16). The Chickasaw's stone tool industry appears to have been reorganized in the early eighteenth century to emphasize well-made scrapers, to accommodate the demand for processed hides (Johnson 1997; Johnson et al. 2008). Changes were also observed in the landscape. An increase in fire frequency has been noted in the Coastal Plain of Alabama and Georgia in the early eighteenth century, and is inferred to have been caused, in part, by the use of fire in deer drives, which could encompass large areas (Foster and Cohen 2007). Wild game continued to be preferred by southeastern peoples, and it was only after the collapse of the deerskin trade that some Native groups intensified their use of introduced domestic animals (Pavao-Zuckerman 2007; Vanderwarker et al. 2007; Ward and Davis 1999:256). Goods obtained in exchange for hides frequently found their way into mortuary contexts; indicating some individuals and households were achieving considerable wealth, further undermining traditional authority structures already weakened by disease (Ward and Davis 1999:254–255; Waselkov 1993; Wesson 2008).

A Continuing Presence

Native peoples are present in the Southeast in large numbers, as are descendant communities and peoples in other parts of the country. Many of these groups are federally recognized nations and have responsibility for implementing tribal and federal preservation laws on tribal lands and in overseeing the stewardship of cultural resources (e.g., NATHPO 2012; Stapp and Burney 2002). Tribal preservation programs with Tribal Historic Preservation

Officers (THPOs) are in place throughout the region and beyond, including with the Poarch Band of the Creek Indians in Alabama, the Seminole Tribe of Florida, the Jena Band of Choctaw Indians and the Tunica-Biloxi Tribe in Louisiana, the Eastern Band of Cherokee Indians in North Carolina, and the Catawba Indian Nation in South Carolina. Oklahoma has the largest number of Indian Nations, since this is where many southeastern peoples were relocated in the 1830s by the federal government, together with peoples native to the area but with ties to the Southeast, such as the Caddo Nation, the Chickasaw Nation, the Choctaw Nation of Oklahoma, the Muscogee Creek Nation, and the Quapaw Tribe of Oklahoma, to give a partial listing. Many other Native peoples and communities exist that have been denied federal recognition, but that have been recognized at the state level; archaeology has contributed and has the potential to contribute evidence in such cases, and also regarding claims tied to NAGPRA (Campisi 2004; Levy 2001).

The archeological record of southeastern Native peoples, of course, does not end with the end of the colonial period, or upon Removal, and is increasingly the subject of study (Rubertone 2000). Archeological research has been directed to Native American households, and to battlefields and political capitals, like Horseshoe Bend in Alabama (Waselkov 1986), New Echota in Georgia (Elliott et al. 2003), and Fort Armistead along the Trail of Tears in eastern Tennessee (Riggs 2010). Working with Native peoples and ethnographers offers many benefits in the interpretation of these sites, specifically in the interpretation of features or items of material culture (e.g., Moore 1994). A number of Native American archaeologists work full time in the region, in THPO programs and in other settings, although greater participation is warranted given the extent and importance of the archaeological record, and fostering both communication and encouraging professional training are goals of both the SAA and SEAC.

As we have seen, the Native American occupation of the Southeast provides a record of human accomplishment equal to that achieved anywhere on the planet. Starting with initial settlement during the last Ice Age through the development of agriculture and elaborately organized societies in recent millennia, the peoples of the Southeast have much to tell us about what it has meant to be human, about subjects as varied as the colonization of continents to the development of complex societies, and everything imaginable in between. Archaeologists and Native peoples are increasingly working together to bring this record to light, which is critical, since the stories being uncovered and written are for all of our peoples. As Janet Levy (2001:45), in a summary of relationships between Indians and archeologists in the Southeast, noted, "The most fruitful Indian-archaeologist relationships will be those based on long-term, local communication and cooperation."

While establishing sound chronologies and cultural sequences, and carefully reporting finds and fieldwork remains fundamental to the practice of archaeology in the Southeast, the field is increasingly concerned with the people whose past we study. Scholars are now working all over the region, on sites of all eras, and on a wide range of topics from a number of theoretical perspectives. The focus of this research is on the variability that is evident in the archaeological record, and understanding it through the recognition of broad trends, patterns, and processes. Southeastern archaeologists are exploring a wide array of topics, of interest and value to many different publics, including descendant communities, and they are increasingly being assisted in the field and the laboratory by members of these publics. Reporting media are changing rapidly as well, with technical as well as popular summaries of much recent work available online or in books and journals. An innovative early example of the changeover is the *Excavating Occaneechi Town* CD that was released in 1998, reporting on a Contact period site in North Carolina, with numerous interactive features (Davis et al. 1998). Another more recent example is the study of the sixteenth-century Mississippian town at the King site in northwestern Georgia, which includes descriptions, analyses, and interpretations in traditional book format, together with a massive compendium of primary site data on an accompanying CD (Hally 2008). Our understanding of the long record of human achievement in the Southeast is rapidly growing and becoming more open and accessible all the time.

6

Long-Term Futures

Our goal in this volume has been to inform and to inspire students, established colleagues, and the public alike about the great gains southeastern archaeology has made in recent years, and why the Southeast is a great area in which to work. Characterized by an energetic, youthful, and growing population of researchers, Southeastern archaeologists are always looking for new blood to help us better understand the past occupation of region, and to find answers to the big questions of human existence. We believe many of these questions can be answered and that important new questions can be raised and explored in the Southeast, and that our region fosters opportunities for leadership in developing ways in which this may be done. Archaeology in the Southeast was once described as theoretically conservative (Dunnell 1990), but we believe archaeology in the region has the potential to contribute, and indeed is contributing, substantially to the development of archaeological theory, and to knowledge about major trends important in the history and prehistory of humankind. In these last few pages we look to the future, to some of the areas that we hope will attract attention, beyond many of the topics we have touched on so far.

One thing we need to deal with is information. So much fieldwork, analysis, and reporting have occurred in the Southeast in recent years that just keeping track of it all is a major challenge. Fortunately, a great deal of synthesis and interpretation is occurring, in part because many of the archeologists who started their careers in CRM during the '70s and '80s are reaching middle or even old age, and spending more time contemplating data rather than gathering new material. In this regard, the current era is beginning to resemble the two decades following the New Deal, when many reports were written and a number of syntheses were produced. A major difference this time, however, is that the national commitment to archaeology, as reflected in legislation like the National Historic Preservation Act, shows little sign of slowing down, with the result that masses of new information are pouring in all the time. Electronic data storage and manipulation technologies are being used to deal with the flood. Entire state site file, collection, and report records can now be scanned and stored on portable drives that fit into a pocket, and the data in them can be linked to a wide array of environmental and archival information using GIS-based information management approaches. This information can be maintained online, furthermore, making it easily accessible, and eliminating the need for massive archives, save perhaps only as long-term backups, and ensuring information is not lost to mischance like fire or theft. What is needed, of course, is the will and resources to migrate existing paper records to electronic format, and the ability to transcribe this information to new formats and storage media as needed. We will need people skilled in organizing and accessing such materials, making them useful to archaeological research and resource management concerns. Future generations of southeastern archaeologists should be spared the burden of maintaining massive libraries, or worry that the only copies of critical records will be lost or misplaced.

The need for a sustained commitment to archaeology will not go away; far from it, and southeastern archaeologists will need to continue to hone their skills at public education and politics to maintain the high degree of public support they currently enjoy. We need to ensure our work is of interest and relevance to the general public (Stottman 2011), but also to descendant populations, both Native American and those who came after (Swidler et al. 1997). Population growth and development is occurring at a rapid rate in the Southeast and these factors, and the likely impacts of climate change on sea level, biota, and erosion mean that cultural resource management and mitigation will be needed on massive scales in the years ahead. The enforcement of laws and regulations protecting cultural resources by federal, state, and tribal preservation office staff and land managers has resulted in a vast amount of work occurring in the region. Their contributions, and those of the site file managers and curation specialists who maintain the records of archaeological investigations, are critically important, and require our continued advocacy and support. There will also, of course, continue to be a need for highly skilled field and lab workers, people who can think critically and make the right choices to maximize information recovery and the opportunities to interpret this record. Southeastern archaeology has a long tradition of fieldwork and reporting, and closely linking theoretical approaches to the archaeological record, characteristics that will not change in the years to come. Indeed, openness to new ideas and flexibility in thinking will continue to be important hallmarks of professional behavior.

What will be also continue to be needed are overviews of major field projects past and present, as well as local, regional, and topical syntheses of work already accomplished, what it is telling us, and the kinds of questions we should be exploring in the future. A seeming rite of passage for aspiring and newly minted Ph.D.'s within the regional professional community over the past two decades has been writing books and monographs directed to this goal, as recounted in Chapter 1 and after. The production of these volumes has been supported by a number of university presses, research programs, and cultural resource management firms in the region, a contribution whose importance cannot be overstated. Finally, southeastern archaeology and archaeologists can provide important help to understanding and reaching solutions to major challenges facing our civilization, such as climate and environmental change (Anderson et al. 1995; Anderson, Maasch, Sandweiss, and Mayewski 2007; Anderson, Maasch, and Sandewiss 2012; Benson et al. 2009; R. Lewis 2000; Little 2003; Marquardt 1994). How human populations responded to sea-level fluctuations, often through displacement and resettlement, is being explored throughout prehistory in the Southeast, and is a subject of considerable relevance to our own civilization, given projections for sea-level rise in the twenty-first century and after. The dramatic postglacial flooding of the continental shelf and the ca. 1 to 4 m fluctuations in sea level that played out over the last few thousand years hold the potential to offer comparative perspectives on the development and transformation of temporalities, or senses of history and the future, under rapid climatic change (e.g., Sassaman 2012), and by helping to provide empirical data on decline, restructuring, and rebounding of coastal ecosystems, particularly resources of economic importance today, such as oysters, clams, and estuarine and pelagic fisheries. Documenting the coastal archaeological record will, we predict, take on increasing urgency in the decades to come, as will the record of those areas where these populations relocate. How past populations responded to changes in climate and biota and their impacts on the landscape through land clearing, use of fire, and the encouragement or overexploitation of resources offer important lessons for the future (e.g., Smith 2011). The emergence of robust programs of dendroclimatological research in the region and its linkage to the archaeological and historical record, for example, has led to an increased awareness that short-term fluctuations in temperature or rainfall can have significant impacts on crop yields and the societies dependent upon them, including the depopulation or abandonment of fairly large areas.

To conclude, it should be clear from the brief review presented in this volume that southeastern archaeology is a vibrant area of study, with research proceeding in multiple directions, making new and important discoveries all the time and exploring subjects of profound interest and relevance to modern society. We are optimistic about the future of archaeology in the Southeast.

References

Abrams, Marc D., and Gregory J. Nowacki

2008 Native Americans as Active and Passive Promoters of Mast and Fruit Trees in the Eastern USA. *The Holocene* 18:1123–1137.

Adovasio, James M., and C. Andrew Hemmings

2011 Inundated Landscapes and the Colonization of the Northeastern Gulf of Mexico. Paper presented in the session Submerged Prehistoric Sites Archaeology in the Americas: Method, Theory, and Results by Academic and CRM Projects Alike, organized by Michael K. Faught and Peter Leach. Society for American Archaeology 76th Annual Meeting, Sacramento, California.

Adovasio, James M., D. C. Hyland, and Olga Soffer

2004 Perishable Fiber Artifacts and the First Americans: New Implications. In *New Perspectives on the First Americans,* edited by Bradley T. Lepper and Robson Bonnichsen, pp. 157–164. Center for the Study of the First Americans, Texas A&M University Press, College Station.

Adovasio, James M., D. Pedler, J. Donahue, and R. Stuckenrath

1999 No Vestiges of a Beginning nor Prospect for an End: Two Decades of Debate on Meadowcroft Rockshelter. In *Ice Age Peoples of North America,* edited by R. Bonnichsen and K. Turnmire, pp. 416–431. Center for the Study of the First Americans, Corvallis, Oregon.

Alley, Richard B.

2000 The Younger Dryas Cold Interval as Viewed from Central Greenland. *Quaternary Science Reviews* 19:213–226.

Allison, N. L. Bindoff, R.A. Bindschadler, P.M. Cox, N. de Noblet, M.H. England, J.E. Francis, N. Gruber, A.M. Haywood, D.J. Karoly, G. Kaser, C. Le Quéré, T.M. Lenton, M.E. Mann, B.I. McNeil, A.J. Pitman, S. Rahmstorf, E. Rignot, H.J. Schellnhuber, S.H. Schneider, S.C. Sherwood, R.C.J. Somerville, K. Steffen, E.J. Steig, M. Visbeck, and A.J. Weaver

2009 *The Copenhagen Diagnosis, 2009: Updating the World on the Latest Climate Science.* University of New South Wales Climate Change Research Centre (CCRC), Sydney, Australia.

Alt, Susan M.

2002 Identities, Traditions and Diversity in Cahokia's Uplands. *Midcontinental Journal of Archaeology* 27:217–236.

2006 The Power of Diversity: The Roles of Migration and Hybridity in Culture Change. In *Leadership and Polity in Mississippian Society,* edited by Brian M. Butler and Paul D. Welch, pp. 289–308. Occasional Paper No. 33. Center for Archaeological Investigations, Southern Illinois University, Carbondale.

2008 Unwilling Immigrants: Culture, Change, and the "Other" in Mississippian Societies. In *Invisible Citizens: Slavery in Ancient Pre-State Societies,* edited by Catherine M. Cameron, pp. 205–222. University of Utah Press, Salt Lake City.

2010 Complexity in Action(s): Retelling the Cahokia Story. In *Ancient Complexities: New Perspectives in Precolumbian North America,* edited by Susan M. Alt, pp. 119–137. University of Utah Press, Salt Lake City.

2012 Making Mississippian at Cahokia. In *The Oxford Handbook of North American Archaeology,* edited by Timothy R. Pauketat, pp. 497–508. Oxford University Press, Oxford, UK.

Alt, Susan M., Jeffery D. Kruchten, and Timothy R. Pauketat

2010 The Construction and Use of Cahokia's Grand Plaza. *Journal of Field Archaeology* 35:131–146.

Alt, Susan M., and Timothy R. Pauketat

2011 Why Wall Trenches? *Southeastern Archaeology* 30:108–122.

Anderson, David G.

1975 Inferences from Distribution Studies of Prehistoric Artifacts in the Coastal Plain of South Carolina. *Southeastern Archaeological Conference, Bulletin* 18:180–194.

1990 The Paleoindian Colonization of Eastern North America: A View from the Southeastern United States. In *Early Paleoindian Economies of Eastern North America,* edited by Kenneth. B. Tankersley and Barry L. Isaac, pp. 163–216. Research in Economic Anthropology, Supplement 5. JAI Press, Greenwich, Connecticut.

1991a The Bifurcate Tradition in the South Atlantic Region. *Journal of Middle Atlantic Archaeology* 7:91–106.

1991b Examining Prehistoric Settlement Distribution in Eastern North America. *Archaeology of Eastern North America* 19:1–22.

1994 *The Savannah River Chiefdoms: Political Change in the Late Prehistoric Southeast.* University of Alabama Press, Tuscaloosa

1995 Paleoindian Interaction Networks in the Eastern Woodlands. In *Native American Interaction: Multiscalar Analyses and Interpretations in the Eastern Woodlands,* edited by Michael S. Nassaney and Kenneth E. Sassaman, pp. 1–26. University of Tennessee Press, Knoxville.

1996a Models of Paleoindian and Early Archaic Settlement in the Lower Southeast. In *The Paleoindian and Early Archaic Southeast,* edited by David G. Anderson and Kenneth E. Sassaman, pp. 29–45. University of Alabama Press, Tuscaloosa.

1996b Modeling Regional Settlement in the Archaic Period Southeast. In *Archaeology of the Mid–Holocene Southeast,* edited by Kenneth E. Sassaman and David G. Anderson, pp. 157–176. University Press of Florida, Gainesville.

1996c Chiefly Cycling and Large–Scale Abandonments as Viewed from the Savannah River Basin. In *Political Structure and Change in the Prehistoric Southeastern United States,* edited by John F. Scarry, pp. 150–191. University Press of Florida, Gainesville.

1997a Celebrating National Commitments to Archaeology: A National Commitment to Archaeology. In *Common Ground: Archaeology and Ethnography in the Public Interest* 2(1):12–19. (Issue guest editor). National Park Service Archeology and Ethnography Program, Washington, D.C.

1997b The Role of Cahokia in the Evolution of Mississippian Society. In *Cahokia: Domination and Ideology in the Mississippian World,* edited by Timothy R. Pauketat and Thomas E. Emerson, pp. 248–268. University of Nebraska Press, Lincoln.

1998 Swift Creek in a Regional Perspective. In *A World Engraved: Archaeology of the Swift Creek Culture,* edited by J. Mark Williams and Daniel T. Elliott, pp. 274–300. University of Alabama Press, Tuscaloosa.

1999 Examining Chiefdoms in the Southeast: An Application of Multiscalar Analysis. In *Great Towns and Regional Polities in the Prehistoric American Southwest and Southeast,* edited by Jill E. Neitzel, pp. 215–241. Amerind Foundation New World Study Series 3. University of New Mexico Press, Albuquerque.

2001 Climate and Culture Change in Prehistoric and Early Historic Eastern North America. *Archaeology of Eastern North America* 29:143–186.

2002a A History of Archaeological Research in South Carolina. In *Histories of Southeastern Archaeology*, edited by Shannon Tushingham, Jane Hill, and Charles H. McNutt, pp. 145–159. University of Alabama Press, Tuscaloosa.

2002b Evolution of Tribal Social Organization in the Southeast. In *The Archaeology of Tribal Societies*, edited by William A. Parkinson, pp. 246–277. International Monographs in Prehistory, Ann Arbor.

2004 Archaic Mounds and the Archaeology of Southeastern Tribal Societies. In *Signs of Power: The Rise of Cultural Complexity in the Southeast*, edited by Jon L. Gibson and Philip J. Carr, pp. 270–299. University of Alabama Press, Tuscaloosa.

2005 Pleistocene Human Occupation of the Southeastern United States: Research Directions for the Early 21st Century. In *Paleoamerican Origins: Beyond Clovis*, edited by Robson Bonnichsen, Bradley T. Lepper, Dennis Stanford, and Michael R. Waters, pp. 29–43. Texas A&M University Press, College Station.

2010 The End of the Southeastern Archaic: Regional Interaction and Archaeological Interpretation. In *Trend, Tradition, and Turmoil: What Happened to the Southeastern Archaic?* edited by David Hurst Thomas and Matthew C. Sanger, pp. 273–302. Proceedings of the Third Caldwell Conference, St. Catherines Island, Georgia, May 9–11, 2008. Anthropological Papers of the American Museum of Natural History 93, New York, New York.

2012a Paleoindian Archaeology in Eastern North America: Current Approaches and Future Directions. In *In the Eastern Fluted Point Tradition*, edited by Joseph A. M. Gingerich. University of Utah Press, Salt Lake City, in press.

2012b Monumentality in Eastern North America during the Mississippian Period. In *Early New World Monumentality*, edited by Richard L. Burger and Robert M. Rosenswig, pp. 78–108. University Press of Florida, Gainesville.

Anderson, David G., and John E. Cornelison, Jr.

2002 Excavations at Mound A, Shiloh: The 2002 Season. Paper presented at the 59th Annual Meeting of the Southeastern Archaeological Conference, Biloxi, Mississippi. Manuscript on file, Southeast Archeological Center, National Park Service, Tallahassee, Florida.

Anderson, David G., and Robbie Ethridge

2009 On Chiefdoms and Other Archaeological Delusions. *Native South* 2:69–73.

Anderson, David G., and J. Christopher Gillam

2000 Paleoindian Colonization of the Americas: Implications from an Examination of Physiography, Demography, and Artifact Distribution. *American Antiquity* 65:43–66.

Anderson, David G., and Glen T. Hanson

1988 Early Archaic Occupations in the Southeastern United States: A Case Study from the Savannah River Basin. *American Antiquity* 53:262–286.

Anderson, David G., and Virginia Horak (editors)

1995 *Archaeological Site File Management: A Southeastern Perspective*. Interagency Archeological Services Division, National Park Service, Southeast Regional Office, Atlanta, Georgia.

Anderson, David G., and J. W. Joseph

1988 *Prehistory and History along the Upper Savannah River: Technical Synthesis of Cultural Resource Investigations, Richard B. Russell Multiple Resource Area*. Russell Papers, Interagency Archeological Services Division, National Park Service. Atlanta, Georgia.

Anderson, David G., and Robert C. Mainfort, Jr.

2002 An Introduction to Woodland Archaeology in the Southeast. In *The Woodland Southeast*, edited by David G. Anderson and Robert C. Mainfort, Jr., pp. 1–19. University of Alabama Press, Tuscaloosa.

Anderson, David G., and Kenneth E. Sassaman (editors)
1996 *The Paleoindian and Early Archaic Southeast.* University of Alabama Press, Tuscaloosa.

Anderson, David G., and Kenneth E. Sassaman
1996 Modeling Paleoindian and Early Archaic Settlement in the Southeast: A Historical Perspective In *The Paleoindian and Early Archaic Southeast,* edited by David G. Anderson and Kenneth E. Sassaman, pp. 16–28. University of Alabama Press, Tuscaloosa.
2004 Early and Middle Holocene Periods, 9500–3750 B.C. In *Smithsonian Handbook of North American Indians, Volume 14, The Southeast,* edited by Raymond D. Fogelson, pp. 87–100. Smithsonian Institution, Washington, D.C.

Anderson, David G., and Marvin T. Smith
2003 Problems of the Past: Perspectives on Eastern North American Archaeology from Prehistory to the Seventeenth-Century. *Blackwell Companion to Colonial American History,* edited by Daniel Vickers, pp. 1–24. Blackwell Publishers, Ltd., Oxford.

Anderson, David G., and Steven D. Smith
2003 *Archaeology, History, and Predictive Modeling: Research on Fort Polk 1972–2002.* University of Alabama Press, Tuscaloosa.

Anderson, David G., David W. Stahle, and Malcolm R. Cleaveland
1995 Paleoclimate and the Potential Food Reserves of Mississippian Societies: A Case Study from the Savannah River Valley. *American Antiquity* 60:258–286.

Anderson, David G., Kirk A. Maasch, Daniel H. Sandweiss, and Paul A. Mayewski
2007 Climate and Culture Change: Exploring Holocene Transitions. In *Climate Change and Cultural Dynamics: A Global Perspective on Mid–Holocene Transitions,* edited by David G. Anderson, Kirk A. Maasch, and Daniel H. Sandweiss, pp. 1–23. Academic Press, Amsterdam, The Netherlands.

Anderson, David G., Michael Russo, and Kenneth E. Sassaman
2007 Cultural Dynamics in Southeastern North America. In *Climate Change and Cultural Dynamics: A Global Perspective on Mid–Holocene Transitions,* edited by David G. Anderson, Kirk A. Maasch, and Daniel H. Sandweiss, pp. 457–489. Academic Press, Amsterdam, The Netherlands.

Anderson, David G., D. Shane Miller, Stephen J. Yerka, J. Christopher Gillam, Erik N. Johanson, Derek T. Anderson, A.C. Goodyear, and Ashley M. Smallwood
2010 PIDBA (Paleoindian Database of the Americas) 2010: Current Status and Findings. *Archaeology of Eastern North America* 38:1–28.

Anderson, David G., Stephen J. Yerka, and J. Christopher Gillam
2010 Employing High Resolution Bathymetric Data to Infer Possible Migration Routes of Pleistocene Populations. *Current Research in the Pleistocene* 27:60–64.

Anderson, David G., Albert C. Goodyear, James Kennett, and Allen West
2011 Multiple Lines of Evidence for Possible Human Population Decline/Settlement Reorganization during the Early Younger Dryas. *Quaternary International* 242:570–583.

Anderson, David G., John E. Cornelison, Jr., and Sarah C. Sherwood
2012 Archeological Investigations at Shiloh Indian Mounds National Historic Landmark (40HR7) 1999–2004. Manuscript on file, Southeast Archeological Center, National Park Service, Tallahassee, Florida.

Anderson, David G., Kirk A. Maasch, and Daniel H. Sandweiss
2012 Climate Change and Cultural Dynamics: Lessons from the Past for the Future. In *Humans and the Environment: New Archaeological Perspectives for the 21st Century,* edited by Matthew Davies and Freda Nkirote. Oxford University Press, Oxford, in press.

Applegate, Darlene, and Robert C. Mainfort, Jr. (editors)
2005 *Woodland Period Systematics in the Middle Ohio Valley*. University of Alabama Press, Tuscaloosa.

Arco, Lee J., and Anthony L. Ortmann
2010 Jaketown's Buried Landscape: Recent Research at a Poverty Point Settlement in the Yazoo Basin, Mississippi. Paper presented at the 75th Annual Meeting of the Society for American Archaeology, St. Louis, Missouri.

Arco, Lee J., Katie A. Adelsberger, Ling–yu Hung, and Tristram R. Kidder
2006 Alluvial Geoarchaeology of a Middle Archaic Mound Complex in the Lower Mississippi Valley, U.S.A. *Geoarchaeology* 21:591–614.

Ashley, Keith H., and Neill J. Wallis
2006 Northeastern Florida Swift Creek: Overview and Future Research. *The Florida Anthropologist* 59:5–18.

Aten, Lawrence E.
1999 Middle Archaic Ceremonialism at Tick Island, Florida: Ripley P. Bullen's 1961 Excavations at the Harris Creek site. *The Florida Anthropologist* 53:131–200.

Banks, Larry D.
1990 *From Mountain Peaks to Alligator Stomachs: A Review of Lithic Sources in the Trans-Mississippi South, the Southern Plains, and Adjacent Southwest.* Oklahoma Anthropological Society, Memoir #4. Leedy, Oklahoma.

Barker, Alex W.
1999 Chiefdoms and the Economics of Perversity. Ph.D. Dissertation, Department of Anthropology, University of Michigan, Ann Arbor, Michigan

Barker, Alex W., and Timothy R. Pauketat (editors)
1992 *Lords of the Southeast: Social Inequality and the Native Elites of Southeastern North America.* American Anthropological Association, Washington, D.C.

Barker, Alex W., Craig E. Skinner, M. Steven Shackley, Michael D. Glascock, and J. Daniel Rogers
2002 Mesoamerican Origin for an Obsidian Scraper from the Precolumbian Southeastern United States. *American Antiquity* 67:103–108.

Barker, Gary, and John B. Broster
1996 The Johnson Site (40Dv400): A Dated Paleoindian and Early Archaic Occupation in Tennessee's Central Basin. *Journal of Alabama Archaeology* 42(2):97–153.

Barnett, James F., Jr.
2007 *The Natchez Indians: A History to 1735*. University Press of Mississippi, Jackson

Beasley, Virgil Roy, III
2008 Monumentality during the Mid-Holocene in the Upper and Middle St. Johns River Basins, Florida. Ph.D. Dissertation, Department of Anthropology, Northwestern University, Evanston, Illinois.

Beck, Robin A., Jr.
1997 From Joara to Chiaha: Spanish Exploration of the Appalachian Summit Area 1540–1568. *Southeastern Archaeology* 16:162–169.

2003 Consolidation and Hierarchy: Chiefdom Variability in the Mississippian Southeast. *American Antiquity* 68:641–661.

2009 Catawba Coalescence and the Shattering of the Carolina Piedmont, 1540-1675. In *Mapping the Mississippian Shatter Zone: The Colonial Indian Slave Trade and Regional Instability in the American South*, edited by Robbie Ethridge and Sheri Shuck-Hall, pp. 115–141. University of Nebraska Press, Lincoln.

Beck, Robin A., Jr., and David G. Moore
2002 The Burke Phase: A Mississippian Frontier in the North Carolina Foothills. *Southeastern Archaeology* 21:192–205.
Beck, Robin A., Jr., David G. Moore, and Christopher B. Rodning
2006 Identifying Fort San Juan: A Sixteenth-Century Spanish Occupation at the Berry Site, North Carolina. *Southeastern Archaeology* 25:65–77.
Beck, Robin A., Jr., Christopher B. Rodning, and David G. Moore
2011 Limiting Resistance: Juan Pardo and the Shrinking of Spanish La Florida, 1566–1568. In *Enduring Conquests: Rethinking the Archaeology of Resistance to Spanish Colonialism in the Americas*, edited by Matthew Liebmann and Melissa S. Murphy, pp. 19–39. School for Advanced Research Press, Santa Fe, New Mexico.
Belmont, John S.
1984 The Troyville Concept and the Goldmine Site. *Louisiana Archaeology* 9:271–284.
Bender, Barbara
1985 Prehistoric Developments in the American Midcontinent and in Brittany, Northwest France. In *Prehistoric Hunter-Gatherers: The Emergence of Cultural Complexity*, edited by T. Douglas Price and James A. Brown, pp. 21–57. Academic Press, Orlando, Florida.
Bense, Judith A.
1994 *Archaeology of the Southeastern United States: Paleoindian to World War II.* Academic Press, Orlando, Florida.
1998 Santa Rosa-Swift Creek in Northwestern Florida. In *A World Engraved: Archaeology of the Swift Creek Culture*, edited by J. Mark Williams and Daniel T. Elliott, pp. 247–273. University of Alabama Press, Tuscaloosa.
Benson, Larry V., Timothy R. Pauketat, and Edward R. Cook
2009 Cahokia's Boom and Bust in the Context of Climate Change. *American Antiquity* 74:467–483.
Benson, Robert W., Thomas J. Pluckhahn, Thomas H. Gresham, Douglas S. Atkinson, and Karen Payne
2006 *Cultural Resources Overview of the Sumter National Forest.* Francis Marion and Sumter National Forests CRM Report 06-07. Columbia, South Carolina.
Bernardini, Wesley
2004 Hopewell Earthworks: A Case Study in the Referential and Experiential Meaning of Monuments. *Journal of Anthropological Archaeology* 23:331–356.
Bigman, Daniel P., Adam King, and Chester P. Walker
2011 Recent Geophysical Investigations and New Interpretations of Etowah's Palisade. *Southeastern Archaeology* 30:20–37.
Binford, Lewis R.
1964 Archaeological and Ethnohistorical Investigation of Cultural Diversity and Progressive Development among Aboriginal Cultures of Coastal Virginia and North Carolina. Ph.D. Dissertation, Department of Anthropology, University of Michigan, Ann Arbor.
1967 An Ethnohistory of the Nottoway, Meherrin, and Weanok Indians of Southeastern Virginia. *Ethnohistory* 14(3-4):103–218.
1968 Post-Pleistocene Adaptations. In *New Directions in Archaeology*, edited by Sally R. Binford and Lewis R. Binford, pp. 313–341. Aldine, Chicago.
1971 Mortuary Practices: Their Study and Their Potential. In *Approaches to the Social Dimensions of Mortuary Practices*, edited by James A. Brown, pp. 6–29. Memoirs of the Society for American Archaeology, Washington, D.C.

Binkley, Cameron
2007 *Science, Politics, and the "Big Dig": History of the Southeast Archeological Center and the Development of Cultural Resources Management in the Southeast.* Cultural Resources Division, Southeast Regional Office, National Park Service, Atlanta, Georgia.

Bissett, Thaddeus
2010 Linking Resource Abundance, Population, and the Rise of Regional Exchange Networks in the Middle Archaic Midsouth and Lower Midwest. Paper presented at the 67th Annual Meeting of the Southeastern Archaeological Conference, Lexington, KY.

Blackman, Benjamin K., Moira Scascitelli, Nolan C. Kane, Harry H. Luton, David A. Rasmussen, Robert A. Bye, David L. Lentz, and Loren H. Rieseberg
2011 Sunflower Domestication Alleles Support Single Domestication Center in Eastern North America. *Proceedings of the National Academy of Sciences,* 108(34) 14360–14365.

Blair, Elliott H., Lorann S. A. Pendleton, and Peter Francis, Jr.
2009 *The Beads of St. Catherines Island.* Anthropological Papers of the American Museum of Natural History 89, New York.

Blakely, Robert L., and David S. Mathews
1990 Bioarchaeological Evidence for a Spanish-Native American Conflict in the Sixteenth-Century Southeast. *American Antiquity* 55:718–744.

Blanton, Dennis B
1996 Accounting for Submerged Mid-Holocene Archaeological Sites in the Southeast: A Case Study from Chesapeake Bay, Virginia. In *Archaeology of the Mid–Holocene Southeast,* edited by Kenneth E. Sassaman and David G. Anderson, pp. 200–217. University Press of Florida, Gainesville.
2000 Drought as a Factor in the Jamestown Colony, 1607–1612. *Historical Archaeology* 34(4):74–81.

Blanton, Dennis B., and Kenneth E. Sassaman
1989 Pattern and Process in the Middle Archaic of South Carolina. In *Studies in South Carolina Archaeology: Essays in Honor of Robert L. Stephenson,* edited by Albert C. Goodyear and Glen T. Hanson, pp. 53–72. South Carolina Institute of Archaeology and Anthropology, Anthropological Studies 9. Columbia, South Carolina.

Blanton, Dennis B., and David Hurst Thomas
2008 Paleoclimates and Human Responses along the Central Georgia Coast: A Tree-ring Perspective. In *Native American Landscapes of St. Catherines Island, Georgia,* edited by David Hurst Thomas, pp. 799–806. Anthropological Papers of the American Museum of Natural History 88 (nos. 1–3). New York, New York.

Blitz, John H.
1988 The Adoption of the Bow in Prehistoric North America. *North American Archaeologist* 9:123–145.
1993a *Ancient Chiefdoms of the Tombigbee.* University of Alabama Press, Tuscaloosa.
1993b Big Pots for Big Shots: Feasting and Storage in a Mississippian Community. *American Antiquity* 64:577–592.
1999 Mississippian Chiefdoms and the Fission-Fusion Process. *American Antiquity* 64:577–592.
2009 New Perspectives in Mississippian Archaeology. *Journal of Archaeological Research* 18:1–39.
2012 Moundville in the Mississippian World. In *The Oxford Handbook of North American Archaeology,* edited by Timothy R. Pauketat, pp. 534–543. Oxford University Press, Oxford.

Blitz, John H., and Patrick Livingood
2004 Sociopolitical Implications of Mississippian Mound Volume. *American Antiquity* 69:291–301.

Blitz, John H., and Karl G. Lorenz
2006 *The Chattahoochee Chiefdoms.* University of Alabama Press, Tuscaloosa.

Blong, John C.
2012 Paleoindian Toolstone Provisioning and Settlement Organization at the Higgins Site. In *In the Eastern Fluted Point Tradition*, edited by Joseph A. M. Gingerich. University of Utah Press, Salt Lake City, in press.

Bonnichsen, Robson
2005 An Introduction to Paleoamerican Origins. In *Paleoamerican Origins: Beyond Clovis*, edited by Robson Bonnichsen, Bradley T. Lepper, Dennis Stanford, and Michael R. Waters, pp. 297–312. Center for the Study of the First Americans, Texas A&M University Press, College Station.

Boudreaux, Edmond A. III
2007 *The Archaeology of Town Creek.* University of Alabama Press, Tuscaloosa.

Bowen, William R.
1989 An Examination of Subsistence, Settlement, and Chronology during the Early Woodland Kellogg Phase in the Piedmont Physiographic Province of the Southeastern United States. Ph.D. Dissertation, Department of Anthropology, University of Tennessee, Knoxville.

Boyd, C. Clifford Jr., and Gerald F. Schroedl
1987 In Search of Coosa. *American Antiquity* 52:840–844.

Bradley, Bruce A.
1997 Flaked Stone Technology at the Sloan Site. In *Sloan: A Paleoindian Dalton Cemetery in Northeast Arkansas*, edited by Dan F. Morse, pp. 53–57. Smithsonian Institution, Washington, D.C.

Bradley, Bruce A., and Dennis Stanford
2004 The North Atlantic Ice-edge Corridor: A Possible Palaeolithic Route to the New World. *World Archaeology* 36:459–478.

Bradley, James W., Arthur E. Spiess, Richard A. Boisvert, and J. Boudreau
2008 What's the Point: Model Forms and Attributes of Paleoindian Bifaces in the New England–Maritimes Region. *Archaeology of Eastern North America* 36:119–172.

Bradley, Richard
1998 *Significance of Monuments: On the Shaping of Human Experience in Neolithic and Bronze Age Europe.* Routledge, London.

Brain, Jeffrey P.
1970 *The Tunica Treasure.* Papers of the Peabody Museum of Archaeology and Ethnology, Harvard University 71. Cambridge, Massachusetts.

Brain, Jeffrey P., and Ian W. Brown
1982 *Robert S. Neitzel: The Great Sun.* Lower Mississippi Survey Bulletin 9. Peabody Museum, Harvard University Printing Office, Cambridge, Massachusetts.

Brain, Jeffrey P., T. M. Hamilton, and Arthur E. Spiess
1988 *Tunica Archaeology.* Papers of the Peabody Museum of Archaeology and Ethnology, Harvard University 78. Cambridge, Massachusetts.

Braun, David P.
1983 Pots as Tools. In *Archaeological Hammers and Theories*, edited by James A. Moore and Arthur S. Keene, pp. 108–134. Academic Press, New York.

Braun, David P., and Stephen Plog
1982 Evolution of "Tribal" Social Networks: Theory and Prehistoric North American Evidence. *American Antiquity* 47:504–525.
Braund, Kathryn E. H.
1996 *Deerskins and Duffels: The Creek Indian Trade with Anglo-America, 1685-1815*. University of Nebraska Press, Lincoln.
Breitburg, Emmanuel, John B. Broster, Arthur L. Reesman, and Richard G. Stearns
1996 The Coats-Hines Site: Tennessee's First Paleoindian-Mastodon Association. *Current Research in the Pleistocene* 13:6–8.
Bridges, Patricia A.
1989 Changes in Activities with the Shift to Agriculture in the Southeastern United States. *Current Anthropology* 30:385–394.
1991 Degenerative Joint Disease in Hunter-Gatherers and Agriculturalists from the Southeastern United States. *American Journal of Physical Anthropology* 85:375–391.
Brinton, Daniel G.
1859 *Notes on the Floridaian Peninsula: Its Literary History, Indian Tries, and Antiquities*. J. Sabin, Philadelphia.
Broecker, Wallace S.
2001 Was the Medieval Warm Period Global? *Science* 291:1497–1499.
Broecker, Wallace S., George H. Denton, R. Lawrence Edwards, Hai Cheng, Richard B. Alley, and Aaron E. Putnam
2010 Putting the Younger Dryas Cold Event into Context. *Quaternary Science Reviews* 29:1078–1081.
Brooks, Mark J., Barbara E. Taylor, and Andrew H. Ivester
2010 Carolina Bays: Time Capsules of Culture and Climate Change. *Southeastern Archaeology* 29:146–163.
Brose, David S.
1991 *Yesterday's River: The Archaeology of 10,000 Years along the Tennessee-Tombigbee Waterway*. Cleveland Museum of Natural History, Cleveland, Ohio.
1993 Changing Paradigms in the Explanation of Southeastern Prehistory. In *The Development of Southeastern Archaeology*, edited by Jay K. Johnson, pp. 1–17. University of Alabama Press, Tuscaloosa.
1994 Trade and Exchange in the Midwestern United States. In *Prehistoric Exchange Systems in North America*, edited by Timothy G. Baugh and Jonathon E. Ericson, pp. 215–240. Plenum Press, New York.
Brose, David S., and N'omi Greber (editors)
1979 *Hopewell Archaeology: The Chillicothe Conference*. Kent State University Press, Kent, Ohio.
Brose, David S., James A. Brown, and David W. Penny
1985 *Ancient Art of the American Woodland Indians*. Harry N. Abrams, Inc. New York, New York.
Broster, John B., and Mark R. Norton
1996 Recent Paleoindian Research in Tennessee. In *The Paleoindian and Early Archaic Southeast*, edited by David G. Anderson and Kenneth E. Sassaman, pp. 288–297. University of Alabama Press, Tuscaloosa.
Broster, John B., Mark R. Norton, D. Shane Miller, Jesse W. Tune, and Jon D. Baker
2012 Tennessee's Paleoindian Record: The Cumberland and Lower Tennessee River Watersheds. In *In the Eastern Fluted Point Tradition*, edited by Joseph A. M. Gingerich. University of Utah Press, Salt Lake City, in press.

Browman, David L.

2002 The Peabody Museum, Frederic W. Putnam, and the Rise of U.S. Anthropology, 1866–1903. *American Anthropologist* 104(2):508–519.

Browman, David L., and Stephen Williams (editors)

2002 *New Perspectives on the Origins of Americanist Archaeology*. University of Alabama Press, Tuscaloosa.

Brown, Calvin S.

1926 *The Archaeology of Mississippi*. Mississippi Geological Survey, University, Mississippi. Reprinted 1992 by University Press of Mississippi, Jackson.

Brown, Ian W. (editor)

2003 *Bottle Creek: A Pensacola Culture Site in South Alabama*. University of Alabama Press, Tuscaloosa.

Brown, Ian W.

1978 *James Alfred Ford: The Man and His Works*. Special Publication Number 4, Southeastern Archaeological Conference.

1980 *Salt and the Eastern North American Indian: An Archaeological Study*. Lower Mississippi Survey Bulletin No.6. Harvard University, Cambridge, Massachusetts.

1985 *Natchez Indian Archaeology: Culture Change and Stability in the Lower Mississippi Valley*. Archaeological Report No. 15, Mississippi Department of Archives and History, Jackson.

1989 The Calumet Ceremony in the Southeast and Its Archaeological Manifestations. *American Antiquity* 54:311–331.

1994 Recent Trends in the Archaeology of the Southeastern United States. *Journal of Archaeological Research* 2:45–111.

1999a Salt Manufacture and Trade from the Perspective of Avery Island, Louisiana. *Midcontinental Journal of Archaeology* 24:113–151.

1999b Contact, Communication, and Exchange: Some Thoughts on the Rapid Movements of Ideas and Objects. In *Raw Materials and Exchange in the Mid-South*, edited by Evan Peacock and Samuel O. Brookes, pp. 132–141. Archaeological Report No. 29. Mississippi Department of Archives and History, Jackson.

2004 Prehistory of the Gulf Coastal Plain after 500 B.C. In *Smithsonian Handbook of North American Indians, Volume 14, The Southeast,* edited by Raymond D. Fogelson, pp. 574–585. Smithsonian Institution, Washington, D.C.

2006 The Calumet Ceremony in the Southeast as Observed Archaeologically. In *Powhatan's Mantle: Indians in the Colonial Southeast* (revised and expanded edition), edited by Gregory A. Waselkov, Peter H. Wood, and Tom Hatley, pp. 371–419. University of Nebraska Press, Lincoln.

Brown, Ian W., and Vincas P. Steponaitis

2010 *The Peabody Man: Jeffery P. Brain*. Borgo Press, Tuscaloosa, Alabama.

Brown, James A.

1985 Long Term Trends to Sedentism and the Emergence of Complexity in the American Midwest. In *Prehistoric Hunter-Gatherers: The Emergence of Cultural Complexity*, edited by T. Douglas Price and James A. Brown, pp. 201–231. Academic Press, Orlando, Florida.

1989 The Beginnings of Pottery as an Economic Process. In *What's New? A Closer Look at the Process of Innovation*, edited by Sander E. van der Leeuw, pp. 203–224. Unwin Hyman, London.

1996 *The Spiro Ceremonial Center: The Archaeology of Arkansas Valley Caddoan Culture in Eastern Oklahoma.* University of Michigan, Museum of Anthropology, Memoirs 29 (2 vols). Ann Arbor, Michigan.

1997 The Archaeology of Ancient Religion in the Eastern Woodlands. *Annual Review of Anthropology* 26:465–485.

2003 The Cahokia Mound 72-Sub 1 Burials as Collective Representation. *Wisconsin Archaeologist* 84:83–99.

2004a The Cahokia Expansion: Creating Court and Cult. In *Hero, Hawk, and the Open Hand: American Indian Art of the Ancient Midwest and South*, edited by Richard F. Townsend and Robert V. Sharp, pp. 108–127. Art Institute of Chicago, Chicago.

2004b Exchange and Interaction until 1500. In *Smithsonian Handbook of North American Indians, Volume 14, The Southeast,* edited by Raymond D. Fogelson, pp. 677–685. Smithsonian Institution, Washington, D.C.

2006 Where's the Power in Mound Building? In *Leadership and Polity in Mississippian Society*, edited by Brian M. Butler and Paul D. Welch, pp. 197–213. Center for Archeological Investigations, Occasional Paper No. 33. Southern Illinois University, Carbondale.

2011 The Regional Cultural Signature of the Braden Art Style. In *Visualizing the Sacred: Cosmic Visions, Regionalism, and the Art of the Mississippian World*, edited by George E. Lankford, F. Kent Reilly III, and James F. Garber, pp. 37–63. University of Texas Press, Austin.

Brown, James A., and David H. Dye

2007 Severed Heads and Sacred Scalplocks: Mississippian Iconographic Trophies. In *The Taking and Displaying of Human Body Parts as Trophies by Amerindians*, edited by Richard J. Chacon and David H. Dye, pp. 274–294. Plenum, New York.

Brown, James A., and Robert K. Vierra

1983 What Happened in the Middle Archaic? Introduction to an Ecological Approach to Koster Site Archaeology. In *Archaic Hunters and Gatherers in the American Midwest*, edited by James L. Phillips and James A. Brown, pp. 165–196. Academic Press, New York.

Brown, James A., Richard A. Kerber, and Howard D. Winters

1990 Trade and the Evolution of Exchange Relations at the Beginning of the Mississippian Period. In *The Mississippian Emergence*, edited by Bruce D. Smith, pp. 251–174. Smithsonian Institution Press, Washington, D.C.

Broyles, Bettye J.

1966 Preliminary Report: The St. Albans Site (46KA27), Kanawha County, West Virginia. *West Virginia Archaeologist* 19:1–43.

1967 Bibliography of Pottery Type Descriptions From the Eastern United States. *Southeastern Archaeological Conference Bulletin* 4.

1968 Reconstructed Designs from Swift Creek Complicated Stamped Sherds. *Southeastern Archaeological Conference Bulletin* 8:49–74.

1971 *Second Preliminary Report: The St. Albans Site, Kanawha Valley, West Virginia.* Report of Archaeological Investigations 3, West Virginia Geological and Economic Survey, Charleston.

Bruseth, James E.

1991 Poverty Point Development as Seen from the Cedarland and Claiborne Sites, Southern Mississippi. In *The Poverty Point Culture: Local Manifestations, Subsistence Practices, and Trade Networks*, edited by Kathleen M. Byrd, pp. 7–26. Geoscience and Man, Vol. 29. Louisiana State University, Baton Rouge.

Buchanan, Briggs, and Marcus J. Hamilton

2009 A Formal Test of the Origin of Variation in North American Early Paleoindian Projectile Points. *American Antiquity* 74:279–298.

Buikstra, Jane E., and Douglas K. Charles

1999 Centering the Ancestors: Cemeteries, Mounds, and Sacred Landscapes of the Ancient North American Midcontinent. In *Archaeologies of Landscape: Contemporary Perspectives*, edited by Wendy Ashmore and A. B. Knapp, pp. 201–228. Blackwell, Malden, Massachusetts.

Buikstra, Jane E., Douglas K. Charles, and Gordon F. M. Rakita
1998 *Staging Ritual: Hopewell Ceremonialism at the Mound House Site, Greene County, Illinois.* Kampsville Studies in Archaeology and History 1, Center for American Archaeology, Kampsville, Illinois.
Burdin, Richard
2004 Interaction, Exchange, and Social Organization among Hunter-Gatherers in the Mid-continent–Evidence from the Lower Ohio River Valley: Bannerstone Use from 6500 to 3000 B.P. M.A. Thesis, Department of Anthropology, University of Kentucky, Lexington.
Butler, Brian M., and Paul D. Welch (editors)
2006 *Leadership and Polity in Mississippian Society.* Center for Archeological Investigations, Occasional Paper No. 33. Southern Illinois University, Carbondale.
Butler, Brian M., R. Berle Clay, Michael E. Hargrave, Staffan D. Peterson, John E. Schwegman, and Paul D. Welch
2011 A New Look at Kincaid: Magnetic Survey at a Large Mississippian Town. *Southeastern Archaeology* 30:20–37.
Byers, A. Martin, and Dee Ann Wymer (editors)
2010 *Hopewell Settlement Patterns, Subsistence, and Symbolic Landscapes.* University Press of Florida, Gainesville.

Cable, John S.
1996 Haw River Revisited: Implications for Modeling Late Glacial and Early Holocene Hunter-Gatherer Settlement Systems in the Southeast. In *The Paleoindian and Early Archaic Southeast,* edited by David G. Anderson and Kenneth E. Sassaman, pp. 107–148. University of Alabama Press, Tuscaloosa.
Cable, John S., Gail E. Wagner, and Christopher Judge
1999 *Wateree Archaeological Research Project, 1998 Survey and Testing of the Belmont Neck (38KE06), Adamson (38KE11), and Mulberry (38KE12) Sites: Mississippian Occupation in the Wateree River Valley.* South Carolina Department of Archives and History, Columbia, South Carolina.
Caldwell, Joseph R.
1958 *Trend and Tradition in the Prehistory the Eastern United States.* American Anthropological Association Memoir 88. Menasha, Wisconsin.
1964 Interaction Spheres in Prehistory. In *Hopewellian Studies,* edited by Joseph R. Caldwell and Robert L. Hall, pp. 133–143. Illinois State Museum Scientific Paper 12 (6). Springfield, Illinois.
Caldwell, Joseph R., and Catherine McCann
1941 *Irene Mound Site, Chatham County, Georgia.* University of Georgia Press, Athens.
Campisi, Jack
2004 Resurgence and Recognition. In *Smithsonian Handbook of North American Indians, Volume 14, The Southeast,* edited by Raymond D. Fogelson, pp. 760–768. Smithsonian Institution, Washington, D.C.
Carmody, Stephen B.
2009 Hunter/Gatherer Foraging Adaptations during the Middle Archaic Period at Dust Cave, Alabama. M.A. Thesis, Department of Anthropology, University of Tennessee, Knoxville.
2010 The Relationship Between Middle Archaic Foraging Strategies and Complexity in Northwest Alabama. Paper presented at the 67th Annual Meeting of the Southeastern Archaeological Conference, Lexington, Kentucky.
Carniero, Robert L.
1970 A Theory of the Origin of the State. *Science* 169:733–739.

1981 The Chiefdom: Precursor of the State. In *The Transition to Statehood in the New World*, edited by Grant D. Jones and Robert R. Kautz, pp. 37–79. Cambridge University Press, Cambridge, UK.

Carr, Christopher

2005 Historical Insights into the Direction and Limitations of Recent Research on Hopewell. In *Gathering Hopewell: Society, Ritual, and Ritual Interaction*, edited by Christopher Carr and D. Troy Case, pp. 51–70. Kluwer Academic/Plenum Publishers, New York.

Carr, Christopher, and D. Troy Case (editors)

2005 *Gathering Hopewell: Society, Ritual, and Ritual Interaction*. Kluwer Academic/Plenum Publishers, New York.

Carr, Kurt W., James M. Adovasio, and Frank J. Vento

2012 A Report on the 2008 Field Investigations at the Shoop Site (36da20). In *In the Eastern Fluted Point Tradition*, edited by Joseph A. M. Gingerich. University of Utah Press, Salt Lake City, in press.

Carr, Kurt W., R. Michael Stewart, Dennis Stanford, and Michael Frank

2012 The Flint Run Complex: A Quarry Related Paleoindian Complex in the Great Valley of Northern Virginia. In *In the Eastern Fluted Point Tradition*, edited by Joseph A. M. Gingerich. University of Utah Press, Salt Lake City, in press.

Carr, Philip J., Andrew P. Bradbury, and Sarah E. Price (editors)

2012 *Contemporary Lithic Analysis in the Southeast: Problems, Solutions, and Interpretations*. University of Alabama Press, Tuscaloosa, in press.

Carstens, Kenneth C., and Patty Jo Watson (editors)

1996 *Of Caves and Shell Mounds*. University of Alabama Press, Tuscaloosa.

Case, D. Troy and Christopher Carr (editors)

2008 *The Scioto Hopewell and Their Neighbors: Bioarchaeological Documentation and Cultural Understanding*. Springer, New York.

Charles, Douglas K., and Jane E. Buikstra

1983 Archaic Mortuary Sites in the Central Mississippi Drainage: Distribution, Structure, and Behavioral Implications. In *Archaic Hunter-Gatherers in the American Midwest*, edited by James L. Phillips and James A. Brown, pp. 117–145. Academic Press, New York.

Charles, Douglas K., and Jane E. Buikstra (editors)

2006 *Recreating Hopewell*. University Press of Florida, Gainesville.

Charles, Douglas K., Julieann Van Nest, and Jane E. Buikstra

2004 From the Earth: Minerals and Meaning in the Hopewellian World. In *Soils, Stones and Symbols*, edited by Nicole Boivan and Mary A. Owoc, pp. 43–70. University College London Press, London.

Chapman, Jefferson

1973 *The Icehouse Bottom Site–40MR23*. University of Tennessee, Report of Investigations 14. Knoxville, Tennessee.

1975 *The Rose Island Site and the Bifurcate Point Tradition*. Department of Anthropology, University of Tennessee, Report of Investigations 14. Knoxville, Tennessee.

1985 Archaeology and the Archaic Period in the Southern Ridge–and–Valley Province. In *Structure and Process in Southeastern Archaeology*, edited by Roy S. Dickens and H. Trawick Ward, pp. 137–53. University of Alabama Press, Tuscaloosa.

1995 *Tellico Archaeology Revised Edition 12000 Years of Native American History*. University of Tennessee Press, Knoxville.

Chapman, Jefferson, and Gary D. Crites

1987 Evidence for Early Maize (*Zea mays*) from the Icehouse Bottom Site, Tennessee. *American Antiquity* 52:352–354.

Chapman, Jefferson, and Bennie C. Keel

1979 Candy Creek-Connestee Components in Eastern Tennessee and Western North Carolina and their Relationship with Adena-Hopewell. In *Hopewell Archaeology: The Chillicothe Conference*, edited by David S. Brose and N'omi Greber, pp. 157–161. Kent State University Press, Kent, Ohio.

Childs, S. Terry, and Karolyn Kinsey

2002 *A Survey of SHPO Archeological Report Bibliographic Systems, 2002*. National Center for Cultural Resources, National Park Service, Studies in Archaeology and Ethnography 5. Washington, D.C.

Claassen, Cheryl P. (editor)

1992 *Exploring Gender through Archaeology*. Prehistory Press, Madison, Wisconsin.

Claassen, Cheryl P.

1991a Gender, Shellfishing, and the Shell Mound Archaic. In *Engendering Archaeology*, edited by Joan M. Gero and Margaret W. Conkey, pp. 276–300. Basil Blackwell, Oxford.

1991b New Hypotheses for the Demise of the Shell Mound Archaic. In *The Archaic Period in the Mid-South*, edited by Charles McNutt, pp. 66–72. Archaeological Report 24. Mississippi Department of Archives and History, Jackson.

1992 Shell Mounds as Burial Mounds: A Revision of the Shell Mound Archaic. In *Current Archaeological Research in Kentucky*, vol 2, edited by David Pollack and A. G. Henderson, pp. 1–12. Kentucky Heritage Council, Frankfort.

1993 Black and White Woman at Irene Mound. *Southeastern Archaeology* 12:137–147.

1996 A Consideration of the Social Organization of the Shell Mound Archaic. In *Archaeology of the Mid–Holocene Southeast*, edited by Kenneth E. Sassaman and David G. Anderson, pp. 235–258. University Press of Florida, Gainesville.

1998 *Shells*. Cambridge University Press, Cambridge, UK.

1999 Black and White Woman at Irene Mound. In *Grit Tempered: Early Women Archaeologists in the Southeastern United States*, edited by Nancy M. White, Lynne P. Sullivan, and Rochelle A. Marrinan, pp. 92–102. University Press of Florida, Gainesville.

2010 *Feasting with Shellfish in the Southern Ohio Valley: Archaic Sacred Sites and Rituals*. University of Tennessee Press, Knoxville.

2011 Rock Shelters as Women's Retreats: Understanding Newt Kash. *American Antiquity* 76:628–641.

Claassen, Cheryl, and Samuella Sigmann

1993 Sourcing *Busycon* Artifacts of the Eastern United States. *American Antiquity* 58:333–347.

Claassen, Cheryl P., Michael O'Neal, Tamara Wilson, Elizabeth Arnold, and Brent Lansdell

1999 Hearing and Reading Southeastern Archaeology: A Review of the Annual Meetings of SEAC from 1983 through 1995 and the Journal Southeastern Archaeology. *Southeastern Archaeology* 18:85–97.

Claflin, William H., Jr.

1931 *The Stalling's Island Mound, Columbia County, Georgia*. Peabody Museum of American Archaeology and Ethnology Papers 14(1). Cambridge, Massachusetts.

Clark, John E.

2004 Surrounding the Sacred: Geometry and Design of Early Mound Groups as Meaning and Function. In *Signs of Power: The Rise of Cultural Complexity in the Southeast*, edited by Jon L. Gibson and Philip J. Carr, pp. 162–213. University of Alabama Press, Tuscaloosa.

Clark, John E., Jon L. Gibson, and James Ziedler

2010 First Towns in the Americas: Searching for Agriculture, Population Growth, and Other Enabling Conditions. In *Becoming Villagers: Comparing Early Village Societies*, edited by Matthew S. Bandy and Jake R. Fox, pp. 205–245. University of Arizona Press, Tucson.

Clausen, Carl J., H. K. Brooks, and A. B. Wesolowsky

1975a Florida Spring Confirmed as 10,000-Year-Old Early Man Site. *The Florida Anthropologist* 28:1–38.

1975b The Early Man Site at Warm Mineral Springs. *Journal of Field Archaeology* 2:191–213.

Clausen, Carl J., A. D. Cohen, Cesare Emiliani, J. A. Holman, and J. J. Stipp

1979 Little Salt Springs, Florida: A Unique Underwater Site. *Science* 203:609–614.

Clay, R. Berle

1998 The Essential Features of Adena Ritual and Their Implications. *Southeastern Archaeology* 17:1–21.

Clayton, Lawrence A., Vernon James Knight Jr., and Edward C. Moore (editors)

1993 *The De Soto Chronicles: The Expedition of Hernando de Soto to North America in 1539–1543*. 2 vols. University of Alabama Press, Tuscaloosa.

Cobb, Charles R.

2000 *From Quarry to Cornfield: The Political Economy of Mississippian Hoe Production and its Contribution to the Agriculture of Mississippian Communities*. University of Alabama Press, Tuscaloosa.

2003 Mississippian Chiefdoms: How Complex? *Annual Review of Anthropology* 32:63–84.

Cobb, Charles R. (editor)

2003 *Stone Tool Traditions in the Contact Era*. University of Alabama Press, Tuscaloosa.

Cobb, Charles R., and Brian M. Butler

2002 The Vacant Quarter Revisited: Late Mississippian Abandonment of the Lower Ohio Valley. *American Antiquity* 67:625–641.

2006 Mississippian Migration and Emplacement in the Lower Ohio Valley. In *Leadership and Polity in Mississippian Society*, edited by Brian M. Butler and Paul D. Welch, pp. 328–347. Center for Archaeological Investigations, Occasional Paper No. 33. Southern Illinois University, Carbondale.

Cobb, Charles R., and Eric Drake

2008 The Colour of Time: Head Pots and Temporal Convergences. *Cambridge Archaeological Journal* 18:85–93.

Cobb, Charles R., and Bretton Giles

2009 War is Shell: The Ideology and Embodiment of Mississippian Conflict. In *Warfare in Cultural Context: Practice, Agency, and the Archaeology of Violence*, edited by Axel E. Nielsen and William H. Walker, pp. 84–108. University of Arizona Press, Tucson.

Cobb, Charles R., and Patrick H. Garrow

1996 Woodstock Culture and the Question of Mississippian Emergence. *American Antiquity* 61:21–37.

Cobb, Charles R., and Michael S. Nassaney

1991 Introduction: Renewed Perspectives on Late Woodland Stability, Transformation, and Variation in the Southeastern United States. In *Stability, Transformation, and Variation: The Late Woodland Southeast*, edited by Michael S. Nassaney and Charles R. Cobb, pp. 1–10. Plenum Press, New York.

2002 Domesticating Self and Society in the Woodland Southeast. In *The Woodland Southeast*, edited by David G. Anderson and Robert C. Mainfort, Jr., pp. 525–539. University of Alabama Press, Tuscaloosa.

Coe, Joffre L.

1964 *The Formative Cultures of the Carolina Piedmont*. Transactions of the American Philosophical Society 54(5). Philadelphia.

Collins, Michael, Thomas R. Hester, and P. J. Headrick

1992 Engraved Cobbles from the Gault Site. *Current Research in the Pleistocene* 9:3–4.

Condon, Keith W., and Jerome C. Rose
1997 Bioarchaeology of the Sloan Site. In *Sloan: A Paleoindian Dalton Cemetery in Arkansas*, edited by Dan F. Morse, pp. 8–13. Smithsonian Institution, Washington, D.C.
Connaway, John M.
1977 *The Denton Site: A Middle Archaic Occupation in the Northern Yazoo Basin, Mississippi.* Archaeological Papers 4. Mississippi Department of Archives and History, Jackson.
1981 The Keenan Bead Cache, Lawrence County, Mississippi. *Louisiana Archaeology* 8:59–71.
Cook, Edward R., Richard Seager, Mark A. Cane, and David W. Stahle
2007 North American Drought: Reconstructions, Causes, and Consequences. *Earth-Science Reviews* 81:93–134.
Cordell, Ann S.
1984 *Ceramic Technology at a Weeden Island Period Archaeological Site in North Florida.* Ceramic Notes 2. Florida Museum of Natural History, University of Florida, Gainesville.
1992 Technological Investigations of Pottery Variability in Southwest Florida. In *Culture and Environment in the Domain of the Calusa*, edited by William H. Marquardt, pp. 105–189. Monograph 1. Institute of Archaeology and Paleoenvironmental Studies, University of Florida, Gainesville.
2004 Paste Variability and Possible Manufacturing Origins of Late Archaic Fiber-Tempered Pottery from Selected Sites in Peninsular Florida. In *Early Pottery: Technology, Function, Style, and Interaction in the Lower Southeast*, edited by Rebecca Saunders and Christopher T. Hays, pp. 63–104. University of Alabama Press, Tuscaloosa.
Cotter, John L. and John M. Corbett
1951 *Archeology of the Bynum Mounds, Mississippi.* Archaeological Research Series 1. National Park Service, Washington D.C.
Cowan, C. Wesley
1985 Understanding the Evolution of Plant Husbandry in Eastern North America: Lessons from Botany, Ethnography, and Archaeology. In *Prehistoric Food Production in North America*, edited by Richard I. Ford, pp. 205–243. Anthropological Papers 74. Museum of Anthropology, University of Michigan, Ann Arbor.
Cowan, C. Wesley, H. Edwin Jackson, Katherine Moore, A. Nickelhoff, and T. L. Smart
1981 The Cloudsplitter Rockshelter, Menifee County, Kentucky: A Preliminary Report. *Southeastern Archaeological Conference Bulletin* 24:60–76.
Crawford, Jessica
2003 Archaic Effigy Beads: A New Look at Some Old Beads. M.A. Thesis, Department of Sociology and Anthropology, University of Mississippi, Oxford.
Crothers, George M.
1999 Archaic Period Subsistence and Economy: The Green River Shell Midden Sites of Kentucky. Ph.D. Dissertation, Department of Anthropology, Washington University, St. Louis.
2001 Material Mining and Perishable Remains in Mammoth Cave, Kentucky: Examining Social Process during the Early Woodland Period. In *Fleeting Identities: Perishable Material Culture in Archaeological Research*, edited by Penelope B. Drooker, pp. 314–334. Center for Archaeological Investigations, Occasional Paper No. 28. Southern Illinois University, Carbondale.
2004 The Green River in Comparison to the Lower Mississippi Valley during the Archaic: to Build Mounds or Not to Build Mounds? In *Signs of Power: The Rise of Cultural Complexity in the Southeast*, edited by Jon L. Gibson and Philip J. Carr, pp. 86–96. University of Alabama Press, Tuscaloosa.

Crothers, George M. Charles H. Faulkner, Jan F. Simek, Patty Jo Watson, and P. Willey
2002 Woodland Cave Archaeology in Eastern North America. In *The Woodland Southeast*, edited by David G. Anderson and Robert C. Mainfort, Jr., pp. 502–524. University of Alabama Press, Tuscaloosa.
Crowley, Thomas J.
2000 Causes of Climate Change Over the Past 1000 Years. *Science* 289:270–277.
Cushing, Frank Hamilton
1897 Exploration of Ancient Key–Dweller Remains on the Gulf Coast of Florida. *Proceedings of the American Philosophical Society* 25(153):329–448.
Custer, Jay F., John A. Cavallo, and R. Michael Stewart
1983 Lithic Procurement and Paleo-Indian Settlement Patterns on the Middle Atlantic Coastal Plain. *North American Archaeologist* 4:263–275.

Dalan, Rinita A.
1997 The Construction of Mississippian Cahokia. In *Cahokia: Domination and Ideology in the Mississippian World*, edited by Timothy R. Pauketat and Thomas E. Emerson, pp. 89–102. University of Nebraska Press, Lincoln.
Dalan, Rinita A., George R. Holley, William I. Woods, Harold W. Watters Jr., and John A. Koepke
2003 *Envisioning Cahokia: A Landscape Perspective*. Northern Illinois Press, DeKalb.
Dancey, William S., and Paul J. Pacheco (editors)
1997 *Ohio Hopewell Community Organization*. Kent State University Press, Kent, Ohio.
Daniel, Glynn E.
1950 *A Hundred Years of Archaeology*. Gerald Duckworth and Company, London.
Daniel, I. Randolph
1998 *Hardaway Revisited: Early Archaic Settlement in the Southeast*. University of Alabama Press, Tuscaloosa.
2001 Stone Raw Material Availability and Early Archaic Settlement in the Southeastern United States. *American Antiquity* 66:237–265.
Davis, R. P. Stephen, Jr.
1990 *Aboriginal Settlement Patterns in the Lower Little Tennessee River Valley*. Report of Investigations 50, Department of Anthropology, University of Tennessee, Knoxville, and Publications in Anthropology 54, Tennessee Valley Authority, Knoxville, Tennessee.
Davis, R. P. Stephen Jr., and Brett H. Riggs
2004 An Introduction to the Catawba Project. *North Carolina Archaeology* 53:1–41.
Davis, R. P. Stephen Jr., Patrick Livingood, H. Trawick Ward, and Vincas P. Steponaitis
1998 *Excavating Occaneechi Town: Archaeology of an Eighteenth-Century Indian Village in North Carolina*. CD-ROM. University of North Carolina Press, Chapel Hill.
Deagan, Katherine A., and David Hurst Thomas (editors)
2009 *From Santa Elena to St. Augustine: Indigenous Ceramic Variability (A.D. 1400-1700)*: Proceedings of the Second Caldwell Conference, St. Catherines Island, Georgia, March 30-April 1, 2007. Anthropological Papers of the American Museum of Natural History 90. New York, New York.
DeBoer, Warren R.
1988 Subterranean Storage and the Organization of Surplus: The View from Eastern North America. *Southeastern Archaeology* 7:1–20.
1997 Ceremonial Centers from Cayapas (Esmeraldas, Ecuador), to Chillicothe (Ohio, USA). *Cambridge Archaeological Journal* 7:225–253.
2005 Colors for a North American Past. *World Archaeology* 37:66–91.

DeJarnette, David L., E. Kurjack, and Jack Cambron
1962 Excavations at the Stanfield–Worley Bluff Shelter. *Journal of Alabama Archaeology* 8:1–124.

Delcourt, Hazel R., and Paul A. Delcourt
1985 Quaternary Palynology and Vegetational History of the Southeastern United States. In *Pollen Records of Late-Quaternary North American Sediments*, edited by V. M. Bryant and R. G. Holloway, pp. 1–37. American Association of Stratigraphic Palynologists Foundation, Dallas, Texas.

Delcourt, Paul A., and Hazel R. Delcourt
1987 *Long Term Forest Dynamics of the Temperate Zone: A Case Study of Late Quaternary Forests in Eastern North America*. Springer–Verlag Press, New York.
2004 *Prehistoric Native Americans and Ecological Change*. Cambridge University Press, Cambridge, UK.

Delcourt, Paul A., Hazel R. Delcourt, Cecil R. Ison, William E. Sharp, and Kristen J. Gremillion
1998 Prehistoric Human Use of Fire, the Eastern Agricultural Complex, and Appalachian Oak–Chestnut Forests: Paleoecology of Cliff Palace Pond, Kentucky. *American Antiquity* 63:263–278.

Deller, D. Brian, Christopher J. Ellis, and James R. Keron
2009 Understanding Cache Variability: A Deliberately Burned Early Paleoindian Tool Assemblage from the Crowfield site, Southeastern Ontario. *American Antiquity* 74:371–397.

Dent, Richard J.
2002 Paleoindian Occupation of the Upper Delaware Valley; Revisiting Shawnee Minisink and Nearby Sites. In *Ice Age People of Pennsylvania*, edited by Kurt W. Carr and James M. Adovasio, pp. 51–78. Pennsylvania Historical and Museum Commission, Harrisburg.
2007 Seed Collecting and Fishing at the Shawnee-Minisink Site: Everyday Life in the Pleistocene. In *Foragers of the Terminal Pleistocene in North America*, edited by Renee B. Walker and Boyce N. Driskell. pp. 116–131. University of Nebraska Press, Lincoln.

DePratter, Chester B.
1991 *Late Prehistoric and Early Historic Chiefdoms in the Southeastern United States*. Garland Press, New York.
1994 The Chiefdom of Cofitachequi. In *The Forgotten Centuries: Indians and Europeans in the American South, 1521–1704*, edited by Charles M. Hudson and Carmen Chaves Tesser, pp. 197–226. University of Georgia Press, Athens.

DePratter, Chester B., and James D. Howard
1980 Indian Occupation and Geologic History of the Georgia Coast: A 5000 Year Summary. In *Excursions in Southeastern Geology: The Archaeology-Geology of the Georgia Coast*, edited by James D. Howard, Chester B. DePratter, and Robert W. Frey, pp. 1–65. Georgia Geological Society Guidebook 20, Atlanta, Georgia.

Deter-Wolf, Aaron
2004 The Ensworth School Site (40DV184): A Middle Archaic Benton Occupation along the Harpeth River Drainage in Middle Tennessee. *Tennessee Archaeology* 1(1):18–35.

Deter-Wolf, Aaron, Jesse W. Tune, and John B. Broster
2011 Excavations and Dating of Late Pleistocene and Paleoindian Deposits at the Coats-Hines Site, Williamson County, Tennessee. *Tennessee Archaeology* 5(2):142–156.

Diaz-Granádos, Carol
2004 Marking Stone, Land, Body, and Spirit Rock Art and Mississippian Iconography. In *Hero, Hawk, and Open Hand: American Indian Art of the Ancient Midwest and South*, edited by Richard F. Townsend and Robert V. Sharp, pp. 139–149. The Art Institute of Chicago and Yale University Press, New Haven, Connecticut.

Diaz-Granádos, Carol, and James R. Duncan (editors)

2000 *The Petroglyphs and Pictographs of Missouri.* University of Alabama Press, Tuscaloosa.

2004 *The Rock-Art of Eastern North America: Capturing Images and Insight.* University Alabama Press, Tuscaloosa.

Diaz-Granádos, Carol, Marvin W. Rowe, Marian Hyman, James R. Duncan, and John R. Southon

2001 Radiocarbon Dates for Charcoal from Three Missouri Pictographs and Their Associated Iconography. *American Antiquity* 66:481–492.

DiBlasi, Philip J.

1981 A New Assessment of the Archaeological Significance of the Ashworth Site (15Bu236): A Study in the Dynamics of Archaeological Investigation in Cultural Resource Management. M. A. Thesis, Interdisciplinary Studies, University of Louisville, Louisville, Kentucky.

Dickel, David N.

2002 Analysis of Mortuary Patterns. In *Windover: Multidisciplinary Investigations of an Early Archaic Florida Cemetery,* edited by Glen Doran, pp. 73–96. University Press of Florida, Gainesville.

Dickens, Roy S., Jr.

1975 A Processual Approach to Mississippian Origins on the Georgia Piedmont. *Southeastern Archaeological Conference Bulletin* 18:31–42.

1976 *Cherokee Prehistory: The Pisgah Phase in the Appalachian Summit.* University of Tennessee Press, Knoxville.

Dincauze, Dena F.

1993 Pioneering in the Pleistocene Large Paleoindian Sites in the Northwest. In *Archaeology of Eastern North America Papers in Honor of Stephen Williams,* edited by James B. Stoltman, pp. 43–60. Archaeological Report No. 25, Mississippi Department of Archives and History, Jackson.

Dincauze, Dena F., and Victoria Jacobson

2001 The Birds of Summer: Lakeside Routes into Pleistocene New England. *Canadian Journal of Archaeology* 25:121–126.

Dobyns, Henry F.

1983 *Their Number Become Thinned: Native American Population Dynamics in Eastern North America.* University of Tennessee Press, Knoxville.

Doran, Glen H. (editor)

2002 *Windover: Multidisciplinary Investigations of an Early Archaic Florida Cemetery.* University Press of Florida, Gainesville.

Dowd, John T.

1989 *The Anderson Site: Middle Archaic Adaptation in Tennessee's Central Basin.* Tennessee Anthropological Association, Miscellaneous Papers 13. Knoxville.

Dragoo, Don W.

1973 Wells Creek: An Early Man Site in Stewart County, Tennessee. *Archaeology of Eastern North America* 1:1–56.

Driskell, Boyce N., and Renee B. Walker

2007 Making Sense of Paleoindian Subsistence Strategies. In *Foragers of the Terminal Pleistocene in North America,* edited by Renee B. Walker and Boyce N. Driskell, pp. 226–238. University of Nebraska Press, Lincoln.

Drooker, Penelope B.

1992 *Mississippian Village Textiles at Wickliffe.* University of Alabama Press, Tuscaloosa.

2003 Matting and Pliable Fabrics from Bottle Creek. In *Bottle Creek: A Pensacola Culture Site in South Alabama,* edited by Ian W. Brown, pp. 180–193. University of Alabama Press, Tuscaloosa.

Dunbar, James S.
1991 Resource Orientation of Clovis and Suwannee Age Paleoindian Sites in Florida. In *Clovis: Origins and Adaptations*, edited by Robson Bonnichsen and Karen L. Turnmire, pp. 185–213. Center for the Study of the First Americans and Oregon State University, Corvallis.
2006a Pleistocene-Holocene Climate Change: Chronostratigraphy and Geoclimate of the Southeastern United States. In *First Floridians and Last Mastodons: The Page Ladson Site in the Aucilla River*, edited by. S. David Webb, pp. 103–155. Springer, Dordrecht, The Netherlands.
2006b Paleoindian Archaeology. In *First Floridians and Last Mastodons: The Page Ladson Site in the Aucilla River*, edited by. S. David Webb, pp. 403–435. Springer, Dordrecht, The Netherlands.
Dunbar, James S., and C. Andrew Hemmings
2004 Florida Paleoindian Points and Knives. In *New Perspectives on the First Americans*, edited by B. T. Lepper and R. Bonnichsen, pp. 65–72. Center for the Study of the First Americans, Texas A&M University Press, College Station.
Dunbar, James S., and Ben I. Waller
1983 A Distribution of the Clovis/Suwannee Paleoindian Sites of Florida: A Geographic Approach. *The Florida Anthropologist* 36:18–30.
Dunbar, James S., and S. David Webb
1996 Bone and Ivory Tools from Paleoindian Sites in Florida. In *The Paleoindian and Early Archaic Southeast*, edited by David G. Anderson and Kenneth E. Sassaman, pp. 331–353. University of Alabama, Tuscaloosa.
Dunbar, James S., and P.K. Vojnovski
2007 Early Floridians and Late Megamammals Some Technological and Dietary Evidence from Four North Florida Paleoindian Sites. In *Foragers of the Terminal Pleistocene*, edited by Renee B. Walker and Boyce N. Driskell, pp. 167–202. University of Alabama Press, Tuscaloosa.
Dunbar, James S., S. David Webb, and Michael K. Faught
1988 Page-Ladson (8JE591): An Underwater Paleo-Indian Site in Northwestern Florida. *The Florida Anthropologist* 41:442–52.
Dunbar, James S., S. David Webb, and D. Cring
1989 Culturally and Naturally Modified Bones from a Paleoindian site in the Aucilla River, North Florida. In *Bone Modification*, edited by Robson Bonnichsen and M. Sorg, pp. 473–97. Center for the Study of the First Americans, Orono, Maine.
Dunbar, James S., C. Andrew Hemmings, P. K. Vojnovski, S. David Webb, and W. M. Stanton
2005 The Ryan-Harley Site 8Je1004: A Suwannee Point Site in the Wacissa River, North Florida. In *Paleoamerican Origins: Beyond Clovis*, edited by Robson Bonnichsen, Bradley T. Lepper, Dennis Stanford, and Michael R. Waters, pp. 81–96. Center for the Study of the First Americans, Texas A&M University Press, College Station.
Dunnell, Robert C.
1990 The Role of the Southeast in American Archaeology. *Southeastern Archaeology* 9:11–22.
Dye, David H.
1996 Initial Riverine Adaptation in the Midsouth: An Examination of Three Middle Holocene Shell Middens. In *Of Caves and Shell Mounds*, edited by Kenneth C. Carstens and Patty Jo Watson, pp. 140–158. University of Alabama Press, Tuscaloosa.
2004 Art, Ritual, and Chiefly Warfare in the Mississippian World. In *Hero, Hawk, and Open Hand: American Indian Art of the Ancient Midwest and South*, edited by Richard F. Townsend and Robert V. Sharp, pp. 191–205. The Art Institute of Chicago and Yale University Press, New Haven, Connecticut.

2006 The Transformation of Mississippian Warfare: Four Case Studies from the Mid-South. In *The Archaeology of Warfare: Prehistories of Raiding and Conquest*, edited by Elizabeth Arkush and Mark W. Allen, pp. 101–142. University Press of Florida, Gainesville.

2007 Ritual, Medicine, and the War Trophy Iconographic Theme in the Mississippian Southeast. In *Ancient Objects and Sacred Realms: Interpretations of Mississippian Iconography*, edited by F. Kent Reilly, III and James F. Garber, pp. 289–320. University of Texas Press, Austin.

2009 *War Paths, Peace Paths: An Archaeology of Cooperation and Conflict in Native Eastern North America*. AltaMira Press, Lanham, Maryland.

2012 Mississippian Religious Traditions. In *The Cambridge History of Religions in America Volume One, Pre-Columbian Times to 1790.*, edited by Stephen J. Stein. Cambridge University Press, Cambridge, UK.

Dye, David H. (editor)

2008 *Cave Archaeology in the Eastern Woodlands: Papers in Honor of Patty Jo Watson*. University of Tennessee Press, Knoxville.

Dye, David H. and Cheryl Anne Cox (editors)

1990 *Towns and Temples along the Mississippi*. University of Alabama Press, Tuscaloosa.

Dye, David H., and Adam King

2008 Desecrating the Sacred Ancestor Temples: Chiefly Conflict and Violence in the American Southeast. In *North American Indigenous Warfare and Ritual*, edited by Richard J. Chacon and Ruben G. Mendoza, pp. 160–181. University of Arizona Press, Tucson.

Dye, David H., and Patty Jo Watson

2010 Primary Forest Efficiency in the Eastern Woodlands of North America. *Early Georgia* 38:157–165.

Early, Ann M.

2004 Prehistory of the Western Interior After 500 B.C. In *Smithsonian Handbook of North American Indians, Volume 14, The Southeast*, edited by Raymond D. Fogelson, pp. 560–573. Smithsonian Institution, Washington, D.C.

Eastman, Jane M., and Christopher B. Rodning (editors)

2001 *Archaeological Studies of Gender in the Southeastern United States*. University Press of Florida, Gainesville.

Elliott, Daniel T., and Kenneth E. Sassaman

1995 *Archaic Period Archaeology of the Georgia Coastal Plain and Coastal Zone*. University of Georgia Laboratory of Archaeology Series Report Number 35, Georgia Archaeological Research Design Paper No. 11. Athens, Georgia.

Elliott, Daniel T., Karen G. Wood, and Scot J. Keith

2003 *The Archaeology of the New Echota State Historic Site, Gordon Co. Georgia*. Report produced by Southern Research for the Historic Preservation Division, Georgia Department of Natural Resources, Atlanta.

Ellis, Christopher J., and D. Brian Deller

2002 *Excavations at the Caradoc Site (AfHj-104): A Late Paleoindian Ritual Artifact Deposit*. Occasional Publications of the London Chapter, Ontario Archaeological Society No. 8.

Ellis, Christopher J., and Jonathan C. Lothrop (editors)

1989 *Eastern Paleoindian Lithic Resource Use*. Westview Press, Boulder, Colorado.

Ellis, Christopher J., Albert C. Goodyear, Dan F. Morse, and Kenneth B. Tankersley

1998 Archaeology of the Pleistocene-Holocene Transition in Eastern North America. *Quaternary International* 49/50:151–166.

Emerson, Thomas E.

1989 Water, Serpents and the Underworld: An Exploration into Cahokia Symbolism. In *The Southeastern Ceremonial Complex: Artifacts and Analysis*, edited by Patricia Galloway, pp. 45–92. University of Nebraska Press, Lincoln.

1997 *Cahokia and the Archaeology of Power*. University of Alabama Press, Tuscaloosa.

2002 An Introduction to Cahokia 2002: Diversity, Complexity, and History. *Midcontinental Journal of Archaeology* 27:127–148.

2012 Cahokia Interaction and Ethnogenesis in the Northern Midcontinent. In *The Oxford Handbook of North American Archaeology*, edited by Timothy R. Pauketat, pp. 398–409. Oxford University Press, Oxford, UK.

Emerson, Thomas E., and Dale L. McElrath

2001 Interpreting Discontinuity and Historical Process in Midcontinental Late Archaic and Early Woodland Societies. In *The Archaeology of Traditions: Agency and History Before and After Columbus*, edited by Timothy R. Pauketat, pp. 195–217. University Press of Florida, Gainesville.

Emerson, Thomas E., and Randall E. Hughes

2000 Flint Clay Sourcing, the Ozark Highlands, and Cahokian Acquisition. *American Antiquity* 65:79–101.

2003 Crossing Boundaries Between Worlds: Changing Beliefs and Mortuary Practices at Cahokia. *The Wisconsin Archaeologist* 84:73–80.

Emerson, Thomas E., Randall E. Hughes, Mary R. Hynes, and Sarah U. Wisseman

2003 The Sourcing and Interpretation of Cahokia–Style Figurines in the Trans–Mississippi South and Southeast. *American Antiquity* 68:287–313.

Emerson, Thomas E., Dale L. McElrath, and Andrew C. Fortier (editors)

2000 *Late Woodland Societies: Tradition and Transformation across the Midcontinent*. University of Nebraska Press, Lincoln.

2009 *Archaic Societies: Diversity and Complexity Across the Midcontinent*. State University of New York Press, Albany.

Endonino, Jon C.

2008 The Thornhill Lake Archaeological Project: 2005–2008. *The Florida Anthropologist* 61:149–165.

2010 Thornhill Lake: Hunter-Gatherers, Monuments, and Memory. Ph.D. Dissertation, Department of Anthropology, University of Florida, Gainesville.

Engelbrecht, William E., and Carl K. Seyfert

1994 Paleoindian Watercraft: Evidence and Implications. *North American Archaeologist* 15:221–234.

Ethridge, Robbie

2006 Creating the Shatter Zone: Indian Slave Traders and the Collapse of the Southeastern Chiefdoms. In *Light on the Path: The Anthropology and History of the Southeastern Indians*, edited by Thomas J. Pluckhahn and Robbie Ethridge, pp. 207–218. University of Alabama Press, Tuscaloosa.

Ethridge, Robbie, and Charles M. Hudson (editors)

2002 *The Transformation of the Southeastern Indians, 1540–1760*. University Press of Mississippi, Jackson.

Ethridge, Robbie, and Sheri M. Shuck-Hall (editors)

2009 *Mapping the Mississippian Shatter Zone: The Colonial Indian Slave Trade and Regional Instability in the American South*. University of Nebraska Press, Lincoln.

Eubanks, Mary
1997 Reevaluation of the Identification of Ancient Maize Pollen from Alabama. *American Antiquity* 62:139–145.
Ewan, Charles R.
1998 *Hernando de Soto Among the Apalachee: The Archaeology of the First Winter Encampment.* University Press of Florida, Gainesville.

Fagette, Paul
1996 *Digging for Dollars: American Archaeology and the New Deal.* University of New Mexico Press, Albuquerque.
Fairbanks, Charles H.
1946 The Macon Earth Lodge. *American Antiquity* 12:94–108.
Farnsworth, Kenneth B., and Thomas E. Emerson (editors)
1986 *Early Woodland Archaeology.* Center for American Archaeology Press, Kampsville, Illinois.
Faught, Michael K.
1996 Clovis Origins and Underwater Prehistoric Archaeology in Northwestern Florida. Ph.D. Dissertation, Department of Anthropology, University of Arizona, Tucson.
2004a The Underwater Archaeology of Paleolandscapes, Apalachee Bay, Florida. *American Antiquity* 69:275–289.
2004b Submerged Paleoindian and Archaic Sites of the Big Bend, Florida. *Journal of Field Archaeology* 29:273–289.
2006 Paleoindian Archaeology in Florida and Panama: Two Circum-Gulf Regions Exhibiting Waisted Lanceolate Projectile Points. In *Ice Age Occupations of the Americas: A Hemispheric Perspective,* edited by Juliet Morrow, and Christopher Gnecco, pp. 164–183. University Press of Florida, Gainesville.
Faulkner, Charles H.
1986 *The Prehistoric Native American Art of Mud Glyph Cave.* University of Tennessee Press, Knoxville.
1997 Four Thousand Years of Native American Cave Art in the Southern Appalachians. *Journal of Cave and Karst Studies* 59:148–153.
2002 Woodland Cultures of the Elk and Duck River Valleys, Tennessee: Continuity and Change. In *The Woodland Southeast,* edited by David G. Anderson and Robert C. Mainfort, Jr., pp. 185–203. University of Alabama Press, Tuscaloosa.
Faulkner, Charles H., and Major C. R. McCollough
1974 *Excavations and Testing, Normandy Reservoir Salvage Project: 1972 Season.* Report of Investigations 12, Department of Anthropology, University of Tennessee, Knoxville
1982 Excavation at the Jernigan II Site (40CF37). In *Seventh Report on the Normandy Archaeological Project,* edited by Major C. R. McCullough and Charles H. Faulkner, pp. 153–309. Report of Investigations 32, Department of Anthropology, University of Tennessee, Knoxville
Fearn, Miriam L., and Kar-Bui Liu
1995 Maize Pollen of 3500 B.P. from Southern Alabama. *American Antiquity* 62:109–117.
1997 Identification of Maize Pollen: Reply to Eubanks. *American Antiquity* 62:146–148.
Feathers, James K.
2009 Problems of Ceramic Chronology in the Southeast: Does Shell-Tempered Pottery Appear Earlier than We Think? *American Antiquity* 74:113–142.
Feathers, James K., and Evan Peacock
2008 Origins and Spread of Shell–Tempered Ceramics in the Eastern Woodlands: Conceptual and Methodological Frameworks for Analysis. *Southeastern Archaeology* 27:286–293.

Ferring, C. Reid
1995 The Late Quaternary Geology and Archaeology of the Aubrey Clovis Site, Texas. In *Ancient Peoples and Landscapes*, edited by E. Johnson, pp. 273–282. Museum of Texas Tech University, Lubbock.

Fiedel, Stuart J.
1999 Older Than We Thought: Implications of Corrected Dates for Paleoindians. *American Antiquity* 64:95–116.
2001 What Happened in the Early Woodland? *Archaeology of Eastern North America* 29:101–142.
2005 Man's Best Friend- Mammoths Worst Enemy? A Speculative Essay on the Role of Dogs in Paleoindian Colonization and Megafaunal Extinction. *World Archaeology* 37:11–25.
2007 Quacks in the Ice: Waterfowl, Paleoindians, and the Discovery of America. In *Foragers of the Terminal Pleistocene in North America*, edited by Renee B. Walker and Boyce N. Driskell, 1–14. University of Nebraska Press, Lincoln.
2012 Is That All There Is? The Weak Case for Pre-Clovis Occupation of Eastern North America. In *In the Eastern Fluted Point Tradition*, edited by Joseph A. M. Gingerich. University of Utah Press, Salt Lake City, in press.

Fiedel, Stuart J., and Gary Haynes
2004 A Premature Burial: Comments on Grayson and Meltzer's "Requiem for Overkill." *Journal of Archaeological Science* 31:121–131.

Firestone, R.B.., A. West, J. P. Kennett, L. Becker, T. E. Bunch, Z. S. Revay, P. H. Schultz, T. Belgya, D. J. Kennett, J. M. Erlandson, O. J. Dickenson, A. C. Goodyear, R. S. Harris, G. A. Howard, J. B. Kloosterman, P. Lechler, P. A. Mayewski, J. Montgomery, R. Poreda, T. Darrah, S. S. Que Hee, A. R. Smith, A. Stich, W. Topping, J. H. Wittke and W. S. Wolbach
2007 Evidence for an Extraterrestrial Impact 12,900 Years Ago that Contributed to the Megafaunal Extinctions and the Younger Dryas Cooling. *Proceedings of the National Academy of Sciences, USA* 104:16016-16021.

Flannery, Regina
1943 Some Notes on a Few Sites in Beaufort County, South Carolina. *Bureau of American Ethnology, Smithsonian Institution, Bulletin* 133. U.S. Government Printing Office, Washington, D.C.

Fogelson, Raymond D. (editor)
2004 *Smithsonian Handbook of North American Indians, Volume 14, The Southeast.* Smithsonian Institution, Washington, D.C.

Ford, James A.
1936 *Analysis of Indian Village Site Collections from Louisiana and Mississippi.* School of Geology, Louisiana State University, Baton Rouge.
1963 *Hopewell Culture Burial Mounds Near Helena, Arkansas.* Anthropological Papers of the American Museum of Natural History 50 (Part 1), New York, New York.

Ford, James A., and James B. Griffin
1937 (A Proposal for a) Conference on Pottery Nomenclature for the Southeastern United States. Mimeograph. Museum of Anthropology, Ann Arbor, Michigan.

Ford, James A., and Clarence H. Webb
1956 *Poverty Point, a Late Archaic Site in Louisiana.* American Museum of Natural History, Anthropological Papers Vol. 46, Pt. 1. New York, New York.

Ford, James A., and Gordon R. Willey
1941 An Interpretation of the Prehistory of the Eastern United States. *American Anthropologist* 43:325–363.

Fortier, Andrew C., and Dale L. McElrath
2002 Deconstructing the Emergent Mississippian Concept: The Case for the Terminal Late Woodland in the American Bottom. *Midcontinental Journal of Archaeology* 27:171–215.

Foster, H. Thomas, and Arthur D. Cohen
2007 Palynological Evidence of the Effects of the Deerskin Trade on Forest Fires during the Eighteenth Century in Southeastern North America. *American Antiquity* 72:35–51.

Fowler, Melvin R.
1959 *Summary Report of Modoc Rock Shelter: 1952, 1953, 1955, 1956*. Reports of Investigations 8. Illinois State Museum, Springfield.

Fowler, Melvin L. (editor)
1997 *The Cahokia Atlas: A Historical Atlas of Cahokia Archaeology*, Revised Edition. Studies in Archaeology 2, Illinois Transportation Archaeological Research Program. Urbana, Illinois.

Fowler, Melvin L., Jerome Rose, Barbara Vander Leest, and Steven R. Ahler
1999 *The Mound 72 Area: Dedicated and Sacred Space in Cahokia*. Illinois State Museum Reports of Investigations 54, Springfield, Illinois.

Franklin, Jay D.
2008 Big Cave Archaeology in the East Fork Obey River Gorge. In *Cave Archaeology in the Eastern Woodlands: Essays in Honor of Patty Jo Watson*, edited by David H. Dye, pp. 141–155. University of Tennessee Press, Knoxville.

Franklin, Jay D., and Sierra Bow
2009 Archaeological Explorations of the Workshop Rock Shelter, Upper Cumberland Plateau, Tennessee. *Tennessee Archaeology* 4:145–161.

Fritz, Gayle J.
1990 Multiple Pathways to Farming in Precontact Eastern North America. *Journal of World Prehistory* 4:387–435.
1993 Early and Middle Woodland Period Paleoethnobotany. In *Foraging and Farming in the Eastern Woodlands*, edited by C. Margaret Scarry, pp. 39–56. University Press of Florida, Gainesville.
1997 A Three-Thousand-Year-Old Seed Crop from Marble Bluff, Arkansas. In *People, Plants, and Landscapes: Studies in Paleoethnobotany*, edited by Kristen J. Gremillion, pp. 42–62. University of Alabama Press, Tuscaloosa.

Fritz, Gayle J., and Tristram R. Kidder
1993 Recent Investigations into Prehistoric Agriculture in the Lower Mississippi Valley. *Southeastern Archaeology* 12: 1–14.

Futato, Eugene
2004 Late Middle Archaic Biface Caches and Mortuary Practices in the Interior Southeast. Paper presented at the 2004 Poverty Point Gathering The Enigma of the Specialist: Middle and Late Archaic Beads, Big Bifaces, and Caches in the Lower Mississippi Valley and Greater Southeast, Entering the Mind of the Stone. Epps, Louisiana.

Gaertner, Linda M.
1994 Determining the Function of Dalton Adzes from Northeast Arkansas. *Lithic Technology* 19(2):97–109.

Gallay, Alan
2003 *The Indian Slave Trade: The Rise of the English Empire in the American South, 1670–1717*. University of Nebraska Press, Lincoln.

Gallay, Alan (editor)
2009 *Indian Slavery in Colonial America*. University of Nebraska Press, Lincoln.

Gallivan, Martin D.
2003 *James River Chiefdoms: The Rise of Social Inequality in the Chesapeake.* University of Nebraska Press, Lincoln.
2007 Powhatan's Werowocomoco: Constructing Place, Polity, and Personhood in the Chesapeake, A.D. 1200–1609. *American Anthropologist* 109:85–100.
Galloway, Patricia K.
1993 Ethnohistory. In *The Development of Southeastern Archaeology*, edited by Jay K. Johnson, pp. 78–198. University of Alabama Press, Tuscaloosa.
1994 Confederacy as a Solution to Chiefdom Dissolution: Historical Evidence in the Choctaw Case. In *The Forgotten Centuries: Indians and Europeans in the American South, 1521–1704*, edited by Charles M. Hudson and Carmen Chaves Tesser, pp. 393–420. University of Georgia Press, Athens.
1995 *Choctaw Genesis 1500–1700.* University of Nebraska Press, Lincoln.
Galloway, Patricia K. (editor)
1989 *The Southeastern Ceremonial Complex: Artifacts and Analysis.* University of Nebraska Press, Lincoln.
2005 *The Hernando de Soto Expedition: History, Historiography, and "Discovery" in the Southeast*, second edition, University of Nebraska Press, Lincoln.
Gamble, Clive
2007 *Origins and Revolutions: Human Identity in Earliest Prehistory.* Cambridge University Press, Cambridge, UK.
Gardner, Paul
1997 The Ecological Structure and Behavioral Implications of Mast Exploitation Strategies. In *People, Plants, and Landscape: Studies in Paleoethnobotany*, edited by Kristen J. Gremillion, pp. 161–178. University of Alabama Press, Tuscaloosa.
Gardner, William M.
1974 *The Flint Run Paleoindian Complex: A Preliminary Report 1971 through 1973 Seasons.* Occasional Paper No. 1, Archaeology Laboratory. Catholic University of America, Washington, D.C.
1977 Flint Run Paleoindian Complex and its Implications for Eastern North American Prehistory in *Amerinds and their Paleoenvironments in Northeastern North America*, edited by Walter S. Newman and Bert Salwen, pp. 257–263. New York Academy of Sciences, New York, New York.
1989 An Examination of Cultural Change in the Late Pleistocene and Early Holocene (circa 9200 to 6800 B.C.). In *Paleoindian Research in Virginia: A Synthesis*, edited by J. Mark Wittkofski and Theodore R. Reinhart, pp. 5–51. Special Publication 19, Archeological Society of Virginia, Richmond.
Gardner, William M., and R. Verrey
1979 Typology and Chronology of Fluted Points from the Flint Run Area. *Pennsylvania Archaeologist* 49:13–45.
Gavrilets, Sergey, David G. Anderson, and Peter Turchin
2010 Cycling in the Complexity of Early Societies. *Cliodynamics: The Journal of Theoretical and Mathematical History* 1:58–80. Also available at http://escholarship.org/ uc/item/5536t55r
Geertz, Clifford
1980 *Negara: The Theater State in Nineteenth Century Bali.* Princeton University Press, Princeton, New Jersey.
Gell, Alfred
1998 *Art and Agency: An Anthropological Theory.* Clarendon Press, Oxford.

Gibson, Jon L

1993 Ceramics. In *The Development of Southeastern Archaeology*, edited by Jay K. Johnson, pp. 18–35. University of Alabama Press, Tuscaloosa.

1994 Empirical Characterization of Exchange Systems in Lower Mississippi Valley Prehistory. In *Prehistoric Exchange Systems in North America*, edited by Timothy G. Baugh and Jonathon E. Ericson, pp. 127–175. Plenum, New York.

1996 Poverty Point and Greater Southeastern Prehistory: The Culture That Did Not Fit. In *Archaeology of the Mid–Holocene Southeast*, edited by Kenneth E. Sassaman and David G. Anderson, pp. 288–305. University Press of Florida, Gainesville.

2000 *The Ancient Mounds of Poverty Point Place of Rings*. University Press of Florida, Gainesville.

2004 The Power of Beneficent Obligation in First Mound-Building Societies. In *Signs of Power: The Rise of Cultural Complexity in the Southeast*, edited by Jon L. Gibson and Philip J. Carr, pp. 254–269. University of Alabama Press, Tuscaloosa.

2010 "Nothing But the River's Flood": Late Archaic Diaspora or Disengagement in the Lower Mississippi Valley and Southeastern North America. In *Trend, Tradition, and Turmoil: What Happened to the Southeastern Archaic?* Proceedings of the Third Caldwell Conference, St. Catherines Island, Georgia, May 9–11, 2008, edited by David Hurst Thomas and Matthew C. Sanger, pp. 33–42. Anthropological Papers 93. American Museum of Natural History, New York.

Gibson, Jon L., and Philip J. Carr (editors)

2004 *Signs of Power: The Rise of Cultural Complexity in the Southeast*. University of Alabama Press, Tuscaloosa.

Gibson, Jon L., and Mark A. Melancon

2004 In the Beginning: Social Contexts of First Pottery in the Lower Mississippi Valley. In *Early Pottery: Technology, Function, Style, and Interaction in the Lower Southeast*, edited by Rebecca Saunders and Christopher T. Hays, pp. 169–192. University of Alabama Press, Tuscaloosa.

Giles, Bretton

2010 Sacrificing Complexity: Renewal through Ohio Hopewell Rituals. In *Ancient Complexities: New Perspectives in Precolumbian North America*, edited by Susan M. Alt, pp. 73–95. University of Utah Press, Salt Lake City.

2011 The Ritual Mnemonics of Hopewell Symbols: An Analysis of Effigies and Ceremonial Regalia from Tremper, Mound City and Hopewell. Ph.D. Dissertation, Department of Anthropology, State University of New York at Binghamton, Binghamton, New York.

Giles, Bretton, Jennifer Bauder, and Marta P. Alfonso-Durruty

2010 Revisiting the Dead at Helena Crossing, Arkansas. *Southeastern Archaeology* 29:323–340.

Gillam, J. Christopher

1996a Early and Middle Paleoindian Sites in the Northeastern Arkansas Region. In *The Paleoindian and Early Archaic Southeast*, edited by David G. Anderson and Kenneth E. Sassaman, pp. 404–412. University of Alabama Press, Tuscaloosa.

1996b A View of Paleoindian Settlement from Crowley's Ridge. *Plains Anthropologist* 157:273–286.

1999 Paleoindian Settlement in Northeastern Arkansas. In *Papers in Honor of Dan and Phyllis Morse*, edited by Robert C. Mainfort, Jr. and Marvin D. Jeter, pp. 99–118. University of Arkansas Press, Fayetteville.

Gillam, J. Christopher, David G. Anderson, Stephen J. Yerka, and D. Shane Miller

2006 Estimating Pleistocene Shorelines and Land Elevations for North America. *Current Research in the Pleistocene* 23:185–187.

Gilliland, Marion Spjut
1975 *The Material Culture of Key Marco, Florida*. University Press of Florida, Gainesville.
Gingerich, Joseph A.M.
2007 Picking up the Pieces: New Paleoindian Research in the Upper Delaware Valley. *Archaeology of Eastern North America* 35:117–124.
2011 Down to Seeds and Stones: A New Look at the Subsistence Remains from Shawnee-Minisink. *American Antiquity* 76:127–144.
2012 Revisiting Shawnee-Minisink. In *In the Eastern Fluted Point Tradition*, edited by Joseph A. M. Gingerich. University of Utah Press, Salt Lake City, in press.
Gingerich, Joseph A.M. (editor)
2012 *In the Eastern Fluted Point Tradition*. University of Utah Press, Salt Lake City, in press.
Goad, Sharon
1979 Middle Woodland Exchange in the Prehistoric Southeastern United States. In *Hopewell Archaeology: The Chillicothe Conference*, edited by David S. Brose and N'omi Greber, pp. 239–246. Kent State University Press, Kent, Ohio.
Goebel, Ted, Michael R. Waters, and D. H. O'Rourke
2008 The Late Pleistocene Dispersal of Modern Humans in the Americas. *Science* 319:1497–1502
Goldstein, Lynne
2004 An Analysis of Plummets in the Lower Illinois River Valley. In *Aboriginal Ritual and Economy in the Eastern Woodlands: Essays in Honor of Howard Dalton Winters*, edited by Anne-Marie Cantwell, Lawrence A. Conrad, and Jonathan E. Reyman, pp. 73–112. Scientific Papers 30. Illinois State Museum, Springfield.
Goodyear, Albert C.
1974 *The Brand Site: A Techno-functional Study of a Dalton Site in Northeast Arkansas*. Research Series 7. Arkansas Archaeological Survey, Fayetteville.
1979 *A Hypothesis for the Use of Cryptocrystalline Raw Materials among Paleoindian Groups of North America*. South Carolina Institute of Archaeology and Anthropology. Research Manuscript Series 156. University of South Carolina, Columbia.
1982 The Chronological Position of the Dalton Horizon in the Southeastern United States. *American Antiquity* 47:382–395.
1999 The Early Holocene Occupation of the Southeastern United States: A Geoarchaeological Summary. In *Ice Age Peoples of North America*, edited by Robson Bonnichsen and Karen L. Turnmire, pp. 432–481. Center for the Study of the First Americans, Corvallis, Oregon.
2005 Evidence for Pre-Clovis Sites in the Eastern United States. In *Paleoamerican Origins: Beyond Clovis*, edited by Robson Bonnichsen, Bradley T. Lepper, Dennis Stanford, and Michael R. Waters, pp. 103–112. Center for the Study of the First Americans, Texas A&M University Press, College Station.
2006 Recognizing the Redstone Fluted Point in the South Carolina Paleoindian Point Database. *Current Research in the Pleistocene* 23:112–114.
2010 Instrument-Assisted Fluting as a Techno-chronological Marker among North American Paleoindian Points. *Current Research in the Pleistocene* 27:86–88.
Goodyear, Albert C., and Glen T. Hanson (editors)
1989 *Studies in South Carolina Archaeology: Essays in Honor of Robert L. Stephenson*. South Carolina Institute of Archaeology and Anthropology, Anthropological Studies 9. Columbia, South Carolina.
Goodyear, Albert C., James L. Michie, and Tommy Charles
1990 *The Earliest South Carolinians: The Paleoindian Occupation of South Carolina*. The Archaeological Society of South Carolina, Inc., Occasional Papers No. 2. Columbia.

Gougeon, Ramie A.

2006 Different but the Same: Social Integration of Households in Mississippian Chiefdoms. In *Leadership and Polity in Mississippian Society*, edited by Brian M. Butler and Paul D. Welch, pp. 178–194. Center for Archaeological Investigations, Occasional Paper No. 33. Southern Illinois University, Carbondale.

2007 An Architectural Grammar of Late Mississippian Houses in Northwest Georgia. In *Architectural Variability in the Southeast*, edited by Cameron H. Lacquement, pp. 136–152. University of Alabama Press, Tuscaloosa.

Grafenstein, Ulrich von, Helmut Erlenkeuser, Achime Brauer, Jean Jouzel, and Sigfus J. Johnsen

1999 A Mid-European Decadal Isotope-Climate Record from 15,500 to 5000 Years B.P. *Science* 284:1654–1657.

Graham, Russell W., and E. L. Lundelius

1994 *FAUNMAP: A Database Documenting Late Quaternary Distributions of Mammal Species in the United States.* Illinois State Museum Scientific Papers Vol. XXV. Springfield. Available online at http://www.museum.state.il.us/research/faunmap/aboutfaunmap.html.

Graham, Russell W., C. Vance Haynes, Donald Lee Johnson, and Marvin Kay

1981 Kimmswick: A Clovis-Mastodon Association in Eastern Missouri. *Science* 213:1115–1117.

Gramly, Richard M.

2009 *Origin and Evolution of the Cumberland Palaeo-American Tradition.* American Society for Amateur Archaeology, North Andover, Massachusetts.

Grantham, Bill

2002 *Creation Myths and Legends of the Creek Indians.* University Press of Florida, Gainesville.

Grayson, Donald K.

1991 Late Pleistocene Mammalian Extinction in North America: Taxonomy, Chronology, and Explanations. *Journal of World Prehistory* 5:193–231.

2007 Deciphering North American Pleistocene Extinctions. *Journal of Anthropological Research* 63:185–213

Grayson, Donald K., and David J. Meltzer

2002 Clovis Hunting and Large Mammal Extinction: A Critical Review of the Evidence. *Journal of World Prehistory* 16:313–359.

2003 A Requiem for North American Overkill. *Journal of Archaeological Science* 30:585–593.

2004 North American Overkill Continued? *Journal of Archaeological Science* 31:133–136.

Greber, N'omi B.

2006 Enclosures and Communities of Ohio Hopewell: An Essay. In *Recreating Hopewell*, edited by Douglas K. Charles and Jane E. Buikstra, pp. 74–105. University Press of Florida, Gainesville.

Gremillion, Kristen J.

1996 The Paleoethnobotanical Record for the Mid–Holocene Southeast. In *Archaeology of the Mid–Holocene Southeast*, edited by Kenneth E. Sassaman and David G. Anderson, pp. 99–114. University Press of Florida, Gainesville.

1998 Changing Roles of Wild and Cultivated Plant Resources among Early Farmers in Eastern Kentucky. *Southeastern Archaeology* 17:140–57.

2002 The Development and Dispersal of Agricultural Systems in the Woodland Period Southeast. In *The Woodland Southeast*, edited by David G. Anderson and Robert C. Mainfort, Jr., pp. 483–501. University of Alabama Press, Tuscaloosa.

2004a Environment. In *Smithsonian Handbook of North American Indians, Volume 14, The Southeast*, edited by Raymond D. Fogelson, pp. 53–67. Smithsonian Institution, Washington, D.C.

2004b Seed Processing and the Origins of Food Production in Eastern North America. *American Antiquity* 69, 215–33.

2006 Southeastern Food Plants. In *Smithsonian Handbook of North American Indians, Volume 3, Environment, Origins, and Population*, edited by Douglas H. Ubelaker, pp. 388–395. Smithsonian Institution, Washington, D.C.

2011 The Role of Plants in Southeastern Subsistence Economies. In *Subsistence Economies of Indigenous North American Societies*, edited by Bruce D. Smith., pp. 380–400. Smithsonian Institution Scholarly Press, Washington, D.C.

Gremillion, Kristen J. (editor)

1997 *People, Plants, and Landscape: Studies in Paleoethnobotany*. University of Alabama Press, Tuscaloosa.

Gremillion, Kristen J., Jason Windingstad, and Sarah C. Sherwood

2008 Forest Opening, Habitat Use, and Food Production on the Cumberland Plateau, Kentucky: Adaptive Flexibility in Marginal Settings. *American Antiquity* 73:387–411.

Griffin, James B.

1952 Culture Periods in Eastern United States Archeology. In *Archeology of the Eastern United States*, edited by James B. Griffin, pp. 352–364. University of Chicago Press, Chicago.

1961 Some Correlations of Climatic and Cultural Change in Eastern North American Prehistory. *Annals of the New York Academy of Sciences* 95:710–717.

1967 Eastern North American Archaeology: A Summary. *Science* 156:175–191.

1985 Changing Concepts of the Prehistoric Mississippian Cultures of the Eastern United States. In *Alabama and the Borderlands: From Prehistory to Statehood*, edited by R. Reid Badger and Lawrence A. Clayton, pp. 40–63. University of Alabama Press, Tuscaloosa.

Griffin, James B. (editor)

1952 *Archeology of Eastern United States*. University of Chicago Press, Chicago.

Griffin, James B., David J. Meltzer, and Bruce D. Smith

1988 A Mammoth Fraud in Science. *American Antiquity* 53:578–582

Griffin, John W.

1974 *Investigations in Russell Cave, Russell Cave National Monument, Alabama*. National Park Service, Publication in Archeology 13. Washington, D.C.

Grimm, Eric C., and George L. Jacobson

2004 Late Quaternary Vegetation History of the Eastern United States. In *The Quaternary Period in the United States*, edited by Alan R. Gillespie, Stephen C. Porter, and Brian F. Atwater, pp. 381–402. Elsevier, Amsterdam, The Netherlands.

Grissino-Mayer, Henri D.

2009. An Introduction to Dendroarchaeology in the Southeastern United States. *Tree-Ring Research* 65(1): 5–10.

Gunn, Joel D., and David O. Brown (editors)

1982 *Eagle Hill: A Late Quaternary Upland Site in Western Louisiana*. Special Report 12, Center for Archaeological Research, University of Texas at San Antonio, San Antonio.

Guthe, Carl E.

1939 Obituary [of Warren K. Moorehead]. *American Antiquity* 5:65–66.

Haag, William G.

1965 William Snyder Webb, 1882–1964. *American Antiquity* 30:470–473.

1985 Federal Aid to Archaeology in the Southeast, 1933–1942. *American Antiquity* 50:272–280.

Hahn, Steven C.

2004 *The Invention of the Creek Nation, 1670–1763*. University of Nebraska Press, Lincoln.

Hall, Robert L.

1968 The Goddard–Ramey Cahokia Flight: A Pioneering Aerial Photographic Survey. *The Wisconsin Archaeologist* 49(2):75–79.

1997 *An Archaeology of the Soul: North American Indian Belief and Ritual.* University of Illinois Press, Urbana.

Hally, David J. (editor)

1994 *Ocmulgee Archaeology 1936–1986.* University of Georgia Press, Athens.

Hally, David J.

1983 Use Alteration of Pottery Surfaces: An Important Source of Evidence for the Identification of Vessel Function. *North American Archaeologist* 4:3–26.

1986 The Identification of Vessel Function: A Case Study from Northwest Georgia. *American Antiquity* 51:267–295.

1993 The Territorial Size of Mississippian Chiefdoms. In *Archaeology of Eastern North America, Papers in Honor of Stephen Williams*, edited by James B. Stoltman, pp. 143–168. Archaeological Report No. 25. Mississippi Department of Archives and History, Jackson.

1994a An Overview of Lamar Culture. In *Ocmulgee Archaeology 1936–1986*, edited by David J. Hally, pp. 144–174. University of Georgia Press, Athens.

1994b The Chiefdom of Coosa. In *The Forgotten Centuries: Indians and Europeans in the American South, 1521–1704*, edited by Charles M. Hudson and Carmen Chaves Tesser, pp. 227–253. University of Georgia Press, Athens.

1996 Platform-Mound Construction and the Political Stability of Mississippian Chiefdoms. In *Political Structure and Change in the Prehistoric Southeastern United States*, edited by John F. Scarry, pp. 92–127. University Press of Florida, Gainesville.

1999 The Settlement Pattern of Mississippian Chiefdoms in Northern Georgia. In *Settlement Pattern Studies in the Americas: Fifty years since Viru*, edited by Brian R. Billman and Gary M. Feinman, pp. 96–115. Smithsonian Institution Press, Washington, D.C.

2006 Nature of Mississippian Regional Systems. In *Light on the Path: The Anthropology and History of the Southeastern Indians*, edited by Thomas J. Pluckhahn and Robbie Ethridge, pp. 26–42. University of Alabama Press, Tuscaloosa.

2008 *King: The Social Archaeology of a Late Mississippian Town in Northwestern Georgia.* University of Alabama Press, Tuscaloosa.

Hally, David J., and Robert C. Mainfort, Jr.

2004 Prehistory of the Eastern Interior, After 500 B.C. In *Smithsonian Handbook of North American Indians, Volume 14, The Southeast*, edited by Raymond D. Fogelson, pp. 265–285. Smithsonian Institution, Washington, D.C.

Hamilton, Fran E.

1999 Southeastern Archaic Mounds: Examples of Elaboration in a Temporally Fluctuating Environment? *Journal of Anthropological Archaeology* 18:344–355.

Hammerstedt, Scott W.

2005 Mississippian Construction, Labor, and Social Organization in Western Kentucky. Ph.D. Dissertation, Department of Anthropology, Pennsylvania State University.

Hammerstedt, Scott W., Amanda L. Regnier, and Patrick C. Livingood

2010 Geophysical and Archaeological Investigations at the Clement Site, A Caddo Mound Complex in Southeastern Oklahoma. *Southeastern Archaeology* 29:279–291.

Hann, John H.

1988 *Apalachee: The Land Between the Rivers.* University Press of Florida, Gainesville.

Hann, John H., and Bonnie G. McEwan

1998 *The Apalachee Indians and Mission San Luis.* University Press of Florida, Gainesville.

Hantman, Jeffery L.
2001 Monacan History at the Dawn of Colonization: The Archaeology of the Virginia Interior A.D. 1400–1700. In *Societies in Eclipse: Eastern North America at the Dawn of Colonization*, edited by David S. Brose and Robert C. Mainfort, pp. 107–124. Smithsonian Institution Press, Washington, D.C.

Harle, Michaelyn S.
2010 Biological Affinities and the Construction of Cultural Identity for the Proposed Coosa Chiefdom. Ph.D. Dissertation, Department of Anthropology, University of Tennessee, Knoxville.

Harmon, David, Francis P. McManamon, and Dwight T. Pitcaithley (editors)
2006 *The Antiquities Act: A Century of American Archaeology, Historic Preservation, and Nature Conservation*. University of Arizona Press, Tucson.

Haskins, Valerie A., and Nicholas P. Herrmann
1996 Shell Mound Bioarchaeology. In *Of Caves and Shellmounds*, edited by Kenneth C. Carstens and Patty J. Watson, pp. 107–118. University of Alabama Press, Tuscaloosa.

Haynes, C. Vance
1964 Fluted Projectile Points: Their Age and Dispersion. *Science* 145:1408–1413.

Haynes, Gary
2002 *The Early Settlement of North America: The Clovis Era*. Cambridge University Press, Cambridge, UK.

Haynes, Gary (editor)
2009 *American Megafaunal Extinctions at the End of the Pleistocene*. Springer, New York, New York.

Hays, Christopher T., and Richard A. Weinstein
2010 Tchefuncte and Early Woodland. In *Archaeology of Louisiana*, edited by Mark A. Rees, pp. 97–119. Louisiana State University Press, Baton Rouge.

Hegmon, Michelle
2003 Setting Theoretical Egos Aside: Issues and Theory in North American Archaeology. *American Antiquity* 68:213–243.

Hemmings, C. Andrew
2004 The Organic Clovis: A Single Continent-Wide Cultural Adaptation. Ph.D. Dissertation, Department of Anthropology, University of Florida, Gainesville.
2005 An Update on Recent Work at Sloth Hole (8JE121), Aucilla River, Jefferson County, Florida. *Current Research in the Pleistocene* 22:47–49.

Hemmings, C. Andrew, James S. Dunbar, and S. David Webb
2004 Florida's Early–Paleoindian Bone and Ivory Tools. In *New Perspectives on the First Americans*, edited by Bradley T. Lepper and Robson Bonnichsen, pp. 87–92. Center for the Study of the First Americans, Texas A&M University Press, College Station.

Hensley, Christine
1994 The Archaic Settlement System of the Middle Green River Valley. Ph.D. Dissertation, Department of Anthropology, Washington University, St. Louis.

Herbert, Joseph
2009 *Woodland Potters and Archaeological Ceramics of the North Carolina Coast*. University of Alabama Press, Tuscaloosa.

Heye, George G., Frederick W. Hodge, and George H. Pepper
1918 *The Nacoochee Mound in Georgia*. Contributions from the Museum of the American Museum, Heye Foundation 4(3). New York, New York.

Hoak, Megan King
2012 Evaluating Pre-Clovis at the Topper Site through Lithic Debitage Analysis. M.A. Thesis, Department of Anthropology, University of Tennessee, Knoxville. (In preparation)

Hoard, Robert, and Henry W. Chaney

2010 *Olivella* Shells from Kansas Archaeological Sites. *Plains Anthropologist* 55:293–298.

Hodder, Ian

1990 *The Domestication of Europe: Structure and Contingency in Neolithic Societies*. Basil Blackwell, Oxford, UK.

Hofman, Jack

1985 Middle Archaic Ritual and Shell Midden Archaeology: Considering the Significance of Cremations. In *Exploring Tennessee Prehistory: A Dedication to Alfred K. Guthe*, edited by Thomas R. Whyte, C. Clifford Boyd, and Brett H. Riggs, pp. 1–21. Report of Investigations 42. Department of Anthropology, University of Tennessee, Knoxville.

Hogue, S. Homes

1994 The Human Skeletal Remains from Dust Cave. *Journal of Alabama Archaeology* 40:173–191.

Hollenbach, Kandace D.

2005 Gathering in the Late Paleoindian and Early Archaic Periods in the Middle Tennessee River Valley. Ph.D. Dissertation, Department of Anthropology, University of North Carolina, Chapel Hill.

2007 Gathering in the Late Paleoindian Period: Archaeological Remains from Dust Cave, Alabama. In *Foragers of the Terminal Pleistocene*, edited by Renee B. Walker and Boyce N. Driskell, pp. 132–147. University of Alabama Press, Tuscaloosa.

2009 *Foraging in the Tennessee River Valley 12,500 to 8,000 Years Ago*. University of Alabama Press, Tuscaloosa.

Holley, George R.

1999 Late Prehistoric Towns in the Southeast. In *Great Towns and Regional Polities in the Prehistoric American Southwest and Southeast*, edited by Jill E. Neitzel, pp. 22–38. Amerind Foundation New World Study Series 3. University of New Mexico Press, Albuquerque.

Holley, George R., Rinita A. Dalan, and Phillip A. Smith

1993 Investigations in the Cahokia Site Grand Plaza. *American Antiquity* 58:306–319.

Holliday, Vance T., and David J. Meltzer

2010 The 12.9ka ET Impact Hypothesis and North American Paleoindians. *Current Anthropology* 51:575–607

Holt, Julie Zimmerman

2009 Rethinking the Ramey State: Was Cahokia the Center of a Theater State? *American Antiquity* 74:231–254.

Holmes, William H.

1903 Aboriginal Pottery of the Eastern United States. In *Twentieth Annual Report of the Bureau of American Ethnology 1898–1899*, pp. 1–237. Smithsonian Institution, Washington, D.C.

Homsey, Lara K., Renee B. Walker, and Kandace D. Hollenbach

2010 What's for Dinner? Investigating Food-processing Technologies at Dust Cave, Alabama. *Southeastern Archaeology* 29:182–196.

Howe, George

1856 An Essay on the Antiquities of the Congaree Indians of South Carolina. In *Historical and Statistical Information, Respecting the History, Condition and Prospects of the Indian Tribes of the United States; Collected and Prepared Under the Direction of the Bureau of Indian Affairs, per Act of Congress of March 3rd, 1847*. 6 vols., edited by Henry Schoolcraft, Volume IV:155–168. Lippincott, Grambo and Co., Philadelphia.

Hudson, Charles H.

1976 *The Southeastern Indians*. University of Tennessee Press, Knoxville.

1990 *Juan Pardo Expeditions: Exploration of the Carolinas and Tennessee, 1566–1568.* Smithsonian Institution Press, Washington, D.C. Reprinted, 2005, University of Alabama Press, Tuscaloosa.

1997 *Knights of Spain, Warriors of the Sun: Hernando De Soto and the South's Ancient Chiefdoms.* University of Georgia Press, Athens.

Hudson, Charles M., and Carmen Chaves Tesser (editors)

1994 *The Forgotten Centuries: Indians and Europeans in the American South, 1521–1704.* University of Georgia Press, Athens.

Hudson, Charles M., Marvin T. Smith, David J. Hally, Richard Polhemus, and Chester B. DePratter

1985 Coosa: A Chiefdom in the Sixteenth-Century Southeastern United States. *American Antiquity* 50:723–737.

Hudson, Charles M., Robin A. Beck, Chester B. DePratter, Robbie Ethridge, and John E. Worth

2008 On Interpreting Cofitachequi. *Ethnohistory* 55:465–490.

Hutchinson, Dale L.

2004 *Bioarchaeology of the Florida Gulf Coast: Adaptation, Conflict, and Change.* University Press of Florida, Gainesville.

Hutchinson, Dale L., Clark Spencer Larsen, Margaret J. Schoeninger, and Lynette Norr

1998 Regional Variation in the Pattern of Maize Adoption and Use in Florida and Georgia. *American Antiquity* 63:397–416.

Ison, Cecil R.

1988 The Cold Oak Shelter: Providing a Better Understanding of the Terminal Archaic. In *PaleoIndian and Archaic Research in Kentucky,* edited by Charles D. Hockensmith, David Pollack, and Tom Sanders, pp. 205–220. Kentucky Heritage Council, Frankfort.

Jackson, H. Edwin

1991 The Trade Fair in Hunter-Gatherer Interaction: The Role of Intersocietal Trade in the Evolution of Poverty Point Culture. In *Between Bands and States,* edited by Susan A. Gregg, pp. 265–286. Center for Archaeological Investigations, Occasional Paper No. 9. Southern Illinois University, Carbondale.

Jackson, H. Edwin, and Susan L. Scott

1995 The Faunal Record of the Southeastern Elite: The Implications of Economy, Social Relations, and Ideology. *Southeastern Archaeology* 14:103-119.

2001 Archaic Faunal Utilization in the Louisiana Bottomlands. *Southeastern Archaeology* 20:187–196.

2002 Woodland Faunal Exploitation in the Mid-South. In *The Woodland Southeast,* edited by David G. Anderson and Robert C. Mainfort, Jr., pp. 461–482. University of Alabama Press, Tuscaloosa.

2003 Patterns of Elite Faunal Utilization at Moundville, Alabama. *American Antiquity* 68:552–572.

Jacobson, George L. Jr., Thompson Webb III, and Eric C. Grimm

1987 Patterns and Rates of Vegetation Change during the Deglaciation of Eastern North America. In: *North America and Adjacent Oceans during the Last Deglaciation,* edited by William F. Ruddiman, and Herbert E. Wright Jr., pp. 277–288. Geological Society of America, Boulder, Colorado.

Jantz, Richard L., and Douglas W. Owsley

2005 Circumpacific Populations and the Peopling of the New World: Evidence from Cranial Morphometrics. In *Paleoamerican Origins: Beyond Clovis,* edited by Robson Bonnichsen,

Bradley T. Lepper, Dennis Stanford, and Michael R. Waters, pp. 185–193. Center for the Study of the First Americans, Texas A&M University Press, College Station.

Jefferies, Richard W.

1976 *The Tunacunnahee Site: Evidence of Hopewell Interaction in Northwest Georgia.* Anthropological Papers of the University of Georgia 1. Department of Anthropology, University of Georgia, Athens.

1994 The Swift Creek Site and Woodland Platform Mounds in the Southeastern United States. In *Ocmulgee Archaeology, 1936–1986*, edited by David J. Hally, pp. 71–83. University of Georgia Press, Athens.

1995 Late Middle Archaic Exchange and Interaction in the North American Midcontinent. In *Native American Interactions: Multiscalar Analysis and Interpretations in the Eastern Woodlands*, edited by Michael S. Nassaney and Kenneth E. Sassaman, pp. 73–99. University of Tennessee Press, Knoxville.

1996 The Emergence of Long–Distance Exchange Networks in the Southeastern United States. In *Archaeology of the Mid–Holocene Southeast*, edited by Kenneth E. Sassaman and David G. Anderson, pp. 222–234. University Press of Florida, Gainesville.

2004a Regional Scale Interaction Networks and the Emergence of Cultural Complexity along the Northern Margins of the Southeast. In *Signs of Power: The Rise of Cultural Complexity in the Southeast*, edited by Jon L. Gibson and Philip J. Carr, pp. 71–85. University of Alabama Press, Tuscaloosa.

2004b Regional Cultures, 700 B.C.–A.D. 1000. In *Smithsonian Handbook of North American Indians, Volume 14, The Southeast*, edited by Raymond D. Fogelson, pp. 115–127. Smithsonian Institution, Washington, D.C.

2009 *Holocene Hunter-Gatherers of the Lower Ohio River Valley.* University of Alabama Press, Tuscaloosa.

Jefferson, Thomas

1787 *Notes on the State of Virginia.* John Stockdale, London.

Jenkins, Ned J., and Richard A. Krause

2009 The Woodland-Mississippian Interface in Alabama, ca. A.D. 1075–1200: An Adaptive Radiation? *Southeastern Archaeology* 28:202–219.

Jennings, Jesse D.

1994 *Accidental Archaeologist: Memoirs of Jesse D. Jennings.* University of Utah Press, Salt Lake City.

Jennings, Thomas A.

2008a San Patrice: An Example of Late Paleoindian Adaptive Versatility in South-Central North America. *American Antiquity* 73(3):539–559.

2008b *San Patrice Technology and Mobility across the Plains-Woodland Border.* Oklahoma Anthropological Society Memoir 12, Robert E. Bell Monographs in Anthropology No. 5. Sam Noble Oklahoma Museum of Natural History, Norman.

Jenson, Richard E. (editor)

1997 *From Fort Laramie to Wounded Knee In the West That Was by Charles W. Allen.* University of Nebraska Press, Lincoln.

Jeter, Marvin D.

1990 *Edward Palmer's Arkansaw Mounds.* University of Arkansas Press, Fayetteville. Reprinted, 2010, University of Alabama Press, Tuscaloosa.

Jodry, Margaret A.

2005 Envisioning Water Transport Technology in Late-Pleistocene America. In *Paleoamerican Origins: Beyond Clovis*, edited by Robson Bonnichsen, Bradley T. Lepper, Dennis Stanford, and

Michael R. Waters, 133–160. Center for the Study of the First Americans, Texas A&M University Press, College Station.

Johanson, Erik N.

2011 Predictive Modeling in Western Louisiana: Prehistoric and Historic Settlement in the Kisatchie National Forest. M.A. Thesis, Department of Anthropology, University of Tennessee, Knoxville.

Johnson, Leroy, Jr.

1989 *Great Plains Interlopers in the Eastern Woodlands during Late Paleoindian Times*. Office of the State Archaeologist, Report 36. Texas Historical Commission,Austin.

Johnson, Jay K.

1994 Prehistoric Exchange in the Southeast. In *Prehistoric Exchange Systems in North America*, edited by Timothy G. Baugh and Jonathon E. Ericson, pp. 99–126. Plenum, New York.

1997 Stone Tools, Politics, and the Eighteenth-Century Chickasaw in Northeast Mississippi. *American Antiquity* 62:215–230.

2000 Beads, Microdrills, Bifaces, and Blades from the Watson Brake Site in Northeastern Louisiana. *Southeastern Archaeology* 19:95–104.

Johnson, Jay K. (editor)

1993 *The Development of Southeastern Archaeology*. University of Alabama Press, Tuscaloosa.

Johnson, Jay K., and Samuel O. Brookes

1989 Benton Points, Turkey Tails and Cache Blades: Middle Archaic Exchange in the Southeast. *Southeastern Archaeology* 8:134–145.

Johnson, Jay K., John W. O'Hear, Robbie Ethridge, Brad R. Lieb, Susan L. Scott, and H. Edwin Jackson

2008 Measuring Chickasaw Adaptation on the Western Frontier of the Colonial South: A Correlation of Documentary and Archaeological Data. *Southeastern Archaeology* 27:1–30.

Jones, Charles C.

1873 *Antiquities of the Southern Indians, Particularly of the Georgia Tribes*. D. Appleton, New York.

Jones, Joseph

1876 *Explorations of the Aboriginal Remains of Tennessee*. Contributions to Knowledge No. 259. Smithsonian Institution, Washington, D.C.

Jones, Volney T.

1936 Vegetal Remains of Newt Kash Hollow Shelter. In *Rockshelters in Menifee County*, edited by William S. Webb and William D. Funkhouser, pp. 147–165. Reports in Archaeology and Anthropology 3. University of Kentucky, Louisville.

Justice, Noel D.

1987 *Stone Age Spear and Arrow Points of the Midcontinental and Eastern United States A Modern Survey and Reference*. Indiana University Press, Bloomington.

Kane, Sharyn, and Richard Keeton

1994 *Beneath These Waters, Archeological and Historical Studies of 11,500 Years along the Savannah River.* Interagency Archeological Services Division, National Park Service. Atlanta, Georgia.

Keel, Bennie C.

1970 Cyrus Thomas and the Mound Builders. *Southern Indian Studies* 22:3–16.

1976 *Cherokee Archaeology: A Study of the Appalachian Summit*. University of Tennessee Press, Knoxville.

1988 *Advances in Southeastern Archaeology: Contributions of the Federal Archaeology Program*. Southeastern Archaeological Conference Special Publication 6. Morgantown, West Virginia.

Kehoe, Alice B.
1998 *The Land of Prehistory: A Critical History of American Archaeology*. Routledge, New York.

Kelly, John E.
1987 Emergent Mississippian and the Transition from Late Woodland to Mississippian: the American Bottom Case for a New Concept. In *The Emergent Mississippian, Proceedings of the Sixth Mid-South Archaeological Conference, June 6–9, 1985,* edited by Richard A. Marshall, pp. 87–101. Cobb Institute of Archaeology Occasional Papers 87–01, Mississippi State University, State College.
1990 The Emergence of Mississippian Culture in the American Bottom. In *The Mississippian Emergence,* edited by Bruce D. Smith, pp. 113–152. Smithsonian Institution Press, Washington, D.C.
2000 Introduction. *The Cahokia Mounds,* edited by John E. Kelly, pp. 1–57. University of Alabama Press, Tuscaloosa.
2002 Woodland Period Archaeology in the American Bottom. In *The Woodland Southeast,* edited by David G. Anderson and Robert C. Mainfort, Jr., pp. 134–161. University of Alabama Press, Tuscaloosa.
2006 The Ritualization of Cahokia: The Structure and Organization of Early Cahokia Crafts. In *Leadership and Polity in Mississippian Society,* edited by Brian M. Butler and Paul D. Welch, pp. 236–263. Center for Archeological Investigations, Occasional Paper No. 33. Southern Illinois University, Carbondale.

Kelly, John E., Steven J. Ozuk, Douglas K. Jackson, Dale L. McElrath, Fred A. Finney, and Duane Esarey
1984 Emergent Mississippian Period. In *American Bottom Archaeology: A Summary of the FAI-270 Project Contribution to the Culture History of the Mississippi River Valley,* edited by Charles J. Bareis and James W. Porter, pp. 128–157. University of Illinois Press, Urbana.

Kelly, Robert L., and Lawrence C. Todd
1988 Coming into the Country: Early Paleoindian Hunting and Mobility. *American Antiquity* 53(2):231–244.

Kemp, Brian M., and Theodore G. Schurr
2010 Ancient and Modern Genetic Variation in the Americas. In *Human Variation in the Americas: The Integration of Archaeology and Biological Anthropology,* edited by Benjamin M. Auerbach, pp. 12–50. Center for Archaeological Investigations, Occasional Paper 38. Southern Illinois University, Carbondale.

Kidder, Tristram R.
2001 Mapping Poverty Point. *American Antiquity* 67:89–101.
2002 Woodland Period Archaeology of the Lower Mississippi Valley. In *The Woodland Southeast,* edited by David G. Anderson and Robert C. Mainfort, Jr., pp. 66–90. University of Alabama Press, Tuscaloosa.
2004a Prehistory of the Lower Mississippi Valley after 800 B.C. In *Smithsonian Handbook of North American Indians, Volume 14, The Southeast,* edited by Raymond D. Fogelson, pp. 545–559. Smithsonian Institution, Washington, D.C.
2004b Plazas as Architecture: An Example from the Raffman Site, Northeast Louisiana. *American Antiquity* 69:514–532.
2006 Climate Change and the Archaic to Woodland Transition (3000–2500 cal B.P.) in the Mississippi River Basin. *American Antiquity* 71:195–231.
2010 Trend, Tradition, and Transition at the End of the Archaic. In *Trend, Tradition, and Turmoil: What Happened to the Southeastern Archaic?* edited by David Hurst Thomas and Matthew C. Sanger, pp. 23–32. Proceedings of the Third Caldwell Conference, St. Catherines Island,

Georgia, May 9–11, 2008. Anthropological Papers 93. American Museum of Natural History, New York.

2011 Transforming Hunter–Gatherer History at Poverty Point. In *Hunter–Gatherer Archaeology as Historical Process*, edited by Kenneth E. Sassaman and Donald H. Holley Jr., pp. 95–119. University of Arizona Press, Tucson.

2012 Poverty Point. In *The Oxford Handbook of North American Archaeology*, edited by Timothy R. Pauketat, pp. 460–470. Oxford University Press, Oxford, UK.

Kidder, Tristram R., and Kenneth E. Sassaman

2009 The View from the Southeast. In *Archaic Societies: Diversity and Complexity Across the Midcontinent*, edited by Thomas E. Emerson, Dale L. McElrath and Andrew C. Fortier, pp. 667–694. State University of New York Press, Albany.

Kidder, Tristram R., Anthony L. Ortmann, and Lee J. Arco

2008 Poverty Point and the Archaeology of Singularity. *The SAA Archaeological Record* 8(5):9–12.

Kidder, Tristram R., Lee J. Arco, Anthony L. Ortmann, Timothy M. Schilling, C. Boeke, R. Bielitz, and Katie A. Adelsberger

2009 *Poverty Point Mound A: Final Report of the 2005 and 2006 Field Seasons.* Louisiana Division of Archaeology and the Louisiana Archaeological Survey and Antiquities Commission, Baton Rouge.

Kidder, Tristram R., Lori Roe, and Timothy M. Schilling

2010 Early Woodland Settlement and Mound Building in the Upper Taensas Basin, Northeast Louisiana. *Southeastern Archaeology* 29:121–145.

Kimball, Larry

1996 Early Archaic Settlement and Technology: Lessons from Tellico. In *The Paleoindian and Early Archaic Southeast*, edited by David G. Anderson and Kenneth E. Sassaman, pp. 149–186. University of Alabama Press, Tuscaloosa.

Kimball, Larry R., Thomas R. Whyte, and Gary D. Crites

2010 The Biltmore Mound and Hopewellian Mound Use in the Southern Appalachians. *Southeastern Archaeology* 29:44–58

King, Adam (editor)

2007 *Southeastern Ceremonial Complex: Chronology, Content, Context.* University of Alabama Press, Tuscaloosa.

King, Adam

2003a *Etowah: The Political History of a Chiefdom Capital.* University of Alabama Press, Tuscaloosa.

2003b Over a Century of Explorations at Etowah. *Journal of Archaeological Research* 11:279–306.

2004 Power and the Sacred Mound C and the Etowah Chiefdom. In *Hero, Hawk, and Open Hand: American Indian Art of the Ancient Midwest and South*, edited by Richard F. Townsend and Robert V. Sharp, pp. 151–165. The Art Institute of Chicago and Yale University Press, New Haven, Connecticut.

2012 Mississippian in the Deep South: Common Themes in Varied Histories. *The Oxford Handbook of North American Archaeology*, edited by Timothy R. Pauketat, pp. 509–522. Oxford University Press, Oxford, UK.

King, Adam, Chester P. Walker, F. Kent Reilly III, Robert V. Sharp, and Duncan P. McKinnon

2011 Remote Sensing from Etowah's Mound A: Architecture and the Re–Creation of Mississippian Tradition. *American Antiquity* 76:355–371.

King, Thomas F.

2004 *Cultural Resource: Law and Practice.* 2nd edition. AltaMira Press, New York.

Kintz, Theresa
1997 A View from the Trenches. *Common Ground: Archaeology and Ethnography in the Public Interest* 2(1):49–53. National Park Service Archeology and Ethnography Program, Washington, D.C.
Klippel, Walter E., and William H. Bass (editors)
1984 *Averbuch: A Late Mississippian Manifestation in the Nashville Basin.* 2 vols. Report prepared for the National Park Service, Southeast Regional Office, Atlanta, Georgia.
Knight, Vernon J. Jr. (editor)
2009 *The Search for Mabila: The Decisive Battle between Hernando de Soto and Chief Tascalusa.* University of Alabama Press, Tuscaloosa.
Knight, Vernon J. Jr.
1986 The Institutional Organization of Mississippian Religion. *American Antiquity* 51:675–687.
1990 *Excavation of the Truncated Mound at the Walling Site: Middle Woodland Culture and Copena in the Tennessee Valley.* Alabama State Museum of Natural History Report of Investigations 56. University of Alabama Press, Tuscaloosa.
1994 The Formation of the Creeks. In *The Forgotten Centuries: Indians and Europeans in the American South, 1521–1704*, edited by Charles M. Hudson and Carmen Chaves Tesser, pp. 373–392. University of Georgia Press, Athens.
1996 Introduction: The Expeditions of Clarence B. Moore to Moundville in 1905 and 1906. In *The Moundville Expeditions of Clarence Bloomfield Moore*, edited by Vernon J. Knight, Jr., pp. 1–20. University of Alabama Press, Tuscaloosa.
1998 Moundville as a Diagrammatic Ceremonial Center. In *Archaeology of the Moundville Chiefdom*, edited by Vernon J. Knight and Vincas P. Steponaitis, pp. 44–62. Smithsonian Institution Press, Washington, D.C.
2001 Feasting and the Emergence of Platform Mound Ceremonialism in Eastern North America. In *Feasts: Archaeological and Ethnographic Perspectives on Food, Politics, and Power*, edited by Michael Dietler and Brian Hayden, pp. 311–333. Smithsonian Institution Press, Washington, D.C.
2006 Farewell to the Southeastern Ceremonial Complex. *Southeastern Archaeology* 25:1–5.
2010 *Mound Excavations at Moundville: Architecture, Elites and Social Order.* University of Alabama Press, Tuscaloosa.
Knight, Vernon James, Jr., and Vincas P. Steponaitis
1998 A New History of Moundville. In *Archaeology of the Moundville Chiefdom*, edited by Vernon J. Knight and Vincas P. Steponaitis, pp. 1–25. Smithsonian Institution Press, Washington, D.C.
Knight, Vernon J., Jr., James A. Brown, and George E. Lankford
2001 On the Subject Matter of Southeastern Ceremonial Complex Art. *Southeastern Archaeology* 20:129–141.
Knox, James C.
1983 Responses of River Systems to Holocene Climates. In *Late Quaternary Environments of the United States. Vol. 2: The Holocene*, edited by Herbert E. Wright, Jr., pp. 26–41. University of Minnesota, Minneapolis.
Koerner, Shannon D., Henri Grissino-Mayer, Lynne P. Sullivan, and Georgina G. Deweese
2009 Dendroarchaeological Approach to Mississippian Cultural Occupational History in Eastern Tennessee, USA. *Tree-Ring Research* 65:81–90.
Koldehoff, Brad and John A. Walthall
2004 Settling In: Hunter-Gatherer Mobility during the Pleistocene-Holocene Transition in the Central Mississippi Valley. In *Aboriginal Ritual and Economy in the Eastern Woodlands: Essays in*

Honor of Howard Dalton Winters, edited by A-M. Cantwell, L. A. Conrad, and J. E. Reyman, pp. 49–72. Scientific Papers 30. Illinois State Museum, Springfield.

2009 Dalton and the Early Holocene Midcontinent: Setting the Stage. In *Archaic Societies: Diversity and Complexity Across the Midcontinent*, edited by Thomas E. Emerson, Dale L. McElrath and Andrew C. Fortier, pp. 137–151. State University of New York Press, Albany.

Kozuch, Laura

2002 *Olivella* Beads from Spiro and the Plains. *American Antiquity* 67:697–709.

Krech, Shepard III

2009 *Spirits of the Air: Birds and American Indians in the South.* University of Georgia Press, Athens.

Kroeber, Alfred L.

1927 Disposal of the Dead. *American Anthropologist* 29:308–315.

Kuttruff, Jenna Tedrick

1993 Mississippian Period Status Differentiation through Textile Analysis: A Caddoan Example. *American Antiquity* 58:125–145.

Kuttruff, Carl

1997 Louisiana's Lost Heritage: The Monte Sano Mounds. *Louisiana Archaeological Conservancy* 7(2):4–6.

Kwachka, Patricia B. (editor)

1994 *Perspectives on the Southeast: Linguistics, Archaeology, and Ethnohistory.* University of Georgia Press, Athens.

Lacquement, Cameron H. (editor)

2007 *Architectural Variability in the Southeast.* University of Alabama Press, Tuscaloosa.

Lafferty, Robert H. III

1994 Prehistoric Exchange in the Lower Mississippi Valley. In *Prehistoric Exchange Systems in North America*, edited by Timothy G. Baugh and Jonathon E. Ericson, pp. 177–214. Plenum, New York.

Lambeck, Kurt, Tezer M. Estat, and Emma-Kate Potter

2002 Links between Climate and Sea Levels for the Past Three Million Years. *Nature* 419:199–206.

Lambeck, Kurt, Yusuke Yokoyama, and Tony Purcell

2002 Into and Out of the Last Glacial Maximum: Sea-level Change during Oxygen Isotope Stages 3 and 2. *Quaternary Science Review* 21:343–360.

Lambert, Patricia M. (editor)

2000 *Bioarchaeological Studies of Life in the Age of Agriculture A View from the Southeast.* University of Alabama Press, Tuscaloosa.

Lankford, George E.

2004 World on a String: Some Cosmological Components of the Southeastern Ceremonial Complex. In *Hero, Hawk, and Open Hand: American Indian Art of the Ancient Midwest and South*, edited by Richard F. Townsend and Robert V. Sharp, pp. 207–217. The Art Institute of Chicago and Yale University Press, New Haven, Connecticut.

2007 *Reachable Stars: Patterns in the Ethnoastronomy of Eastern North America.* University of Alabama Press, Tuscaloosa.

Lankford, George E. (editor)

1987 *Native American Legends: Southeastern Legends—Tales from the Natchez, Caddo, Biloxi, Chickasaw, and Other Nations.* August House, Little Rock, Arkansas. Reprinted, 2011, University of Alabama Press, Tuscaloosa.

Lankford, George E., F. Kent Reilly III, and James F. Garber (editors)
2011 *Visualizing the Sacred: Cosmic Visions, Regionalism, and the Art of the Mississippian World.* University of Texas Press, Austin.
Lapham, Heather A.
2005 *Hunting for Hides: Deerskins, Status, and Cultural Change in the Protohistoric Appalachians.* University of Alabama Press, Tuscaloosa.
2006 Southeast Animals. In *Smithsonian Handbook of North American Indians, Volume 3, Environment, Origins, and Population*, edited by Douglas H. Ubelaker, pp. 396–404. Smithsonian Institution, Washington, D.C.
2011 Animals in Southeastern Native American Subsistence Economies. In *Subsistence Economies of Indigenous North American Societies*, edited by Bruce D. Smith, pp. 401–429. Smithsonian Institution Scholarly Press, Washington, D.C.
Larsen, Clark S. (editor)
1990 *The Archaeology of Mission Santa Catalina de Guale, Part 2: Biocultural Interpretations of a Population in Transition.* Anthropological Papers of the American Museum of Natural History 68. New York, New York.
2001 *Bioarchaeology of Spanish Florida: The Impact of Colonialism.* University Press of Florida, Gainesville.
Larsen, Clark S., and David Hurst Thomas
1979 Mortuary Archaeology on the Georgia Coast. In *The Anthropology of St. Catherines Island: 2. The Refuge-Deptford Mortuary Complex*, edited by David Hurst Thomas and Clark S. Larsen, pp. 8–12 Anthropological Papers 56(1). American Museum of Natural History, New York.
Larson, Lewis H.
1994 The Case for Earth Lodges in the Southeast. In *Ocmulgee Archaeology 1936–1986*, edited by David J. Hally, pp. 105–115. University of Georgia Press, Athens.
1998 Introduction. In *The Georgia and South Carolina Expeditions of Clarence Bloomfield Moore*, edited by Lewis H. Larson, pp. 1–85. University of Alabama Press, Tuscaloosa.
Ledbetter, R. Jerald
1995 *Archaeological Investigations at Mill Branch Sites 9WR4 and 9WR11, Warren County, Georgia.* Technical Report No. 3, Interagency Archeological Services Division, National Park Service, Atlanta.
Leigh, David S.
2006 Terminal Pleistocene Braided to Meandering Transition in Rivers of the Southeastern USA. *Catena* 66:155–160.
2008 Late Quaternary Climates and River Channels of the Atlantic Coastal Plain, USA *Geomorphology* 101:90–108
Leigh, David S., Pradeep Srivastava, and George A. Brook
2004 Late Pleistocene Braided Rivers of the Atlantic Coastal Plain, USA. *Quaternary Science Reviews* 23:65–84.
Lekson, Stephen H., and Peter N. Peregrine
2004 A Continental Perspective for North American Archaeology. *SAA Archaeological Record* 4(1):15–19.
Lepper, Bradley T.
1998 Ancient Astronomers of the Ohio Valley. *Timeline* 15:2–11.
2006 The Great Hopewell Road and the Role of the Pilgrimage in the Hopewell Interaction Sphere. In *Recreating Hopewell*, edited by Douglas K. Charles and Jane E. Buikstra, pp. 122–133. University Press of Florida, Gainesville.

Lepper, Bradley T., and Robert E. Funk
2006 Paleo-Indian: East. In *Smithsonian Handbook of North American Indians, Volume 3, Environment, Origins, and Population*, edited by Douglas H. Ubelaker, pp. 171–193. Smithsonian Institution, Washington, D.C.
Levi-Strauss, Claude
1963 *Structural Anthropology*. Basic Books, New York.
Levy, Janet E.
2001 The Archaeologists'—and Indians'—New World. In *Anthropologists and Indians in the New South*, edited by Rachel A. Bonney and J. Anthony Parades, pp. 29–45. University of Alabama Press, Tuscaloosa.
Lewis, R. Barry (editor)
1996 *Kentucky Archaeology*. University of Press of Kentucky, Lexington.
Lewis, R. Barry
2000 Sea-Level Rise and Subsidence Effects on Gulf Coast Archaeological Site Distributions. *American Antiquity* 65:525–541.
Lewis, R. Barry, and Charles B. Stout (editors)
1998 *Mississippian Towns and Sacred Spaces Searching for an Architectural Grammar*. University of Alabama Press, Tuscaloosa.
Lewis, R. Barry, Charles Stout, and Cameron B. Wesson
1998 The Design of Mississippian Towns. In *Mississippian Towns and Sacred Spaces: Searching for an Architectural Grammar*, edited by R. Barry Lewis and Charles Stout, pp. 1–21. University of Alabama Press, Tuscaloosa.
Lewis, Thomas M. N., and Madeline Kneberg
1946 *Hiwassee Island: An Archaeological Account of Four Tennessee Indian Peoples. Partially Based on Field Reports by Charles H. Nash.* University of Tennessee Press, Knoxville.
Lindauer, Own, and John H. Blitz
1997 Higher Ground: The Archaeology of North American Platform Mounds. *Journal of Archaeological Research* 5:169–207.
Lipo, Carl P., James K. Feathers, Robert C. Dunnell
2005 Temporal Data Requirements, Luminescence Dates, and the Resolution of Chronological Structure of Late Prehistoric Deposits in the Central Mississippi River Valley. *American Antiquity* 70:527–544.
Little, Keith J.
2003 Late Holocene Climactic Fluctuations and Culture Change in Southeastern North America. *Southeastern Archaeology* 22:9–32.
Livingood, Patrick C.
2008 Recent Discussions in Late Prehistoric Southern Archaeology. *Native South* 1:1–26.
2010 *Mississippian Polity and Politics on the Gulf Coastal Plain: A View from the Pearl River, Mississippi*. University of Alabama Press, Tuscaloosa.
2012 No Crows Made Mounds: Do Cost-Distance Calculations of Travel Time Improve Our Understanding of Southern Appalachian Polity Size? In *Least Cost Analysis of Social Landscapes: Archaeological Case Studies for Beginners and Experts Alike*, edited by Devin A. White, and Sarah L. Surface-Evans, pp. 174–187. University of Utah Press. Salt Lake City.
Loebel, Thomas J.
2012 Endscrapers, Use-wear, and Early Paleoindians in Eastern North America. In *In the Eastern Fluted Point Tradition*, edited by Joseph A. M. Gingerich. University of Utah Press, Salt Lake City, in press.

Logan, Wilfred

1952 Graham Cave: An Archaic Site in Montgomery County, Missouri. *Memoir of the Missouri Archaeological Society* 2:1–86.

Lopinot, Neal H., Jack H. Ray, and Michael D. Conner

1998 *The 1997 Excavations at the Big Eddy Site (23CE426) in Southwest Missouri.* Southwest Missouri State University, Center for Archaeological Research Special Publication No. 2, Springfield.

2000 *The 1999 Excavations at the Big Eddy Site (23CE426).* Southwest Missouri State University, Center for Archaeological Research, Special Publication No. 3, Springfield.

Lorenz, Karl G.

2000 The Natchez of Southwest Mississippi. In *Indians of the Greater Southeast: Historical Archaeology and Ethnohistory*, edited by Bonnie G. McEwan, pp. 152–158. University Press of Florida, Gainesville.

Lowery, Darren L.

2002 *A Time of Dust: Archaeological and Geomorphological Investigations at the Paw Paw Cove Paleo-Indian Site Complex in Talbot County, Maryland.* Maryland Historical Trust, Crownsville, Maryland.

Lydick, Christopher M.

2008 Sensor Fusion: Integrated Remote Sensing Surveys at Shiloh Mounds National Historic Landmark, Shiloh, Tennessee. M.A. Thesis, Department of Anthropology, Florida State University, Tallahassee.

Lynott, Mark J., Thomas W. Boutton, James E. Price, and Dwight E. Nelson

1986 Stable Carbon Isotopic Evidence for Maize Agriculture in Southeast Missouri and Northeast Arkansas. *American Antiquity* 51:51–65.

Lynott, Mark J., Hector Neff, James E. Price, James W. Cogswell, and Michael D. Glascock

2000 Inferences about Prehistoric Ceramics and People in Southeast Missouri: Results of Ceramic Compositional Analysis. *American Antiquity* 65:103–126.

Lyon, Eugene

1996 *A New Deal for Southeastern Archaeology.* University of Alabama Press, Tuscaloosa.

McAvoy, Joseph M.

1992 *Nottoway River Survey Part I: Clovis Settlement Patterns; The 30 Year Study of a Late Ice Age Hunting Culture on the Southern Interior Coastal Plain of Virginia.* Archeological Society of Virginia Special Publication Number 28, Richmond.

McAvoy, Joseph M., and Lynn D. McAvoy

1997 *Archaeological Investigations of Site 44SX202, Cactus Hill, Sussex County, Virginia.* Virginia Department of Historic Resources, Research Report Series No. 8, Richmond.

McDonald, Jerry N.

2000 An Outline of the Pre-Clovis Archeology of SV-2, Saltville, Virginia, with Special Attention to a Bone Tool Dated 14,510 yr BP. *Jeffersonia: Contributions from the Virginia Museum of Natural History* 9:1–59.

McElrath, Dale L., and Thomas E. Emerson

2009 Concluding Thoughts on the Archaic Occupation of the Eastern Woodlands. In *Archaic Societies: Diversity and Complexity Across the Midcontinent*, edited by Thomas E. Emerson, Dale L. McElrath and Andrew C. Fortier, pp. 841–855. State University of New York Press, Albany.

2012 Reenvisioning Eastern Woodlands Archaic Origins. In *The Oxford Handbook of North American Archaeology*, edited by Timothy R. Pauketat, pp. 448–459. Oxford University Press, Oxford, UK.

McElrath, Dale L., Andrew C. Fortier, and Thomas E. Emerson
2009 An Introduction to the Archaic Societies of the Midcontinent. In *Archaic Societies: Diversity and Complexity Across the Midcontinent*, edited by Thomas E. Emerson, Dale L. McElrath and Andrew C. Fortier, pp. 3–21. State University of New York Press, Albany.
McEwan, Bonnie G. (editor)
1993 *The Spanish Missions of "La Florida"*. University Press of Florida, Gainesville.
2000 *Indians of the Greater Southeast: Historical Archaeology and Ethnohistory*. University Press of Florida, Gainesville.
McGahey, Samuel O.
2005 Prehistoric Stone Bead Manufacture: The Loosa Yokena Site, Warren County, Mississippi. *Mississippi Archaeology* 40:3–30.
McGimsey, Charles R., III.
1972 *Public Archaeology*. Seminar Press, New York.
McGimsey, Charles R., III, and Hester A. Davis
1977 *The Management of Archaeological Resources: The Airlie House Report*. Special Publication, Society for American Archaeology, Washington, D.C.
McGimsey, Charles R.
2010 Marksville and Middle Woodland. In *Archaeology of Louisiana*, edited by Mark A. Rees, pp. 120–134. Louisiana State University Press, Baton Rouge.
McNutt, Charles H. (editor)
1996 *Prehistory of the Central Mississippi Valley*. University of Alabama Press, Tuscaloosa.
McNutt, Charles H.
2008 The Benton Phenomenon and Middle Archaic Chronology in Adjacent Portions of Tennessee, Mississippi, and Alabama. *Southeastern Archaeology* 27:45–60.
Mainfort, Robert C. Jr.
1986 *Pinson Mounds: A Middle Woodland Ceremonial Site*. Research Series 7. Tennessee Department of Conservation, Division of Archaeology,Nashville.
1996 Pinson Mounds and the Middle Woodland Period in the Midsouth and Lower Mississippi Valley. In *A View from the Core: A Synthesis of Ohio Hopewell Archaeology*, edited by Paul J. Pacheco, pp. 370–391. Ohio Archaeological Council, Columbus.
2001 The Late Prehistoric and Protohistoric Periods in the Central Mississippi Valley. In *Societies in Eclipse: Archaeology of the Eastern Woodland Indians, A.D. 1400–1700*, edited by David S. Brose, C. Wesley Cowan, and Robert C. Mainfort, Jr., pp. 173–189. Smithsonian Institution Press, Washington, D.C.
2003 Assessing Late Period Phases in the Central Mississippi Valley. *Southeastern Archaeology* 22:176–184.
Mainfort, Robert C. Jr., and Lynne P. Sullivan (editors)
1998 *Ancient Earthen Enclosures of the Eastern Woodlands*. University Press of Florida, Gainesville.
Mainfort, Robert C., Jr., James W. Cogswell, Michael J. O'Brien, Hector Neff, and Michael D. Glascock
1997 Neutron Activation Analysis of Pottery from Pinson Mounds and Nearby Sites in Western Tennessee: Local Production vs. Long-Distance Importation. *Midcontinental Journal of Archaeology* 22:43–68.
Maki, David, and Ross C. Fields
2010 Multisensor Geophysical Survey Results from the Pine Tree Mound Site: A Comparison of Geophysical and Excavation Data. *Southeastern Archaeology* 29:292–309.
Marceaux, Shawn, and David H. Dye
2007 Hightower Anthropomorphic Marine Shell Gorgets and Duck River Sword-form Flint Bifaces: Middle Mississippian Ritual Regalia in the Southern Appalachians. In *Southeastern*

Ceremonial Complex: Chronology, Content, Style, edited by Adam King, pp. 165–184. University of Alabama Press, Tuscaloosa.

Marcoux, Jon Bernard

2008 Cherokee Households and Communities in the English Contact Period. Ph.D. Dissertation, Department of Anthropology, University of North Carolina, Chapel Hill.

2010 *Pox, Empire, Shackles, and Hides: The Townsend Site, 1670–1715*. University of Alabama Press, Tuscaloosa.

Marcoux, Jon Bernard, and Gregory D. Wilson

2010 Categories of Complexity and the Preclusion of Practice. In *Ancient Complexities: New Perspectives in Precolumbian North America,* edited by Susan M. Alt, pp. 138–152. University of Utah Press, Salt Lake City.

Marquardt, William H.

1988 Politics and Production among the Calusa of South Florida. In *Hunters and Gatherers. Volume 1: History, Evolution, and Social Change in Hunting and Gathering Societies*, edited by Tim Ingold, David Riches, and James Woodburn, pp. 161–188. Explorations in Anthropology, University College, London. Berg Publishers, Ltd., London.

1994 The Role of Archaeology in Raising Environmental Consciousness: An Example from Southwest Florida. In *Historical Ecology: Cultural Knowledge and Changing Landscapes*, edited by C. L. Crumley, pp. 203–221. School of American Research, Santa Fe, New Mexico.

2010a Shell Mounds in the Southeast: Middens, Monuments, Temple Mounds, Rings, or Works? *American Antiquity* 75:551–570.

2010b Mounds, Middens, and Rapid Climate Change during the Archaic–Woodland Transition in the Southeastern United States. In *Trend, Tradition, and Turmoil: What Happened to the Southeastern Archaic?* Proceedings of the Third Caldwell Conference, St. Catherines Island, Georgia, May 9–11, 2008, edited by David Hurst Thomas and Matthew C. Sanger, pp. 253–271. Anthropological Papers 93. American Museum of Natural History, New York.

Marquardt, William H., and Patty Jo Watson (editors)

2005 *Archaeology of the Middle Green River Region, Kentucky*. Institute of Archaeology and Paleoenvironmental Studies Monograph 5. University Press of Florida, Gainesville.

Marrinan, Rochelle

2010 Two Late Archaic Period Shell Rings, St. Simon's Island, Georgia. In *Trend, Tradition, and Turmoil: What Happened to the Southeastern Archaic?* edited by David Hurst Thomas and Matthew C. Sanger, pp. 71–102. Proceedings of the Third Caldwell Conference, St. Catherines Island, Georgia, May 9–11, 2008. American Museum of Natural History, New York.

Marsh, Alan

1998 Swift Creek Site Excavations: The Works Progress Administration and Black Labor. In *A World Engraved: Archaeology of the Swift Creek Culture*, edited by J. Mark Williams and Daniel T. Elliott, pp. 12–18. University of Alabama Press, Tuscaloosa.

Marshall, James A.

1996 Towards a Definition of the Ohio Hopewell Core and Periphery Utilizing the Geometric Earthworks. In *A View from the Core: A Synthesis of Ohio Hopewell Archaeology*, edited by Paul J. Pacheco, pp. 210–220. Ohio Archaeological Council, Columbus.

Martin-Siebert, Erica K. (editor)

2004 *The Earliest Americans (Paleoindian) Theme Study for the Eastern United States* (David G. Anderson, David S. Brose, Dena F. Dincauze, Michael J. Shott, Robert S. Grumet, and Richard C. Waldbauer). National Historic Landmarks Survey, National Park Service, Washington D.C.

Means, Bernard K. (editor)

2012 *Shovel Ready: Archaeology and Roosevelt's New Deal for America*. The University of Alabama Press, Tuscaloosa, in press.

Meeks, Scott C.

1999 The "Function" of Stone Tools in Prehistoric Exchange Systems: A Look at Benton Interaction in the Mid-South. In *Raw Materials and Exchange in the Mid-South, Proceedings of the Mid-South Archaeological Conference, Jackson, Mississippi*, edited by Evan Peacock and Samuel O. Brooks, pp. 29–43. Mississippi Department of Archives and History, Archaeological Report 29. Mississippi Department of Archives and History, Jackson.

2000 *The Use and Function of Late Middle Archaic Projectile Points in the Midsouth*. Report of Investigations 77. Office of Archaeological Research, University of Alabama, Tuscaloosa.

2009 Understanding Cultural Pattern and Process in the Tennessee River Valley: The Role of Cultural Resources Management Investigations in Archaeological Research. In *TVA Archaeology: 75 Years of Prehistoric Site Research*, edited by Erin Pritchard, pp. 269–297. University of Tennessee Press, Knoxville.

Meeks, Scott C., and David G. Anderson

2012 Drought, Subsistence Stress, and Population Dynamics: Assessing Mississippian Abandonment of the Vacant Quarter. In *Living on the Land: Investigating the Complex Relationships among Soils, Climate and Society in the Americas*, edited by John D. Wingard and Susan Hayes. University Press of Colorado, Boulder, in press.

Meltzer, David J.

1985 North American Archaeology and Archaeologists, 1879–1934. *American Antiquity* 50:249–260.

1988 Late Pleistocene Human Adaptations in Eastern North America. *Journal of World Prehistory* 2:1–53.

1989 Why Don't We Know When the First People Came to North America? *American Antiquity* 54:471–490.

2002 What Do You Do When No One's Been There Before? Thoughts on the Exploration and Colonization of New Lands. In *The First Americans: The Pleistocene Colonization of the New World*, edited by Nina G. Jablonski, pp. 27–58. Memoir of the California Academy of Sciences, Number 27, San Francisco.

2003 Peopling of North America. *Development in Quaternary Science* 1:539–563

2004 Modeling the Initial Colonization of the Americas Issues of Scale, Demography, and Landscape Learning. In *The Settlement of the American Continents: A Multidisciplinary Approach to Human Biogeography*, edited by C. M. Barton, G. A. Clark, D. R. Yesner, and G. A. Pearson, pp. 123–137. University of Arizona Press, Tucson.

2009 *First Peoples in a New World: Colonizing Ice Age America*. University of California Press, Berkeley.

Meltzer David J., and Vance T. Holliday

2010 Would North American Paleoindians Have Noticed Younger Dryas Age Climate Changes? *Journal of World Prehistory* 23:1–41.

Mikell, Greg, and Rebecca Saunders

2007 Coastal Archaic Sites in Southern Walton County, Florida: Implications Concerning Estuarine Adaptation on the Northern Gulf Coast. *Southeastern Archaeology* 26(2):169–195.

Milanich, Jerald T.

1971 The Deptford Phase: An Archaeological Reconstruction. Ph.D. Dissertation, Department of Anthropology, University of Florida, Gainesville.

1994 *Archaeology of Pre-columbian Florida*. University Press of Florida, Gainesville.

1999 *Laboring in the Fields of the Lord: Spanish Missions and Southeastern Indians*. Smithsonian Institution Press, Washington, D.C.

2002 Weeden Island Cultures. In *The Woodland Southeast*, edited by David G. Anderson and Robert C. Mainfort, Jr., pp. 318–352. University of Alabama Press, Tuscaloosa.

2004a Prehistory of Florida After 500 B.C. In *Smithsonian Handbook of North American Indians, Volume 14, The Southeast*, edited by Raymond D. Fogelson, pp. 191–203. Smithsonian Institution, Washington, D.C.

2004b Prehistory of the Lower Atlantic Coast After 500 B.C. In *Smithsonian Handbook of North American Indians, Volume 14, The Southeast*, edited by Raymond D. Fogelson, pp. 229–237. Smithsonian Institution, Washington, D.C.

Milanich, Jerald T., and Charles M. Hudson.

1993 *Hernando de Soto and the Indians of Florida*. University Press of Florida, Gainesville.

Milanich, Jerald T., Ann Cordell, V. James Knight, Jr., Timothy Kohler, and Brenda Sigler-Lavelle

1984 *McKeithen Weeden Island: The Culture of Northern Florida, A.D. 200–900*. Academic Press, New York.

1997 *Archaeology of Northern Florida A.D. 200–900*. University Press of Florida, Gainesville.

Miller, Carl F.

1956 Life 8,000 Years Ago Uncovered in an Alabama Cave. National Geographic 110(4):542–558.

Miller, D. Shane

2010 *Clovis Excavations at Topper 2005–2007: Examining Site Formation Processes at an Upland Paleoindian Site along the Middle Savannah River.* Occasional Papers 1 Southeastern Paleoamerican Survey South Carolina Institute of Archaeology and Anthropology, University of South Carolina. Columbia.

2011 Rivers, Rocks and Eco-Tones: Modeling Clovis Landscape-Use in the Southeastern United States. Paper presented at the 76th Annual Meeting of the Society for American Archaeology, Sacramento, California.

Miller, D. Shane, and Joseph A.M. Gingerich

2012 Paleoindian Chronology and the Eastern Fluted Point Tradition. In *In the Eastern Fluted Point Tradition*, edited by Joseph A. M. Gingerich. University of Utah Press, Salt Lake City, in press.

Miller, D. Shane, and Albert C. Goodyear III

2008 A Probable Hafted Uniface from the Clovis Occupation at the Topper Site, 38AL23, Allendale County, South Carolina. *Current Research in the Pleistocene* 25:75–77.

Miller, D. Shane, and Ashley M. Smallwood

2012 Beyond Stages: Modeling Clovis Biface Production at the Topper Site (38AL23), South Carolina. In *Contemporary Lithic Analysis in the Southeast: Problems, Solutions, and Interpretations*, edited by Philip J. Carr, Andrew P. Bradbury, and Sarah E. Price. University of Alabama Press, Tuscaloosa, in press.

Miller, James J.

1998 *An Environmental History of Northeast Florida.* University Press of Florida, Gainesville.

Milner, George R.

1998 *The Cahokia Chiefdom: The Archaeology of a Mississippian Society*. Smithsonian Institution Press, Washington, D.C.

1999 Warfare in Prehistoric and Early Historic Eastern North America. *Journal of Archaeological Research* 7:105–151.

2004a *The Mound Builders: Ancient Peoples of Eastern North America*. Thames and Hudson, London.

2004b Old Mounds, Ancient Hunter–Gatherers, and Modern Archaeologists. In *Signs of Power: The Rise of Cultural Complexity in the Southeast*, edited by Jon L. Gibson and Philip J. Carr, pp. 300–316. University of Alabama Press, Tuscaloosa.

2012 Mound-Building Societies of the Midsouth and Southeast. In *The Oxford Handbook of North American Archaeology*, edited by Timothy R. Pauketat, pp. 437–447. Oxford University Press, Oxford, UK.

Milner, George R., and Richard W. Jefferies
1998 The Read Archaic Shell Midden in Kentucky. *Southeastern Archaeology* 17 119–132.

Milner, George R., and George Chaplin
2010 Eastern North American Population at ca. A.D. 1500. *American Antiquity* 75:707–726.

Milner, George R., David G. Anderson, and Marvin T. Smith
2001 The Distribution of Eastern Woodlands Peoples at the Prehistoric and Historic Interface. In *Societies in Eclipse: Archaeology of the Eastern Woodland Indians, A.D. 1400–1700,* edited by David S. Brose, C. Wesley Cowan, and Robert C. Mainfort, Jr., pp. 9–18. Smithsonian Institution Press, Washington, D.C.

Milner, George R., Clark Spencer Larsen, Dale L. Hutchinson, Matthew A. Williamson and Dorothy A. Humpf
2000 Conquistadors, Excavators, or Rodents: What Damaged the King Site Skeletons? *American Antiquity* 65:355–363.

Mitchem, Jeffrey M.
1996 Investigations of the Possible Remains of de Soto's Cross at Parkin. *The Arkansas Archeologist* 35:87–95. Arkansas Archeological Society, Fayetteville.

Mooney, James
1900 *Myths of the Cherokee.* Smithsonian Institution, Bureau of American Ethnology Annual Report 19:1–576, Washington, D.C.

Moore, Christopher R.
2010 A Macroscopic Investigation of Technological Style and the Production of Middle to Late Archaic Fishhooks at the Chiggerville, Read, and Baker Sites, Western Kentucky. *Southeastern Archaeology* 29:197–221.

Moore, Christopher R., and Victoria G. Dekle
2010 Hickory Nuts, Bulk Processing, and the Advent of Early Horticultural Economies in Eastern North America. *World Archaeology* 42:595–608.

Moore, Christopher R., Mark J. Brooks, Andrew H. Ivester, and Terry A. Ferguson
2010 Geoarchaeological Investigations of Carolina Bays in South Carolina: Methodological Approaches for Interpreting Site Formation Processes, Archaeostratigraphy and Geochronology. *Geological Society of America Abstracts with Programs* 42(1):70.

Moore, Clarence B.
1898 Certain Aboriginal Mounds of the Savannah River. *Journal of the Academy of Natural Sciences of Philadelphia* 11:167–172.
1910 Antiquities of the St. Francis, White, and Black Rivers, Arkansas. *Journal of the Academy of Natural Sciences of Philadelphia* 14:255–364.

Moore, David G.
2002 *Catawba Valley Mississippian: Ceramics, Chronology, and Catawba Indians.* University of Alabama Press, Tuscaloosa.

Moore, David G., Robin A. Beck, Jr., and Christopher B. Rodning
2005 Pardo, Joara, and Fort San Juan Revisited. In *Juan Pardo Expeditions: Exploration of the Carolinas and Tennessee, 1566–1568, Revised Edition,* by Charles M. Hudson, pp. 343–349. University of Alabama Press, Tuscaloosa.

Moore, John H.
1994 Ethnoarchaeology of the Lamar Peoples. In *Perspectives on the Southeast, Linguistics, Archaeology, and Ethnohistory,* edited by Patricia Kwachka, pp. 126-141. University of Georgia Press, Athens.

Moore, Michael C.
2004 Early Investigations at Gordontown (40DV6): Results of an 1877 Exploration Sponsored by the Peabody Museum, Harvard University. *Tennessee Archaeology* 1:1–15.

2005 *The Brentwood Library Site: A Mississippian Town on the Little Harpeth River, Williamson County, Tennessee.* Research Series No. 15. Tennessee Department of Environment and Conservation, Division of Archaeology, Nashville.

Moore, Michael C., and Emanuel Breitburg

1998 *Gordontown: Salvage Archaeology at a Mississippian Town in Davidson County, Tennessee.* Research Series No. 11. Tennessee Department of Environment and Conservation, Division of Archaeology, Nashville.

Moore, Michael C., and Kevin E. Smith

2001 *Archaeological Investigations at the Rutherford–Kizer Site: A Mississippian Mound Center in Sumner County, Tennessee.* Research Series No. 13. Tennessee Department of Environment and Conservation, Division of Archaeology, Nashville.

2009 *Archaeological Expeditions of the Peabody Museum in Middle Tennessee, 1877–1884.* Research Series No. 16. Tennessee Department of Environment and Conservation, Division of Archaeology, Nashville.

Moore, Michael C., Emanuel Breitburg, Kevin E. Smith, and Mary Beth Trubitt

2006 One Hundred Years of Archaeology at Gordontown: A Fortified Mississippian Town in Middle Tennessee. *Southeastern Archaeology* 25:89–109.

Moorehead, Warren K.

1914 *The American Indian in the United States Period 1850–1914 The Present Condition of the American Indian; His Political History and Other Topics A Plea for Justice.* The Andover Press, Andover, Massachusetts.

1923 *The Cahokia Mounds: A Preliminary Report.* University of Illinois Bulletin 21, No. 6, pt. 1, University of Illinois, Urbana

1929 *The Cahokia Mounds.* University of Illinois Bulletin, Vol. 26, No. 4. Urbana. Reprinted, 2000. University of Alabama Press, Tuscaloosa.

Moorehead, Warren K., Charles C. Willoughby, Margaret E. Ashley, Zelia Nuttall, and Frank Collins Baker

1932 *Etowah Papers.* Yale University Press and Phillips Academy, New Haven, Connecticut and Andover, Massachusetts.

Morey, Darcy F.

2010 *Dogs: Domestication and Development of a Social Bond.* Cambridge University Press, Cambridge, UK.

Morrow, Juliet E.

1995 Clovis Projectile Point Manufacture: A Perspective from the Ready/Lincoln Hills Site, 11JY46, Jersey County, Illinois. *Midcontinental Journal of Archaeology* 20:167–191.

1996 The Organization of Early Paleoindian Lithic Technology in the Confluence Region of the Mississippi, Illinois, and Missouri Rivers. Ph.D. Dissertation, Department of Anthropology, Washington University, St. Louis.

Morrow, Juliet E., and Toby A. Morrow

1999 Geographic Variation in Fluted Projectile Points: A Hemispheric Perspective. *American Antiquity* 64:215–230.

Morse, Dan F.

1971 The Hawkins Cache: A Significant Dalton Find in Northeast Arkansas. *Arkansas Archaeologist* 12:9-20.

1973 Dalton Culture in Northeast Arkansas. *The Florida Anthropologist* 26(1):23–38.

1975a Paleoindian in the Land of Opportunity: Preliminary Report on the Excavations at the Sloan Site (3GE94). In *The Cache River Archaeological Project: An Experiment in Contract Archaeology,* assembled by Michael B. Schiffer and John H. House, pp. 93–113. Research Series 8. Arkansas Archaeological Survey, Fayetteville.

1975b Reply to Schiffer. In *The Cache River Archaeological Project: An Experiment in Contract Archaeology*, assembled by Michael B. Schiffer and John M. House, pp. 113–119. Research Series 8. Arkansas Archaeological Survey, Fayetteville.

1977 Dalton Settlement Systems: Reply to Schiffer (2). *Plains Anthropologist* 22:149–158.

1986a McCarty (3-Po-467): A Tchula Period Site Near Marked Tree, Arkansas. In *The Tchula Period in the Mid-South and Lower Mississippi Valley*, edited by David H. Dye and Ronald C. Brister, pp. 70–92. Archaeological Report 17. Mississippi Department of Archives and History, Jackson.

1986b Preliminary Investigation of the Pinson Mounds Site: 1963 Field Season. In *Pinson Mounds, A Middle Woodland Ceremonial Center*, edited by Robert C. Mainfort, Jr., pp. 96–119. Research Series 7. Tennessee Department of Conservation, Division of Archaeology, Nashville.

1997 *Sloan: A Paleoindian Dalton Cemetery in Arkansas*. Smithsonian Institution, Washington, D.C.

Morse, Dan F., and Albert C. Goodyear, III

1973 The Significance of the Dalton Adze in Northeast Arkansas. *Plains Anthropologist* 18:316–22.

Morse, Dan F., and Phyllis A. Morse (editors)

1980 *Excavation, Data Interpretation and Report on the Zebree Homestead Site, Mississippi County, Arkansas*. Arkansas Archeological Survey, Fayetteville.

Morse, Dan F., and Phyllis A. Morse

1983 *Archaeology of the Central Mississippi Valley*. Academic Press, Orlando, Florida.

1990 The Spanish Exploration of Arkansas. In *Columbian Consequences, Volume 2: Archaeological and Historical Perspectives on the Spanish Borderlands East*, edited by David Hurst Thomas, pp. 197–210. Smithsonian Institution Press, Washington, D.C.

Morse, Dan F., David G. Anderson, and Albert C. Goodyear

1996 The Pleistocene–Holocene Transition in the Eastern United States. In *Humans at the End of the Ice Age: The Archaeology of the Pleistocene–Holocene Transition*, edited by Lawrence Guy Straus, Berit Valentin Eriksen, Jon Erlandson, and David R. Yesner, pp. 319–338. Plenum Press, New York.

Morse, Phyllis A.

1993 The Parkin Archaeological Site and Its Role in Determining the Route of de Soto Expedition. In *The Expedition of Hernando de Soto West of the Mississippi, 1541–1543 Proceedings of the DeSoto Symposia 1988 and 1990*, edited by Gloria A. Young and Michael P. Hoffman, pp. 58–67. University of Arkansas Press, Fayetteville.

Muller, Jon

1986 *Archaeology of the Lower Ohio River Valley*. Academic Press, Orlando, Florida.

1997 *Mississippian Political Economy*. Plenum Press, New York.

Munson, Patrick

1986 Hickory Silviculture: a Subsistence Revolution in the Prehistory of Eastern North America. Paper presented at the Conference on Emergent Horticultural Economies of the Eastern Woodlands. Carbondale, Illinois.

1990 Folsom Fluted Projectile Points East of the Great Plains and Their Biogeographical Correlates. *North American Archaeologist* 11:255–272.

Murowchick, Robert E.

1990 A Curious Sort of Yankee: Personal and Professional Notes on Jeffries Wyman (1814–1874). *Southeastern Archaeology* 9:55–66.

Nassaney, Michael S., and Charles R. Cobb (editors)
1991 *Stability, Transformation, and Variation: The Late Woodland Southeast.* Plenum Press, New York.
Nassaney, Michael S., and Kendra Pyle
1999 The Adoption of the Bow and Arrow in Eastern North America: A View from Central Arkansas. *American Antiquity* 64:243–263.
Nassaney, Michael S., and Kenneth E. Sassaman (editors)
1995 *Native American Interactions: Multiscalar Analysis and Interpretations in the Eastern Woodlands.* University of Tennessee Press, Knoxville.
NADB-Reports
2011 National Archeological Database, Reports Module. Electronic document, http://cast.uark.edu/other/nps/nadb/, accessed 31 December 2011
NATHPO
2012 National Association of Tribal Historic Preservation Officers. Electronic document, http://www.nathpo.org/mainpage.html, accessed 1 January 2012.
National Trust
2008 *The National Forest System: Cultural Resources at Risk: An Assessment and Needs Analysis.* National Trust for Historic Preservation, Washington, D.C.
Neitzel, Jill E. (editor)
1999 *Great Towns and Regional Polities in the Prehistoric American Southwest and Southeast.* University of New Mexico Press, Albuquerque.
Neitzel, Robert S.
1966 *Archaeology of the Fatherland Site: The Grand Village of the Natchez.* Anthropological Papers 51(1). American Museum of Natural History, New York.
1983 *The Grand Village of the Natchez Revisited: Excavations of the Fatherland Site, Adams County, Mississippi, 1972.* Archaeological Report No. 12. Mississippi Department of Archives and History, Jackson.
Nolan, Kevin C., and Robert A. Cook
2010 Volatile Climate Conditions Cahokia Comment on Benson, Pauketat and Cook 2009. *American Antiquity* 75:975–983.
Norton, Mark R., and John B. Broster
2004 The Sogom Site (40DV68): A Mississippian Farmstead on Cockrill Bend, Davidson County, Tennessee. *Tennessee Archaeology* 1(1): 2–17.

O'Brien, Michael J. (editor)
1998 *Changing Perspectives on the Archaeology of the Central Mississippi Valley.* University of Alabama Press, Tuscaloosa.
O'Brien, Michael J., and R. Lee Lyman
1998 *James A. Ford and the Growth of Americanist Archaeology.* University of Missouri Press, Columbia.
1999a *Seriation, Stratigraphy, and Index Fossils The Backbone of Archaeological Dating.* Kluwer Academic/Plenum Publishers, New York, New York.
1999b The Bureau of American Ethnology and Its Legacy to Southeastern Archaeology. *Journal of the Southwest* 41:407–440.
O'Brien, Michael J., and W. Raymond Wood
1998 *The Prehistory of Missouri.* University of Missouri Press, Columbia.
O'Brien, Michael J., J. Darwent, and R. Lee Lyman
2001 Cladistics is Useful for Reconstructing Archaeological Phylogenies: Paleoindian Points from the Southeastern United States. *Journal of Archaeological Science* 28:1115–1136.

O'Brien, Michael J., R. Lee Lyman, and Robert C. Dunnell
1997 *The Rise and Fall of Culture History*. Plenum Press, New York.
O'Donoughue, Jason M.
2007 Paleoindian Settlement in the Southeastern United States: Insights from Examining Regional Databases. *Current Research in the Pleistocene* 24:126–129.
2008 Living in the Low Country: Modeling Archaeological Site Location in the Francis Marion National Forest, South Carolina. M.A. Thesis, Department of Anthropology, University of Tennessee, Knoxville.
Ortman, Anthony L.
2007 The Poverty Point Mounds: Analysis of the Chronology, Construction History, and Function of North America's Largest Hunter-Gatherer Monuments. Ph.D. Dissertation, Department of Anthropology, Tulane University, New Orleans, Louisiana.
2010 Placing Poverty Point Mounds in their Temporal Context. *American Antiquity* 75:657–678.

Pauketat, Timothy R. (editor)
2001 *The Archaeology of Traditions: Agency and History Before and After Columbus*. University Press of Florida, Gainesville.
2012 *The Oxford Handbook of North American Archaeology*. Oxford University Press, Oxford, UK.
Pauketat, Timothy R.
1991 *The Ascent of Chiefs: Cahokia and Mississippian Politics in Ancient North America*. University of Alabama Press, Tuscaloosa.
1997 Cahokian Political Economy. In *Cahokia: Domination and Ideology in the Mississippian World*, edited by Timothy R. Pauketat and Thomas E. Emerson, pp. 30–51. University of Nebraska Press, Lincoln.
2001 Practice and History in Archaeology: An Emerging Paradigm. *Anthropological Theory* 1:73–98.
2003 Resettled Farmers and the Making of a Mississippian Polity. *American Antiquity* 68:39–66.
2004 *Ancient Cahokia and the Mississippians*. Cambridge University Press, Cambridge, UK.
2007 *Chiefdoms and Other Archaeological Delusions*. AltaMira Press, Lanham, Maryland.
2009 *Cahokia: Ancient America's Great City on the Mississippi*. Penguin Press, New York.
2012 Questioning the Past in North America. In *The Oxford Handbook of North American Archaeology*, edited by Timothy R. Pauketat, pp. 3–17. Oxford University Press, Oxford, UK.
Pauketat, Timothy R., and Susan M. Alt
2003 Mounds, Memory, and Contested Mississippian History. In *Archaeologies of Memory*, edited by R. Van Dyke and S. Alcock, pp. 151–179. Blackwell, Oxford.
2004 The Making and Meaning of a Mississippian Axe-head Cache. *Antiquity* 78:779–797.
Pauketat, Timothy R., and Thomas E. Emerson (editors)
1997 *Cahokia: Domination and Ideology in the Mississippian World*. University of Nebraska Press, Lincoln.
Pauketat, Timothy R., and Thomas E. Emerson
1991 The Ideology of Authority and the Power of the Pot. *American Anthropologist* 93:919–941.
1997 Introduction: Domination and Ideology in the Mississippian World. In *Cahokia: Domination and Ideology in the Mississippian World*, edited by Timothy R. Pauketat and Thomas E. Emerson, pp. 1–29. University of Nebraska Press, Lincoln.

Pauketat, Timothy R., and Neal H. Lopinot
1997 Cahokian Population Dynamics. In *Cahokia: Domination and Ideology in the Mississippian World*, edited by Timothy R. Pauketat and Thomas E. Emerson, pp. 103–123. University of Nebraska Press, Lincoln.
Pauketat, Timothy R., Lucretia S. Kelly, Gayle J. Fritz, Neal H. Lopinot, Scott Elias, and Eve Hargrave
2002 The Residues of Feasting and Public Ritual at Cahokia. *American Antiquity* 67:257–279.
Pavao-Zuckerman, Barnet
2007 Deerskins and Domesticates: Creek Subsistence and Economic Strategies in the Historic Period. *American Antiquity* 72:5–33.
Payne, Claudine
1994 Mississippian Capitals: An Archaeological Investigation of Precolumbian Political Structure. Ph.D. Dissertation, University of Florida.
Peacock, Evan
2002 Shellfish Use during the Woodland Period in the Middle South. In *The Woodland Southeast*, edited by David G. Anderson and Robert C. Mainfort, Jr., pp. 444–460. University of Alabama Press, Tuscaloosa.
Peacock, Evan, Philip J. Carr, Sarah E. Price, John Underwood, William L. Kingery, and Michael Lilly
2010 Confirmation of an Archaic-Period Mound in Southwest Mississippi. *Southeastern Archaeology* 29:355–369.
Pearson, Charles E., Thomas C. C. Birchett, and Richard A. Weinstein
2000 An Aptly Named Steamboat: Clarence B. Moore's Gopher. *Southeastern Archaeology* 19:82–86.
Peebles, Christopher S. (editor)
1983 *Prehistoric Agricultural Communities in West Central Alabama: Excavations in the Lubbub Creek Archaeological Locality*. Museum of Anthropology, University of Michigan, Ann Arbor.
Peebles, Christopher S.
1990 From History to Hermeneutics: The Place of Theory in the Late Prehistory of the Southeast. *Southeastern Archaeology* 9:23–34.
Peebles, Christopher S., and Susan M. Kus
1977 Some Archaeological Correlates of Ranked Societies. *American Antiquity* 42:421–448.
Perdue, Theda
1998 *Cherokee Women: Gender and Culture Change, 1700–1835*. University of Nebraska Press, Lincoln.
Peregrine, Peter N., and Stephen H. Lekson
2006 Southeast, Southwest, Mexico: Continental Perspectives on Mississippian Polities. In *Leadership and Polity in Mississippian Society*, edited by Brian M. Butler and Paul D. Welch, pp. 351–364. Center for Archeological Investigations, Occasional Paper No. 33. Southern Illinois University, Carbondale.
2012 The North American Oikoumene. In *The Oxford Handbook of North American Archaeology*, edited by Timothy R. Pauketat, pp. 64–72. Oxford University Press, Oxford, UK.
Phillips, James L., and James A. Brown (editors)
1983 *Archaic Hunter-Gatherers in the American Midwest*. Academic Press, New York.
Phillips, Philip
1970 *Archaeological Survey in the Lower Yazoo Basin, Mississippi 1949–1955*, 2 vols. Papers of the Peabody Museum of American Archaeology and Ethnology 60. Harvard University, Cambridge, Massachusetts.

Phillips, Philip, and James A. Brown
1978 *Pre-Columbian Shell Engravings from the Craig Mound at Spiro, Oklahoma*. Peabody Museum of American Archaeology and Ethnology, Harvard University, Cambridge, Massachusetts.
Phillips, Philip, James A. Ford, and James B. Griffin
1951 *Archaeological Survey in the Lower Mississippi Alluvial Valley 1940–1947*. Papers of the Peabody Museum of American Archaeology and Ethnology 25. Harvard University, Cambridge, Massachusetts. Reprinted, 2003. University of Alabama Press, Tuscaloosa.
Pluckhahn, Thomas J.
1996 Joseph Caldwell's Summerour Mound (9FO16) and Woodland Platform Mounds in the Southeastern United States. *Southeastern Archaeology* 15:191–211.
2003 *Kolomoki: Settlement, Ceremony, and Status in the Deep South, c. 350 to 750 AD*. University of Alabama Press, Tuscaloosa.
2007 Reflections on Paddle Stamped Pottery: Symmetry Analysis of Swift Creek Paddle Designs. *Southeastern Archaeology* 26:1–11.
2010 Practicing Complexity (Past and Present) at Kolomoki. In *Ancient Complexities: New Perspectives in Precolumbian North America,* edited by Susan M. Alt, pp. 52–72. University of Utah Press, Salt Lake City.
Pluckhahn, Thomas J., and Robbie Ethridge (editors)
2006 *Light on the Path: The Anthropology and History of the Southeastern Indians.* University of Alabama Press, Tuscaloosa.
Pluckhahn, Thomas J., Robbie Ethridge, Jerald T. Milanich, and Marvin T. Smith
2006 Introduction. In *Light on the Path: The Anthropology and History of the Southeastern Indians*, edited by Thomas J. Pluckhahn and Robbie Ethridge, pp. 1–25. University of Alabama Press, Tuscaloosa.
Pluckhahn, Thomas J., Victor D. Thompson, and Brent R. Weisman
2010 Toward a New View of History and Process at Crystal River. *Southeastern Archaeology* 29:164–182.
Pollack, David
2008 *The Archaeology of Kentucky: An Update*. Kentucky Heritage Council, Frankfort.
Potter, Stephen R.
1993 *Commoners, Tribute, and Chiefs The Development of Algonquin Culture in the Potomac Valley*. University Press of Virginia, Charlottesville.
Powell, John W.
1894 Report of the Director. In *12th Annual Report of the Bureau of Ethnology 1890–'91*, pp. xix–xlviii. Smithsonian Institution, Washington, D.C.
Powell, Mary Lucas, Patricia S. Bridges, and Ann Marie Wagner Mires (editors)
1991 *What Mean These Bones?: Studies in Southeastern Bioarchaeology.* University of Alabama Press, Tuscaloosa.
Prasciunas, Mary M.
2011 Mapping Clovis Projectile Points, Behavior, and Bias. *American Antiquity* 76:107–126.
Prentice, Guy
1986 An Analysis of the Symbolism Expressed by the Birger Figurine. *American Antiquity* 51:239–266.
2000 *Ancient Indian Architecture of the Lower Mississippi Delta: A Study of Earthworks.* Southeast Archeological Center, National Park Service, Tallahassee, Florida.
Pritchard, Erin E., and Todd M. Ahlman
2009 *TVA Archaeology: Seventy–Five Years of Prehistoric Site Research*. University of Tennessee Press, Knoxville.

Purdy, Barbara A., Kevin S. Jones, John J. Mecholsky, Gerald Bourne, Richard C. Hulbert Jr., Bruce J. MacFadden, Krista L. Church, Michael W. Warren, Thomas F. Jorstad, Dennis J. Stanford, Melvin J. Wachowiak, and Robert J. Speakman

2011 Earliest Art in the Americas: Incised Image of a Proboscidean on a Mineralized Extinct Animal Bone from Vero Beach, Florida. *Journal of Archaeological Science* 38:2908–2913.

Pursell, Corin

2004 Geographic Distribution and Symbolism of Colored Mound Architecture in the Mississippian Southeast. M.A. Thesis, Department of Anthropology, Southern Illinois University, Carbondale.

Putnam, Frederic Ward

1878 *Archaeological Explorations in Tennessee*. Eleventh Annual Report of the Peabody Museum of American Archaeology and Ethnology, pp. 305-360. Harvard University, Cambridge, Massachusetts.

Quinn, Rhonda L., Bryan D. Tucker, and John Krigbaum

2008 Diet and Mobility in Middle Archaic Florida; Stable Isotope and Faunal Data from the Harris Creek Archaeological Site (8vo24), Tick Island. *Journal of Archaeological Science* 35:2346–2356.

Rafferty, Janet, and Evan Peacock (editors)

2008 *Time's River: Archaeological Syntheses from the Lower Mississippi Valley*. University of Alabama Press, Tuscaloosa.

Randall, Asa R.

2010 Remapping Histories: Archaic Period Community Construction along the St. Johns River, Florida. Ph.D. Dissertation, Department of Anthropology, University of Florida, Gainesville.

2011 Remapping Archaic Social Histories along the St. John's River in Florida. In *Hunter–Gatherer Archaeology as Historical Process*, edited by Kenneth E. Sassaman and Donald H. Holley Jr., pp. 120–142. University of Arizona Press, Tucson.

Randall, Asa R., and Kenneth E. Sassaman

2010 Emergent Complexities during the Archaic in Northeast Florida. In *Ancient Complexities: New Perspectives in Precolumbian North America*, edited by Susan Alt, pp. 8–31. University of Utah Press, Salt Lake City.

Rasmussen, S. O., K. K. Andersen, A. M. Svensson, J. P. Steffensen, B. M. Vinther, H. B. Clausen, M.-L. Siggaard-Andersen, S. J. Johnsen, L. B. Larsen, D. Dahl-Jensen, M. Bigler, R. Röthlisberger, H. Fischer, K. Goto-Azuma, M. E. Hansson, and U. Ruth

2006 A New Greenland Ice Core Chronology for the Last Glacial Termination. *Journal of Geophysical Research* 111(D6):1–16.

Ray, Jack H.

2007 *Ozarks Chipped-Stone Resources: A Guide to Identification, Distribution, and Prehistoric Use of Cherts and Other Siliceous Raw Materials*. Special Publications, No. 8. Missouri Archaeological Society, Springfield.

Ray, Jack H., and Neal H. Lopinot

2000 Excavations of Pre-Clovis Age Deposits. In *The 1999 Excavations at the Big Eddy Site (23CE426)*, edited by Neal H. Lopinot, Jack H. Ray, and Michael D. Conner, pp. 82–112. Special Publication No. 3. Center for Archaeological Research, Southwest Missouri State University, Springfield.

Ray, Jack H., Neal H. Lopinot, Edward R. Hajic, and Rolfe D. Mandel

1998 The Big Eddy Site: A Multicomponent Paleoindian Site on the Ozark Border, Southwest Missouri. *Plains Anthropologist* 43(163):73–81.

Redfield, Alden
1971 *Dalton Project Notes*, Vol. 1. Museum of Anthropology, University of Missouri, Columbia.
Redmond, Elsa M., and Charles S. Spencer
2012 Chiefdoms at the Threshold: The Competitive Origins of the Primary State. *Journal of Anthropological Archaeology* 31:22–37.
Rees, Mark A. (editor)
2010 *Archaeology of Louisiana*. Louisiana State University Press, Baton Rouge.
Rees, Mark A.
2012 Monumental Landscape and Community in the Southern Lower Mississippi Valley during the Late Woodland and Mississippi Periods. In *The Oxford Handbook of North American Archaeology*, edited by Timothy R. Pauketat, pp. 483–496. Oxford University Press, Oxford, UK.
Rees, Mark A., and Patrick C. Livingood (editors)
2006 *Plaquemine Archaeology*. University of Alabama Press, Tuscaloosa.
Reilly, F. Kent III
2004 People of Earth, People of Sky: Visualizing the Sacred in Native American Art of the Mississippian Period. In *Hero, Hawk, and Open Hand: American Indian Art of the Ancient Midwest and South*, edited by Richard F. Townsend and Robert V. Sharp, pp. 125–137. The Art Institute of Chicago and Yale University Press, New Haven, Connecticut.
Reilly, F. Kent III, and James F. Garber (editors)
2007 *Ancient Objects and Sacred Realms: Interpretations of Mississippian Iconography*. University of Texas Press, Austin.
Reilly, F. Kent III, and James F. Garber
2007 Introduction. In *Ancient Objects and Sacred Realms: Interpretations of Mississippian Iconography*, edited by F. Kent Reilly and James Garber, pp. 1–7. University of Texas Press, Austin.
Reinhart, Theodore R. and Mary Ellen N. Hodges (editors)
1990 *Early and Middle Archaic Research in Virginia: A Synthesis*. Special Publication No. 22. Archeological Society of Virginia, Richmond.
1991 *Late Archaic and Early Woodland Research in Virginia: A Synthesis*. Special Publication No. 23. Archeological Society of Virginia, Richmond.
1992 *Middle and Late Woodland Research in Virginia: A Synthesis*. Special Publication No. 29. Archeological Society of Virginia, Richmond.
Reitz, Elizabeth J.
1993 Zooarchaeology. In *The Development of Southeastern Archaeology*, edited by Jay K. Johnson, pp. 109–131. University of Alabama Press, Tuscaloosa.
2004 "Fishing Down the Food Web": A Case Study from St. Augustine, Florida, USA. *American Antiquity* 69:63–83.
Rice, Prudence M.
1987 *Pottery Analysis: A Sourcebook*. University of Chicago Press, Chicago.
1996a Recent Ceramic Analysis: 1. Function, Style, and Origins. *Journal of Archaeological Research* 4:133–163.
1996b Recent Ceramic Analysis: 2. Composition, Production, and Theory. *Journal of Archaeological Research* 4:165–202.
Ricklis, Robert A.
1988 Archeological Investigations at the McKinzie Site (41NU221), Nueces County, Texas: Description and Contextual Interpretations. *Bulletin of the Texas Archeological Society* 58(for 1987):1–76.

Riggs, Brett H.
2010 Fort Armistead, Lost and Found: The Archeology of a Removal Period army Post on the Cherokee National Forest. Paper Presented at the Annual Meeting of the Southeastern Archeological Conference, Lexington, Kentucky.
Riley, Thomas J., Gregory R. Walz, Charles J. Bareis, Andrew C. Fortier, and Kathryn E. Parker
1994 Accelerator Mass Spectrometry (AMS) Dates Confirm Early *Zea Mays* in the Mississippi River Valley. *American Antiquity* 59:490–498
Roberts, Frank H. H.
1940 Developments in the Problem of the North American Paleo-Indian. Essays in Historical Anthropology of North America. *Smithsonian Miscellaneous Collections* 100:51–116. Washington, D.C.
Robinson, Brian S., and Jennifer C. Ort
2011 Paleoindian and Archaic Period Traditions: Particular Explanations from New England. In *Hunter–Gatherer Archaeology as Historical Process*, edited by Kenneth E. Sassaman and Donald H. Holley Jr., pp. 209–226. University of Arizona Press, Tucson.
Robinson, Brian S., Jennifer C. Ort, William A. Eldridge, Adrian L. Burke, and Bernard G. Pelletier
2009 Paleoindian Aggregation and Social Context at Bull Brook. *American Antiquity* 74:424–447.
Rodning, Christopher B.
1999 Archaeological Perspectives on Gender and Women in Traditional Cherokee Society. *Journal of Cherokee Studies* 20:3–27.
2007 Building and Rebuilding Cherokee Houses and Townhouses in Southwestern North Carolina. In *The Durable House: Architecture, Ancestors, and Origins*, edited by Robin A. Beck, Jr., pp. 464–484. Center for Archaeological Investigations, Occasional Paper No. 35. Southern Illinois University, Carbondale.
2009 Mounds, Myths, and Cherokee Townhouses in Southwestern North Carolina. *American Antiquity* 74:627–663.
2010 Architectural Symbolism and Cherokee Townhouses. *Southeastern Archaeology* 29:59–79.
Rodning, Christopher B., Robin A. Beck, Jr., and David G. Moore
2012 Conflict, Violence, and Warfare in La Florida. In *Native and Imperial Transformations: Sixteenth-Century Entradas in the American Southwest and Southeast*, edited by Clay Mathers, Jeffrey M. Mitchem, and Charles M. Haecker. University of Arizona Press, Tucson, in press.
Roe, Lori M., and Timothy M. Schilling
2010 Coles Creek. In *Archaeology of Louisiana*, edited by Mark A. Rees, pp. 157–171. Louisiana State University Press, Baton Rouge.
Rogers, J. Daniel, and George Sabo III
2004 Caddo. In *Smithsonian Handbook of North American Indians, Volume 14, The Southeast*, edited by Raymond D. Fogelson, pp. 616–631. Smithsonian Institution, Washington, D.C.
Rogers, J. Daniel, and Bruce D. Smith (editors)
1995 *Mississippian Communities and Households*. University of Alabama Press, Tuscaloosa.
Rolingson, Martha A.
2002 Plum Bayou Culture of the Arkansas–White River Basin. In *The Woodland Southeast*, edited by David G. Anderson and Robert C. Mainfort, Jr., pp. 44–65. University of Alabama Press, Tuscaloosa.
2004 Prehistory of the Central Mississippi Valley and Ozarks After 500 B.C. In *Smithsonian Handbook of North American Indians, Volume 14, The Southeast*, edited by Raymond D. Fogelson, pp. 534–544. Smithsonian Institution, Washington, D.C.

Rolingson, Martha A., and Robert C. Mainfort, Jr.
2002 Woodland Period Archaeology in the Central Mississippi Valley. In *The Woodland Southeast,* edited by David G. Anderson and Robert C. Mainfort, Jr., pp. 20–43. University of Alabama Press, Tuscaloosa.
Romain, William F.
2000 *Mysteries of the Hopewell: Astronomers, Geometers, and Magicians of the Eastern Woodlands.* University of Akron Press, Akron, Ohio.
Rubertone, Patricia E.
2000 The Historical Archeology of Native Americans. *Annual Review of Anthropology* 29:425–446.
Ruby, Bret J., and Christine M. Shriner
2005 Ceramic Vessel Compositions and Styles as Evidence of the Local and Nonlocal Social Affiliations of Ritual Participants at the Mann Site, Indiana. In *Gathering Hopewell Society, Ritual, and Ritual Interaction,* edited by Christopher Carr and D. Troy Case, pp. 553–572. Kluwer Academic/Plenum Publishers, New York.
Rudes, Blair A., Thomas J. Blumer, and J. Alan May
2004 Catawba and Neighboring Groups. In *Smithsonian Handbook of North American Indians, Volume 14, The Southeast,* edited by Raymond D. Fogelson, pp. 301–318. Smithsonian Institution, Washington, D.C.
Rudolph, James L
1984 Earthlodges and Platform Mounds: Changing Public Architecture in the Southeastern United States. *Southeastern Archaeology* 4:33–46.
Russo, Michael
1994 Why We Don't Believe in Archaic Ceremonial Mounds and Why We Should: The Case from Florida. *Southeastern Archaeology* 13:93–109.
1996a Southeastern Preceramic Archaic Ceremonial Mounds. In *Archaeology of the Mid–Holocene Southeast,* edited by Kenneth E. Sassaman and David G. Anderson, pp. 259–287. University Press of Florida, Gainesville.
1996b Southeastern Mid–Holocene Coastal Settlements. In *Archaeology of the Mid–Holocene Southeast,* edited by Kenneth E. Sassaman and David G. Anderson, pp. 177–199. University Press of Florida, Gainesville.
2004 Measuring Shell Rings for Social Inequality. In *Signs of Power: The Rise of Cultural Complexity in the Southeast,* edited by Jon L. Gibson and Philip J. Carr, pp. 26–70. University of Alabama Press, Tuscaloosa.
2006 *Archaic Shell Rings of the Southeast.* U.S. National Historic Landmark Theme Study submitted to the National Park Service, Washington D.C.
2010 Shell Rings and Other Settlement Features as Indicators of Cultural Continuity Between the Late Archaic and Woodland periods of Coastal Florida. In *Trend, Tradition, and Turmoil: What Happened to the Southeastern Archaic?* edited by David Hurst Thomas and Matthew C. Sanger, pp. 149–172. Proceedings of the Third Caldwell Conference, St. Catherines Island, Georgia, May 9–11, 2008. Anthropological Papers 93. American Museum of Natural History, New York.
Russo, Michael, and Gregory Heide
2001 Shell Rings of the Southeast US. *Antiquity* 75(289):491–492.
Russo, Michael, and Rebecca Saunders
1999 Identifying the Early Use of Coastal Fisheries and the Rise of Social Complexity in Shell Rings and Arcuate Middens on Florida's Northeast Gulf Coast. Manuscript submitted to the National Geographic Society, Washington, D.C. Also available at http://www.nps.gov/seac/shellrings/NatlGeo_Report1.pdf.

Sahlins, Marshall D.
1963 Poor Man, Rich Man, Big-Man, Chief: Political Types in Melanesia and Polynesia. *Comparative Studies in Society and History* 5:285–303
Sain, Douglas A.
2011 *Clovis Blade Technology at the Topper Site (38AL23) Assessing Lithic Attribute Variation and Regional Patterns of Technological Organization.* Occasional Papers 2. Southeastern Paleoamerican Survey, South Carolina Institute of Archaeology and Anthropology, University of South Carolina. Columbia.
Sanders, Thomas N.
1990 *Adams: The Manufacturing of Flaked Stone Tools at a Paleoindian Site in Western Kentucky.* Persimmon, Buffalo, New York.
Sanger, Matthew C.
2010 Leaving the Rings: Shell Ring Abandonment and the End of the Late Archaic. In *Trend, Tradition, and Turmoil: What Happened to the Southeastern Archaic?* edited by David Hurst Thomas and Matthew C. Sanger, pp. 201–215. Proceedings of the Third Caldwell Conference, St. Catherines Island, Georgia, May 9–11, 2008. Anthropological Papers 93. American Museum of Natural History, New York.
Sanger, Matthew C., and David Hurst Thomas
2010 The Two Rings of St. Catherines Island: Some Preliminary Results from the St. Catherines and McQueen Shell Rings. In Trend, In *Trend, Tradition, and Turmoil: What Happened to the Southeastern Archaic?* edited by David Hurst Thomas and Matthew C. Sanger, pp. 45–69. Proceedings of the Third Caldwell Conference, St. Catherines Island, Georgia, May 9–11, 2008. Anthropological Papers 93. American Museum of Natural History, New York.
Sassaman, Kenneth E.
1993 *Early Pottery in the Southeast: Tradition and Innovation in Cooking Technology.* University of Alabama Press, Tuscaloosa.
1995 The Cultural Diversity of Interactions among Mid-Holocene Societies of the American Southeast. In *Native American Interaction: Multiscalar Analyses and Interpretations in the Eastern Woodlands*, edited by Michael S. Nassaney and Kenneth E. Sassaman, pp. 174–204. University of Tennessee Press, Knoxville.
2001a Hunter-Gatherers and Traditions of Resistance. In *The Archaeology of Traditions: Agency and History Before and After Columbus*, edited by Timothy R. Pauketat, pp. 218–236. University Press of Florida, Gainesville.
2001b Articulating Hidden Histories of the Mid-Holocene. In *Archaeology of the Appalachian Highlands*, edited by Lynne P. Sullivan and Susan Prezanno, pp. 102–120. University of Tennessee Press, Knoxville.
2002 Woodland Ceramic Beginnings. In *The Woodland Southeast*, edited by David G. Anderson and Robert C. Mainfort, Jr., pp. 398–420. University of Alabama Press, Tuscaloosa.
2004a Common Origins and Divergent Histories in the Early Pottery Traditions of the American Southeast. In *Early Pottery: Technology, Function, Style, and Interaction in the Lower Southeast*, edited by Rebecca Saunders and Christopher T. Hays, pp. 23–39. University of Alabama Press, Tuscaloosa.
2004b Complex Hunter-Gatherers in Evolution and History: A North American Perspective. *Journal of Archaeological Research* 12:227–280.
2005a Structure and Practice in the Archaic Southeast. In *North American Archaeology*, edited by Timothy R. Pauketat and Diane DiPaolo Loren, pp. 79–107. Blackwell Publishing, Ltd., Malden, Massachusetts.
2005b Poverty Point as Structure, Event, Process. *Journal of Archaeological Method and Theory* 12:335–364.

2006a *People of the Shoals: Stallings Culture of the Savannah River Valley.* University Press of Florida, Gainesville.

2006b Dating and Explaining Soapstone Vessels: A Comment on Truncer. *American Antiquity* 71:141–156.

2010a *The Eastern Archaic, Historicized.* AltaMira Press, Lanham, Maryland.

2010b Getting from the Late Archaic to Early Woodland in Three Middle Valleys (those being the Savannah, St. Johns, and Tennessee). In *Trend, Tradition, and Turmoil: What Happened to the Southeastern Archaic?* edited by David Hurst Thomas and Matthew C. Sanger, pp. 229–235. Proceedings of the Third Caldwell Conference, St. Catherines Island, Georgia, May 9–11, 2008. Anthropological Papers of the American Museum of Natural History 93, New York, New York.

2011 History and Alterity in the Eastern Archaic. In *Hunter–Gatherer Archaeology as Historical Process,* edited by Kenneth E. Sassaman and Donald H. Holley Jr., pp. 187–208. University of Arizona Press, Tucson.

2012 Drowning Out the Past: How Humans Historicize Water as Water Historicizes Them. In *Big Histories, Human Lives: Tackling Problems of Scale in Archaeology,* edited by John E. Robb and Timothy R. Pauketat. School for Advanced Research, Santa Fe, in press.

Sassaman, Kenneth E., and David G. Anderson (editors)

1996 *Archaeology of the Mid–Holocene Southeast.* University Press of Florida, Gainesville.

Sassaman, Kenneth E., and David G. Anderson

2004 Late Holocene Period, 3750 to 650 B.C. In *Smithsonian Handbook of North American Indians, Volume 14, The Southeast,* edited by Raymond D. Fogelson, pp. 101–114. Smithsonian Institution, Washington, D.C.

Sassaman, Kenneth E., and Michael Heckenberger

2004 Crossing the Symbolic Rubicon in the Southeast. In *Signs of Power: The Rise of Cultural Complexity in the Southeast,* edited by Jon L. Gibson and Philip J. Carr, pp. 214–233. University of Alabama Press, Tuscaloosa.

Sassaman, Kenneth E., and Asa R. Randall

2007 The Cultural History of Bannerstones in the Savannah River Valley. *Southeastern Archaeology* 26:196–211.

2012 Shell Mounds of the Middle St. Johns Basin, Northeast Florida. In *Early New World Monumentality,* edited by Richard L. Burger and Robert M. Rosenswig, pp. 53–77. University Press of Florida, Gainesville.

Sassaman, Kenneth E., and Wictoria Rudolphi

2001 Communities of Practice in the Early Ceramic Traditions of the American Southeast. *Journal of Anthropological Research* 57:407–425.

Sassaman, Kenneth E., Glen T. Hanson, and Tommy Charles

1988 Raw Material Procurement and the Reduction of Hunter-Gatherer Range in the Savannah River Valley. *Southeastern Archaeology* 7:79–94.

Sassaman, Kenneth E., Mark J. Brooks, Glen T. Hanson, and David G. Anderson

1990 *Native American Prehistory of the Middle Savannah River Valley: A Synthesis of Archaeological Investigations on the Savannah River Site, Aiken and Barnwell Counties, South Carolina.* Savannah River Archaeological Research Papers 1. South Carolina Institute of Archaeology and Anthropology, University of South Carolina, Columbia.

Sassaman, Kenneth E., Meggan E. Blessing and Asa R. Randall

2006 Stallings Island Revisited: New Observations on Occupational History, Community Patterning, and Subsistence Technology. *American Antiquity* 71:539–566.

Sassaman, Kenneth E., Paulette S. McFadden, and Micah P. Mones

2010 *Lower Suwannee Archaeological Survey 2009–2010: Investigations at Cat Island (8DI29), Little Bradford Island (8DI32), and Richards Island (8LV137).* Technical Report 10. Laboratory of Southeastern Archaeology, Department of Anthropology, University of Florida, Gainesville.

Saucier, Roger

1994 *Geomorphology and Quaternary Geological History of the Lower Mississippi Valley.* U.S. Army Engineer Waterways Experiment Station, Vicksburg, Mississippi.

Saunders, Joe W.

2004 Are We Fixing to Make the Same Mistake Again? In *Signs of Power: The Rise of Cultural Complexity in the Southeast,* edited by Jon L. Gibson and Philip J. Carr, pp. 146–161. University of Alabama Press, Tuscaloosa.

2010 Late Archaic? What the Hell Happened to the Middle Archaic? In *Trend, Tradition, and Turmoil: What Happened to the Southeastern Archaic?* Proceedings of the Third Caldwell Conference, St. Catherines Island, Georgia, May 9–11, 2008, edited by David Hurst Thomas and Matthew C. Sanger, pp. 237–243. Anthropological Papers 93. American Museum of Natural History, New York.

Saunders, Joe W., Thurman Allen, and Roger T. Saucier

1994 Four Archaic? Mound Complexes in Northeast Louisiana. *Southeastern Archaeology* 13:134–153.

Saunders, Joe W., Rolfe D. Mandel, Roger T. Saucier, E. Thurman Allen, C. T. Hallmark, Jay K. Johnson, H. Edwin Jackson, Charles M. Allen, Gary L. Stringer, Douglas S. Frink, James K. Feathers, Stephen Williams, Kristen J. Gremillion, Malcolm F. Vidrine, and Reca Jones

1997 A Mound Complex in Louisiana at 5400–5000 Years before the Present. *Science* 277:1796–1799.

Saunders, Joe W., Thurman Allen, Dennis LaBatt, Reca Jones, and David Griffing

2001 An Assessment of the Antiquity of the Lower Jackson Mound. *Southeastern Archaeology* 20:67–77.

Saunders, Joe W., Rolfe D. Mandel, C. G. Sampson, Charles M. Allen, E. Thurman Allen, Daniel A. Bush, James K. Feathers, Kristen J. Gremillion, C. T. Hallmark, H. Edwin Jackson, Jay K. Johnson, Reca Jones, Roger T. Saucier, Gary L. Stringer, and Malcolm F. Vidrine

2005 Watson Brake: A Middle Archaic Mound Complex in Northeast Louisiana. *American Antiquity* 70:631–668

Saunders, Rebecca

1994 The Case for Archaic Mound Sites in Southeastern Louisiana. *Southeastern Archaeology* 13(2):118–134.

1998 Swift Creek Phase Design Assemblages from Two Sites on the Georgia Coast. In *A World Engraved: Archaeology of the Swift Creek Culture,* edited by J. Mark Williams and Daniel T. Elliott, pp. 154–180. University of Alabama Press, Tuscaloosa.

2000 *Stability and Change in Guale Indian Pottery, A.D. 1300–1702.* University of Alabama Press, Tuscaloosa.

2004 Stratigraphy at the Rollins Shell Ring Site: Implications for Ring Function. *The Florida Anthropologist* 57(4):249–270.

Saunders, Rebecca (editor)

2002 *The Fig Island Ring Complex (38CH42): Coastal Adaptation and the Question of Ring Function in the Late Archaic.* Report prepared for the South Carolina Department of Archives and History, Columbia.

Saunders, Rebecca, and Christopher T. Hays (editors)

2004 *Early Pottery: Technology, Function, Style, and Interaction in the Lower Southeast.* University of Alabama Press, Tuscaloosa.

Saunt, Claudio
2004 History until 1776. In *Smithsonian Handbook of North American Indians, Volume 14, The Southeast*, edited by Raymond D. Fogelson, pp. 128–138. Smithsonian Institution, Washington, D.C.
Scarry, C. Margaret (editor)
1993 *Foraging and Farming in the Eastern Woodlands.* University Press of Florida, Gainesville.
Scarry, John F. (editor)
1996 *Political Structure and Change in the Prehistoric Southeastern United States.* University Presses of Florida, Gainesville.
Scarry, John F., and Bonnie G. McEwan
1995 Domestic Architecture in Apalachee Province: Apalachee and Spanish Residential Styles in the Late Prehistoric and Early Historic Period Southeast. *American Antiquity* 60:482–495.
Schiffer, Michael B.
1975a Some Further Comments on the Dalton Settlement Pattern Hypothesis. In *The Cache River Archaeological Project: An Experiment in Contract Archaeology*, assembled by Michael B. Schiffer and John H. House, pp. 103–112. Research Series No. 8. Arkansas Archaeological Survey, Fayetteville.
1975b An Alternative to Morse's Dalton Settlement Pattern Hypothesis. *Plains Anthropologist* 20:253–66.
Schiffer, Michael B., and John H. House
1975 *Cache River Archeological Project: An Experiment in Contract Archeology.* Arkansas Archeological Survey Research Series 8. Fayetteville.
Schmidt, Christopher W., Rachel Lockhart Sharkey, Christopher Newman, Anna Serrano, Melissa Zolnierz, Jeffrey A. Plunkett, and Anne Bader
2010 Skeletal Evidence of Cultural Variation: Mutilation Related to Warfare and Mortuary Treatment. In *Human Variation in the Americas: The Integration of Archaeology and Biological Anthropology*, edited by Benjamin M. Auerbach, pp. 215–237. Center for Archaeological Investigations, Occasional Paper 38. Southern Illinois University, Carbondale.
Schneider, Alan L., and Bonnichsen, Robson
2005 Where Are We Going? Public Policy and Science. In *Paleoamerican Origins: Beyond Clovis*, edited by Robson Bonnichsen, Bradley T. Lepper, Dennis Stanford, and Michael R. Waters, pp. 297–312. Center for the Study of the First Americans, Texas A&M University Press, College Station.
Schroeder, Sissel
2009 Viewing Jonathan Creek Through Ceramics and Radiocarbon Dates: Regional Prominence in the Thirteenth Century. In *TVA Archaeology: Seventy-five Years of Prehistoric Site Research*, edited by Erin E. Pritchard and Todd M. Ahlman, pp. 145–180. University of Tennessee Press, Knoxville.
Schroedl, Gerald F.
2000 Cherokee Ethnohistory and Archaeology from 1540 to 1838. In *Indians of the Greater Southeast: Historical Archaeology and Ethnohistory*, edited by Bonnie G. McEwan, pp. 202–241. University Press of Florida, Gainesville.
2001 Cherokee Archaeology Since the 1970s. In *Archaeology of the Appalachian Highlands*, edited by Lynne P. Sullivan and Susan C. Prezzano, pp. 278–297. University of Tennessee Press, Knoxville.
Schroedl, Gerald F., C. Clifford Boyd, and R. P. Stephen Davis
1990 Explaining Mississippian Origins in East Tennessee. In *The Mississippian Emergence*, edited by Bruce D. Smith, pp. 175–196. Smithsonian Institution Press, Washington, D.C.

Schuldenrein, Joseph

1996 Geoarchaeology and the Mid-Holocene Landscape History of the Greater Southeast. In *Archaeology of the Mid–Holocene Southeast*, edited by Kenneth E. Sassaman and David G. Anderson, pp. 3–27. University Press of Florida, Gainesville.

Sears, Elsie O., and William H. Sears

1976 Preliminary Report on Prehistoric Corn Pollen from Fort Center, Florida. *Southeastern Archaeological Conference Bulletin* 19:53–56.

Sears, William A.

1956 *Excavations at Kolomoki Final Report.* University of Georgia, Series in Anthropology 5, University of Georgia Press, Athens.

1973 The Scared and Secular in Prehistoric Ceramics. In *Variation in Anthropology, Essays in Honor of John McGregor*, edited by Donald W. Lathrop and Jody Douglas, pp. 31–42. Illinois Archaeological Survey, Urbana.

1982 *Fort Center: An Archaeological Site in the Lake Ockeechobee Basin.* University Press of Florida, Gainesville, Florida.

1992 Mea culpa. *Southeastern Archaeology* 11:66–71.

Seeman, Mark F.

1995 When Words are not Enough: Hopewell Interregionalism and the Use of Material Symbols in the GE Mound. In *Native American Interaction: Multiscalar Analyses and Interpretations in the Eastern Woodlands*, edited by Michael S. Nassaney and Kenneth E. Sassaman, pp. 122–143. University of Tennessee Press, Knoxville.

Setzler, Frank M. and William D. Strong

1936 Archaeology and Relief. *American Antiquity* 1:301–309.

Shapiro, Gary, and John H. Hann

1990 The Documentary Image of the Council Houses of Spanish Florida Tested by Excavations at the Mission of San Luis de Talimali. In *Columbian Consequences, Volume 2: Archaeological and Historical Perspectives on the Spanish Borderlands East*, edited by David Hurst Thomas, pp. 511–526. Smithsonian Institution Press, Washington, D.C.

Shapiro, Gary, and Bonnie G. McEwan

1992 *Archaeology at San Luis, Part One: The Apalachee Council House.* Florida Archaeology 6. Bureau of Archaeological Research, Tallahassee.

Sherwood, Sarah C.

2006 *Geoarchaeological Study of the Mound A Stratigraphy, Shiloh National Military Park, Hardin County, Tennessee*. Manuscript on file, Southeast Archeological Center, National Park Service, Tallahassee, Florida.

Sherwood, Sarah C., and Jefferson Chapman

2005 The Identification and Potential Significance of Early Holocene Prepared Clay Surfaces: Examples from Dust Cave and Icehouse Bottom. *Southeastern Archaeology* 24:70–82.

Sherwood, Sarah C., and Tristram R. Kidder

2011 The DaVincis of Dirt: Geoarchaeological Perspectives on Native American Mound Building in the Mississippi River Basin. *Journal of Anthropological Archaeology* 30:69–87.

Sherwood, Sarah C., Boyce Driskell, Asa R. Randall, and Scott Meeks

2004 Chronology and Stratigraphy at Dust Cave, Alabama. *American Antiquity* 69:533–554

Shields, Ben M.

2010 Middle and Late Archaic Mortuary Practices: Inclusion and Exclusion in the Middle Tennessee River Valley. Paper presented at the 67th Annual Meeting of the Southeastern Archaeological Conference, Lexington, Kentucky.

Shippie, J. Mett

1966 The Archaeology of the Arnold Research Cave, Callaway County, Missouri. *Missouri Archaeologist* 28.

Shott, Michael J.

2005 Representativity of the Midwestern Paleoindian Site Sample. *North American Archaeologist* 25:189–212.

Silverberg, Robert

1968 *Mound Builders of Ancient America: The Archaeology of a Myth.* New York Graphic Society, Greenwich, Connecticut.

Simek, Jan F., and Alan Cressler

2004 Images in Darkness: Prehistoric Cave Art in Southeast North America. In *Discovering North American Rock Art*, edited by Lawrence L. Loendorf, Christopher Chippendale, and David S. Whitley, pp. 93–113. University of Arizona Press, Tucson.

2008 On the Backs of Serpents: Prehistoric Cave Art in the Southeastern Woodlands. In *Cave Archaeology in the Eastern Woodlands: Essays in Honor of Patty Jo Watson*, edited by David H. Dye, pp. 169–191. University of Tennessee Press, Knoxville.

Simek, Jan F., Jay D. Franklin, and Sarah C. Sherwood

1998 The Context of Early Southeastern Prehistoric Cave Art: A Report on the Archaeology of 3rd Unnamed Cave. *American Antiquity* 63:663–677.

Simek, Jan F., Charles H. Faulkner, Todd Ahlman, Brad Cresswell, and Jay D. Franklin

2001 The Context of Late Prehistoric Cave Art: The Art and Archaeology of 11th Unnamed Cave, Tennessee. *Southeastern Archaeology* 20:142–153.

Simon, Mary L.

2009 A Regional and Chronological Synthesis of Archaic Period Plant Use in the Midcontinent. In *Archaic Societies: Diversity and Complexity across the Midcontinent*, edited by Thomas E. Emerson, Dale L. McElrath and Andrew C. Fortier, pp. 81–114. State University of New York Press, Albany.

Smallwood, Ashley M.

2010 Clovis Biface Technology at the Topper site, South Carolina: Evidence for Variation and Technological Flexibility. *Journal of Archaeological Science* 37:2413–2425.

2011 Clovis Technology and Settlement in the American Southeast. Ph.D. Dissertation, Department of Anthropology, Texas A&M University. College Station.

2012 Clovis Technology and Settlement in the American Southeast: Using Biface Analysis to Evaluate Dispersal Models. *American Antiquity*, in press.

Smallwood, Ashley M., D. Shane Miller, and Douglas A. Sain

2012 Topper Site, South Carolina: An Overview of the Clovis Lithic Assemblage from the Topper Hillside. In *In the Eastern Fluted Point Tradition*, edited by Joseph A. M. Gingerich. University of Utah Press, Salt Lake City, in press.

Smith, Betty A.

1979 The Hopewell Connection in Southwest Georgia. In *Hopewell Archaeology: The Chillicothe Conference*, edited by David S. Brose and N'omi Greber, pp. 239–246. Kent State University Press, Kent, Ohio.

Smith, Bruce D.

1984 Mississippian Expansion: Tracing the Historical Development of an Explanatory Model. *Southeastern Archaeology* 3(1):13–32.

1985 Introduction to the 1985 Edition. *Report on the Mound Explorations of the Bureau of Ethnology*, by Cyrus Thomas (originally published in 1894). Classics of Smithsonian Anthropology Series 7, pp. 5-19. Smithsonian Institution Press, Washington, D.C.

1986 The Archaeology of the Southeastern United States: From Dalton to De Soto, 10,500–500 B.P. *Advances in World Archaeology* 5:1–92.

1987 Independent Domestication of Indigenous Seed-Bearing Plants in Eastern North America. In *Emergent Horticultural Economies of the Eastern Woodlands*, edited by William F. Keegan, pp. 3–47. Center for Archaeological Investigations, Occasional Paper No. 7. Southern Illinois University, Carbondale.

1992 *Rivers of Change: Essays on Early Agriculture in Eastern North America*. Smithsonian Institution Press, Washington, D.C.

2001a Low-Level Food Production. *Journal of Archaeological Research* 9:1–43

2001b Documenting Plant Domestication: The Consilience of Biological and Archaeological Approaches. *Proceedings of the National Academy of Sciences USA* 98:1324–1326.

2006 Eastern North America as an Independent Center of Plant Domestication. *Proceedings of the National Academy of Sciences USA* 103:1223–1228

2011 Resource Resilience, Human Niche Construction, and the Long-Term Sustainability of Pre-Columbian Subsistence Economies in the Mississippi River Valley Corridor. *Journal of Ethnobiology* 29:167–183.

Smith, Bruce D. (editor)

1978 *Mississippian Settlement Patterns*. Academic Press, New York

1990 *The Mississippian Emergence*. Smithsonian Institution Press, Washington, D.C.

Smith, Bruce D., and Richard A. Yarnell

2009 Initial Formation of an Indigenous Crop Complex in Eastern North America at 3800 B.P. *Proceedings of the National Academy of Sciences USA* 106:6561–6566.

Smith, Karen Y., and Fraser D. Neiman

2007 Frequency Seriation, Correspondence Analysis, and Woodland Period Ceramic Assemblage Variation in the Deep South. *Southeastern Archaeology* 26:47–72.

Smith, Kevin E.

1992 The Middle Cumberland Region: Mississippian Archaeology in North Central Tennessee. Ph.D. Dissertation, Department of Anthropology, Vanderbilt University, Nashville, Tennessee. University Microfilms International, Ann Arbor.

Smith, Kevin E., and James V. Miller

2009 *Speaking with the Ancestors: Mississippian Stone Statuary of the Tennessee–Cumberland Style*. University of Alabama Press, Tuscaloosa.

Smith, Maria O.

1993 Physical Anthropology. In *The Development of Southeastern Archaeology*, edited by Jay K. Johnson, pp. 53–77. University of Alabama Press, Tuscaloosa.

1996 Biocultural Inquiry into Archaic Period Populations of the Southeast: Trauma and Occupational Stress. In *Archaeology of the Mid–Holocene Southeast*, edited by Kenneth E. Sassaman and David G. Anderson, pp. 134–154. University Press of Florida, Gainesville.

Smith, Marvin T.

1987 *Archaeology of Aboriginal Culture Change in the Interior Southeast: Depopulation during the Early Historic Period*. University of Florida Press, Gainesville.

1994 Aboriginal Depopulation in the Postcontact Southeast. In *The Forgotten Centuries: Indians and Europeans in the American South, 1521–1704*, edited by Charles M. Hudson and Carmen Chaves Tesser, pp. 257–275. University of Georgia Press, Athens.

2000 *Coosa: The Rise and Fall of a Southeastern Mississippian Chiefdom*. University Press of Florida, Gainesville.

Smith, Marvin T., and Mary Elizabeth Good

1982 *Early Sixteenth Century Glass Beads in the Spanish Colonial Trade*. Cottonlandia Museum Publications, Greenwood, Mississippi.

Smith, Marvin T., and J. Mark Williams

1994 Mississippian Mound Refuse Disposal Patterns and Implications for Archaeological Research. *Southeastern Archaeology* 13:27–35.

Smith, Marvin T., Robbie Franklyn Ethridge, and Charles M. Hudson (editors)

2002 *The Transformation of the Southeastern Indians, 1540–1760.* University Press of Mississippi, Jackson.

Snow, Frankie

1975 Swift Creek Designs and Distributions: A South Georgia Study. *Early Georgia* 3(2):38–59.

1998 Swift Creek Design Investigations: The Hartford Case. In *A World Engraved: Archaeology of the Swift Creek Culture,* edited by J. Mark Williams and Daniel T. Elliott, pp. 61–98. University of Alabama Press, Tuscaloosa.

Snow, Frankie, and Keith Stephenson

1998 Swift Creek Designs: A Tool for Monitoring Interaction. In *A World Engraved: Archaeology of the Swift Creek Culture,* edited by J. Mark Williams and Daniel T. Elliott, pp. 99–111. University of Alabama Press, Tuscaloosa.

Solobik, Kristin D., Kristen J. Gremillion, Patricia L. Whitten, and Patty Jo Watson

1996 Technical Note: Sex Determination of Prehistoric Human Paleofeces. *American Journal of Physical Anthropology* 101:283–290.

South, Stanley A.

1977 *Method and Theory in Historical Archaeology.* Academic Press, New York.

1980 *The Discovery of Santa Elena.* South Carolina Institute of Archaeology and Anthropology, Research Manuscript Series 165. University of South Carolina, Columbia,

2005a *An Archaeological Evolution.* Springer, New York.

2005b *Archaeology on the Roanoke.* University of North Carolina, Research Laboratories of Archaeology Monograph 4, Chapel Hill.

South, Stanley A., and Chester B. DePratter

1996 *Discovery at Santa Elena: Block Excavation, 1993.* South Carolina Institute of Archaeology and Anthropology, Research Manuscript Series 222. University of South Carolina, Columbia.

Speth, John D., Khori Newlander, Andrew A. White, Ashley K. Lemke, and Lars E. Anderson

2010 Early Paleoindian Big-game Hunting in North America: Provisioning or Politics? *Quaternary International* 30:1–29.

Squier, Ephraim George, and Edwin H. Davis

1848 *Ancient Monuments of the Mississippi Valley.* Smithsonian Contributions to Knowledge 1. Washington, D.C.

SRARP Staff

2003 *25 Years of Discovering the Past The Savannah River Research Program A Silver Anniversary Retrospective 1978–2003.* Savannah River Archaeological Research Program, South Carolina Institute of Archaeology and Anthropology, University of South Carolina, Columbia.

Stafford, Thomas W., Jr., Holmes A. Semken, Jr., Russell W. Graham, Walter F. Klippel, Anstasia Markova, Nikolai G. Smirnov, and John Southon

1999 First Accelerator Mass Spectrometry ^{14}C Dates Documenting Contemporaneity of Nonanalog Species in Late Pleistocene Mammal Communities. *Geology* 27:903–906.

Stahle, David W., Edward R. Cook, and James W. C. White

1985 Tree-Ring Dating of Baldcypress and the Potential for Millennia-Long Chronologies in the Southeast. *American Antiquity* 50:796–802.

Stahle, David W., Malcolm K. Cleaveland, Dennis B. Blanton, Matthew D. Therrell, and David A. Gay

1998 The Lost Colony and Jamestown Droughts. *Science* 280:564–567.

Stahle, David W., Falko K. Fye, Edward R. Cook, and R. Daniel Griffin

2007 Tree-Ring Reconstructed Megadroughts over North America Since AD 1300. *Climate Change* 83:133–149.

Stanford, Dennis J.

1991 Clovis Origins and Adaptations: An Introductory Perspective. In *Clovis Origins and Adaptations*, edited by Robson Bonnichsen and Karen L. Turnmire, pp. 1–13. Center for the Study of the First Americans, Oregon State University, Corvallis.

Stanford, Dennis J., and Bruce A. Bradley

2002 Ocean Trails and Prairie Paths? Thoughts about Clovis Origins. In *The First Americans: The Pleistocene Colonization of the New World*, edited by Nina G. Jablonski, pp. 255–271. Memoir of the California Academy of Sciences, Number 27, San Francisco.

2012 *Across Atlantic Ice: The Origin of America's Clovis Culture*. University of California Press, Berkeley.

Stapp, Darby C., and Michael S. Burney

2002 *Tribal Cultural Resource Management: The Full Circle to Stewardship*. AltaMira Press, Walnut Creek, California.

Steere, Benjamin A.

2011 The Archaeology of Houses and Households in the Native Southeast. Ph.D. Dissertation, Department of Anthropology, University of Georgia, Athens, Georgia.

Steffensen, J. P., K. K. Andersen, M. Bigler, H. Clausen, D. Dahl-Jensen, H. Fischer, K. Goto-Azuma, M. Hansson, S. Johnsen, J. Jouzel, V. Masson-Delmotte, T. Popp, S. Rasmussen, R. Rothlisberger, U. Ruth, B. Stauffer, M.-L. Siggaard-Andersen, A. Sveinbjörnsdóttir, A. Svensson, and J. W. C. White

2008 High Resolution Greenland Ice Core Data show Abrupt Climate Change Happens in Few Years. *Science* 321:680–684.

Steinen, Karl T.

2006 Kolomoki: Cycling, Settlement Patterns and Culture Change in a Late Middle Woodland Society. In *Recreating Hopewell*, edited by Douglas K. Charles and Jane E. Buikstra, pp. 178–189. University Press of Florida, Gainesville.

Stephenson, Keith L., Judith A. Bense, and Frankie Snow

2002 Some Aspects of Deptford and Swift Creek of the South Atlantic and Gulf Coastal Plains. In *The Woodland Southeast*, edited by David G. Anderson and Robert C. Mainfort, Jr., pp. 318–351. University of Alabama Press, Tuscaloosa.

Steponaitis, Vincas P.

1978 Location Theory and Complex Chiefdoms: A Mississippian Example. In *Mississippian Settlement Patterns*, edited by Bruce D. Smith, pp. 417–453. Academic Press, New York.

1981 Settlement Hierarchies and Political Complexity in Nonmarket Societies: The Formative Period of the Valley of Mexico. *American Anthropologist* 83:320–363.

1983 *Ceramics, Chronology, and Community Pattern: An Archaeological Study at Moundville*. Academic Press, New York. Reprinted, 2009, University of Alabama Press, Tuscaloosa.

1986 Prehistoric Archaeology in the Southeastern United States, 1970–1985. *Annual Review of Anthropology* 15:363–404.

Steponaitis, Vincas P., and David T. Dockery III

2011 Mississippian Effigy Pipes and the Glendon Limestone. *American Antiquity* 76:345–354.

Steponaitis, Vincas P., and Vernon J. Knight Jr.

2004 Moundville Art in Historical and Social Context. In *Hero, Hawk, and Open Hand: American Indian Art of the Ancient Midwest and South*, edited by Richard F. Townsend and Robert V. Sharp, pp. 167–181. The Art Institute of Chicago and Yale University Press, New Haven, Connecticut.

Steponaitis, Vincas P., M. James Blackman, and Hector Neff

1996 Large-Scale Patterns in the Chemical Composition of Mississippian Pottery. *American Antiquity* 61:555–572.

Steponaitis, Vincas P., Stephen Williams, R. P. Stephen Davis, Jr., Ian W. Brown, Tristram R. Kidder, and Melissa Salvanish (editors)

2002 *LMS Archives Online*. Electronic document, http://rla.unc.edu/archives/lms1/, accessed 1 January 2012.

Steponaitis, Vincas P., William H. Marquardt, Vernon J. Knight, R. P. Stephen Davis, Kenneth E. Sassaman, Robert C. Mainfort, Jr., and Gregory A. Waselkov

2003 The Editors Speak: Reminiscences of the Editors of the Journal Southeastern Archaeology on the Occasion of its Twentieth Anniversary. *Southeastern Archaeology* 22:1–8.

Steponaitis, Vincas P., Samuel E. Swanson, George Wheeler, and Penelope B. Drooker

2011 The Provenance and Use of Etowah Palettes. *American Antiquity* 76:81–106.

Stojanowski, Christopher M. (editor)

2010 *Bioarchaeology of Ethnogenesis in the Colonial Southeast*. University Press of Florida, Gainesville.

Stoltman, James B.

1973 The Southeastern United States. In *The Development of North American Archaeology: Essays in the History of Regional Traditions*, edited by James B. Fitting, pp. 115–150. Anchor Press, Garden City, New Jersey.

2004 History of Archaeological Research. In *Smithsonian Handbook of North American Indians, Volume 14, The Southeast*, edited by Raymond D. Fogelson, pp. 14–30. Smithsonian Institution, Washington, D.C.

Stoltman, James B., and Frankie Snow

1998 Cultural Interaction within Swift Creek Society: People, Pots, and Paddles. In *A World Engraved: Archaeology of the Swift Creek Culture*, edited by J. Mark Williams and Daniel T. Elliott, pp. 130–153. University of Alabama Press, Tuscaloosa.

Stottman, M. Jay (editor)

2011 *Archaeologists as Activists: Can Archaeologists Change the World?* University of Alabama Press, Tuscaloosa.

Stout, Charles, and R. Barry Lewis

1998 The Town as Metaphor. In *Mississippian Towns and Sacred Spaces: Searching for an Architectural Grammar*, edited by Berry R. Lewis and Charles Stout, pp. 227–241. University of Alabama Press, Tuscaloosa

Straus, Lawrence G.

2000 Solutrean Settlement of North America? A Review of Reality. *American Antiquity* 65:219–226.

Straus, Lawrence G., David J. Meltzer, and Ted Goebel

2005 Ice Age Atlantis: Exploring the Solutrean–Clovis 'Connection'. *World Archaeology* 37:507–532.

Styles, Bonnie W., and Walter E. Klippel

1996 Mid–Holocene Faunal Exploitation in the Southeastern United States. In *Archaeology of the Mid–Holocene Southeast*, edited by Kenneth E. Sassaman and David G. Anderson, pp. 115–133. University Press of Florida, Gainesville.

Sullivan, Lynne P.
1987 The Mouse Creek Phase Household. *Southeastern Archaeology* 6:16–29.
1994 Madeline Kneberg Lewis: An Original Southeastern Archaeologist. In *Women in Archaeology*, edited by Cheryl Claassen, pp. 110–119. University of Pennsylvania Press, Philadelphia.
1995 Mississippian Household and Community Organization in Eastern Tennessee. In *Mississippian Communities and Households*, edited by J. Daniel Rogers and Bruce D. Smith, pp. 99–123. University of Alabama Press, Tuscaloosa.
2006 Gendered Contexts of Mississippian Leadership in Southern Appalachia. In *Leadership and Polity in Mississippian Society*, edited by Brian M. Butler and Paul D. Welch, pp. 264–285. Center for Archeological Investigations, Occasional Paper No. 33, Southern Illinois University, Carbondale.
2007 A WPA Déjà Vu on Mississippian Architecture. In *Architectural Variability in the Southeast: Comprehensive Case Studies of Mississippian Structures*, edited by Cameron H. Lacquement, pp. 117–135. University of Alabama Press, Tuscaloosa.

Sullivan, Lynne P., and S. Terry Childs
2003 *Curating Archaeological Collections: From the Field to the Repository*. Alta Mira Press, Walnut Creek, California.

Sullivan, Lynne P., and Michaelyn S. Harle
2009 Mortuary Practices and Cultural Identity at the Turn of the Sixteenth Century in Eastern Tennessee. In *Mississippian Mortuary Practices: Beyond Hierarchy and the Representationist Perspective*, edited by Lynne P. Sullivan and Robert C. Mainfort, Jr., pp. 234–249. University Press of Florida, Gainesville.

Sullivan, Lynne P., and Robert C. Mainfort, Jr. (editors)
2010 *Mortuary Practices: Beyond Hierarchy and the Representationist Perspective*. University Press of Florida, Gainesville.

Sullivan, Lynne P., and Susan C. Prezzano (editors)
2001 *Archaeology of the Appalachian Highlands*. University of Tennessee Press, Knoxville.

Sullivan, Lynne P., and Christopher B. Rodning
2001 Tradition, and Social Negotiation in Southern Appalachian Chiefdoms. In *The Archaeology of Traditions: History and Agency Before and After Columbus*, edited by Timothy R. Pauketat, pp. 107–120. University Press of Florida, Gainesville.
2011 Residential Burial, Gender Roles, and Political Development in Late Prehistoric and Early Cherokee Cultures of the Southern Appalachians. In *Residential Burial: A Multiregional Exploration*, edited by Ron L. Adams and Stacie M. King, pp. 79–97. Archaeological Papers of the American Anthropological Association 20, Washington, D.C.

Sullivan, Lynne P., Thomas M. N. Lewis, and Madeline K. Lewis
1995 *The Prehistory of the Chickamauga Basin in Tennessee*. 2 vols. University of Tennessee Press, Knoxville

Sullivan, Lynne P., Bobby R. Braly, Michaelyn S. Harle, and Shannon D. Koerner
2011 Remembering New Deal Archaeology in the Southeast: A Legacy in Museum Collections, In *Museums and Memory*, edited by Margaret Williamson Huber, pp. 64–107. Newfound Press, University of Tennessee Libraries, Knoxville.

Surovell, Todd A.
2000 Early Paleoindian Women, Children, Mobility, and Fertility. *American Antiquity* 65:493–509.

Swanton, John R.
1939 *Final Report of the United States De Soto Expedition Commission*. House Document No. 71, 76th Congress, 1st Session. U.S. Government Printing Office, Washington, D.C.

Swidler, Nina, Kurt Dongoske, Roger Anyon, and Alan Downer, (editors)
1997 *Native Americans and Archaeologists: Stepping Stones to Common Ground.* AltaMira Press, Lanham. Maryland.

Tankersley, Kenneth B.
1990 Late Pleistocene Lithic Exploitation in the Midwest and Midsouth: Indiana, Ohio, and Kentucky. In *Early Paleoindian Economies of Eastern North America*, edited by Kenneth B. Tankersley and Barry L. Isaac, pp. 259–99. Research in Economic Anthropology, Supplement 5. JAI, Greenwich, Connecticut.
1996 Prehistoric Salt Mining in the Mammoth Cave System. In *Of Caves and Shell Mounds*, edited by Kenneth Carstens and Patty Jo Watson, pp. 33-39. University of Alabama Press, Tuscaloosa.
2004 The Concept of Clovis and the Peopling of North America. In: *The Settlement of the American Continents: A Multidisciplinary Approach to Human Biogeography*, edited by C. Michael Barton, Geoffrey A. Clark, David R. Yesner, and Georges A. Pearson, pp. 49–63. University of Arizona Press, Tucson.

Thomas, Cyrus
1894 Report on the Mound Explorations of the Bureau of Ethnology. In *12th Annual Report of the Bureau of Ethnology 1890–'91*, pp. 3–742. Smithsonian Institution, Washington, D.C.

Thomas, David Hurst (editor)
1990 *Columbian Consequences, Vol. 2: Archaeological and Historical Perspectives on the Spanish Borderlands East.* Smithsonian Institution Press, Washington, D.C.
2008 *Native American Landscapes of St. Catherines Island, Georgia.* Anthropological Papers of the American Museum of Natural History, 88 (nos. 1–3). New York, New York.

Thomas, David Hurst
1987 *The Archaeology of Mission Santa Catalina de Guale, Part 1: Search and Discovery.* Anthropological Papers of the American Museum of Natural History 63. New York, New York.
1993 *Historic Period Indian Archaeology of the Georgia Coastal Zone.* University of Georgia, Laboratory of Archaeology Series Report Number 31, Georgia Archaeological Research Design Paper No. 8, Athens.
2008 Late Holocene Sea Levels and the Changing Archaeological Landscape of St. Catherines Island. In *Native American Landscapes of St. Catherines Island, Georgia*, edited by David Hurst Thomas, pp. 42–47. Anthropological Papers 88 (nos. 1–3). American Museum of Natural History, New York.

Thomas, David Hurst, and Matthew C. Sanger (editors)
2010 *Trend, Tradition, and Turmoil: What Happened to the Southeastern Archaic?* Proceedings of the Third Caldwell Conference, St. Catherines Island, Georgia, May 9–11, 2008. Anthropological Papers 93. American Museum of Natural History, New York.

Thompson, Victor D.
2006 Questioning Complexity: The Prehistoric Hunter-Gatherers of Sapelo Island, Georgia. Ph.D. Dissertation, Department of Anthropology, University of Kentucky, Lexington, Kentucky.
2007. Articulating Activity Areas and Formation Processes at the Sapelo Island Shell Ring Complex. *Southeastern Archaeology* 26:91–107.
2010 The Rhythms of Space–Time and the Making of Monuments and Places during the Archaic. In *Trend, Tradition, and Turmoil: What Happened to the Southeastern Archaic?* edited by David Hurst Thomas and Matthew C. Sanger, pp. 217–228. Proceedings of the Third Caldwell Conference, St. Catherines Island, Georgia, May 9–11, 2008. Anthropological Papers 93. American Museum of Natural History, New York.

Thompson, Victor D., and Fred T. Andrus
2011 Evaluating Mobility, Monumentality, and Feasting at the Sapelo Shell Ring Complex. *American Antiquity* 76:315–343.
Thompson, Victor D., and Thomas J. Pluckhahn
2010 History, Complex Hunter-Gatherers, and the Mounds and Monuments of Crystal River, Florida, USA: A Geophysical Perspective. *Journal of Island and Coastal Archaeology* 5(1):33–51.
Thompson, Victor D., and John Turck
2009 Adaptive Cycles of Coastal Hunter-Gatherers. *American Antiquity* 74:255–278.
2010 Island Archaeology and the Native American Economies (2500 B.C.–A.D. 1700) of the Georgia Coast. *Journal of Field Archaeology* 35:283–297.
Thompson, Victor D., and John E. Worth
2011 Dwellers by the Sea: Native American Adaptations along the Southern Coasts of Eastern North America. *Journal of Archaeological Research* 19:51–101.
Thompson, Victor D., M. D. Reynolds, B. Haley, Richard Jefferies, Jay K. Johnson, and L. Humphries
2004 The Sapelo Shell Rings: Shallow Geophysics on a Georgia Sea Island. *Southeastern Archaeology* 23:192–201.
Thompson, Victor D., Kristen J. Gremillion, and Thomas J. Pluckhahn
2012 Challenging the Evidence for Prehistoric Wetland Maize Agriculture at Fort Center, Florida. *American Antiquity* (In Press).
Thruston, Gates P.
1890 *The Antiquities of Tennessee and the Adjacent States and the State of Aboriginal Society in the Scale of Civilization Represented by Them: A Series of Historical and Ethnological Studies*. R. Clarke & Company, Cincinnati, Ohio.
Thulman, David K.
2006 A Reconstruction of Paleoindian Social Organization in North Central Florida. Ph.D. Dissertation, Department of Anthropology, Florida State University, Tallahassee.
2008 A Typology of Fluted Points from Florida. *The Florida Anthropologist* 60:63–75.
2009 Freshwater Availability as the Constraining Factor in the Middle Paleoindian Occupation of North-Central Florida. *Geoarchaeology* 24:243–276.
Townsend, Richard F., and Robert V. Sharp (editors)
2004 *Hero, Hawk, and Open Hand: American Indian Art of the Ancient Midwest and South*. The Art Institute of Chicago and Yale University Press, New Haven, Connecticut.
Trocolli, Ruth
2002 Mississippian Chiefs: Women and Men of Power. In *The Dynamics of Power*, edited by Maria O'Donovan, pp. 168–187. Center for Archaeological Investigations, Occasional Paper No. 30. Southern Illinois University, Carbondale
Truncer, James
2004 Steatite Vessel Age and Occurrence in Temperate Eastern North America. *American Antiquity* 69:487–513.
Tucker, Bryan
2009 Isotopic Investigations of Archaic Period Subsistence and Settlement in the St. Johns River Drainage, Florida. Ph.D. Dissertation, Department of Anthropology, University of Florida, Gainesville.
Tune, Jesse W.
2010 The Wells Creek Clovis? Site: A Reanalysis and Reinterpretation. M.A. Thesis, Department of Anthropology, American University, Washington D.C.

Turck, John
2011 Geoarchaeological Analysis of Two Back-barrier Islands and their Relationship to the Changing Landscape of Coastal Georgia, U.S.A. Ph.D. Dissertation, Department of Anthropology, University of Georgia, Athens.
Tushingham, Shannon, Jane Hill, and Charles H. McNutt (editors)
2002 *Histories of Southeastern Archaeology*. University of Alabama Press, Tuscaloosa.

Ubelaker, Douglas H.
2006 Population Size, Contact to Nadir. In *Smithsonian Handbook of North American Indians, Volume 3, Environment, Origins, and Population*, edited by Douglas H. Ubelaker. Smithsonian Institution, Washington, D.C.

Van Nest, Julie, Douglas K. Charles, Jane E. Buikstra, and David L. Asch
2001 Sod Blocks in Illinois Hopewell Mounds. *American Antiquity* 66:633–650.
VanDerwarker, Amber M., and Kandace R. Detwiler
2002 Gendered Practice in Cherokee Foodways: A Spatial Analysis of Plant Remains from the Coweeta Creek site. *Southeastern Archaeology* 21:21–28.
VanDerwarker, Amber M., C. Margaret Scarry, and Jane M. Eastman
2007 Menus for Families and Feasts: Household and Community Consumption of Plants at Upper Saratown, North Carolina. In *We Are What We Eat: Archaeology, Food, and Identity*, edited by Katheryn C. Twiss, pp. 16–58. Center for Archaeological Investigations, Occasional Paper No. 32. Southern Illinois University, Carbondale.

Waguespack, Nicole M., and Todd A. Surovell
2003 Clovis Hunting Strategies, or How to Make Out on Plentiful Resources. *American Antiquity* 68:333–352.
Walker, Karen Jo
2000 The Material Culture of Precolumbian Fishing: Artifacts and Fish Remains from Coastal Southwest Florida. *Southeastern Archaeology* 19:24–45.
Walker, Renee B.
2000 *Subsistence Strategies at Dust Cave: Changes from the Late Paleoindian through Middle Archaic Occupations*. Report of Investigations No. 78. University of Alabama, Office of Archaeological Services, Tuscaloosa.
2007 Hunting in the Late Paleoindian Period: Faunal Remains from Dust Cave. In *Foragers of the Terminal Pleistocene in North America*, edited by Renee B. Walker and Boyce N. Driskell, pp. 99–115. University of Nebraska Press, Lincoln.
Walker, Renee B., and Boyce N. Driskell (editors)
2007 *Foragers of the Terminal Pleistocene in North America*. University of Nebraska Press, Lincoln.
Walker, Renee B., Kandace R. Detwiler, Scott C. Meeks, and Boyce N. Driskell
2001 Berries, Bones, and Blades: Reconstructing Late Paleoindian Subsistence Economy at Dust Cave, Alabama. *Midcontinental Journal of Archaeology* 26:169–197
Walker, Winslow M.
1936 *The Troyville Mounds, Catahoula Parish, Louisiana*. Bureau of American Ethnology Bulletin 113. U.S. Government Printing Office, Washington, D.C.
Wallis, Neill J.
2007 Defining Swift Creek Interaction: Earthenware Variability at Ring Middens and Burial Mounds. *Southeastern Archaeology* 26:212–231.

2008 Networks of History and Memory: Creating a Nexus of Social Identity in Woodland Period Mounds on the Lower St. Johns River, Florida. *Journal of Social Archaeology* 8:236–271.

2009 Locating the Gift: Swift Creek Exchange Along the Atlantic Coast, A.D. 200 to 800. Ph.D. Dissertation, Department of Anthropology, University of Florida, Gainesville.

2011 *The Swift Creek Gift: Vessel Exchange on the Atlantic Coast.* University of Alabama Press, Tuscaloosa.

Walthall, John A.

1980 *Prehistoric Indians of the Southeast: Archaeology of Alabama and the Middle South.* University of Alabama Press, Tuscaloosa.

1998a Rockshelters and Hunter–Gatherer Adaptation to the Pleistocene/Holocene Transition. *American Antiquity* 63:223–238.

1998b Overwintering Strategy and Early Holocene Hunter-Gatherer Mobility in Temperate Forests. *Midcontinental Journal of Archaeology* 23:1–22.

1999 Mortuary Behavior and Early Holocene Land Use in the North American Midcontinent. *North American Archaeologist* 20:1–30.

Walthall, John A., and Thomas E. Emerson (editors)

1992 *Calumet and Fleur-de-Lys: Archaeology of Indian and French Contact in the Midcontinent.* Smithsonian Institution Press, Washington, D.C.

Walthall, John A., and George R. Holley

1997 Mobility and Hunter-Gatherer Toolkit Design: Analysis of a Dalton Lithic Cache. *Southeastern Archaeology* 16:152–161.

Walthall, John A., and Brad Koldehoff

1998 Hunter–Gatherer Interaction and Alliance Formation: Dalton and the Cult of the Long Blade. *Plains Anthropologist* 43:257–273.

Ward, H. Trawick, and R. P. Stephen Davis, Jr.

1999 *Time before History: The Archaeology of North Carolina.* University of North Carolina Press, Chapel Hill.

Waring, Antonio J., Jr.,

1968 A History of Georgia Archaeology. In *The Waring Papers: The Collected Works of Antonio J. Waring, Jr.*, edited by Stephen Williams, pp. 288–299. Peabody Museum Papers Vol. 58. The Peabody Museum, Harvard University, Cambridge, Massachusetts.

Waring, Antonio J., Jr., and Preston Holder

1945 A Prehistoric Ceremonial Complex in the Southeastern United States. *American Anthropologist* 47:1–34.

Waselkov, Gregory A.

1986 A Reinterpretation of the Creek Indian Barricade at Horseshoe Bend. *Journal of Alabama Archeology* 32:94–107.

1993 Historic Creek Indian Responses to European Trade and the Rise of Political Factions, in *Ethnohistory and Archaeology: Approaches to Postcontact Change in the Americas*, edited by J. Daniel Rogers and Samuel M. Wilson, pp. 123–131. Plenum Press, New York.

2004 Exchange and Interaction since 1500. In *Smithsonian Handbook of North American Indians, Volume 14, The Southeast,* edited by Raymond D. Fogelson, pp. 686–696. Smithsonian Institution, Washington, D.C.

2009 What Do Spanish Expeditionary Artifacts of Circa 1540 Look Like and How Often Are They Preserved? In *The Search for Mabila: The Decisive Battle between Hernando de Soto and Chief Tascalusa*, edited by Vernon James Knight Jr., pp. 94-106. University of Alabama Press, Tuscaloosa.

Waselkov, Gregory A., and Marvin T. Smith

2000 Upper Creek Archeology. In *Indians of the Greater Southeast: Historical Archaeology and Ethnohistory*, edited by Bonnie G. McEwan, pp. 242–264. University Press of Florida, Gainesville.

Waselkov, Gregory A., John W. Cottier, and Craig T. Sheldon

1990 *Archaeological Excavations at the Early Historic Creek Indian Town of Fusihatchee: Phase 1, 1988–1989*. Report to the National Science Foundation, Grant No. BNS-8718934. Washington, D.C.

Waselkov, Gregory A., Peter H. Wood, and Tom Hatley (editors)

2006 *Powhatan's Mantle: Indians in the Colonial Southeast* (revised and expanded edition). University of Nebraska Press, Lincoln.

Waters, Michael R., and Thomas W. Stafford, Jr.

2007 Redefining the Age of Clovis: Implications for the Peopling of the Americas. *Science* 315:1122–1126.

Waters, Michael R., Steven L. Forman, Thomas W. Stafford, Jr., and John Foss

2009 Geoarchaeological Investigations at the Topper and Big Pine Tree sites, Allendale County, South Carolina. *Journal of Archaeological Science* 36:1300–1311.

Waters, Michael R., S. L. Forman, Thomas A. Jennings, L. C. Nordt, S. G. Driese, J. M. Feinberg, J. L. Keene, Jessie Halligan, A. Lindquist, J. Pierson, C. T. Hallmark, Michael B. Collins, and J. E. Wiederhold

2011 The Buttermilk Creek Complex and the Origins of Clovis at the Debra L. Friedkin Site, Texas. *Science* 331:1599–1603.

Watson, Patty Jo

1969 *The Prehistory of Salts Cave, Kentucky*. Illinois State Museum Report of Investigations 16. Springfield.

1974 *Archaeology of the Mammoth Cave Area*. Academic Press, New York.

1985 The Impact of Early Horticulture in the Upland Drainages of the Midwest and Midsouth. In *Prehistoric Food Production in North America*, edited by Richard I. Ford, pp. 99–147. Anthropological Papers 74. Museum of Anthropology, University of Michigan, Ann Arbor.

1990 Trend and Tradition in Southeastern Archaeology. *Southeastern Archaeology* 9:43–54.

2005 WPA Excavations in the Middle Green River Region: A Comparative Account. In *Archaeology of the Middle Green River Region, Kentucky*, edited by William H. Marquardt and Patty Jo Watson, pp. 515–628. Institute of Archaeology and Paleoenvironmental Studies Monograph 5. University Press of Florida, Gainesville.

Watson, Patty Jo, and Mary C. Kennedy

1991 The Development of Horticulture in the Eastern Woodlands of North America: Women's Roles. In *Engendering Archaeology*, edited by Joan M. Gero and Margaret W. Conkey, pp. 255–275. Blackwell, Chicago.

Watts, William A., Eric C. Grimm, and T. C. Hussey

1996 Mid-Holocene Forest History of Florida and the Coastal Plain of Georgia and South Carolina. In *Archaeology of the Mid–Holocene Southeast*, edited by Kenneth E. Sassaman and David G. Anderson, pp. 28–38. University Press of Florida, Gainesville.

Wauchope, Robert

1966 *Archaeological Survey of Northern Georgia*. Memoir 21. Society for American Archaeology, Salt Lake City, Utah.

Weaver, Andrew J, Oleg A. Saenko, Peter U. Clark, and Jerry X. Mitrovica

2003 Meltwater Pulse 1A from Antarctica as a Trigger of the Bølling-Allerød Warm Interval. *Science* 299:1709–1713.

Webb, Thompson III, Patrick J. Bartlein, S. P. Harrison, and K. H. Anderson

1993 Vegetation, Lake Level, and Climate Change in Eastern North America. In *Global Climates since the Last Glacial Maximum*, edited by Herbert E. Wright, Jr., John E. Kutzbach, Thompson Webb III, William F. Ruddiman, F. Alayne Street-Perrott, and Patrick J. Bartlein, pp. 415–467. University of Minnesota Press, Minneapolis.

Webb, S. David

2006 *First Floridians and Last Mastodons: The Page Ladson Site in the Aucilla River*. Springer, Dordrecht, The Netherlands.

Webb, S. David, Jerald T. Milanich, R. Alexon, and James S. Dunbar

1984 A *Bison antiquus* Kill Site, Wacissa River, Jefferson County, Florida. *American Antiquity* 49:384–92.

Webb, William S.

1938 An Archaeological Survey of the Norris Basin in Eastern Tennessee. *Bureau of American Ethnology Bulletin* 118. Smithsonian Institution, Washington, D.C.

1939 An Archaeological Survey of Wheeler Basin on the Tennessee River in Northern Alabama. *Bureau of American Ethnology Bulletin* 122. Smithsonian Institution, Washington, D.C.

1946 *Indian Knoll*. University of Tennessee Press, Knoxville.

Webb, William S., and David DeJarnette

1942 *An Archeological Survey of the Pickwick Basin in the Adjacent Portions of the States of Alabama, Mississippi and Tennessee*. Bulletin 129. Bureau of American Ethnology, Washington, D.C.

Webster, Gary S.

2008 Culture History: A Cultural-Historical Approach. In *Handbook of Archaeological Theories*, edited by R. Alexander Bentley, Herbert D G. Maschner, and Christopher Chippindale, pp. 11–27. AltaMira Press, Lanhan, Maryland.

Weinstein, Richard A.

1986 Tchefuncte Occupation in the Lower Mississippi Delta and Adjacent Coastal one. In *The Tchula Period in the Mid-South and Lower Mississippi Valley*, edited by David H. Dye and R. C. Brister, pp. 102–127. Archaeological Report 17. Mississippi Department of Archives and History, Jackson.

Welch, Paul D.

1990 Mississippian Emergence in West-Central Alabama. In *The Mississippian Emergence*, edited by Bruce D. Smith, pp. 197–226. Smithsonian Institution Press, Washington, D.C.

1991 *Moundville's Economy*. University of Alabama Press, Tuscaloosa.

2006 *Archaeology at Shiloh Indian Mounds, 1899–1999*. University of Alabama Press, Tuscaloosa.

Welch, Paul D., and C. Margaret Scarry

1995 Status-Related Variation in Foodways in the Moundville Chiefdom. *American Antiquity* 60:397–419.

Welch, Paul D., David G. Anderson, and John E. Cornelison, Jr.

2006 SEAC Fieldwork in 1999. In *Archaeology at Shiloh Indian Mounds, 1899–1999*, by Paul D. Welch, pp. 231–251. University of Alabama Press, Tuscaloosa.

Wentz, Rachel K., and John A. Gifford

2007 Florida's Deep Past: The Bioarchaeology of Little Salt Spring (8SO18) and its Place among Florida's Mortuary Ponds. *Southeastern Archaeology* 26:330–337.

Wesler, Kit, and Victoria Fortner

2001 *Excavations at Wickliffe Mounds*. University of Alabama Press, Tuscaloosa.

Wesson, Cameron B.
2008 *Households and Hegemony: Early Creek Prestige Goods, Symbolic Capital, and Social Power.* University of Nebraska Press, Lincoln.
Wesson, Cameron B. and Mark A. Rees (editors)
2002 *Between Contacts and Colonies: Archaeological Perspectives on the Protohistoric Southeast.* University of Alabama Press, Tuscaloosa.
Whalen, Gail, and Michael E. Price
1998 The Elusive Women of Irene: The WPA Excavation of a Savannah Indian Mound. *Georgia Historical Quarterly* 82: 608–626.
Wheat, Amber
2012 Survey of Professional Opinions Regarding the Peopling of the Americas. *The SAA Archaeological Record,* in press.
White, Max E.
1988 *Georgia's Indian Heritage: The Prehistoric Peoples and Historic Tribes of Georgia.* W. H. Wolfe Associates, Roswell, Georgia.
White, Nancy M. (editor)
2005 *Gulf Coast Archaeology: The Southeastern United States and Mexico.* University Press of Florida, Gainesville.
White, Nancy M., and Richard A. Weinstein
2008 The Mexican Connection and the Far West of the U.S. Southeast. *American Antiquity* 73:227–277.
White, Nancy M., Lynne P. Sullivan, and Rochelle Marrinan (editors)
1999 *Grit-Tempered: Early Women Archaeologists in the Southeastern United States.* University Press of Florida, Gainesville.
Widmer, Randolph J.
1988 *The Evolution of Calusa: A Nonagricultural Chiefdom of the Southwest Florida Coast.* University of Alabama Press, Tuscaloosa.
2002 The Woodland Archaeology of South Florida. In *The Woodland Southeast,* edited by David G. Anderson and Robert C. Mainfort, Jr., pp. 373–397. University of Alabama Press, Tuscaloosa.
Willey, Gordon R.
1949 *Archaeology of the Florida Gulf Coast.* Smithsonian Miscellaneous Collections 113. Washington, D.C.
Willey, Gordon R., and Philip Phillips
1958 *Method and Theory in American Archaeology.* University of Chicago, Chicago.
Willey, Gordon R., and Jeremy A. Sabloff
1993 *A History of American Archaeology.* 3rd edition. W. H. Freeman Company, New York.
Williams, J. Mark
1994 The Origins of the Macon Plateau Site. In *Ocmulgee Archaeology 1936–1986,* edited by David J. Hally, pp. 130–137. University of Georgia Press, Athens.
1995 Chiefly Compounds. In *Mississippian Communities and Households,* edited by J. Daniel Rogers and Bruce D. Smith, pp. 124–134. University of Alabama Press, Tuscaloosa.
Williams, J. Mark, and Daniel T. Elliott (editors)
1998 *A World Engraved: Archaeology of the Swift Creek Culture.* University of Alabama Press, Tuscaloosa.
Williams, J. Mark, and Jennifer Freer
1998 Shrines of the Prehistoric South: Patterning in the Middle Woodland Mound Distribution. In *A World Engraved: Archaeology of the Swift Creek Culture,* edited by J. Mark Williams and Daniel T. Elliott, pp. 36–47. University of Alabama Press, Tuscaloosa.

Williams, J. Mark, and Gary Shapiro (editors)
1990 *Lamar Archaeology: Mississippian Chiefdoms in the Deep South.* University of Alabama Press, Tuscaloosa.

Williams, J. Mark, and Victor Thompson
1999 A Guide to Georgia Indian Pottery Types. *Early Georgia* 27(1):1–167.

Williams, John W., Bryan N. Shuman, and Thompson Webb III
2001 Dissimilarity Analyses of Late-Quaternary Vegetation and Climate in Eastern North American. *Ecology* 82(12): 3346–3362.

Williams, John W., Bryan N. Shuman, and Thompson Webb III T., P. J. Bartlein, and P. L. Leduc
2004 Late-Quaternary Vegetation Dynamics in North America: Scaling from Taxa to Biomes. *Ecological Monographs* 74:309–334.

Williams, Stephen
1983 Some Ruminations on the Current Strategy of Archaeology in the Southeast. *Southeastern Archaeological Conference Bulletin* 21:72–81.

1990 The Vacant Quarter and Other Late Events in the Lower Valley. In *Towns and Temples Along the Mississippi*, edited by David H. Dye and Cheryl A. Cox, pp. 170–180. University of Alabama Press, Tuscaloosa.

2001 The Vacant Quarter Hypothesis and the Yazoo Delta. In *Societies in Eclipse: Archaeology of the Eastern Woodland Indians, A.D. 1400–1700*, edited by David S. Brose, C. Wesley Cowan, and Robert C. Mainfort, Jr., pp. 191–203. Smithsonian Institution Press, Washington, D.C.

2003 Introduction to the 2003 Edition. *Archaeological Survey in the Lower Mississippi Alluvial Valley, 1940–1947*, by Philip Phillips, James Alfred Ford, and James Bennett Griffin, pp. xi–xxxii. University of Alabama Press, Tuscaloosa.

Wilson, Gregory D.
2008 *The Archaeology of Everyday Life at Early Moundville.* University of Alabama Press, Tuscaloosa.

2010 Community, Identity, and Social Memory at Moundville. *American Antiquity* 75:3–18.

2012 Living with War: The Impact of Chronic Violence in the Mississippian-Period Central Illinois Valley. In *The Oxford Handbook of North American Archaeology*, edited by Timothy R. Pauketat, pp. 523–533. Oxford University Press, Oxford, UK.

Wilson, Gregory D., Jon B. Marcoux, and Brad Koldehoff
2006 Square Pegs in Round Holes: Organizational Diversity between Early Moundville and Cahokia. In *Leadership and Polity in Mississippian Society*, edited by Brian M. Butler and Paul D. Welch, pp. 43–72. Center for Archeological Investigations, Occasional Paper No. 33. Southern Illinois University, Carbondale.

Winters, Howard
1968 Value Systems and Trade Cycles of the Late Archaic in the Midwest. In *New Directions in Archaeology*, edited by Sally R. Binford and Lewis R. Binford, pp. 175–221. Aldine, Chicago.

1969 *The Riverton Culture.* Illinois State Museum, Reports of Investigation 13. Springfield, Illinois.

Wittkofski, J. Mark, and Theodore R. Reinhart (editors)
1989 *Paleoindian Research in Virginia: A Synthesis.* Special Publications No. 19. Archeological Society of Virginia, Richmond.

Wood, M. Jared
2009 Mississippian Chiefdom Organization: A Case Study from the Savannah River Valley. Ph.D. Dissertation, Department of Anthropology, University of Georgia, Athens.

Wood, W. Dean, and William R. Bowen
1995 *Woodland Period Archaeology of Northern Georgia.* Georgia Archaeological Research Design Paper 9. Report 33. Laboratory of Archaeology, University of Georgia, Athens.
Worth, John E.
1997 *The Struggle for the Georgia Coast: An Eighteenth Century Retrospective on the Guale and Mocama.* The Archaeology of Mission Santa Catalina de Guale Series 4, Anthropological Papers of the American Museum of Natural History 75, New York, New York.
1998a *The Timucuan Chiefdoms of Spanish Florida, Volume 1, Assimilation.* University Press of Florida, Gainesville.
1998b *The Timucuan Chiefdoms of Spanish Florida, Volume 2, Resistance and Destruction.* University Press of Florida, Gainesville.
2002 Spanish Missions and the Persistence of Chiefly Power. In *The Transformation of the Southeastern Indians, 1540–1760,* edited by Robbie Ethridge and Charles M. Hudson, pp. 39–64. University Press of Mississippi, Jackson, Mississippi.
2004 Guale. In *Smithsonian Handbook of North American Indians, Volume 14, The Southeast,* edited by Raymond D. Fogelson, pp. 238–244. Smithsonian Institution, Washington, D.C.
Wright, Alice P., and Edward R. Henry (editors)
2012 *Social Landscapes of the Early and Middle Woodland Southeast.* Manuscript under review.
Wright, Herbert E., Jr.
1992 Patterns of Holocene Climate Change in Midwestern United States. *Quaternary Research* 38:129–134
Wright, Henry T.
1984 Prestate Political Formations. In *On the Evolution of Complex Societies, Essays in Honor of Harry Hoijer,* 1982, edited by Timothy K. Earle, pp. 41–78. Undena Press, Malibu, California.
Wyman, Jeffries
1875 *Fresh Water Shell Mounds of the St. John's River, Florida.* Memoirs of the Peabody Academy of Science 1(4). Salem, Massachusetts.

Yarnell, Richard A.
1974 Plant Foods and Cultivation of the Salts Cavers. In *Archaeology of the Mammoth Cave Area,* edited by Patty Jo Watson, pp. 113–122. Academic Press, New York.
Yarnell, Richard A., and M. Jean Black
1985 Temporal Trends Indicated by a Survey of Archaic and Woodland Plant Remains from Southeastern North America. *Southeastern Archaeology* 4:93–106.
Yerkes, Richard, and Linda M. Gaertner
1997 Microwear Analysis of Dalton Artifacts. In *Sloan: A Paleoindian Dalton Cemetery in Arkansas,* edited by Dan F. Morse, pp. 58–71. Smithsonian Institution, Washington, D.C.
Young, Gloria A., and Michael P. Hoffman (editors)
1993 *The Expedition of Hernando de Soto West of the Mississippi, 1541–1543.* University of Arkansas Press, Fayetteville.

Index

CPSIA information can be obtained
at www.ICGtesting.com
Printed in the USA
LVHW090107260321
682548LV00008B/66

9 780932 839435